W9-CEK-001

NUMBER TWO HUNDRED AND TWENTY-FIVE

THE OLD FARMER'S ALMANAC

CALCULATED ON A NEW AND IMPROVED PLAN FOR THE YEAR OF OUR LORD

Being 1st after Leap Year and (until July 4) 241st year of American Independence

FITTED FOR BOSTON AND THE NEW ENGLAND STATES, WITH SPECIAL CORRECTIONS AND CALCULATIONS TO ANSWER FOR ALL THE UNITED STATES.

Containing, besides the large number of Astronomical Calculations and the Farmer's Calendar for every month in the year, a variety of NEW, USEFUL, & ENTERTAINING MATTER.

ESTABLISHED IN 1792
BY ROBERT B. THOMAS (1766–1846)

We ever feel grateful for the indulgent preference which our friends and patrons have heretofore shown for our little manual.
–Robert B. Thomas, in *The 1829 (Old) Farmer's Almanac*

ISSN 0078-4516

Library of Congress Card No. 56-29681

Cover illustration by Steven Noble • Original wood engraving (above) by Randy Miller

THE OLD FARMER'S ALMANAC • DUBLIN, NH 03444 • 603-563-8111 • ALMANAC.COM

CONTENTS

14

20

30

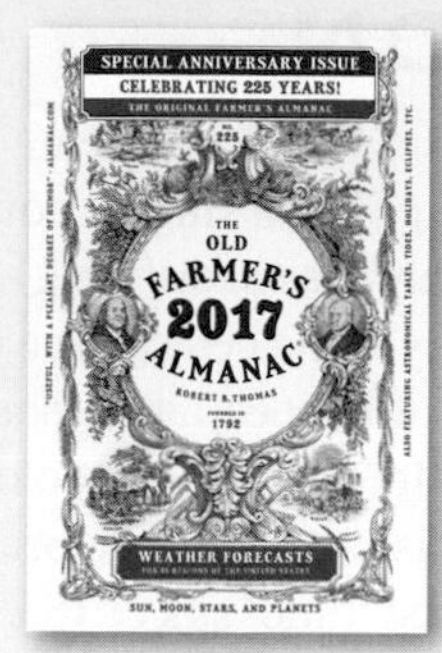

SPECIAL ANNIVERSARY SECTION

GARDENING

HISTORY

HUSBANDRY

MISCELLANY

NATURE

ROMANCE

WEATHER

IN CELEBRATION

With this edition, your modest annual, often described as America's most popular reference, celebrates its quasquibicentennial anniversary. No small word for no small achievement: The term means "a quarter [century] more than 200 years" and refers to this Almanac's 225 years of continuous publication—a record unmatched by any other periodical in North America.

Well in advance of this auspicious occasion, we began planning ways to make this edition special. These talks evolved into the package in your hands.

Like a gift, it comes wrapped—this year, with a "new" cover. Well, not *new*. Be assured, we would never change the cover, but did you notice the brighter, crisper seasonal depictions? The lifelike portraits of Benjamin Franklin and this Almanac's founder, Robert B. Thomas? The delicate lines in the fruit of the harvest and the filigree of the frame? Illustrator Steven Noble has updated our look by harkening back to our earliest designs.

A close eye will also discern the polished type. Sam Berlow of The Font Bureau designed our custom font. Ben Scott and Lainey Fink of Bluerock Design created our new logo, which evokes the Almanac's heritage and tradition yet sets it squarely in the 21st century.

You'll also see a new style of weather forecast pages. We think that you'll find them at least 80 percent more attractive than the traditionally 80 percent–accurate forecasts they represent. If you're wondering: Not a single snowflake or sunny day was sacrificed.

Our anniversary is the centerpiece of this edition, and it echoes throughout. First, we salute Mr. Thomas. His colorful life story, in his own words, appears here (for the first time since 1833), with select reproduced pages from the first edition: Frontispiece, "Preface," recipes for ailments (do not try these at home!), and Calendar Pages. (Oh, and don't get ftreffed out over those "f's" that appear where the letter "s" would normally fall. The "long-s" was commonplace back in the old days.)

The preceding 224 editions of this column, plus a few legendary incidents, inspired the article titled "225 Years of Love, Luck, and Tradition"—an entertaining chronicle of the stunning events, stirring predictions, and profound observations that have occurred over the years and been recorded on these pages.

Happy 225th, Mr. Thomas, and thank you for your wonderful Almanac. Be it ever and always as you set forth: "useful, with a pleasant degree of humor"!

–J. S., June 2016

However, it is by our works and not our words that we would be judged. These, we hope, will sustain us in the humble though proud station we have so long held in the name of

Your obedient servant,

Rob. B. Thomas.

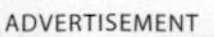
ADVERTISEMENT

PATRIOT PANTRY

SURVIVAL
SEED VAULT
Garden in a can!

THE WHITE HOUSE

WASHINGTON

May 10, 2016

In 1792, The Old Farmer's Almanac published its first edition, launching one of America's most iconic publications. More than two centuries have since gone by—and the world has changed dramatically—but The Almanac still holds a special place in the heart of American culture, enduring as an important part of our Nation's story.

Across generations, The Almanac has been a source of practical information, from homespun wisdom and home remedies to gardening advice and weather forecasts. It has inspired our curiosity about science and our enthusiasm for knowledge, and it has continuously fueled the American spirit of ingenuity and invention.

I offer my congratulations to The Almanac on this historic 225th edition, and I send my best wishes for the years to come.

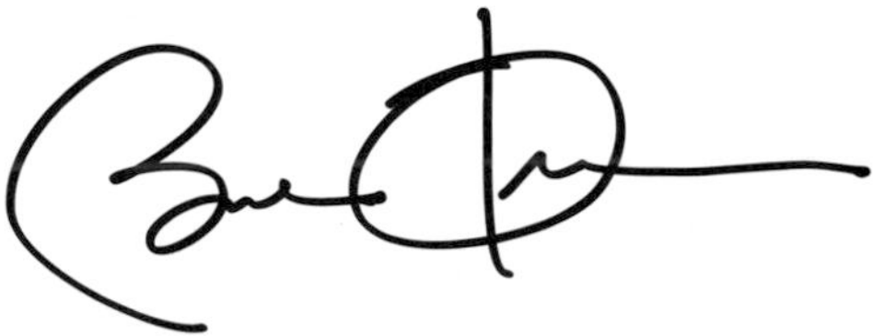

We greatly appreciate this generous and thoughtful message from U.S. President Barack Obama.

PRIME MINISTER · PREMIER MINISTRE

The 225th Anniversary of the Old Farmer's Almanac

It is with great pleasure that I join everyone in wishing the Old Farmer's Almanac my warmest congratulations on occasion of their 225th Anniversary.

Since its establishment in 1792, the Old Farmer's Almanac has continuously engaged North Americans with useful and discerning content, including localized insights into weather, farming, astronomy, and a wide range of other subjects that are central to our daily lives.

Canada derives its strength from our diversity, and it is important that we follow the events and issues that impact every corner of our communities. We are fortunate that the Old Farmer's Almanac, a publication that reflects and celebrates our diversity, continues to be a resource for Canadians of all backgrounds after 225 years in print.

Ottawa
2016

We greatly appreciate this generous and thoughtful message from Canadian Prime Minister Justin Trudeau.

2017 TRENDS

GARDENING

People no longer need to own big lots to garden. . . . Indoor gardening—hydroponic, soilless mixes, or otherwise—is going to explode.
–Katie Dubow, Garden Media Group

EXOTIC EATS

"We're 'growing international,' with veggies once seen only in restaurants and specialty markets. Fennel 'dust' [pollen], radicchio [Italian chicory], and kohlrabi [German turnip] are popping up everywhere," says Chelsey Fields, vegetable product manager, W. Atlee Burpee & Co.

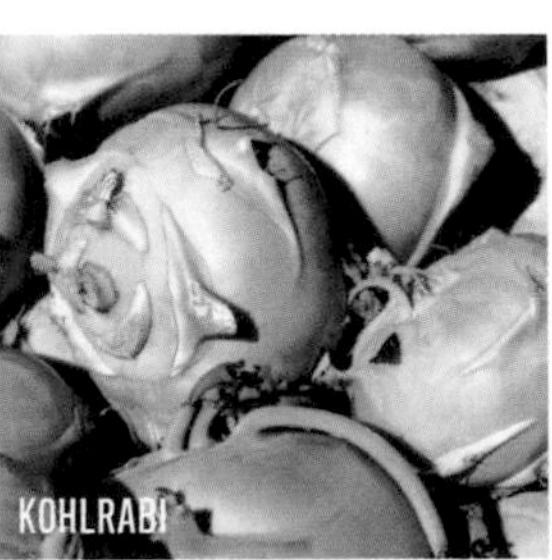

TOP CROPS

- In plots: Rainbow Mix beets, 'Infinite Gold' melons, 'Firecracker' tomatoes, 'Pinstripe' eggplants, 'Little SnapPea Crunch' peas
–Park Seed Company

- 'Pretty N Sweet' multicolor miniature peppers, 'Parisian Gherkin' cucumbers, 'Bopak' bok choy, 'Dolce Fresca' basil
–Ted Pew, horticulturist, Minnesota Landscape Arboretum

- In pots: 'Baby Cakes', a thornless blackberry

BY THE NUMBERS

18,000: total of U.S. and Canadian community gardens (est.)

$120 billion: annual cost to eradicate invasive species in the U.S.

$13.8 billion: total annual U.S. horticulture sales—floriculture, nursery, and specialty crops

$1.8 million: total annual Canadian horticulture and nursery sales

Photos, from top: Ryan Somma/Leafy Greenhouse/Wikimedia; Media Bakery

that fruits in summer and fall

- Indoors: Revolution™ Bicolor Yellow Orange gerbera, 'Rapido White' campanula, 'Bandera Purple' lavender

–Ball Horticultural Company

FROM LAB TO LANDSCAPE

Bioengineering buffs are designing new plants by changing their genetics. In development: blue roses; plants that glow with DNA from jellyfish or fireflies; fragrant mosses to use as air fresheners.

CRAVING CONSTANT COLOR?

Folks at the Minnesota Landscape Arboretum recommend . . .

- hybridized annuals that bloom compactly and repeatedly: 'Summer Jewel White' salvia, 'Trilogy Red' petunia, 'Brocade Cherry Night' geranium, SunPatiens® Spreading Shell Pink impatiens

'SUMMER JEWEL WHITE' SALVIA

- plants with colored leaves to extend growing periods: 'Solar Shadow' coleus; 'Phasion', 'Bengal Tiger', and 'Intrigue' cannas; 'Bishop of Llandaff' dahlia

BUZZWORD
Foodscaping: where edibles replace traditional lawn and shrubs

PEOPLE ARE TALKING ABOUT . . .

- drought-tolerant fescue grasses that require less mowing
- mite- and disease-resistant "superbees"
- cocker spaniels trained to sniff out invasive weeds
- Women who garden at least twice a week have less stress and fatigue and feel more friendly and energetic. "This explains the benefits that gardeners often perceive and widely describe."

–Dr. Charles L. Guy, professor, plant physiology and biochemistry, University of Florida

(continued)

GARDENING IN 1792

Wealthy folks had flower and tree "pleasure" gardens. Every household kept a kitchen garden at least ¼ acre in size, tended by the women and children and full of vegetables and herbs for food and medicine, says Tom Kelleher, historian, Old Sturbridge Village, Massachusetts.

Photo: courtesy of Park Seed Company

MONEY MATTERS

As our lives become increasingly digital, we yearn for things that feel real and authentic. We're whipping up homemade jam, jewelry, knitted ditties, spice rubs, and bath salt concoctions.

–Kit Yarrow, PhD, professor emerita, Golden Gate University, San Francisco

PEOPLE ARE TALKING ABOUT . . .

- buying an automobile from a coin-operated, glass tower vending machine that holds up to 20 cars
- "van pooling" with coworkers in company-supplied vehicles to save money and reduce stress
- groups of volunteers repairing gadgets, appliances, lawn mowers, and TVs at no charge
- Web sites for locating items/tools to borrow in your own neighborhood
- renting classic arcade games by the month

BY THE NUMBERS

46%: households with two parents working full-time

$351,000: average price of newly built home

14.6 million Americans are self-employed

(continued)

MONEY MATTERS IN 1792

"There was little social safety net, and no old-age pensions or Social Security. Land had value that could support you in illness, misfortune, or old age," says Kelleher. Wealthy folks traded on the New York Stock Exchange, founded under a buttonwood tree on May 17, 1792.

Photo: Thinkstock

ON THE FARM

Farmers are recognizing that transparency is no longer optional. Farmers and ranchers must show what we do and, just as important, talk about how the practices we use help us to do other things consumers expect, such as keeping our animals safe, conserving natural resources, and being productive so that food remains affordable.

–Vincent "Zippy" Duvall, president, American Farm Bureau Federation

FARMERS ARE GROWING . . .

- smaller: More farmers' markets, CSAs, and farm stores mean that even ½ acre plots can be profitable.
- more humanely by switching from confinement livestock systems to free-range, with portable fencing, pasture drinkers (livestock water systems), range feeders for poultry and pigs, and solar chargers to power fences and drinkers.

–Forrest Pritchard, author, Gaining Ground: A Story of Farmers' Markets, Local Food, and Saving the Family Farm

FARM TECH'S FUTURE

- X-rays inventory flowing grain, making truck scales obsolete
- satellites are tracking herds, and automated weighing stations are transmitting data, signaling when cattle are ready for market
- 57,299 farms produce on-site renewable energy: solar, geo-exchange, wind, small hydro, or bio-gas
- data, provided by drones, help farmers use precise amounts of fertilizer, pesticides, and water. "This should result in higher

BY THE NUMBERS

3.2 million: total U.S. farmers

58: average age of U.S. farmers

110,000: number of farmers and ranchers under 35

28% of young farmers say that student loans impede their ability to grow their business

70% of young farmers rent land

78% of young farmers did not grow up on a farm

Photo: Thinkstock

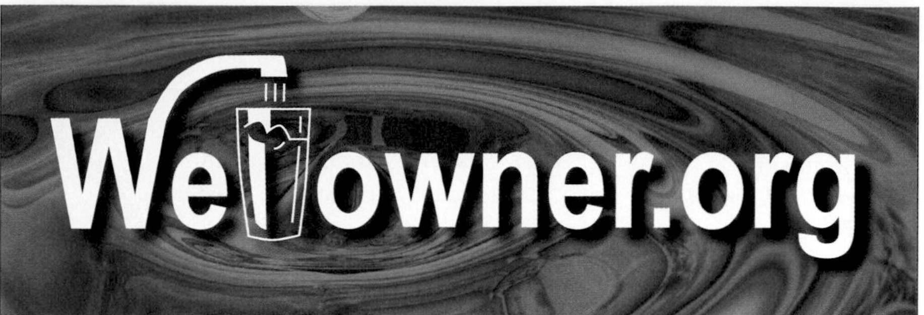

Got well water?
Get peace of mind.

Visit **WellOwner.org/info** to find free help on water testing, improving water quality, maintenance, and more:

- Monthly tip sheets
- Hotline
- Well owners' manuals
- Well financing video
- Lessons
- Webinars
- Smartphone app.

Protect your investment. Protect your family.

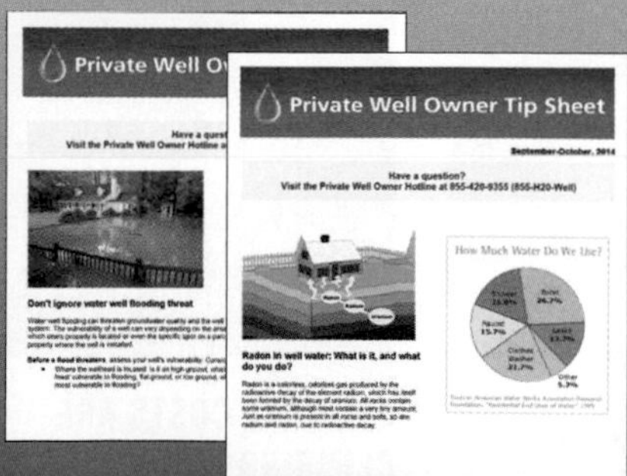

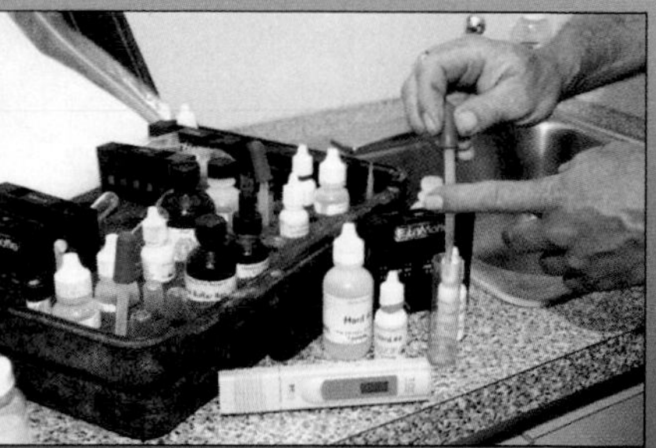

Visit WellOwner.org/info today!

production, lower costs, and a better environment."
–Mark O'Neill, Pennsylvania Farm Bureau

- robotic milking systems are replacing dairy farmworkers
- sales of agricultural robots are estimated to top $16.3 billion by 2020

FARMING IN 1792

Ours was an agrarian society: 90% of Americans were farmers (under 1% are today). The threshing machine enabled farmers to separate plant grain from stalks and husks, eliminating a slow and laborious task. Tobacco growers began diversifying by planting wheat.

PEOPLE ARE TALKING ABOUT . . .

- databases that match landowners who want to sell with beginning farmers who want to buy
- "slow money" investors: those willing to wait for a return on investments in new farms and existing farms that go organic

WAYS FARMERS ARE TRANSPARENT

- veggies are being planted in pickup truck beds, then driven to schools and fairs to demonstrate how produce can be grown anywhere
- Web cams livestream the daily lives of livestock
- farmers host tours for consumers and food bloggers

OUR ANIMAL FRIENDS

Millennials are taking the "pet step": Couples, roommates, and friends are getting pets together as the next step in their lives.

–Tierra Bonaldi, pet lifestyle expert, American Pet Products Association

BY THE NUMBERS

37% of dogs vacation with owners

45% of pets get birthday gifts

54% of dogs are overweight (est.)

PET CARE COSTS ARE CLIMBING . . .

"Spending on boarding and daycare, dog walking, pet waste

Photo: Thinkstock

PETS IN 1792

Cats and dogs were common in homes for a practical purpose: They helped with rodent control. A wealthy person's pet was a squirrel in a cage.

removal services, grooming, training, and pet-sitting is growing," says Bonaldi. Then there's the annual . . .

- $379 million for flea/tick products
- $2.6 billion for dog treats
- $476 million for cat treats

It's money well spent: Pet owners visit a doctor 0.6 times less than non-pet people.

IT'S A DOG'S LIFE

Canine pastimes include . . .

- taking acting classes
- learning to file their own nails
- snacking from specialty food trucks

PEOPLE ARE TALKING ABOUT . . .

- beds with a pet mattress attached, so that dogs can sleep beside owners
- cat and small-dog backpacks allowing owners to bring pets everywhere
- "cat cafes," where people congregate to spend time with furry felines

GOOD EATS

Consumers are looking for products that appear to be fresh, real, and less processed. There is heightened demand for greater transparency in what's in our foods and beverages—where they're from, how they're made, and how safe they are.

–Laurie Demeritt, CEO, The Hartman Group

Photos, from top: S. Pierce; Thinkstock

BUY NOT, WASTE NOT

Supermarket employees are asking shoppers what they plan to serve and telling them exactly how much food to buy—all to discourage food waste.

FOOD IN 1792

"Growing prosperity and improved transportation led to more variety in people's diets," says Kelleher. Spices, sugar, and citrus were increasingly available to diets that were seasonal, repetitive, and heavy on meat and starch. Home cooks had only European cookbooks at hand; American ones had not yet been published.

BY THE NUMBERS

25% of us grocery-shop online

61% of us enjoy grocery shopping

46% of meals are eaten alone

PEOPLE ARE TALKING ABOUT . . .

- cooking oil made from algae
- food seasoned or made with invasive weeds or species: garlic mustard or kudzu, feral hogs, Asian carp, lion fish
- roasted peanuts treated with enzymes to make them hypoallergenic
- cricket flour in snack bars

AROUND THE HOUSE

Clients want a home that will keep them as healthy as possible, with cleaner air, more natural light, and construction with building materials that are low in volatile organic compounds.

–Matt Tinder, American Institute of Architects

THE IDEAL MODEL HOME HAS . . .

- a bright white or charcoal exterior
- one or two emerald green or dark blue walls in an ivory-color room
- soft blue and gray patterned floors
- rose-gold plumbing fixtures

THE IDEAL HEALTHY HOME HAS . . .

- "floating" flooring to help posture
- stone pathways to help joints *(continued)*

Photo: Thinkstock

HOME SWEET HOME IN 1792

Candle boxes and wall sconces provided light. Cooks used reflector ovens, bake pans, and biscuit cutters. "Light and unbreakable tinware was gaining in popularity," says Kelleher. The average family burned 20 cords of wood annually.

- mood-enhancing scent dispensers
- spa equipment (e.g. pedicure chairs)
- chromatherapy tubs (bathwater changes color)
- lots of natural light

NICHES ARE NICE

"People are trying to get a little office space anywhere they can—in mudrooms, closets, entryway walls, or kitchen nooks."

–Amy Panos, deputy editor, Home Design

21ST-CENTURY HOME CONSTRUCTION

"We can build our homes the same way we build our cars: in a controlled factory setting utilizing robotic technology and expert craftsmen and technicians. This way, we can achieve greater quality control, better use of materials, more precision in the production process, and greater integration of technology throughout."

–Joseph Wheeler, co-director, Virginia Tech Center for Design Research

IT'LL BE BETTER IN THE BATHROOM

- vanity heights will adjust to the user, based on fingerprint recognition
- mirrors will display body weight
- toilets will have heated seats and nighttime lighting

IT'LL BE COZIER IN THE KITCHEN

- dishwashers will text when out of soap
- pantries will report low supplies
- ovens will identify food, then cook it
- coffeemakers will "talk" with toothbrushes, to brew at the correct time
- backsplashes will display recipes

IT'LL BE COMFY IN ALL QUARTERS

- living rooms will go "techless" (no TV or gadgets), with seating to encourage conversation
- solar panels will unfurl in sunlight
- lighting will adapt, getting warmer for reading, dimmer for movie-watching, brighter for housecleaning

MOST TALKED-ABOUT TWO-FERS

- the "his and hers" house, with separate entries, bedrooms, kitchens, and living rooms
- partially submerged floating homes

(continued)

Photo: Thinkstock

COLLECTOR'S CORNER

New collectors covet objects associated more with the present than the past.
–Timothy Gordon, appraiser, Missoula, Montana

BAD NEWS, BOOMERS

"The Baby Boomer generation is downsizing an avalanche of 'stuff,' and the younger generations are simply not interested in taking on much of it."
–Gary Piattoni, appraiser, Evanston, Illinois

ONE TRUE THING

"As people search for the greater meaning and purpose of life amid world turmoil, collectors will seek vintage figures, icons, and books relating to their beliefs."
–Piattoni

BECAUSE YOU CAN'T TAKE IT WITH YOU . . .

Collectors are using treasures: riding vintage bicycles, playing early video games, sitting on/storing things in antique furniture. "The repurposing trend is environmentally friendly, which is very important to Millennials."
–LaGina Austin, senior appraiser, Skinner Auctioneers

TECH WORTH KEEPING

"It's going to be smaller items, not big and clunky items like fax machines. Quality and importance is what to look for," says George Glastris, an appraiser in Chicago, Illinois. For example:

- flip phones in original boxes
- computer mice
- MiniDisc players

"As technology progresses, collectors will look back on early tools with nostalgia.

(continued)

COLLECTIBLES IN 1792

A 1792 penny was precious 225 years ago, but not nearly so much as it is today. In that year, Robert Birch engraved one of the first U.S. coins. The "Birch cent" displays "Miss Liberty" surrounded by the words "Liberty Parent of Science & Industry." It sold for almost $2.6 million in January 2015.

Photo, top: Thinkstock

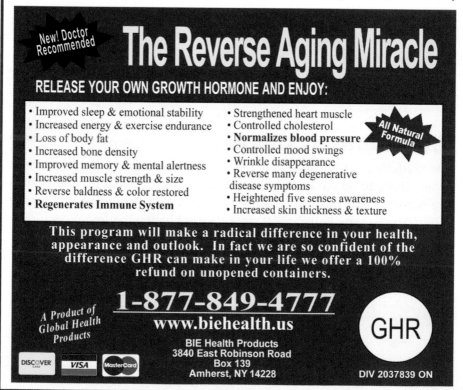

Younger generations will discover them with the same wonder now afforded old typewriters," says Piattoni. Think hand tools without plastic:

- wooden planes
- optical surveyor levels
- brace hand drills
- plumb bobs

CASHING IN . . .
Hobbyist currency collectors are paying cash for U.S. bills with serial numbers in patterns, e.g., ascending (12345 . . .), descending (98765 . . .), or repeating (121212 . . .) and anniversary dates, zip codes, and the like.

BY THE NUMBERS

2.5: fewer walking/biking days enjoyed per week per household for each additional car owned

5.5: years of additional longevity enjoyed today compared to 1950

7.5: years of additional longevity, on average, enjoyed by people with positive attitudes about aging

4,400 physicians provide "concierge" medicine

30% of American adults sleep 6 hours or less a night

TO OUR HEALTH

The manner in which we access healthcare is changing rapidly. Having to show up at an office or leave a [phone] message is quickly going by the wayside. We'll have instant access to physicians via email, text, and videoconferencing.

–Dr. Mark H. Greenawald, professor and vice chair of Family and Community Medicine, Virginia Tech Carilion School of Medicine

MIRACLES OF SCIENCE

- devices strapped to arms or legs that turn energy from everyday movements into electricity
- stretchable gels worn on the skin that monitor temperature and administer medicine
- electronic devices that, once swallowed, measure vital signs and send the data to our doctors

Photo: Thinkstock

PEOPLE ARE TALKING ABOUT . . .

- sitting as the new smoking
- eating fermented foods rich in probiotics like kefir, sauerkraut, miso, and kimchi to boost helpful microbes
- volunteering—because it also helps our health and stress level

HEALTH CARE IN 1792

Doctors were scarce; healthcare was women's duty. They relied on medicinal herbs, guidebooks, word-of-mouth, and handwritten records of tried-and-true remedies. Frequent baths were considered hazardous to health. Rotten teeth were pulled by whoever was available.

CULTURE CUES

The auto industry continues its march from a hardware business to a software business, prompting such innovations as practical semi-autonomy and car-to-car connectivity.

–Eddie Alterman, editor-in-chief, Car and Driver

SIGNS OF THE TIMES

- lasers will beam high-speed Internet to the Moon
- 18% of Americans say that they've seen a ghost

(continued)

BY THE NUMBERS

2: Canada's place in *U.S. News & World Report*'s Best Countries ranking

30 minutes: travel time, New York City to London, on proposed new high-speed jet with four wings and two rockets

57 million Americans live in a multigenerational home

4.9 billion: number of connected devices in use worldwide

Photo: Thinkstock

- an ocean-cleaning system will funnel plastic trash into barriers, to be collected and reused

THE GOING IS GETTING GOOD

- battery-powered aircraft will take off and land vertically, steered with a joystick
- electric aircraft will consume no fuel and emit no pollutants
- after landing, aircraft will drive like a car

OUR TOYS AND JOYS

- typewriters with clicking keys and an Internet connection
- faux indoor slopes for skiing and snowboarding

- hotel guest rooms under the ocean

BUZZWORD

Middlescence: the stage of life between middle and old age

- digital handwriting text fonts
- underground parks, where mirrors direct sunlight into solar collectors so that plants can grow

PEOPLE ARE TALKING ABOUT . . .

- umbrellas attached to wrists for texting in the rain
- front-end car cameras for parking in tight spots and scouting rough terrain
- beer billboards dispensing samples to passersby, and benches dispensing candy to sitters
- waterproof books to read while bathing

(continued)

PASTIMES IN 1792

Adult amusements included church picnics; card games, horse racing, and cockfights that might invite small wagers; whittling; knife throwing; and jumping high enough to click the heels three times in the air. Children were entertained with shadow pictures on a wall; finding "figures" in a fire's flame; and footraces, swimming, fishing, and boating.

Photo: courtesy of Deep Ocean Technology

THE FIRST FASHION COLLECTION PRINTED ENTIRELY USING HOME 3-D PRINTERS

OUR PASSION FOR FASHION

As the hardware becomes more affordable and the software becomes easier to use, we can expect to see 3-D clothing being produced at home.

–Amanda Hallay, fashion merchandising professor, LIM College, New York City

THIS IS SO OVER

- grungy stiletto heels, black mesh stockings, smudgy eye makeup that signals rock chic

THIS IS SO COOL

- candy-color prints, images of animals and rainbows, positive slogans on Ts, tote bags about peace and forgiveness

–Hallay

LOOK OUT, LADIES

"The strong colors—and [padded] shoulders—of 1980s fashion are going to take over. We'll see lots of pop art colors and abstract prints: techno colors and patterns—royal blue, magenta, and bright yellow."

–Suzanne Cotton, department chair of fashion design, Columbus College of Art and Design

BY THE NUMBERS

75% of women put on comfortable clothes as soon as they get home

86% of women will sacrifice style for comfort

GARMENTS ARE GOING GREEN

"Customers want to buy garments from a company that is doing good for the world," says Cotton. Designers are using more recycled and discarded materials than ever, and brands are encouraging customers

Photo: courtesy of Danit Peleg

to return unwanted garments for recycling into other fashions.

ROMANTIC STYLES RULE

"Expect to see—and wear—Victorian high-neck, ruffled blouses and A-line skirts; jewel tones of amethyst, burgundy, eggplant, forest green, midnight blue, and crimson; and three-quarter-length horse-riding coats."

–Steve Faerm, associate professor of fashion, Parsons School of Design

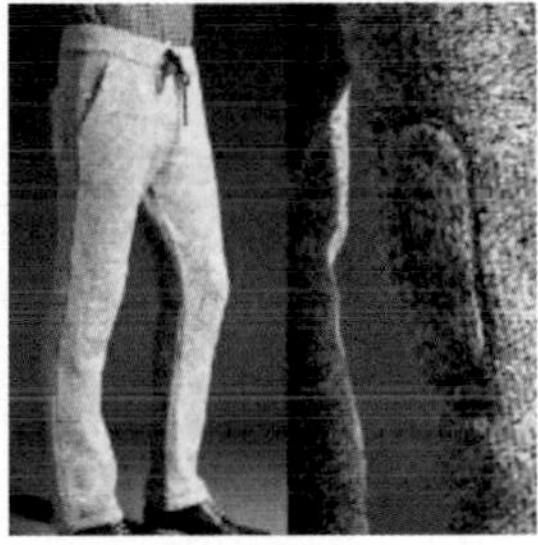

GET READY, GUYS

"Men will be wearing traditional, outdoorsy looks but with slimmer, sleeker cuts. Everything is body-conscious without being tight," says Mark-Evan Blackman of Fashion Institute of Technology (FIT). Think tailored wool jogging pants and quilted wool shirts as jackets.

BUZZWORD
Uni-wardrobe: clothes for any gender
–Steve Faerm

GO BOLD OR GO HOME

"Pink—from pastel to fuchsia—is going to become much bigger in menswear," says Mark Woodman, past president, Color Marketing Group. Also looming large: bright orange, yellow, red, and blue (think socks); and vibrant florals (notably in neckties and pocket squares).

ACCESSORIES WILL GET AMAZING

- sensors and wires in clothing will send texts with the swipe of a cuff
- rings will have memory drives
- earrings will have video screens

PEOPLE ARE TALKING ABOUT . . .

- pizza necklaces, bearing a ready-to-eat slice, sealed in plastic
- sneakers that warm feet and have a flashlight or wheels that shoot sparks when at certain angles
- ladies leaving home in silk or satin PJs, with dressy heels or sandals ■

Stacey Kusterbeck, a frequent contributor to *The Old Farmer's Almanac,* writes about popular culture from New York State.

FASHION IN 1792

"The full coats that men had worn for most of the 1700s were becoming more formfitting tailcoats," says Kelleher. Styles were simpler: The colonial tricorne hat had become the bicorne. Men had their clothing tailor-made; women hand-sewed theirs.

Photo: Trendhunter

Call In the Pollinators

*Love fruit and vegetables?
Love flowers? Plant to
lure pollinators to your garden.*

BY CYNTHIA VAN HAZINGA

*Mankind will not survive
the honeybees' disappearance for
more than five years.*

–ALBERT EINSTEIN, GERMAN-BORN AMERICAN PHYSICIST
(1879–1955)

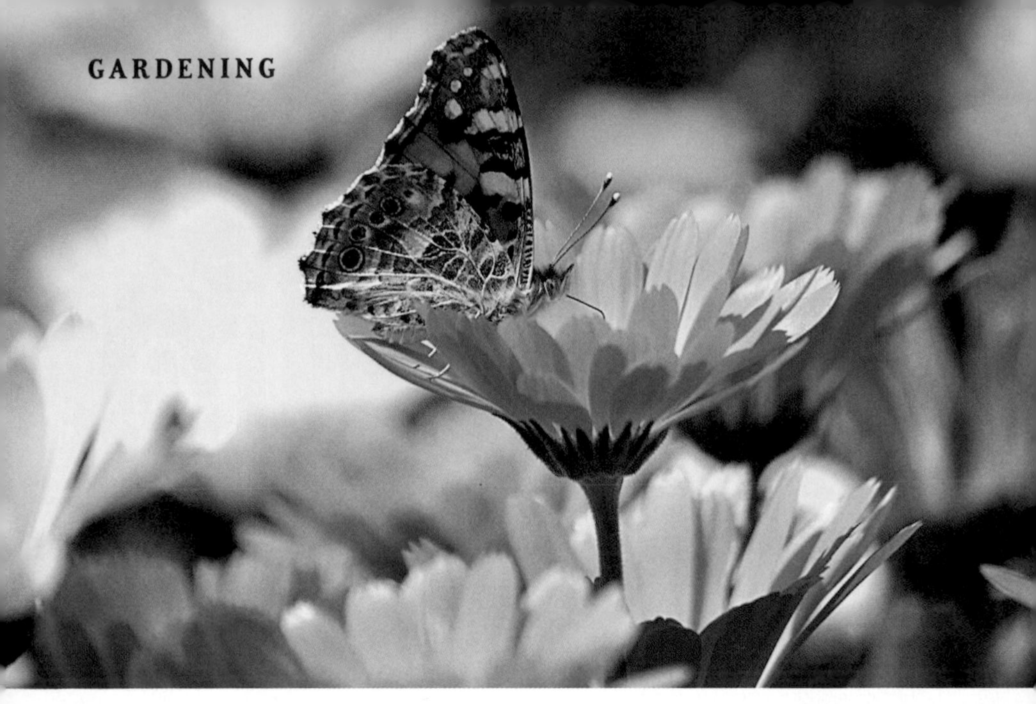

THANK A HONEYBEE or other pollinator for every third bite of food that you eat. Without native bees and their winged cousins (moths, butterflies, flies, and a few beetles)—plus birds and bats—fresh-grown food production would plummet. Many favorite flowers would be rare; many wildflowers would become extinct. You can help nature's crop dusters—and ensure lush, productive plants—by providing, enhancing, and protecting pollinator habitats. Here's how to set the scene and plant to pull in pollinators.

Create a Natural Setting

Pollinators are attracted to floral landscapes that resemble nature.

- Garden in sun: Insects love it and need shelter from strong winds.
- Cultivate native plants: They are four times more attractive to native bees than exotics. They also usually thrive with minimum attention.
- Plant in clumps: Clusters of one species draw more pollinators than scattered flowers.
- Aim for bloom from early spring to fall, with at least three species blooming in each season.
- Select flowers in many bright colors and shapes. Pollinators come in different sizes and with different tongue lengths, so they will need to feed on flowers of different shapes.
- Forgo pollenless cultivars and modern hybrids, especially those with double petals. Choose common plants and heirloom varieties of perennials and herbs—good sources of nectar or pollen.

(continued)

Roses

• Forget the manicured lawn and garden. Leave some open sandy ground, brush piles, and old tree stumps (perhaps at the yard's edges) as nesting and overwintering sites.
• Do not use pesticides, even "organic" insecticides.

Pollinator Plants for Edible Gardens

These colorful flowers and kitchen herbs are magnets for specific pollinators. Vegetable gardeners should include at least a few in edible beds.

Basil: attracts honeybees, solitary bees, and bumblebees to its small purple or white flowers.

Bee balm: nectar-rich flowers attract bumblebees, honeybees, butterflies, and hummingbirds.

Black-eyed Susan: lures bees, butterflies, beetles, wasps, and hoverflies.

Cilantro: loved by honeybees, hoverflies, parasitic wasps, and tachinid flies.

Coneflower: bumblebees relish the many varieties, as do honeybees, butterflies, moths, beetles, hoverflies, and syrphid flies.

Cosmos: lures lacewings, pirate bugs, bees, birds, and butterflies.

Milkweed: a nectar source for the monarch butterfly and food

Oregano

Milkweed

source for its larvae; also attracts buckeye butterflies.

Oregano: a mint-family herb, it attracts bees and butterflies.

Sunflower: flower heads host multiple species of bees, wasps, beetles, and flies.

Sweet alyssum: attracts hoverflies (the larvae consume aphids), other tiny flies, wasps, and many types of bees.

Zinnia: attracts bumblebees, plus swallowtail, monarch, and painted lady butterflies.

Sunflowers

Zinnias

Plants for Particular Pollinator Gardens

Flower forms and plant traits lure certain pollinators. Here's how and why particular plants call to them—and thus how you can call them into your garden:

Honeybee flowers, such as iris, mountain laurel, violets, roses, blackberries and other brambles, and hooded skullcap, have nectar, a sweet or minty scent, abundant pollen, nectar guides (a contrasting ultraviolet strip), and landing platforms to attract bees, which prefer blue, purple, yellow, or white blooms. These blooms are brightly colored and open in daytime. Skillful honeybees are almost universal pollinators, learn quickly, and retain a memory of the flowers they have visited.

Bumblebee flowers, such as monkshood (which grows only where there are bumblebees), snapdragons, bottle gentian, and ladies'

Bees by the Numbers

You've probably heard: Bee colonies have been dying off since 2006 (in part due to colony collapse disorder/CCD); according to some reports, CCD has claimed one-third of the bees in the United States. The U.S. Department of Agriculture reported a loss of 42.1 percent of managed bee colonies between April 2014 and April 2015.

tresses orchids, have lures similar to those of honeybee flowers but also have deep nectaries and can bear bumblebees' comparatively great weight. Some also have trigger flowers that fuse male and female reproductive organs into a floral column that snaps forward quickly when touched, covering bumblebees with pollen.

Butterfly flowers, such as sweet William, asters, sedum, daisies, butterfly weed, lantana, marigolds, purple coneflowers, and zinnias, have scent, nectar, and nectar guides. They have deep nectaries and long throats suited to butterflies' long tongues and always a perch or landing surface. Butterflies favor brightly colored red, orange, and yellow flowers in clusters that are open during the day. Butterflies taste with their feet and don't get much pollen on their bodies.

Bird flowers, such as columbine, agastache, salvia, penstemon, trumpet creepers, and bee balm, have copious nectar and deep tubular nectaries. They can be odorless. These flowers are shaped to accommodate whirring wings. Their petals are thick enough to resist the beaks of birds, and their stems are strong enough for perching. Bright colors, especially red, attract nectar-eating birds.

Moth flowers, such as honeysuckle, evening primrose, Madonna lily, night-blooming jasmine, mayapples, and some yucca species, have a strong, sweet scent and considerable nectar. Many bloom in clusters and open in late afternoon. They have long, narrow throats and are usually white or light-color to shine at night. Hawkmoths (with

tongues as long as their bodies) are pollinators of night-blooming plants, including datura, tufted evening primrose, and sweet four o'clock. The female yucca moth rolls pollen into a ball and stuffs it into the flowers that it visits.

Fly flowers, such as goldenrod and Queen Anne's lace, catnip, and orchids, attract flies, which are generalist pollinators. Flies (and gnats and mosquitoes, which pollinate small bog orchids) visit small, pale to dark brown or purple flowers that bloom in shade and in seasonally moist habitats; the blooms are sometimes flecked with translucent patches. Hoverflies and syrphid flies head for sweet alyssum; carrion flies go for wild ginger flowers, which are dull in color and smell like rotting meat. Some flowers in this category, including many orchids and Venus's-flytraps, catch flies with curious mechanisms, which enhance their effectiveness in pollination.

Bat flowers often have white or pale nocturnal blooms that are large and bell-shape, such as the agave plant and the saguaro cactus. They include the flowers of more than 300 species of fruit, including mangoes, bananas, and guavas. Many of these flowers have large amounts of dilute nectar and emit a strong smell—a fruity, fermenting, or musky odor. Bats are very important pollinators in tropical or desert climates and use chemical cues to locate food sources. ■

Perils to Today's Pollinators

- **Insecticides kill plants and bees; climate change narrows their range.**
- **Light pollution harms nocturnal pollinators, including hawkmoths and fireflies.**
- **Habitat loss threatens monarch butterflies and hummingbirds.**
- **The population of once-common monarch butterflies is plummeting due to lack of native milkweed. In 2014, the number of monarchs migrating to Mexico was the lowest ever recorded.**

Cynthia Van Hazinga, a frequent contributor to Old Farmer's Almanac publications, grows pollinator plants in her New Hampshire garden.

HARVEST A HELPING OF HISTORY

HEIRLOOM VEGETABLES TURN BACK TIME AND TURN UP FLAVOR.

BY SUSAN PEERY

ILLUSTRATION BY KRISTIN KEST

Americans in 1792 gardened the way their European ancestors had and grew most of the same crops: peas, beans, cabbages, carrots, beets, turnips, greens, and onions, plus a few not widely known today, such as scorzonera, cardoons, skirrets, and orach. They also grew flint corn, pumpkins, potatoes, sweet potatoes, and other native crops.

A MOST IMPORTANT TASK WAS TO SAVE SEEDS FROM THE BEST SPECIMENS OF EACH CROP.

Few grew tomatoes, sugar snap peas, sweet corn, or brussels sprouts, all bred or popularized in the 19th century or later. But they likely mixed herbs among their vegetables to keep both at hand "for Meate or Medicine," as the Pilgrims would have said. They harvested continuously, pickling, drying, fermenting, root cellaring, salting, and otherwise preserving anything they or their livestock couldn't eat on the spot.

Wealthy gardeners ordered seeds from merchants in Europe; the advent of large mail-order seed companies was a century away. For others, a most important task was to save seeds from the best specimens of each crop. The mysteries of genetics in plant breeding not yet having been revealed, practiced gardeners knew how to grow plants successfully in their soil, their climate.

Thanks to our ancestral seed-savers and the generations that followed, we still can grow vegetables that are direct descendants of the old types. These "heirlooms" and others are widely available from seed houses. Most are open-pollinated (can be saved and will reproduce faithfully); some, like the popular Amish 'Brandywine' pink tomato, have also been hybridized to improve certain traits. Here are some heirlooms to try.

(continued)

GARDENING FOR FLAVOR

Love the earthy taste of **beets?** Try 'Bull's Blood' (related to an old French variety, 'Crapaudine'), a deliciously sweet dark red beet with beautiful red-purple leaves, or the striking 'Chiogga', an old Italian variety with concentric red and white stripes.

For the bite of a good, crisp, sweet **radish,** go for 'Watermelon Radish', an antique from China that has a white exterior and a burst of eponymous pink in the center.

Thomas Jefferson liked **peppers.** The most curious of gardeners, he gave seeds from a small, bright-red hot pepper grown at Monticello to plantsman Bernard McMahon, who introduced it as 'McMahon's Red Bird' pepper in 1813. Jefferson also grew the sweet 'Bull Nose Bell' pepper, which had arrived here from India in the 1700s.

People have craved a crisp, citrusy **cucumber** that doesn't need peeling for ages. Small, round (2-inch-diameter) 'Lemon' cucumber was introduced here

SIMPLE TOMATO SEED-SAVING

Few gardeners in 1792 would have been growing tomatoes, except perhaps in the Carolinas and Virginia, where they were regarded as both an ornamental and a culinary vegetable. The plant, native to South America, became widely known in the 19th century and has exploded in popularity since then. It is the rare gardener today who does not grow at least one variety of tomato. Seed catalogs list many heirloom varieties—take your pick.

Saving the seeds of tomatoes can be cumbersome, involving fermentation to separate the pulp and seeds; thank the gardeners at Strawbery Banke, a living history museum in Portsmouth, New Hampshire, for this easier way:

Take seeds from your best open-pollinated specimens, smear the pulpy mix onto brown paper bags, and let the bags dry in the hot sun. When all of the moisture has evaporated, the seeds may be removed and stored in a cool, dry place for planting the following spring.

For more on seed-saving, see page 58.

TURNIPS WERE WIDELY GROWN FROM CANADA TO VIRGINIA IN THE 17TH AND 18TH CENTURIES.

in the early 1890s, having already been grown in the Middle East for centuries.

FOR FUN

Every gardener likes a good story. The white-flesh 'Gilfeather' **turnip**—actually, a cross between a turnip and a rutabaga—was developed in Wardsboro, Vermont, in the late 1800s. Its seeds were guarded jealously by its breeder, a farmer named John Gilfeather. Some seeds eventually escaped his hoard, and the secret was out. The flavor is mild and sweet, not sulfurous as some turnips can be. Turnips were widely grown from Canada to Virginia in the 17th and 18th centuries to feed people and livestock and only lost favor when the white potato was introduced in the 19th century.

Jefferson also grew many different **beans** at Monticello—for field crops, ornamental plantings, eating fresh, and drying. Every garden should have at least one type of bean, if space allows. For drying, you can't go wrong with open-pollinated 'Hutterite' (grown in North America since the 1870s), 'Jacob's Cattle', or 'Silver Cloud Cannellini' (white kidney). Fresh bean lovers could try 'Red Noodle' yardlong bean, an Asian specialty that is delicious in stir-fries and does best in warm gardening zones. 'Mountaineer White Half Runner', a German pole bean brought to South Carolina 200 years ago, is another tasty fresh bean.

Peas can be sown as early as soil can be worked: Valentine's Day in the mid-Atlantic region, Patriots Day (mid-April) in New England, or after the first crocus blooms anywhere. In the heritage gardens at Colonial Williamsburg, gardeners plant 'Prince Albert', a shelling (not snap) pea developed in the 1830s and thought to be descended

Thanks to BetterWOMAN, I'm winning the battle for Bladder Control.

All Natural
Clinically-Tested Herbal Supplement

- Reduces Bladder Leaks
- Reduces Urinary Frequency
- Safe and Effective – No Known Side Effects
- Costs Less than Traditional Bladder Control Options
- Sleep Better All Night
- **Live Free of Worry, Embarrassment, and Inconvenience**

You don't have to let bladder control problems control you.
Call now!

Frequent nighttime trips to the bathroom, embarrassing leaks and the inconvenience of constantly searching for rest rooms in public – for years, I struggled with bladder control problems. After trying expensive medications with horrible side effects, ineffective exercises and undignified pads and diapers, I was ready to resign myself to a life of bladder leaks, isolation and depression. But then I tried **BetterWOMAN**.

When I first saw the ad for BetterWOMAN, I was skeptical. So many products claim they can set you free from leaks, frequency and worry, only to deliver disappointment. When I finally tried BetterWOMAN, I found that it actually works! It changed my life. Even my friends have noticed that I'm a new person. And because it's all natural, I can enjoy the results without the worry of dangerous side effects. Thanks to BetterWOMAN, I finally fought bladder control problems and I won!

Also Available: **BetterMAN**®
The 3-in-1 Formula Every Man Needs –
Better **BLADDER**, Better **PROSTATE**, and Better **STAMINA!**
Order online at www.BetterMANnow.com.

Limited Time Offer

Call Now & Ask How To Get A

FREE BONUS BOTTLE

CALL TOLL-FREE 1-888-821-0401
or order online: www.BetterWOMANnow.com

These statements have not been evaluated by the FDA. This product is not intended to diagnose, treat, cure or prevent any disease.
Use as directed. Individual results may vary.

from 'Hotspur', the most popular pea of the 18th century. 'Prince Albert' and other heirloom peas (look for late-season 'Marrowfat', similar to 'Champion of England') are shelling peas that usually require pea sticks, fences, or trellises for support.

The glory of the firmament comes to Earth in the gold-spattered green rind and foliage of the juicy **watermelon** 'Moon and Stars' (aka 'Sun, Moon, and Stars'), a legendary melon dating from the 1800s. In fact, this melon was believed to have been lost: Kent Whealy, founder of the Seed Savers Exchange in Decorah, Iowa, searched for it for years before finding it on Merle Van Doren's farm in Macon, Missouri, in 1980.

A LEGENDARY MELON DATING FROM THE 1800s WAS BELIEVED TO HAVE BEEN LOST.

FOR THE FUTURE

When you grow heirloom vegetables, you help to sustain the genetic diversity that enriches life. Because heirloom vegetables are not bred for the mass market, we can expect complex, local flavors to delight the palate.

Many of the heirloom seeds on the market today harken back to old varieties, such as those brought here by immigrants from Europe and Asia or carried west by pioneers in the 19th century, yet have evolved to survive in new locations. The **scarlet runner bean,** for example, is native to cool and humid areas of Mexico and Guatemala. It was introduced in England by botanist John Tradescant in the early 17th century and returned to the New World as an ornamental and culinary bean in the 18th century. It still adorns garden arbors and flavors soups, its uses little changed over the centuries. 'Painted Lady', a bicolor heirloom runner bean, dates from the 1880s. ■

Susan Peery gardens in Nelson, New Hampshire, and loves to experiment with traditional gardening methods and plants. Like all gardeners, she invokes the mantra "Wait 'til next year!"

DRY-FARM FOR TASTY TOMATOES

. . . and save water doing it.

BY JOAN MORRIS

Photo: Food and Drink/SuperStock

DRY FARMING means growing food without irrigation or, in the case of a household, with minimal water. Records indicate that the practice thrived in Mesopotamia in the 3rd millennium B.C. In North America, the method dates only from the early 1800s. For today's home gardener, dry farming is an easy method that will reduce water use in the garden and produce some amazingly tasty tomatoes.

The technique takes some advance work. The idea is to create a lush growing bed that will retain water and provide a healthy medium for the plants. The best way to do this is to begin in the fall or winter by growing a cover crop in the beds that you plan to use.

The crop can be fava beans, clover, rye, wheat, legumes, or a mixture of plants that grow well in the cooler months and fix nitrogen in the soil. In the early spring, you'll chop down the crop, cut it into small pieces, and work it, as well as the roots, into the bed. Then add 2 to 4 inches of compost and fertilizer. Organic fertilizers—aged cow, horse, chicken or rabbit manure—are good choices. (Chicken manure needs to be aged 6 to 12 months before using because it is so high in nitrogen, phosphorus, and potassium that it can burn your plants.)

By the time you're ready to put in your

PROVIDE HEALTHY SOIL WITH THESE COVER CROPS

 Photos, clockwise from top left: Pixabay; Smoerrebrood/Wikimedia; Pixabay; David Monniaux/Wikimedia; Dwight Burdette/Wikimedia; Harrak/Wikimedia

seedlings, the plant material will have begun to compost, creating a rich, loamy soil.

If you didn't plan ahead with a cover crop, no worries. In the spring, work 3 to 4 inches or more of compost into your beds before planting.

CHOOSING the right variety of plant is important. This method works best with medium- to small-tomato varieties. The big, 3-pound slicers just take too long to develop, and the bed won't be able to support them. In general, pick varieties that have a shorter growing season and produce smaller fruit.

To further reduce your water use, try growing determinate tomatoes that have a fixed production time.

Plant your seedlings, mulch your beds, and water as normal for about a month. When the plants are established and begin to set fruit, cut off the water—and leave it off. You'll be tempted, but step away from the hose faucet. However, you will need to add compost or fertilizer throughout the growing season on a regular basis for your plants.

The production life of the dry-farmed tomato is shorter and the fruit will be smaller, but the flavors will be concentrated. Be aware, too, that toward the end of the season, the foliage may start looking sad, but the fruit will continue to grow. ■

Joan Morris, a columnist and writer for northern California's Bay Area News Group, is learning firsthand about the challenges of drought farming.

GO FISH!

Yet one more way to plant tomatoes

This planting method works in any weather condition but is especially recommended in drought.

Dig a hole as deep as the tomato transplant is tall. Add into the hole a handful of a good organic vegetable fertilizer, a handful of bonemeal, a handful of worm castings, a small fish head if you have one or fish meal if you don't, some crushed eggshells, and two or three uncoated aspirins. Tomatoes are susceptible to a number of diseases, and studies indicate that the aspirin may boost the plant's immune system.

Before planting, cut the leaves off the main stem, leaving just the top third of the plant intact. Bury the plant in the hole, leaving only the top above ground. Roots will form along the buried stem where the leaves had been, which will give the plant a stronger root system, able to take up water and nutrients more easily. These strong roots also will seek out water in the deeper regions of your bed. *–J. M.*

Photo: Media Bakery

SOW GOOD!

SEEDS SAVED FROM THIS YEAR'S PLANTS CAN YIELD EVEN BETTER RESULTS NEXT SEASON.

By Julie MacIsaac

Photo: Gary Smith/GAP Photos

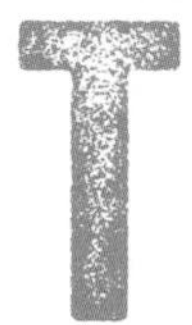

TY AND JANICE Shelton own a farm and run an organic market garden in Lac La Biche County, Alberta. Their fresh produce—potatoes, beans, peas, tomatoes, and kale—is sold in organic grocery chains in Edmonton as well as at their local farmers' market. They've seen a steady increase in demand for their good-looking, tasty vegetables, and one reason for this, they say, is that they save and use seed from their own plants.

"We got hailed out one year," Janice says. The summer's crops had been pulverized in the field by golf ball–size hail. "I was looking at all of our peas and beans, knowing that they couldn't be sold, and wondering what to do. I thought, 'I know! I'll save them for seed.' I'm actually thankful for that hail."

The Sheltons and gardeners everywhere find that the benefits of saving seeds from the healthiest and most robust plants more than justify the extra effort. "Our seeds outperform the seeds we buy by 50 percent, easily. The plants are heartier, more vigorous, and adapted to our climate," notes Ty, adding that he even finds them to be more resistant to insects. "A plant raises a seed, and it instinctually raises this seed to be adapted to our conditions. This is what plants do."

Some commonly homegrown seeds are tomatoes, beans, peas, and lettuce. If these are among your favorites, follow these steps to become a master seed-saver.

STORE SEEDS IN AIRTIGHT GLASS JARS TO KEEP OUT MOISTURE.

Photo: GAP Photos

SAVE "SELFIES"

Self-pollinating plants (we're calling them "selfies") contain both the male and female reproductive parts, and pollination happens inside the plant. This prevents cross-pollination—when pollen from the male plant of one variety fertilizes the female plant of another, resulting in a new variety.

(continued)

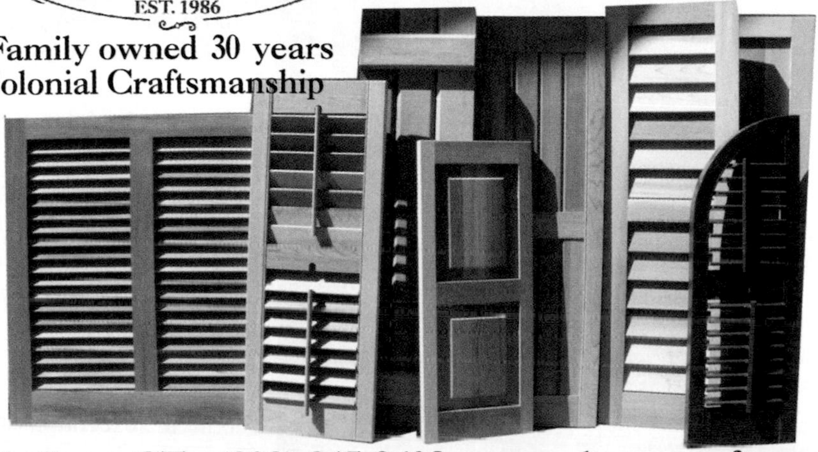

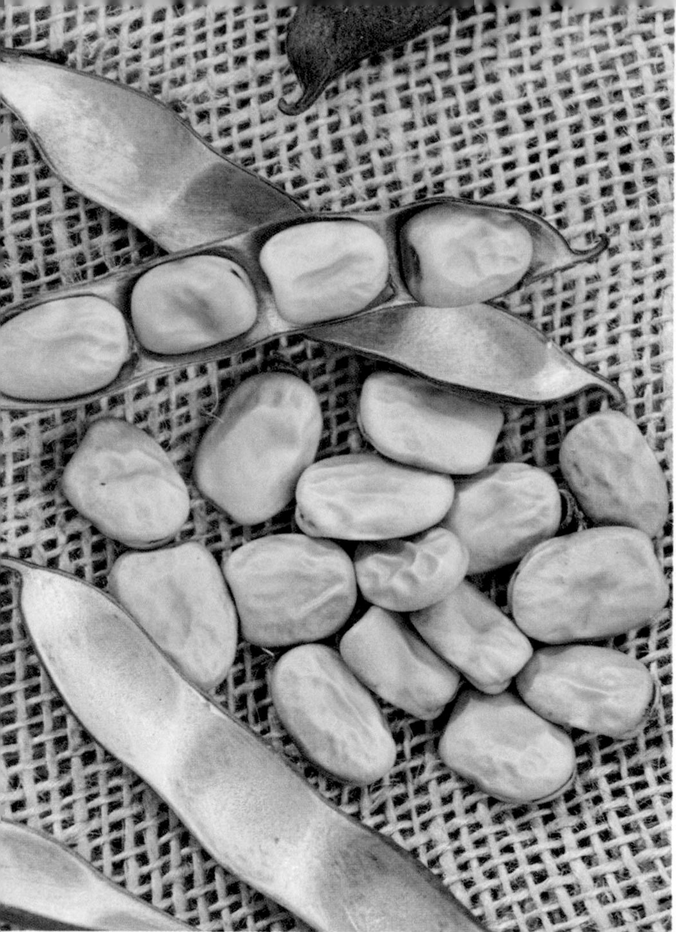

HARVESTING PEAS, BEANS, AND LETTUCE SEEDS IN DRY WEATHER SPEEDS UP THE DRYING PROCESS.

Heirloom vegetables are good choices.

Do not save the seeds of hybrid plants. First-generation hybrids take the best characteristics from both parent plants to produce delicious fruit. Second-generation hybrids rarely show the same traits and are often poor producers.

COLLECT CONTAINERS

Use the growing period to gather materials. Set aside margarine, yogurt, and ice cream containers for harvesting your seeds. Wash out old pickle, mayonnaise, or jelly jars for storing your dried seeds; airtight glass jars keep out moisture. (Plastic containers are permeable, and seeds can germinate if they're exposed to moisture, as well as warmth or light.) Save mesh bags, such as those that store-bought onions come in; fine mesh is handy for sifting the chaff from lettuce seeds. Clean a couple of window screens; they're a well-ventilated surface on which to dry seeds. Baking trays or dinner plates can also be used.

PICK PATIENTLY

With the exception of tomatoes, pick your seed crops as late into the season as possible. Seeds are attached to the parent fruit and receive nourishment until harvest. To allow extra growing time for beans, peas, and lettuce, consider adding time to the beginning of the growth cycle by starting plants indoors. Harvest tomatoes for seed when you pick them to eat.

HARVEST DRY

Always harvest peas, beans, and lettuce seeds in dry weather. This speeds up the drying process and prevents mold. Pick peas and beans when pods are

Photo: Gary Smith/GAP Photos

For more on tomato seed–saving, see page 46.

SCOOP OUT TOMATO SEEDS AND PULP.

brown, dry, and crackly to the touch. Lettuce flowers form seed heads about 6 weeks after harvest-to-eat time. Gather seed heads before wind carries them away.

SEPARATE SELECTIVELY

Remove beans and peas from their pods when they are completely dry.

Release lettuce seeds from the chaff by using fine mesh.

Scoop out tomato seeds and pulp and set the rest of the tomato aside for eating. Put the seeds and pulp into a small container and add a few drops of water. Leave the container at room temperature for 3 to 4 days while the pulp around the seeds ferments. Use a fine sieve to drain and rinse the seeds. Place the seeds on a plate or screen to dry.

DRY DILIGENTLY

Dry seeds completely before storing them. In humid conditions, turn a fan on low near your seeds to aid the process. Large seeds require a longer drying time than smaller ones. Stir the seeds occasionally. Seeds are dry when they are hard to the touch.

SET ASIDE TILL SPRING

Store seeds in labeled airtight glass jars in a cold, dark place. Do not freeze them; if even a few molecules of moisture are trapped inside a seed, the frost will damage it.

With this, you've taken the first step toward planting next year's garden—one that will be populated with crops that are ready to face the unique challenges of your soil and climate. ■

Julie MacIsaac is a public relations professional and freelance writer from Alberta who loves to exercise her green thumb in her spare time.

Photo: Thomas Alamy/GAP Photos

Mangrove Mysteries Explained

BY DOUG ALDERSON

Visitors to Florida's coast below Cedar Key on the Gulf side or Cape Canaveral along the eastern shore occasionally find the ocean view obscured and beach access denied by dense green masses of trees with exposed, tangled roots that seem to be in motion.

(continued)

Photo: Stock Connection/SuperStock

These are red mangroves, broadleaf evergreen trees aptly named "walking trees" for the roots that prop them up as if in stride above water. While some vacationers may find them a hindrance, locals value these subtropical trees for their beauty, unusual traits, and protection. They are the first line of defense against hurricanes, helping to absorb the tremendous wave action and winds associated with the storms.

Of the 80-plus species of mangroves worldwide, only three exist in Florida: red, black, and white; these occupy nearly 470,000 acres. Rather than pass by these natural wonders, visitors should try moseying up and taking a much closer look.

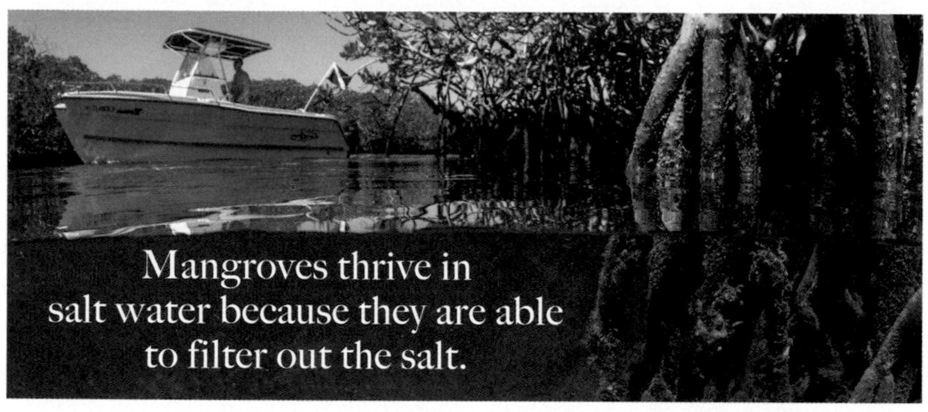
Mangroves thrive in salt water because they are able to filter out the salt.

At a slightly higher elevation than red mangroves are black mangroves. These trees are distinguished by leaves with hairy undersides and roots with fingerlike projections. The digits provide oxygen to its underwater roots. On even higher ground are white mangroves, easily identified by their leaves—yellow-green in color and elliptical in shape. White mangroves have no visible aerial root systems but are strongly rooted in the ground.

Mangroves thrive in salt water because they are able to filter out the salt. Both black and white mangroves take in ocean water through their roots and exude salt from the water through their leaves. Some say that white salt residue on the foliage gives the white mangrove its name.

Scientists are less sure about the purpose of two pimple-size bumps, or nectaries, at the stem base of each white mangrove leaf. Some think that these glands simply get rid of more salt, while others suggest that they secrete sugar to attract ants, which help to control harmful insects. (Red mangroves separate most of the fresh water from salt at their roots' surface.)

These trees propagate in unique fashion. Seeds sprout (germinate) while attached to the tree. A few months later, the seeds (technically, propagules) drop to root near the tree base, or they drift away to other locations on tides and currents.

The cigar-shape seedlings of red mangroves can remain viable for up

Photo: Image Source/SuperStock

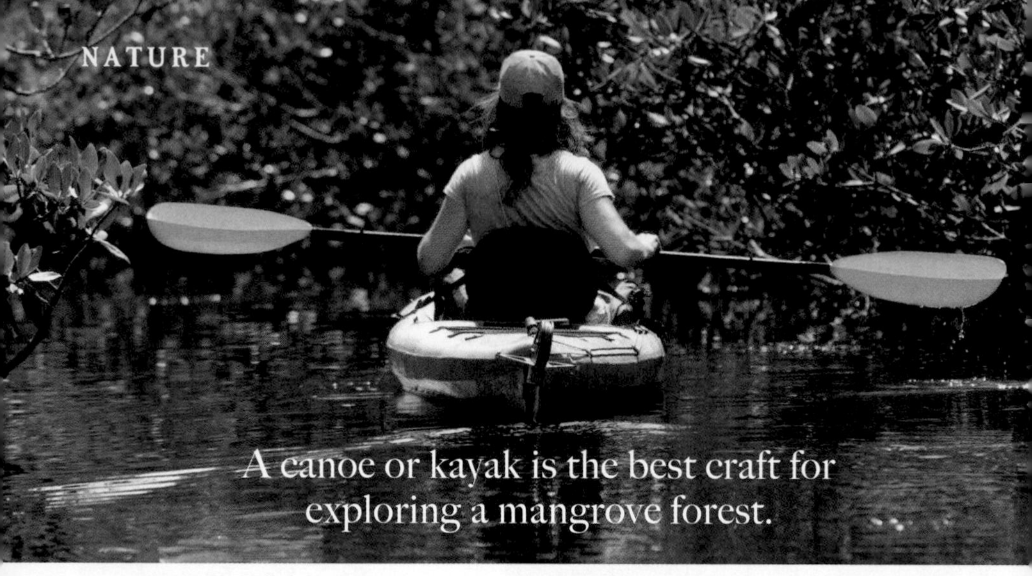

A canoe or kayak is the best craft for exploring a mangrove forest.

to a year while bobbing in the ocean; the black mangroves' lima-bean-shape propagule, for about 110 days; and the pea-size seed of the white mangroves, about 1 month.

A mature mangrove forest is an otherworldly jungle. It is thick and nearly impenetrable in places. However, a maze of canopied mangrove tunnels often leads to small coves that can be home to myriad sea life and birds.

Mangrove forests are ideal feeding and nursery grounds for fish—snapper, snook, tarpon, redfish, sheepshead, mullet, cobia, and more (up to 230 fish species!), plus shrimp, oysters, and barnacles. (Barnacles, which populate intertidal zones, cling to the plants' roots.) The roots provide shelter from predators, and mangrove tree litter—leaves, bark, and wood—forms the base of a rich marine food source.

More than 190 bird species flock to Florida mangroves. In wading bird rookeries, the thick green forests are alive with the calls and cries of juvenile birds. Adults fly in and out on feeding runs and often bicker with other birds over coveted branches. Brown pelicans, great blue herons, brilliant white great egrets, stunning pink roseate spoonbills, and other species all perch, nest, and feed in the mangroves, as do ospreys, hawks, peregrine falcons, and bald eagles—the top echelon of aerial hunters fittingly occupying the topmost branches.

Unique among them all is the mangrove cuckoo, whose extended range

DID YOU KNOW?
The buttonwood tree, often found in mangrove forests, is considered a mangrove species by some scientists. This Florida native evergreen, often used as a specimen or shade tree, tolerates full sun, sandy soil, and brackish areas.

Photo: Seth Resnick/SuperStock

More than 190 bird species flock to Florida mangroves.

includes Mexico, South America, and the Caribbean but only U.S. habitat is the South Florida mangroves.

A canoe or kayak is the best craft for exploring a mangrove forest, but be sure to check tide charts before venturing out. Low tide makes these areas too shallow for navigation. If trapped, potentially for hours, visitors are doubly vulnerable. Those who can not or do not move are at the mercy of winged pests such as mosquitoes and no-see-ums. Some movement, along with the effective application of insect repellent, is preferable.

While the red mangroves' tangle of roots makes close examination difficult while out of a boat, low tide has its benefits. It is sometimes possible to walk through a black or white mangrove forest at low tide. The air usually smells heavily of salt and decomposing vegetation, while underfoot is a tangle of sea grasses or mud.

The surface will likely be pocked with thousands of fiddler crab burrows that help to aerate the sediment. These tiny creatures race away from unexpected visitors. The males wave an oversize pincer, which someone once likened to a fiddle, hence the name. Other crabs commonly seen include the purple marsh crab, mud crab, great land crab, and climbing mangrove tree crab (near the water's edge).

A close look along mangrove branches may reveal flowering orchids and bromeliads, along with squirrel tree frogs, green anoles, and orange-brown, mangrove salt marsh snakes. Life abounds in a mangrove forest!

Because their many attributes are now largely recognized, mangroves have some degree of protection under Florida law and are faring better than they have in the past, when developers destroyed vast forests.

The largest protected area of mangroves is in the storied Ten Thousand Islands in southwest Florida. Historically,

Photo: FLPA/SuperStock

Gulf Stream currents deposited quartz sand in deeper water offshore. Eventually, the accumulating sand created shoals near the surface. Long red mangrove seedlings floated in on the tide and took hold. Jigsaw-shape mangrove islands were the end result, and today a maze of several hundred islands—not 10,000—dots the watery landscape.

There is evidence that mangroves are expanding their range as global temperatures warm. Because of fewer freezing days and nights, mangrove forests along Florida's east coast doubled in size between New Smyrna Beach and St. Augustine from 1984 to 2011. Researchers point out that this is not necessarily a good trend, since mangroves are invading salt marsh habitats that are also valuable nursery grounds for a variety of marine creatures.

Also, as the sea level rises, mangroves will likely need to retreat inland but may end up being hemmed in by development. Another climate-related study found that the shade provided by mangroves is benefiting corals growing beneath them by reducing high levels of solar radiation, thus deterring coral bleaching that can kill corals—one more reason to appreciate the valuable role of mangroves in Florida's coastal ecology. ■

Doug Alderson is the author of several Florida outdoor and nature books, including his latest, *Wild Florida Adventures* (CreateSpace, 2014). To learn more, go to www.dougalderson.net.

MURDER IN THE MANGROVES

A century ago, desperadoes found the labyrinth of mangrove islands and tunnels in Florida's Ten Thousand Islands to be good places to evade capture.

"Down in the mazes of the Ten Thousand Islands, one will sometimes meet men who turn their faces away and will merely smile if you ask them their names," wrote Nevin O. Winter in 1918 in *Florida, the Land of Enchantment.* "Sometimes they kill men whom they fear are after them, and occasionally they slay each other either in a drunken quarrel or for the purpose of robbery."

The collection of outlaws included The Hermit, who allegedly had a hideaway with slaves and a harem of women. The most infamous renegade was Ed Watson, immortalized by author Peter Matthiessen in his novel *Shadow Country.* Watson had allegedly killed Belle Starr in Oklahoma and a man in Arcadia in southwest Florida before fleeing to the islands in the early 1880s.

He continued to have run-ins with the law for attempted and alleged murders until the autumn of 1910, when he came to tie up his boat at the Chokoloskee landing. A mob gathered and accused him of killing one of his own hired hands. They demanded Watson's gun, and his short temper flared. He raised his shotgun and pressed the trigger. The gun misfired. The crowd then opened fire, ending another chapter in the state's colorful history. *–D. A.*

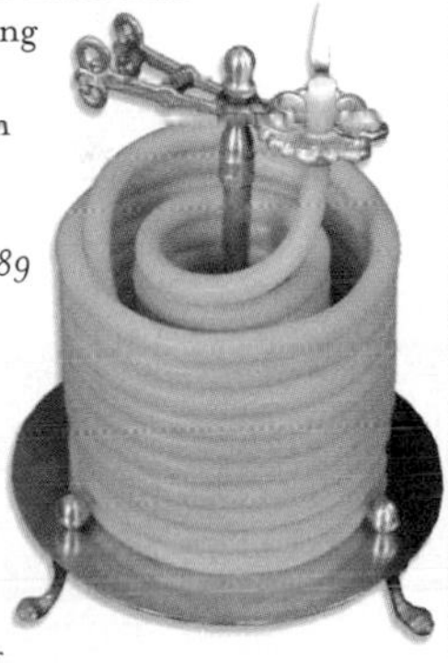

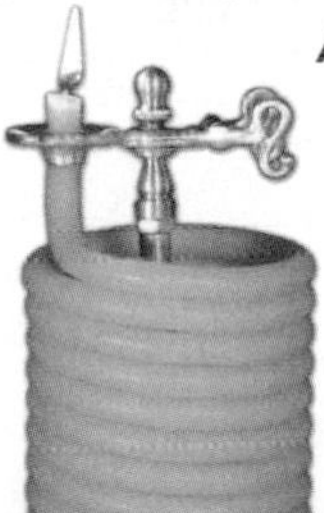

FOR BEST FISHING DAYS, SEE PAGE 172

HOME WATERS
RIVERS THAT RUN IN THE MIND

Our roving angler casts his current thoughts.

BY BOB SCAMMELL

EVERY ANGLER NEEDS A HOME WATER, not just the developers of the concept—angling authors or expert fishermen who write. By definition, home water should be close enough to home that you can fish it so often that it starts running in your mind.

In "To Know a River," a chapter in Roderick Haig-Brown's masterpiece, *A River Never Sleeps,* many anglers first encounter a concept of home water: ". . . knowing a river intimately is a very large part of the joy of fly-fishing." Yet the author admits he does not know nearly as much about the Campbell River as he would like, even though he fearlessly named the river beside which he lived on Vancouver Island.

Other writers believe that to name your home water is to destroy it, and they resort to outrageous sophistry to explain their secrecy. For example, Steven A. Griffin, in his essay "Night Shift," admits that he knows how to get to his home water, but he pretends not to know its name: "It's more important to know the river than its name." *(continued)*

Photo: Tetra Images/SuperStock

Home water not necessarily meaning superb fishing is an idea taken to the ultimate absurdity in an essay by humorist Stephen Leacock. The prime virtue of "My Fishpond" is that it contains no fish whatsoever: "It's the idea of the thing that counts, not the reality. You don't need fish for fishing . . . ."

Paul Schullery writes in "Home River," from his book *Mountain Time:* "A home river is that rarest of friends, the one who frequently surprises you with new elements of personality without ever seeming a stranger."

Many of us won't be dragged away from our home waters lest we miss a single surprise, as Paul O'Neil explains "In Praise of Trout—and Also Me": "I have invested so many hours of frustration in the Esopus and its tributaries that the prospect of losing even one unlikely dividend because of absence is more than I can quite bring myself to contemplate."

My home waters are where I'd rather get skunked than catch the limit anywhere else. I have two home waters.

One, 230 miles from home, is Pincher Creek, a small southern Alberta foothills stream flowing past the century-old, two-story log home of my spouse for the first 3 years of her life. Pincher has never skunked me; its feisty rainbow trout are always famished.

The other, Prairie Creek—a river, really,

"KNOWING A RIVER INTIMATELY IS A VERY LARGE PART OF THE JOY OF FLY-FISHING."

Photo: Mint Images/SuperStock

only 60 miles from home—flows through the boreal forest and aspen parkland south of Rocky Mountain House, Alberta, through our Stump Ranch and past our cabin on its bank. It is moody, often muddy, and its trophy brown trout skunk me as often as not.

Angling boasts the richest literature of all human recreations. Immersed in it, anglers will discover unknown but hallowed home waters that they must fish.

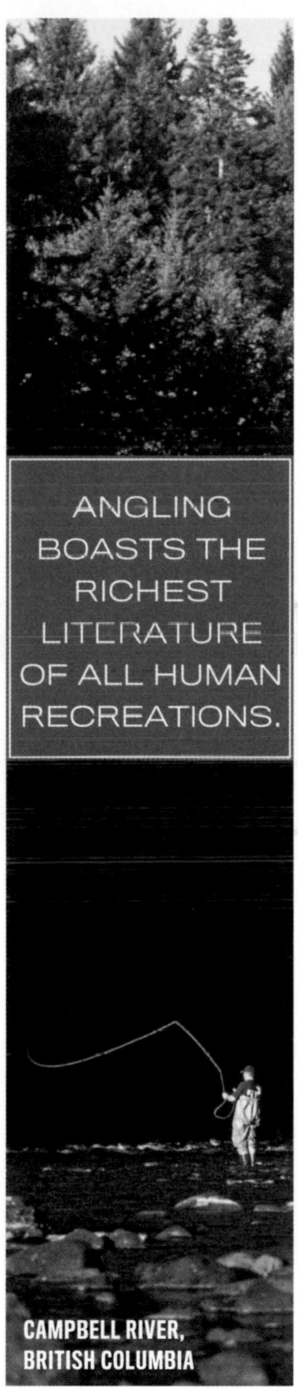
ANGLING BOASTS THE RICHEST LITERATURE OF ALL HUMAN RECREATIONS.
CAMPBELL RIVER, BRITISH COLUMBIA

My first home water pilgrimage was to Haig-Brown's beloved Campbell River in British Columbia, the province to our west. I hooked a summer steelhead that I waded and wallowed to follow as it surged back to sea, until I slipped the light fantastic on too many of the Campbell's famously slimy boulders, lost a *pas de deux* with my piscatorial partner, and ended up swimming for my life.

My sodden hulk hove up on a beach where a tall, gangly gent stood puffing a pipe. I knew in a flash that it was not St. Nick but Haig-Brown himself, out on a July Sunday morning stroll.

"So, there's still some summer-runs around," he commented, before soothing my shattered soul by admitting that his river occasionally baptized him, too. My rubber-sole waders and slippery boulders were a deadly combination, he said, and then this angling god gave how-to gospel on installing felt, even tire studs, on wader soles.

My next pilgrimage was to Montana, neighbor to the south, and the Madison River, which, from its start at Madison Junction in Yellowstone National Park, flows 183 miles west to join the Missouri River at Three Forks. Angling author Charlie Brooks starts and ends his "My Part of the River" chapter in *The Living River* with this: "One can not own a river or even a part of it, except in one's heart . . . the part of the Madison

Photo: Chris Cheadle/All Canada Photos/SuperStock

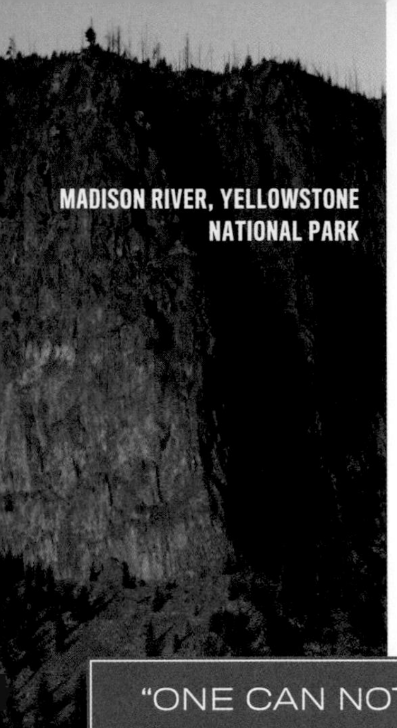

River in Yellowstone National Park belongs to me, also to 220 million Americans, but few know and love it as I do. . . . I doubt if I know myself why it is so important to me, I only know that it is."

I fished with Charlie on the Madison's three Barn Holes, just inside the park's west boundary. I was treated to a tutorial on Charlie's unique technique for getting huge stone fly nymph imitations to bump along the bottom of really fast and deep river holes: hands up as though beseeching heaven, then bowing to the river gods as the nymphs drift deeply by. I also learned why a pioneering catch-and-release angler always wore a huge creel cobbled from an old-time canvas water bag: to cool the sody pop, of course.

"ONE CAN NOT OWN A RIVER OR EVEN A PART OF IT, EXCEPT IN ONE'S HEART."

In 1987, I made the ultimate angler's pilgrimage: to the final home water of the father of all anglers, Izaak Walton, author of our bible, *The Compleat Angler,* first published in 1653 and released in more than 300 editions since.

On a day when thick mist blotched the line between air and water, I fished the Winchester College beat of England's River Itchen. Off to the right, behind the fog, was #7 Dome Alley, Walton's last home, and Winchester Cathedral, where he is buried and honored with a glowing stained glass window depicting him in two riverside scenes, one inscribed "Study to be quiet," the other "In everything give thanks." Now, whenever I fish that beat of the Itchen in my mind, I'm never skunked as I was so royally that day.

"You could not step twice into the same river, for other waters are ever flowing on," declared Heraclitus, a Greek philosopher of

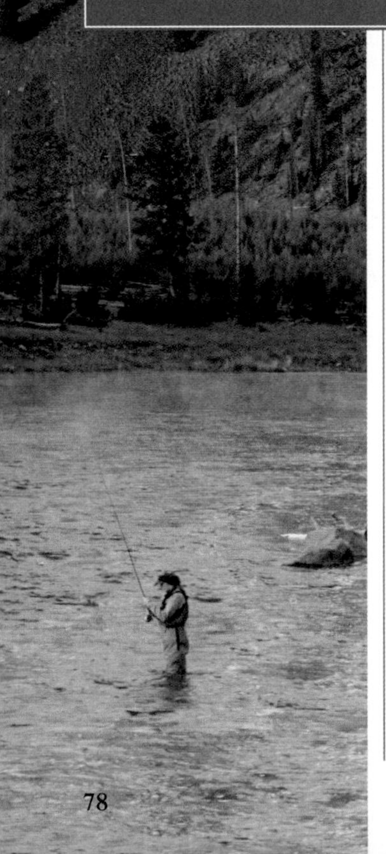

Photo: Drew Rush/Exactostock/SuperStock

the 6th century B.C.

He was wrong, if that river is home water running in your mind, just as you memorized it.

At home, you can "Study to be quiet" by fishing a river running in your mind and "In everything give thanks" that it beats the puffing and moaning of TV's piscatorial-porn fishing shows. (That's not shallow counsel: I once co-starred in a TV fishing show segment.)

The writer-fishermen and angler-authors don't mention another great benefit of home waters running in the mind. Who hasn't heard the lullaby of running water and napped beside a stream? Tossing and turning, sleepless, and far from any running water, fishing home waters that run in my mind has become a more interesting, effective, and healthy soporific than the common nostrums: counting sheep or taking pills.

I usually start on Pincher Creek with a trout or two from the Swimming Hole, wade up and take a 14-incher from the Pump House Pool, fish downstream from above the Corner Backwater and miss the rosy flash of—maybe—a 16–inch rainbow, then hike upstream to the Long Cut Bank. But I never get there before sleep overtakes me. ■

WHO HASN'T HEARD THE LULLABY OF RUNNING WATER AND NAPPED BESIDE A STREAM?

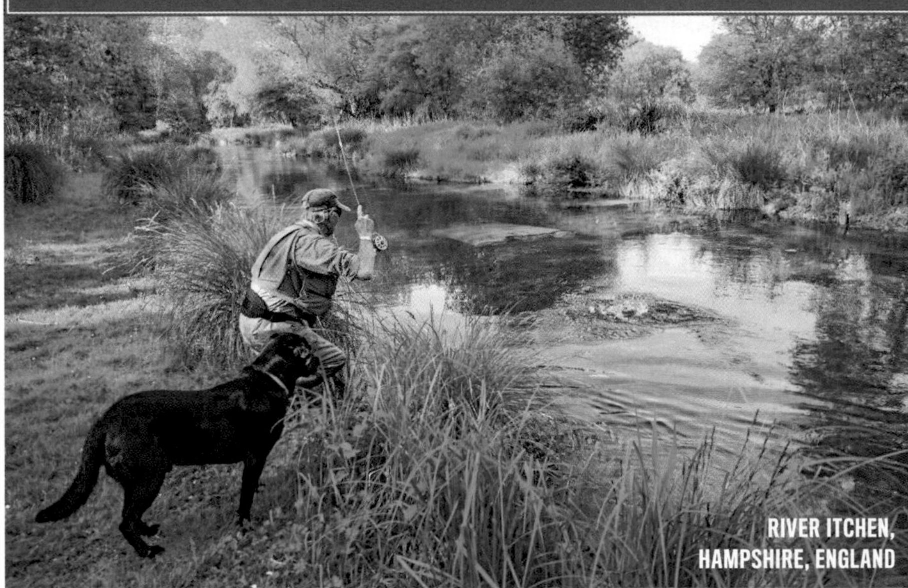

RIVER ITCHEN, HAMPSHIRE, ENGLAND

Bob Scammell is a winner of The Roderick Haig-Brown Award and a former member of Canada's World Fly-Fishing Championship team.

Photo: David Lambroughton/All Canada Photos/SuperStock

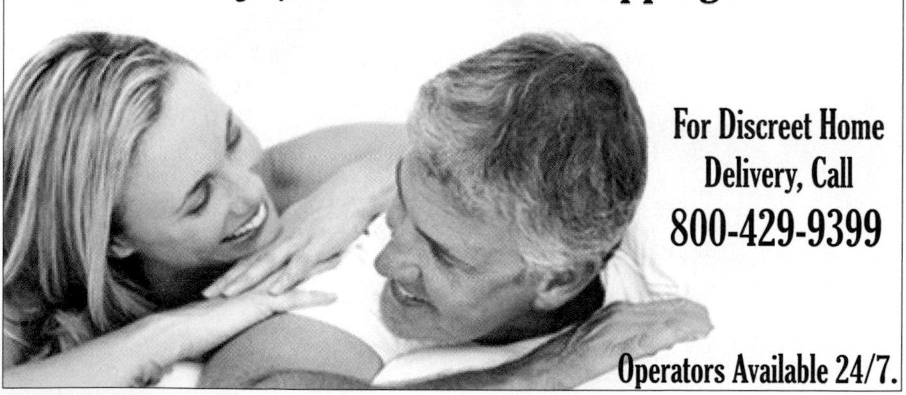

HISTORY
GEORGE WASHINGTON'S EGGNOG
(recipe, page 259)

Almanac Snacks

COMPILED BY SARAH PERREAULT
PHOTOGRAPHY BY BECKY LUIGART-STAYNER

Just as birthdays are marked with special and favorite foods, so it is for the Almanac's 225th anniversary. We chose these recipes to capture the flavor of the Almanac through its most popular topic areas and bring the party home to each of you. Cook, eat, and enjoy!

(continued)

ASTRONOMY
CINNAMON STARS
(recipe, page 259)

NATURE
LADYBUG CUPCAKES
(recipe, page 258)

Photos: food stylist, Ana Kelly; prop stylist, Jan Gautro

GARDENING

Harvest Relish

Turn the bounty of the garden into a condiment to keep and share.

- 5 cups coarsely chopped green bell pepper
- 3 cups coarsely chopped red bell pepper
- 4 cups coarsely chopped onions
- 4 cups coarsely chopped cabbage
- ½ cup pickling salt
- 6 cups sugar
- 2 tablespoons mustard seed
- 1 tablespoon celery seed
- 1½ teaspoons turmeric
- 4 cups apple cider vinegar

1. Combine chopped vegetables. Sprinkle with salt. Set aside overnight.
2. Rinse and drain vegetables, discarding liquid. Put vegetables into a stockpot.
3. In a bowl, combine sugar, spices, vinegar, and 2 cups water. Whisk to blend. Pour over vegetables. Bring to a boil. Reduce heat and simmer for 3 minutes.
4. Pack into sterilized jars, seal, and process in a hot water bath.

Makes about 5 quarts.

HUSBANDRY

Piggy Dip

Go hog-wild when the gang comes over!

your favorite dip
(guacamole, hummus, ranch)
small pretzels
triangle tortilla chips
pimentos

1. Fill a small bowl with dip. Place a pretzel "snout" in the center of dip. Stand two tortilla chip "ears" upright and touching at the bowl's edge. Near the pretzel, place two pimento "eyes." Repeat in other bowls.

2. Serve with tortilla chips, crackers, or veggie sticks.

SEE RECIPES for Weather: Snow Pudding, Nature: Ladybug Cupcakes, Calendar: Day-After-Thanksgiving Hash, Home Remedies: Granny's Chicken Soup, History: George Washington's Eggnog, and Astronomy: Cinnamon Stars **STARTING ON PAGE 258.**

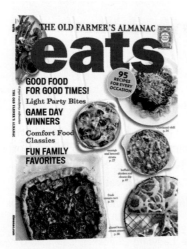

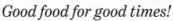

THIRD PRIZE: $100
TATER-CRUSTED CHEESE AND MUSHROOM PIE

SECOND PRIZE: $150
SEACOST SCALLOP PIE

Photo: Becky Luigart-Stayner; food stylist, Ana Kelly; prop stylist, Jan Gautro

The Savory Pie Contest Winners

Many thanks to the hundreds of you who submitted recipes! Tell us at Almanac.com/Feedback whether you too think that they're winners.

(continued)

FIRST PRIZE: $250
SPICED LAMB PIE

FIRST PRIZE: $250

Spiced Lamb Pie

1 medium onion, chopped
2 cloves garlic, diced
1 teaspoon olive oil
1 pound ground lamb
¼ cup chicken stock
3 tablespoons pine nuts
3 tablespoons golden raisins
2 tablespoons tomato paste
2 teaspoons fennel seeds
1 teaspoon cardamom powder
1 teaspoon ground cinnamon
1 teaspoon ground coriander
¾ teaspoon ground ginger
salt and freshly ground black pepper, to taste
4 tablespoons (½ stick) melted butter
9 sheets phyllo pastry
1 egg, for egg wash
sesame seeds
torn mint leaves

1. In a skillet over medium heat, cook onion and garlic in olive oil until soft. Add lamb and cook until browned. Drain the pan. Add remaining ingredients, except butter, phyllo, egg, sesame seeds, and mint. Cook for at least 10 minutes. Mixture should be moist but not runny. If it's dry, add a little stock. Set aside to cool.

2. Preheat oven to 350°F.

3. Lightly brush melted butter on one sheet of phyllo pastry, edges first, then the center. Cover with another phyllo sheet and butter it the same way. Repeat, making three layers.

4. Spread lamb mixture thinly along the edge of the buttered pastry, leaving about 2 inches on each side. Fold the sides inward, then, starting from the edge with meat, roll the pastry into a tight cylinder shape.

5. Repeat, making three cylinders.

6. Form cylinders into one spiral shape (start from the center). To join cylinder ends, rub a wet finger along the seams (cylinders may not join smoothly). Brush entire spiral with egg wash. Sprinkle with sesame seeds and torn mint leaves. Bake for 25 minutes, or until pastry is golden.

Makes 4 servings.

–Eden Dranger, Los Angeles, California

SECOND PRIZE: $150

Seacoast Scallop Pie

BOTTOM CRUST:
1½ cups flour
1 teaspoon salt
½ teaspoon baking powder
4 tablespoons shortening
4 tablespoons (½ stick) unsalted butter
3 tablespoons ice-cold water
1 tablespoon white vinegar

TOP CRACKER CRUST:
1½ cups finely crushed buttery crackers
2 tablespoons fresh lemon juice
4 tablespoons (½ stick) unsalted butter, melted

FILLING:
4 tablespoons (½ stick) butter
1 pound sea scallops, diced
¼ cup flour
1 cup chicken broth
1 cup half-and-half
½ teaspoon freshly ground black pepper
½ cup shredded Havarti cheese

(continued)

FOR BOTTOM CRUST:

1. In a food processor, combine flour, salt, and baking powder. Add shortening and butter and pulse 10 times. Add ice water and vinegar. Process only enough to moisten dough and have it just come together. Shape dough into a ball. Wrap in plastic and refrigerate for 30 minutes.

FOR TOP CRACKER CRUST:

1. In a bowl, combine crackers and lemon juice. Stir in butter until evenly mixed. Set aside.

FOR FILLING:

1. In a saucepan over medium heat, melt butter. Add scallops and cook until opaque. Remove scallops from saucepan and set aside.

2. Reduce heat to low. Add flour to pan. Cook, stirring constantly, for 2 minutes, then add chicken broth, half-and-half, and pepper. Simmer for 5 to 10 minutes, or until thickened. Stir scallops and Havarti into sauce mixture. Continue cooking for 5 minutes.

TO ASSEMBLE:

1. Preheat oven to 375°F.

2. Roll out dough and put into a 9- or 9½-inch round pie plate. Pour scallop mixture into crust. Top with cracker crust. Bake for 1 hour, or until top is golden brown and filling is bubbling.

Makes 6 to 8 servings.

–Denise LaRoche, Farmington, New Hampshire

THIRD PRIZE: $100

Tater-Crusted Cheese and Mushroom Pie

8 ounces fresh mushrooms, finely chopped
¼ cup finely chopped shallots
1 tablespoon olive oil
¼ cup finely chopped parsley
2 tablespoons finely chopped mixed fresh herbs, such as oregano, sage, and thyme
1 tablespoon butter
½ teaspoon freshly ground black pepper
16 ounces frozen Tater Tots, thawed
3 ounces fontina cheese, grated (about 1 cup)
3 ounces Gruyère cheese, grated (about 1 cup)
¾ cup finely crushed potato chips

1. Preheat oven to 425°F.

2. In a skillet over medium heat, combine mushrooms and shallots. Drizzle with olive oil. Cook, stirring occasionally, until pan is dry and mushrooms are golden, about 12 minutes. Stir in parsley, herbs, butter, and pepper. Continue cooking until butter has melted. Set aside.

3. Mash Tater Tots into a 9-inch pie plate. Press firmly, covering bottom and sides, to form a shell. Press fontina onto the Tater Tots to cover. Add mushroom filling. Sprinkle with Gruyère, then with potato chips. Cover loosely with foil. Bake for 25 minutes, removing foil after 20 minutes.

Makes 8 servings.

–Jennifer Burke, San Francisco, California

ENTER THE 2017 RECIPE CONTEST: SWEET POTATOES

Got a great sweet potato recipe that your family and friends love? It could win! See contest rules on page 242.

A CHRONOLOGICAL OF WEATHER PHENOMENA,

with occasional bursts

It is amazing to consider how little was known about the weather when our founder, Robert B. Thomas, published his first Almanac 225 years ago. The entire sky was the last piece of nature to be scientifically classified. No one could explain what the sky was made of (it was thought to be weightless), how clouds managed to stay airborne, why winds shifted direction, what dew was. There was little sense that storms moved along certain paths and that weather was not simply random. The few people who kept meticulous daily weather records did not have a standard language for describing atmospheric conditions or any way to share or analyze their data.

Moreover, the firmament was widely considered to be the domain of God; weather events were often interpreted as divine punishment or benevolence. Until Benjamin Franklin's experiments with his kite and insights into electricity (1752), it took fancy theological footwork to explain why church steeples, usually the highest points in a town, were so often struck by God's wrath in the form of lightning.

TORM HITS 5 STATES

Illustration: Tim Robinson

COMPENDIUM FACTS, AND FORECASTS

of mirth and mayhem

The infant science of meteorology had not progressed much since the 4th century B.C., when Aristotle, in his treatise *Meteorologica,* stated that all activity in what he called the "meteoric zone"—that vast and mysterious territory between Earth and the Moon—was governed by two types of exhalations: hot and dry (which produced shooting stars and the Milky Way) versus cool and wet (which clung to the ground as rain and snow). "Weather" was a collision of exhalations: capricious, unpredictable events, best explained by poets and priests thusly, for example: "St. Swithin's Day if thou dost rain, for 40 days it will remain."

Thomas's first forecasts, based mostly on observations of nature and cycles, were penned just as science was on the verge of understanding and predicting weather. The combination of new technology and standardized data collection in the 19th century moved forecasting from Aristotle toward AccuWeather. Here are some of the highlights of that transition and the weather endured through it.

–Susan Peery

(continued)

1600s

1612: Galileo Galilei begins to study sunspots, key to the solar science behind the Almanac weather forecasts.

1643: Italian physicist Evangelista Torricelli develops a working barometer.

1700s

1717: Four snowstorms in 10 days drop 3 to 4 feet of snow on New England. Puritan Cotton Mather writes: "As mighty a snow as perhaps has been known in the memory of man is at this time lying on the ground."

1724: Daniel G. Fahrenheit of Gdansk, Germany (now Poland), invents the temperature scale that bears his name.

1742: Sweden's Anders Celsius invents his 100-point temperature scale.

1743: Benjamin Franklin, in Philadelphia, receives a letter from his brother in Boston describing an eclipse that Franklin was unable to see due to overcast skies. The brother wrote that inclement weather followed, leading Franklin to deduce that storms travel.

1747–48: New England experiences 25 to 30 snowstorms, with depths of 4 to 5 feet in some areas.

1772: George Washington and Thomas Jefferson both record about 3 feet of snow at their Virginia residences.

1786: Heavy rains on the Delaware and Susquehanna rivers cause The Great Pumpkin Flood, with "heavy pumpkins tumbling downstream like great orange cannonballs."

1800s

1802: English chemist Luke Howard classifies clouds, giving weather observers an invaluable tool and bringing "God's wilderness" into the realm of science.

1805: Francis Beaufort proposes his eponymous wind force scale.

1814: After a 3-year study, W. C. Wells establishes that dew is a product of condensation.

1816: Volcanic ash from an eruption of Mt. Tambora in the Dutch East Indies in 1815 blocks the Sun's light and heat, resulting in "The Year Without a Summer" from New England to Georgia.

(continued)

Photos: Wikimedia

KENYON®
ELECTRIC GRILLS
10% OFF
USE CODE: OFA10
WEATHER RESISTANT CONSTRUCTION
FIRE SAFE & FLAME FREE
500°F+ IN UNDER 7 MINUTES
PROUDLY HANDCRAFTED IN CONNECTICUT
www.CookWithKenyon.com
860.664.4906

" At Bastyr I learned critical ways that nutrition plays a role in natural medicine and health care. "
Lisa Holman, MS (2014)
Create a Healthier World
Naturopathic Medicine • Acupuncture • Nutrition • Psychology • Herbal Sciences
BASTYR UNIVERSITY
Bastyr.edu/StudyHerbs • 855-4-BASTYR • Seattle • San Diego

1817: Alexander von Humboldt publishes the first global climate analysis as a map of average temperatures.

1821: The Great September Gale pounds New York City and New England. William C. Redfield of Connecticut observes from felled trees that severe storm winds rotate, leading to our modern understanding of hurricanes.

1836: On December 20, in central Illinois, a sudden cold snap from 40° to 0°F reportedly causes chickens to freeze in their tracks.

1843: Samuel Heinrich Schwabe notices an approximately 10-year cycle in the number of sunspots. Later observers prove that the cycle averages 11.3 years.

1849: The Smithsonian Institution provides weather instruments to telegraph companies, which return weather reports for maps. By 1860, 500 weather stations are involved.

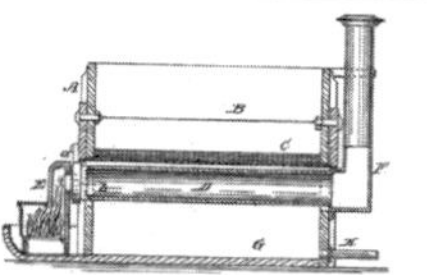

1869: Nicholas H. Borgfeldt patents a snow-melting device to clear streets.

1869: The Saxby Gale, predicted by Briton Stephen Saxby in 1868, roars through Maine and New Brunswick, setting wind speed and rain records.

1870: President Ulysses S. Grant orders the U.S. Army Signal Service to make weather reports; these are the roots of a national weather service.

1873: Frogs rain on Kansas City, Missouri.

1877: Live, footlong alligators land on a farm in South Carolina.

1881: Abbott L. Rotch begins North America's oldest continuous weather record log at Blue Hill Meteorological Observatory in Milton, Massachusetts.

1885: Wilson A. "Snowflake" Bentley, of Jericho, Vermont, takes the first photo of a snowflake crystal, beginning a lifelong study eventually showing that no two snowflakes are alike.

1888: In January, a "blue norther" northern Great Plains storm drops temperatures to −20°F, killing hundreds of children returning home from school and homesteaders caught in the open.

1889: 10 inches of rain in 24 hours burst the South Fork Dam and send 20 million tons of water downstream in The Johnstown (Pa.) Flood.

1894: New Jersey's William Eddy makes the first temperature observations aloft by flying a self-recording thermometer on five kites.

1895: *The New York Times:* "Geologists think that the world may be frozen up again."

Photos, this page: William C. Redfield and snow-melting device, Wikimedia; all others, Thinkstock
Photos, opposite page: *Titanic,* Regina Cyclone, and Silver Lake, Colorado, Wikimedia; all others, Thinkstock

1898: Hailstones weighing up to 11 ounces hammer Chicago in July.

1899: Swedish immigrant Victor Wickstrom, skilled in weather prognostication through pig spleen analysis, arrives in Saskatchewan. He teaches his son Ernest, who shares the lore with his son, Glen ("Gus"). In the 1950s and '60s, Gus refines and popularizes the art. Following his death in 2007, nephew Jeff Woodward continues the practice.

1900s

1900: A May thunderstorm dumps rain—and fish—on Olneyville, Rhode Island.

1900: The Galveston (Tex.) Hurricane overwashes the island city with 15 feet of water; 6,000 lives are lost.

1912: RMS *Titanic* hits an iceberg and sinks. *The New York Times:* "An ice age is encroaching." *Los Angeles Times:* "The human race will have to fight for its existence against cold."

1912: George E. Hale observes two 11-year Schwabe solar cycles in close synchrony—a double sunspot, or Hale, cycle.

1912: The Regina (Sask.) Cyclone leaves 2,500 of the city's citizens homeless.

1913: The Great Lakes' Black Sunday Storm sinks 12 ships. The crew members of a surviving vessel lash themselves to the mast—and freeze to death.

1915: Cloud seeder Charles Mallory ("The Rain Man") Hatfield is hired by San Diego, California, and a torrent of 28 inches ("Hatfield's Flood") arrives.

1921: Then-world-record 1-day snowfall of 76 inches drops on Silver Lake, Colorado.

1923: *The Washington Post:* "The Ice Age Is Coming Here." *Chicago Tribune:* "Scientist Says Arctic Ice Will Wipe Out Canada and Parts of Europe and Asia, and Switzerland Would Be Entirely Obliterated."

STORM HITS 5 STATES;
1,000 DEAD, 3,000 HURT

Tornado Travels Path of 700 Miles, Causing Greatest Loss In Indiana, Illinois and Missouri.

Towns Are Wiped Out, Fire Adding to Horror Havoc; Thousands Made Homeless; Troops Called Out.

1925: The Great Tri-State Tornado rips through Missouri, Illinois, and Indiana, on a path up to 1 mile wide over almost 220 miles.

1930: A hailstone containing an 8-inch gopher turtle falls near Vicksburg, Mississippi.

1931: Drought and depleted soils create conditions conducive to 5 years of the great dust storms of America's midwestern Dust Bowl.

1933: Ottawa records −39°C (−38°F) on December 29.

1933: *The New York Times:* "America is in longest warm spell since 1776, with temperatures in a 25-year rise."

(continued)

1935: 60-mph winds blow dirt across Oklahoma on Black Sunday, April 14.

1935: The world's meteorologists set three decades as the basis for "average" comparisons.

1936: Elvis Presley, age 1½, survives an April tornado that wipes out homes near his own in Tupelo, Mississippi.

1936: A July heat wave—44°C (111°F)—in Manitoba and Ontario causes fruit to bake on trees. In Syracuse, New York, a woman fries an egg on the sidewalk when temps top 100°F.

1938: January in Saskatchewan is so cold that cattle reportedly walk while they pee, lest icicles freeze them in place.

1938: The Great New England Hurricane wreaks havoc, with waves up to 30 feet high on the Rhode Island coast.

1938: Baseball-size hail falls on Washington, D.C., in April.

1939: *TIME:* ". . . weathermen have no doubt that the world, at least for the time being, is growing warmer."

1947: A 10-day blizzard from Calgary to Winnipeg causes people to dig tunnels to outhouses.

1947: Snag, Yukon Territory, records −63°C (−81°F), North America's coldest temperature.

1948: Dr. C. H. Curran, curator of insects at NYC's American Museum of Natural History, begins to study the bands on woolly bear caterpillars *(Pyrrharctia isabella)*. He postulates that the wider the brown midsection, the milder the coming winter will be.

1948: Manitoba cold reportedly causes chimney smoke to freeze and choke out the fire below.

1949: Joanne M. Simpson is the first woman to earn a Ph.D. in meteorology.

1950s: U.S. National Weather Bureau adopts 30-year comparison base but advances it a decade every 10 years.

1950: Cloud seeder Wallace E. Howell is hired by New York City. Showers and fog delay his first flight. More rain, plus an April snowstorm, follow. Reservoirs eventually fill to 99 percent capacity, but locals are skeptical about Howell's impact on the precipitation.

1950: The Storm of the Century sends hurricane-force winds and heavy snow across 22 states.

(continued)

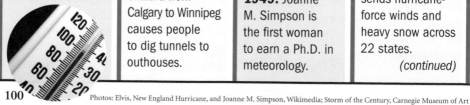

Photos: Elvis, New England Hurricane, and Joanne M. Simpson, Wikimedia; Storm of the Century, Carnegie Museum of Art

ADVERTISEMENT
POST & BEAM
BARNS | GARAGES | PAVILIONS
gctimberframes.com
(860) 454-9103
Build Services &
Timber Frame Kits
GREAT COUNTRY
TIMBER FRAMES

1952: *The New York Times:* "Melting glaciers are the trump card of global warming."

1953: "Heavy squall and that's not all" on the Almanac's June Calendar Pages portends the Great Worcester (Mass.) Tornado that lasts 84 minutes, travels 46 miles, and ultimately kills 94 people.

1954: Hurricane Hazel dumps 300 million tons of rain on Toronto.

1954: CBC-TV, with chalk-tossing meteorologist Percy Saltzman, makes its debut. He becomes the first Canadian weathercaster to use radar and satellite imagery.

1956: Sweden's Carl-Gustaf Rossby, expert in large-scale atmospheric motions (e.g., jet streams), appears on *TIME* magazine's cover.

1960: NASA launches *TIROS-1,* the first successful U.S. weather satellite.

1962: Dianne W. Clatto becomes the first full-time African-American TV weathercaster, at KSD, St. Louis, Mo.

1967: With a game-time temperature of −13°F (windchill: −46°F), "The Ice Bowl"—aka the NFL Championship game in Green Bay, Wisconsin, on New Year's Eve—is won by the home team Packers over the Dallas Cowboys, 21–17.

1967: Canada's greatest 1-day rainfall—489.2 mm (19.26 inches)—deluges Ucluelet Brynnor Mines, British Columbia.

1969: A tide during Hurricane Camille leaves a watermark 25 feet high in a Pass Christian, Mississippi, building.

1969: Herbert Saffir and Bob Simpson formulate their eponymous hurricane scale to describe storm intensity based on wind strength.

1960s–70s: When the brutal cold that prevailed worldwide in the 1960s continues into the '70s, *TIME* and *Newsweek* report on the coming ice age.

1970: The U.S. Weather Bureau becomes the National Weather Service.

1971: Montreal's Snowstorm of the Century leaves behind second-story drifts and 500,000 truckloads of snow.

1976–79: The U.S. and many other parts of the Western Hemisphere experience the coldest contiguous winters on record.

1977: "Human Lightning Rod" Roy C. Sullivan of Virginia survives the world-record seventh (and last) strike to hit him.

Photos: Hurricane Camille, NOAA; Snowstorm of the Century, Wikimedia

1978: The New England Blizzard drops 30 to 36 inches of snow, paralyzing the region for a week.

The South Middlesex News

5 DAYS IN FEBRUARY

a storm you'll never forget

1978: Some Los Angeles, California, swimming pool owners report ice on the water surface in December.

1979: Winooski, Vermont: "Plan for the Study of Dome Over Town Is Approved" (to protect the city from cold).

1980: Brutal summer heat wave hits much of the U.S. (See 1979: Winooski residents now realize that they would have fried to death.)

1983: Children are thawed off their playground equipment in Moosomin, Saskatchewan, as temperatures drop to −42°C (−44°F).

1983: Hurricane Alicia fulfills the Almanac prophecy of "tropical storm may bring torrential rains" to the Gulf Coast and Texas.

1988: Record heat and drought in the eastern and central U.S. cause over $40 billion in crop losses.

1991: Cold from Canada, a Midwest low-pressure system, and Hurricane Grace in the Atlantic become the Halloween Northeaster ("The Perfect Storm"), with 30- to 40-foot waves, massive destruction, and the loss of the crew of the *Andrea Gail.*

1992: As the Almanac predicts ("a possible hurricane crossing southern Florida at the end of August"), Hurricane Andrew makes landfall at Homestead, Florida, on August 24.

1993: A superstorm brings 43 inches of snow to Syracuse, New York, in March. The Almanac reads: "Wintry conditions will set in and persist through March, bringing well above-normal precipitation and snowfall."

1994: −43°C (−45°F) in Kapuskasing, Ontario, causes car tires to fall off their rims.

1995: Ocean liner *Queen Elizabeth 2* is hit with a world-record 98-foot-high wave off Newfoundland during Hurricane Luis.

1997: The 1998 Almanac predicts: "The year ahead may be the warmest on record overall, with a mild winter in much of the country." Winter 1997–98 is the U.S.'s second-warmest to date, with well below-normal snowfall.

1997: The Great April Fool's Day Snowstorm in New York and New England is presaged by the Almanac: "A big snowstorm may serve as nature's April Fool's joke."

1997: The Almanac forecasts a "tropical storm in late May, threatening the [Florida] Keys before the official start of the hurricane season on June 1." The first storm is on May 31.

(continued)

Photos: Tropical storm, NOAA; all others, Wikimedia

1998: The Ice Storm of the Century hits eastern Canada, taking down 120,000 km (almost 75,000 miles) of power lines and millions of trees.

1998: *The New York Times:* "Earth Temperature in 1998 Is Reported at Record High."

2000s

2003: Hurricane Isabel picks up frog eggs in the U.S. South and deposits them in Berlin, Connecticut.

2005: On August 29, Hurricane Katrina floods New Orleans, Louisiana, and wreaks havoc in Mississippi.

2007: Despite the bitter cold throughout much of the Southern Hemisphere, NASA's James Hansen declares 2007 the second warmest year on record.

2008: Freezing rain on December 11–12 produces ½ to 1½ inches of ice from Maine to Pennsylvania.

2008: *International Herald Tribune:* "Snow Day In Baghdad." The coldest weather since 1964 hits the Middle East, while China experiences unusually heavy snow and freezing temperatures.

2010: A Miami, Fla., chill to 35°F causes iguanas to enter a torporic state and fall out of trees.

2013: An October 4–5 blizzard drops up to 44 inches of snow in South Dakota's Black Hills, killing thousands of cattle.

2014: Over November 17–19, more than 5 feet of lake-effect snow fall on parts of Buffalo, New York. One to 4 feet more follow on November 19–20.

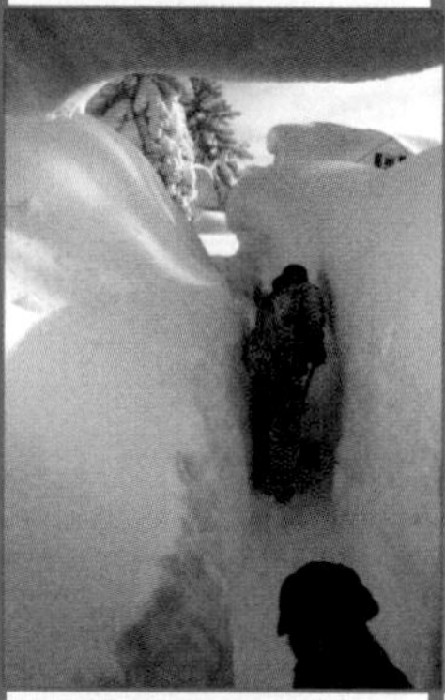

2014–15: Globally, December through February is warmest on record (since 1880) according to NOAA, topping previously hottest 2007 by 0.05 degree F (0.03 degree C).

2015: Seasonal snowfall at Logan Airport in Boston, Massachusetts, breaks an all-time record with a total of 110.6 inches.

2015: NASA declares July the warmest on record, at 1.46 degrees F (0.81 degree C) above the 20th-century average.

2015: October 1 begins a new "water year" in California and the fifth year of drought, including the third driest year since record-keeping began in 1896.

2016: NOAA declares 2015 the hottest year in 136 years of record-keeping. ■

–compiled by Jack Burnett

Jack Burnett is the managing editor of *The Old Farmer's Almanac.*

Photos: Hurricane Katrina, NOAA; Buffalo, NY, Tanya Weston Muscato; all others, Wikimedia

HOME RESOURCE

GARDEN • HOME • FOOD • GIFTS

UNIQUE PRODUCTS AND SERVICES TO FILL YOUR EVERY NEED

Millie's PIEROGI

Homemade Pierogi

We make and ship fully-cooked pierogi with these popular fillings: cabbage, potato & cheese, prune, blueberry, potato & onion, farmer's cheese, or potato & cheese w/kielbasa.

Box of 6 trays $45.00
Box of 10 trays $68.00
Polish Party Pack $69.00

Plus S&H. One dozen pierogi/tray.

129 Broadway • Chicopee Falls, MA 01020
800-743-7641 • MilliesPierogi.com

Say Hello to the Last Litter Box You Will Ever Buy

The highest rated automatic self-cleaning litter box just got better. Say goodbye to the litter box smell and enjoy the freedom from scooping litter.

888-227-8650 • Litter-Robot.com

HARD-TO-FIND Traditional Moveable Louver Shutters

Quality hardwoods custom made to your size!

Shuttercraft.com

203-245-2608

Madison, CT

Shelves That Slide

Custom pullout shelves for your cabinets

Sliding trash and recycle centers, tip out trays, lazy susans and wire pullouts. Order online, call or email for a free catalog.

ShelvesThatSlide.com
800-598-7390

Gothic Arch Greenhouses

Most Trusted Name in Greenhouses & Supplies

Serving the horticultural industry since 1946. The leading provider offering a huge selection of top-quality greenhouse kits & supplies to suit the needs of growers large & small.

800-531-4769 • GothicArchGreenhouses.com

Farm Fresh Vegetables Without the Farm™

The GrowBox™ automatically waters and adds the correct amount of fertilizer every day, keeps weeds out, and even shows you the best spacing for your plants. Stellar results are 100% Guaranteed or your money back.

Grow Box

800-519-1955 • AGardenPatch.com/FF

Southern Exposure Seed Exchange

Specializing in heirloom seeds.

Our 700+ varieties offer remarkable flavor and superior disease and pest resistance.

Heirloom • Organic Non-GMO

SouthernExposure.com

WINTER 2016–17

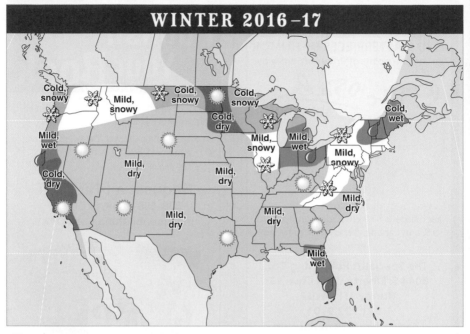

These weather maps correspond to the winter (November through March) and summer (June through August) predictions in the General Weather Forecast (opposite). Forecast terms here represent deviations from the normals; learn more on page 217.

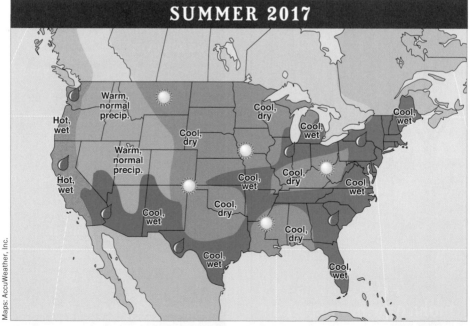

SUMMER 2017

Maps: AccuWeather, Inc.

2016-17

The General Weather Report and Forecast

FOR REGIONAL FORECASTS, SEE PAGES 220-237.

What's shaping the weather? Solar Cycle 24, the smallest in more than 100 years, is well into its declining phase after reaching double peaks in late 2011 and early 2014. As solar activity continues to decline from these low peaks toward the minima in early 2019, we expect temperatures in much of the nation to be much colder than last winter but still above normal. The winter of 2016–17 will feature above-normal snowfall in the North, along the spine of the Appalachians, and in northern Illinois but below-normal snowfall in other areas.

With last winter's strong El Niño being replaced by a moderate La Niña this winter, cold air masses will be able to build in Canada and move southward into the United States. Other important factors in the coming weather patterns include the Atlantic Multidecadal Oscillation (AMO) in a continued warm phase, the North Atlantic Oscillation (NAO) in a cold phase, and the Pacific Decadal Oscillation (PDO) in the early stages of its warm cycle. Oscillations are linked ocean–atmosphere patterns that influence the weather over periods of weeks to years.

WINTER will be much colder than last winter, but still above normal, in much of the eastern two-thirds of the nation. The exceptions will be in a swath from North Dakota to Maine, which will have below-normal temps. Most of the Pacific states will have below-normal temps, with above-normal temps in the Intermountain region and Desert Southwest. Snowfall will be above normal from southern New England and western New York southwestward through the Appalachians; from eastern Minnesota eastward to the UP (Upper Peninsula) of Michigan and southward to St. Louis, Missouri; and from central North Dakota westward to the Pacific. We expect below-normal snowfall in most other places that normally receive snow. Precipitation will be below normal across most of the southern two-thirds of the nation and above normal in the North, with the primary exceptions being above-normal rainfall in northern California, southern Oregon, portions of the western Lower Lakes region, and Florida. With rainfall below normal in most of California, the drought there will continue.

SPRING will be cooler than normal in the Northeast and Desert Southwest, but warmer than normal in most other areas. Spring precipitation will be below normal from the Upper Midwest southward to the Deep South, in the Pacific Northwest and Intermountain regions, and in the Lower Lakes and above normal elsewhere.

SUMMER temperatures will be above normal in the Pacific and Intermountain states but below normal elsewhere. Rainfall will be below normal in much of the Ohio Valley, Deep South, Upper Midwest, Heartland, High Plains, and Oklahoma and northern Texas and near or above normal elsewhere.

HURRICANE SEASON will be more active along the Atlantic seaboard than along the Gulf Coast. The best chances for a major hurricane strike are in mid-June from Florida to New England and in late August and early September from Florida to North Carolina.

AUTUMN will be warmer than normal from southern New England to Florida, in the Upper Midwest, and from Texas eastward and cooler than normal in most other areas. Precipitation will be below normal in Florida and the Southeast and near or above normal elsewhere.

To learn how we make our weather predictions, turn to page 217 and to get a summary of the results of our forecast for last winter, turn to page 218.

THE OLD FARMER'S ALMANAC

Established in 1792 and published every year thereafter

ROBERT B. THOMAS, *founder* (1766–1846)

YANKEE PUBLISHING INC.

EDITORIAL AND PUBLISHING OFFICES

P.O. Box 520, 1121 Main Street, Dublin, NH 03444
Phone: 603-563-8111 • Fax: 603-563-8252

CONTACT US

We welcome your questions and comments about articles in and topics for this Almanac. Mail all editorial correspondence to Editor, The Old Farmer's Almanac, P.O. Box 520, Dublin, NH 03444-0520; fax us at 603-563-8252; or contact us through Almanac.com/Feedback. *The Old Farmer's Almanac* can not accept responsibility for unsolicited manuscripts and will not acknowledge any hard-copy queries or manuscripts that do not include a stamped and addressed return envelope.

All printing inks used in this edition of *The Old Farmer's Almanac* are soy-based. This product is recyclable. Consult local recycling regulations for the right way to do it.

Thank you for buying this Almanac! We hope that you find it "useful, with a pleasant degree of humor." Thanks, too, to everyone who had a hand in it, including advertisers, distributors, printers, and sales and delivery people.

OUR CONTRIBUTORS

Bob Berman, our astronomy editor, is the director of Overlook Observatory in Woodstock and Storm King Observatory in Cornwall, both in New York. In 1976, he founded the Catskill Astronomical Society. Bob has led many aurora and eclipse expeditions, venturing as far as the Arctic and Antarctic.

Tim Clark, a retired high school English teacher from New Hampshire, wrote the Farmer's Calendar essays that appear in this edition. His recordings of them are available free at Almanac.com/Podcast. He has composed the weather doggerel on the Calendar Pages since 1980.

Bethany E. Cobb, our astronomer, earned a Ph.D. in astronomy at Yale University and is an Assistant Professor of Honors and Physics at George Washington University. She also conducts research on gamma-ray bursts and follows numerous astronomy pursuits, including teaching astronomy to adults at the Osher Lifelong Learning Institute at UC Berkeley. When she is not scanning the sky, she enjoys playing the violin, figure skating, and reading science fiction.

Celeste Longacre, our astrologer, often refers to astrology as "a study of timing, and timing is everything." A New Hampshire native, she has been a practicing astrologer for more than 25 years. Her book, *Celeste's Garden Delights* (2015), is available for sale on her Web site, www.celestelongacre.com.

Michael Steinberg, our meteorologist, has been forecasting weather for the Almanac since 1996. In addition to college degrees in atmospheric science and meteorology, he brings a lifetime of experience to the task: He began predicting weather when he attended the only high school in the world with weather Teletypes and radar.

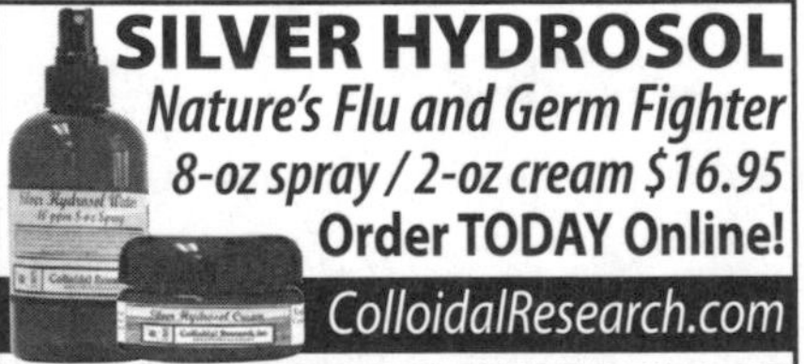

THE OLD FARMER'S ALMANAC

Established in 1792 and published every year thereafter

ROBERT B. THOMAS, *founder* (1766–1846)

YANKEE PUBLISHING INC.
P.O. Box 520, 1121 Main Street, Dublin, NH 03444
Phone: 603-563-8111 • Fax: 603-563-8252

PUBLISHER *(23rd since 1792)*: Sherin Pierce
EDITOR IN CHIEF: Judson D. Hale Sr.

FOR DISPLAY ADVERTISING RATES
Go to Almanac.com/AdvertisingInfo or
Call 800-895-9265, ext. 109

Stephanie Bernbach-Crowe • 914-827-0015
Steve Hall • 800-736-1100, ext. 320
Susan Lyman • 646-221-4169

FOR CLASSIFIED ADVERTISING
Almanac.com/Advertising

AD PRODUCTION COORDINATOR: Janet Grant

PUBLIC RELATIONS
Quinn/Brein • 206-842-8922
ginger@quinnbrein.com

CONSUMER MAIL ORDERS
Call 800-ALMANAC (800-256-2622)
or go to Almanac.com/Shop

CONSUMER MARKETING MANAGER:
Kate McPherson • 800-895-9265, ext. 188

RETAIL SALES
Stacey Korpi, 800-895-9265, ext. 160
Janice Edson, ext. 126

DISTRIBUTORS
NATIONAL: Curtis Circulation Company
New Milford, NJ
BOOKSTORE: Houghton Mifflin Harcourt
Boston, MA

The Old Farmer's Almanac publications are available for sales promotions or premiums. Contact Beacon Promotions, info@beaconpromotions.com.

YANKEE PUBLISHING INCORPORATED

Jamie Trowbridge, *President;* Judson D. Hale Sr., *Senior Vice President;* Paul Belliveau, Jody Bugbee, Judson D. Hale Jr., Brook Holmberg, Sherin Pierce, *Vice Presidents.*

PRINTED IN U.S.A.

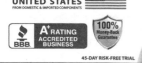

Eclipses

■ There will be four eclipses in 2017, two of the Sun and two of the Moon. Solar eclipses are visible only in certain areas and require eye protection to be viewed safely. Lunar eclipses are technically visible from the entire night side of Earth, but during a penumbral eclipse, the dimming of the Moon's illumination is slight. See the Astronomical Glossary, **page 126,** for explanations of the different types of eclipses.

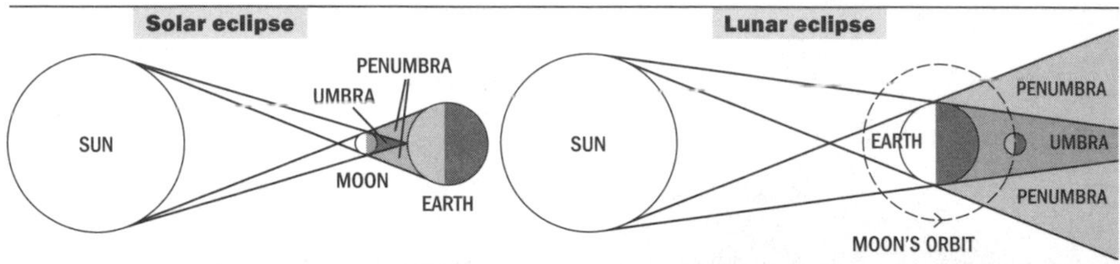

February 10: Penumbral eclipse of the Moon. This eclipse will be visible from North America. The Moon will enter the penumbra at 5:32 P.M. EST and leave it at 9:55 P.M.

February 26: Annular eclipse of the Sun. This eclipse will not be visible from North America but can be viewed from the southeastern Pacific Ocean, southern half of South America, southern Africa, and Antarctica.

August 7: Partial eclipse of the Moon. This eclipse will not be visible from North America but can be seen from the western Pacific Ocean, Oceania, Australia, New Zealand, Asia, Africa, Europe, and the easternmost tip of South America.

August 21: Total eclipse of the Sun. This eclipse will be visible from North America. It will begin at 11:47 A.M. EDT and end at 5:04 P.M. All regions of North America will be able to view a partial eclipse at some point during this time span (exact times depend on specific locations). The total eclipse—viewable for up to 2 minutes and 40 seconds at most—will be visible only along a narrow path running southeastward from Oregon to South Carolina and crossing through parts of Idaho, Wyoming, Nebraska, Kansas, Missouri, Illinois, Kentucky, Tennessee, and North Carolina. Cities that will experience totality include Salem, OR; Lincoln, NE; Kansas City, Jefferson City, and St. Louis, MO; Nashville, TN; and Columbia and Charleston, SC. For more details, **see page 130**. The next total solar eclipse visible from North America will occur in 2024.

Full-Moon Dates (Eastern Time)

	2017	2018	2019	2020	2021
Jan.	12	1 & 31	21	10	28
Feb.	10	–	19	9	27
Mar.	12	1 & 31	20	9	28
Apr.	11	29	19	7	26
May	10	29	18	7	26
June	9	28	17	5	24
July	9	27	16	5	23
Aug.	7	26	15	3	22
Sept.	6	24	14	2	20
Oct.	5	24	13	1 & 31	20
Nov.	4	23	12	30	19
Dec.	3	22	12	29	18

The Moon's Path

The Moon's path across the sky changes with the seasons. Full Moons are very high in the sky (at midnight) between November and February and very low in the sky between May and July.

Next Total Eclipses of the Sun

July 2, 2019: visible from South America and the South Pacific Ocean.
December 14, 2020: visible from South America and Antarctica.

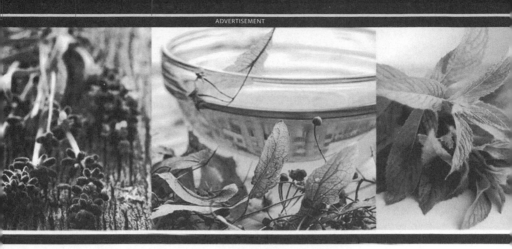

Bright Stars

Transit Times

■ This table shows the time (EST or EDT) and altitude of a star as it transits the meridian (i.e., reaches its highest elevation while passing over the horizon's south point) at Boston on the dates shown. The transit time on any other date differs from that of the nearest date listed by approximately 4 minutes per day. To find the time of a star's transit for your location, convert its time at Boston using Key Letter C **(see Time Corrections, page 252)**.

–Beth Krommes

Star	Constellation	Magnitude	Time of Transit (EST/EDT) **Bold = P.M.** Light = A.M. Jan. 1	Mar. 1	May 1	July 1	Sept. 1	Nov. 1	Altitude (degrees)
Altair	Aquila	0.8	**12:50**	8:58	5:58	1:58	**9:50**	**5:50**	56.3
Deneb	Cygnus	1.3	**1:40**	9:48	6:48	2:48	**10:40**	**6:41**	92.8
Fomalhaut	Psc. Aus.	1.2	**3:56**	**12:04**	9:04	5:04	1:01	**8:57**	17.8
Algol	Perseus	2.2	**8:06**	**4:14**	**1:14**	9:14	5:11	1:11	88.5
Aldebaran	Taurus	0.9	**9:33**	**5:41**	**2:42**	10:42	6:38	2:38	64.1
Rigel	Orion	0.1	**10:12**	**6:20**	**3:20**	11:20	7:16	3:17	39.4
Capella	Auriga	0.1	**10:14**	**6:22**	**3:23**	11:23	7:19	3:19	93.6
Bellatrix	Orion	1.6	**10:22**	**6:30**	**3:31**	11:31	7:27	3:27	54.0
Betelgeuse	Orion	var. 0.4	**10:52**	**7:00**	**4:01**	**12:01**	7:57	3:57	55.0
Sirius	Can. Maj.	–1.4	**11:42**	**7:50**	**4:50**	**12:50**	8:47	4:47	31.0
Procyon	Can. Min.	0.4	12:40	**8:44**	**5:44**	**1:45**	9:41	5:41	52.9
Pollux	Gemini	1.2	12:46	**8:50**	**5:51**	**1:51**	9:47	5:47	75.7
Regulus	Leo	1.4	3:09	**11:13**	**8:13**	**4:13**	**12:09**	8:10	59.7
Spica	Virgo	var. 1.0	6:25	2:33	**11:29**	**7:30**	**3:26**	11:26	36.6
Arcturus	Boötes	–0.1	7:15	3:23	12:24	**8:20**	**4:16**	**12:16**	66.9
Antares	Scorpius	var. 0.9	9:29	5:37	2:37	**10:33**	**6:30**	**2:30**	21.3
Vega	Lyra	0	11:36	7:44	4:44	12:44	**8:36**	**4:36**	86.4

Rise and Set Times

■ To find the time of a star's rising at Boston on any date, subtract the interval shown at right from the star's transit time on that date; add the interval to find the star's setting time. To find the rising and setting times for your city, convert the Boston transit times above using the Key Letter shown at right before applying the interval **(see Time Corrections, page 252)**. The directions in which the stars rise and set, shown for Boston, are generally useful throughout the United States. Deneb, Algol, Capella, and Vega are circumpolar stars—they never set but appear to circle the celestial north pole.

Star	Interval (h. m.)	Rising Key	Rising Dir.*	Setting Key	Setting Dir.*
Altair	6 36	B	EbN	E	WbN
Fomalhaut	3 59	E	SE	D	SW
Aldebaran	7 06	B	ENE	D	WNW
Rigel	5 33	D	EbS	B	WbS
Bellatrix	6 27	B	EbN	D	WbN
Betelgeuse	6 31	B	EbN	D	WbN
Sirius	5 00	D	ESE	B	WSW
Procyon	6 23	B	EbN	D	WbN
Pollux	8 01	A	NE	E	NW
Regulus	6 49	B	EbN	D	WbN
Spica	5 23	D	EbS	B	WbS
Arcturus	7 19	A	ENE	E	WNW
Antares	4 17	E	SEbE	A	SWbW

*b = "by"

The Twilight Zone

Twilight is the time when the sky is partially illuminated preceding sunrise and again following sunset. The ranges of twilight are defined according to the Sun's position below the horizon. **Civil twilight** occurs when the Sun's center is between the horizon and 6 degrees below the horizon (visually, the horizon is clearly defined). **Nautical twilight** occurs when the center is between 6 and 12 degrees below the horizon (the horizon is distinct). **Astronomical twilight** occurs when the center is between 12 and 18 degrees below the horizon (sky illumination is imperceptible). When the center is at 18 degrees (**dawn** or **dark**) or below, there is no illumination.

Length of Astronomical Twilight (hours and minutes)

LATITUDE	Jan. 1 to Apr. 10	Apr. 11 to May 2	May 3 to May 14	May 15 to May 25	May 26 to July 22	July 23 to Aug. 3	Aug. 4 to Aug. 14	Aug. 15 to Sept. 5	Sept. 6 to Dec. 31
25°N to 30°N	1 20	1 23	1 26	1 29	1 32	1 29	1 26	1 23	1 20
31°N to 36°N	1 26	1 28	1 34	1 38	1 43	1 38	1 34	1 28	1 26
37°N to 42°N	1 33	1 39	1 47	1 52	1 59	1 52	1 47	1 39	1 33
43°N to 47°N	1 42	1 51	2 02	2 13	2 27	2 13	2 02	1 51	1 42
48°N to 49°N	1 50	2 04	2 22	2 42	—	2 42	2 22	2 04	1 50

TO DETERMINE THE LENGTH OF TWILIGHT: The length of twilight changes with latitude and the time of year. See the **Time Corrections, page 252,** to find the latitude of your city or the city nearest you. Use that figure in the chart above with the appropriate date to calculate the length of twilight in your area.

TO DETERMINE WHEN DAWN OR DARK WILL OCCUR: Calculate the sunrise/sunset times for your locality using the instructions in **How to Use This Almanac, page 138.** Subtract the length of twilight from the time of sunrise to determine when dawn breaks. Add the length of twilight to the time of sunset to determine when dark descends.

EXAMPLE:

Boston, Mass. (latitude 42°22')

Sunrise, August 1	**5:37 A.M. EDT**
Length of twilight	**– 1 52**
Dawn breaks	**3:45 A.M.**
Sunset, August 1	**8:03 P.M. EDT**
Length of twilight	**+1 52**
Dark descends	**9:55 P.M.**

Principal Meteor Showers

SHOWER	BEST VIEWING	POINT OF ORIGIN	DATE OF MAXIMUM*	NO. PER HOUR**	ASSOCIATED COMET
Quadrantid	**Predawn**	**N**	**Jan. 4**	**25**	**—**
Lyrid	Predawn	S	Apr. 22	10	Thatcher
Eta Aquarid	Predawn	SE	May 4	10	Halley
Delta Aquarid	Predawn	S	July 30	10	—
Perseid	**Predawn**	**NE**	**Aug. 11–13**	**50**	**Swift-Tuttle**
Draconid	Late evening	NW	Oct. 9	6	Giacobini-Zinner
Orionid	Predawn	S	Oct. 21–22	15	Halley
Taurid	Late evening	S	Nov. 9	3	Encke
Leonid	Predawn	S	Nov. 17–18	10	Tempel-Tuttle
Andromedid	Late evening	S	Nov. 25–27	5	Biela
Geminid	**All night**	**NE**	**Dec. 13–14**	**75**	**—**
Ursid	Predawn	N	Dec. 22	5	Tuttle

May vary by one or two days* ***Moonless, rural sky* **Bold = *most prominent*

The Visible Planets

■ Listed here for Boston are viewing suggestions for and the rise and set times (EST/EDT) of Venus, Mars, Jupiter, and Saturn on specific days each month, as well as when it is best to view Mercury. Approximate rise and set times for other days can be found by interpolation. Use the Key Letters at the right of each listing to convert the times for other localities **(see pages 138 and 252).** *For all planet rise and set times by zip code, visit* **Almanac.com/Astronomy.**

Venus

This is a very unusual year for the brightest planet. It is vividly visible the first 11 months of 2017; in most years, it is lost in solar glare about a third of the time. This is because it has no superior conjunction this year and goes behind the Sun only in December. January begins with Venus nicely high in the west and steadily brightening. It reaches greatest brilliancy in February at a shadow-casting magnitude –4.8, then rapidly plunges downward in March for its inferior conjunction on the 25th. Venus quickly returns as a morning star in April and shines at its brightest at the end of that month and in early May. Remaining conspicuous before dawn until November, it has no tight conjunctions with the Moon in 2017 but does offer a super-close meeting with Mars on October 5.

Date		Time	Key	Date		Time	Key	Date		Time	Key	Date		Time	Key
Jan. 1	**set**	**8:15**	B	Apr. 1	rise	5:26	C	July 1	rise	2:37	B	Oct. 1	rise	4:35	B
Jan. 11	**set**	**8:32**	C	Apr. 11	rise	4:50	C	July 11	rise	2:32	B	Oct. 11	rise	4:59	C
Jan. 21	**set**	**8:46**	C	Apr. 21	rise	4:22	C	July 21	rise	2:32	A	Oct. 21	rise	5:23	C
Feb. 1	**set**	**8:54**	C	May 1	rise	4:00	C	Aug. 1	rise	2:38	A	Nov. 1	rise	5:50	D
Feb. 11	**set**	**8:55**	D	May 11	rise	3:42	C	Aug. 11	rise	2:49	A	Nov. 11	rise	5:15	D
Feb. 21	**set**	**8:45**	D	May 21	rise	3:26	C	Aug. 21	rise	3:04	A	Nov. 21	rise	5:41	E
Mar. 1	**set**	**8:26**	D	June 1	rise	3:09	B	Sept. 1	rise	3:26	B	Dec. 1	rise	6:06	E
Mar. 11	**set**	**7:44**	D	June 11	rise	2:56	B	Sept. 11	rise	3:48	B	Dec. 11	rise	6:31	E
Mar. 21	rise	6:18	B	June 21	rise	2:45	B	Sept. 21	rise	4:11	B	Dec. 21	rise	6:52	E
												Dec. 31	rise	7:09	E

Mars

Mars comes close to Earth every 26 months, so it alternates years of brilliancy. This is one of its "off" years. Still, it starts 2017 at a respectable magnitude 1, in Aquarius, and meets the crescent Moon on January 2. It is an easy naked-eye object as it floats a third of the way up the southwestern sky at nightfall. Each month finds it dimmer and lower. By May, it is closer to magnitude 2 and quite low, vanishing by month's end. It invisibly sidles behind the Sun on July 26; starts to appear as a dim, low morning star in September; and has super-close conjunctions with Mercury on September 16 and Venus on October 5. Slowly brightening, it rises 4 hours before the Sun at year's end.

Date		Time	Key	Date		Time	Key	Date		Time	Key	Date		Time	Key
Jan. 1	**set**	**9:17**	B	Apr. 1	**set**	**10:06**	E	July 1	**set**	**8:58**	E	Oct. 1	rise	4:48	C
Jan. 11	**set**	**9:17**	C	Apr. 11	**set**	**10:03**	E	July 11	**set**	**8:42**	E	Oct. 11	rise	4:42	C
Jan. 21	**set**	**9:16**	C	Apr. 21	**set**	**10:00**	E	July 21	**set**	**8:24**	E	Oct. 21	rise	4:35	C
Feb. 1	**set**	**9:15**	C	May 1	**set**	**9:56**	E	Aug. 1	rise	5:26	B	Nov. 1	rise	4:27	C
Feb. 11	**set**	**9:14**	D	May 11	**set**	**9:51**	E	Aug. 11	rise	5:20	B	Nov. 11	rise	3:20	C
Feb. 21	**set**	**9:13**	D	May 21	**set**	**9:44**	E	Aug. 21	rise	5:15	B	Nov. 21	rise	3:13	D
Mar. 1	**set**	**9:12**	D	June 1	**set**	**9:35**	E	Sept. 1	rise	5:08	B	Dec. 1	rise	3:06	D
Mar. 11	**set**	**9:10**	D	June 11	**set**	**9:24**	E	Sept. 11	rise	5:02	B	Dec. 11	rise	2:59	D
Mar. 21	**set**	**10:08**	E	June 21	**set**	**9:12**	E	Sept. 21	rise	4:55	B	Dec. 21	rise	2:52	D
												Dec. 31	rise	2:44	E

☞ **Bold = P.M.** ☞ Light = A.M.

Jupiter

Jupiter spends about a year in each zodiacal constellation. This year, it's in Virgo, initially hovering above the blue star Spica. In January, it rises at around midnight and then comes up 2 hours earlier each month. On April 7, Jove reaches its opposition, when it is brightest and out all night long. Jupiter remains perfectly placed for observation throughout the spring and early summer, starts getting low in the west in August, and vanishes behind the Sun in October. By December, it has re-emerged in the east, to rise by 4:00 A.M. in its new home of Libra. Its tightest 2017 conjunctions are with the Moon on April 10, May 7, June 3 and 30, and July 28 and with Venus on November 13.

Jan. 1	rise	12:43	D	Apr. 1	**rise**	**7:34**	C	July 1	set	12:47	C	Oct. 1	**set**	**7:14**	B
Jan. 11	rise	12:08	D	Apr. 11	set	6:16	C	July 11	set	12:09	C	Oct. 11	**set**	**6:39**	B
Jan. 21	**rise**	**11:28**	D	Apr. 21	set	5:34	C	July 21	**set**	**11:28**	C	Oct. 21	**set**	**6:05**	B
Feb. 1	**rise**	**10:47**	D	May 1	set	4:52	C	Aug. 1	**set**	**10:48**	C	Nov. 1	rise	6:54	D
Feb. 11	**rise**	**10:07**	D	May 11	set	4:10	C	Aug. 11	**set**	**10:12**	C	Nov. 11	rise	5:26	D
Feb. 21	**rise**	**9:26**	D	May 21	set	3:29	C	Aug. 21	**set**	**9:36**	C	Nov. 21	rise	4:57	D
Mar. 1	**rise**	**8:52**	D	June 1	set	2:44	C	Sept. 1	**set**	**8:58**	B	Dec. 1	rise	4:29	D
Mar. 11	**rise**	**8:08**	D	June 11	set	2:05	C	Sept. 11	**set**	**8:23**	B	Dec. 11	rise	4:00	D
Mar. 21	**rise**	**8:24**	D	June 21	set	1:26	C	Sept. 21	**set**	**7:48**	B	Dec. 21	rise	3:30	D
												Dec. 31	rise	3:00	D

Saturn

Saturn's famous rings are optimally angled for maximum display this year, letting small telescopes view the entire circumference of the outermost A-ring. However, being in Ophiuchus, it's at a very southerly declination, so it never appears high to North American observers. Saturn opens 2017 low in the east at dawn but rises 2 hours earlier each month and before midnight starting in May. It reaches its nearest approach to Earth on June 15, when it is out all night. Saturn remains well placed all summer. Sinking low in October, it falls into dusk's twilight and is gone until next year. Saturn has striking conjunctions with the Moon on May 13, June 9, July 6, and September 26.

Jan. 1	rise	5:45	E	Apr. 1	rise	1:19	E	July 1	set	4:15	A	Oct. 1	**set**	**10:03**	A
Jan. 11	rise	5:10	E	Apr. 11	rise	12:39	E	July 11	set	3:33	A	Oct. 11	**set**	**9:27**	A
Jan. 21	rise	4:36	E	Apr. 21	**rise**	**11:55**	E	July 21	set	2:51	A	Oct. 21	**set**	**8:50**	A
Feb. 1	rise	3:57	E	May 1	**rise**	**11:15**	E	Aug. 1	set	2:05	A	Nov. 1	**set**	**8:11**	A
Feb. 11	rise	3:22	E	May 11	**rise**	**10:33**	E	Aug. 11	set	1:25	A	Nov. 11	**set**	**6:36**	A
Feb. 21	rise	2:46	E	May 21	**rise**	**9:51**	E	Aug. 21	set	12:45	A	Nov. 21	**set**	**6:01**	A
Mar. 1	rise	2:16	E	June 1	**rise**	**9:05**	E	Sept. 1	**set**	**11:57**	A	Dec. 1	**set**	**5:26**	A
Mar. 11	rise	1:39	E	June 11	**rise**	**8:22**	E	Sept. 11	**set**	**11:19**	A	Dec. 11	**set**	**4:52**	A
Mar. 21	rise	2:01	E	June 21	set	4:57	A	Sept. 21	**set**	**10:41**	A	Dec. 21	rise	7:09	E
												Dec. 31	rise	6:35	E

Mercury

The innermost planet alternately darts from morning to evening sky and back again every few months. To be observed easily, Mercury must be at least 5 degrees above the horizon 40 minutes after sunset or before sunrise. Favorable "evening star" conditions occur in fading twilight from March 18 to April 6 and from July 7 to 26. Mercury is an observable morning star from January 6 to 27 and from September 8 to 24. Mercury and Mars have a dramatic conjunction on September 16, which will be challengingly low to see.

DO NOT CONFUSE ■ *Jupiter with Virgo's brightest star, Spica: Jupiter is much brighter, and Spica is blue.* ■ *Jupiter with Venus in mid-November: Venus is brighter.* ■ *Mercury with Mars in mid-September: Both look orange, but Mercury is much brighter.*

Astronomical Glossary

Aphelion (Aph.): The point in a planet's orbit that is farthest from the Sun.

Apogee (Apo.): The point in the Moon's orbit that is farthest from Earth.

Celestial Equator (Eq.): The imaginary circle around the celestial sphere that can be thought of as the plane of Earth's equator projected out onto the sphere.

Celestial Sphere: An imaginary sphere projected into space that represents the entire sky, with an observer on Earth at its center. All celestial bodies other than Earth are imagined as being on its inside surface.

Circumpolar: Always visible above the horizon, such as a circumpolar star.

Conjunction: The time at which two or more celestial bodies appear closest in the sky. **Inferior (Inf.):** Mercury or Venus is between the Sun and Earth. **Superior (Sup.):** The Sun is between a planet and Earth. Actual dates for conjunctions are given on the **Right-Hand Calendar Pages;** the best times for viewing the closely aligned bodies are given in **Sky Watch** on the **Left-Hand Calendar Pages.**

Declination: The celestial latitude of an object in the sky, measured in degrees north or south of the celestial equator; analogous to latitude on Earth. This Almanac gives the Sun's declination at noon.

Eclipse, Lunar: The full Moon enters the shadow of Earth, which cuts off all or part of the sunlight reflected off the Moon. **Total:** The Moon passes completely through the **umbra** (central dark part) of Earth's shadow. **Partial:** Only part of the Moon passes through the umbra. **Penumbral:** The Moon passes through only the **penumbra** (area of partial darkness surrounding the umbra). See **Eclipses** for more information about eclipses.

Eclipse, Solar: Earth enters the shadow of the new Moon, which cuts off all or part of the Sun's light. **Total:** Earth passes through the umbra (central dark part) of the Moon's shadow, resulting in totality for observers

within a narrow band on Earth. **Annular:** The Moon appears silhouetted against the Sun, with a ring of sunlight showing around it. **Partial:** The Moon blocks only part of the Sun.

Ecliptic: The apparent annual path of the Sun around the celestial sphere. The plane of the ecliptic is tipped 23½° from the celestial equator.

Elongation: The difference in degrees between the celestial longitudes of a planet and the Sun. **Greatest Elongation (Gr. Elong.):** The greatest apparent distance of a planet from the Sun, as seen from Earth.

Epact: A number from 1 to 30 that indicates the Moon's age on January 1 at Greenwich, England; used in calculations for determining the date of Easter.

Equinox: When the Sun crosses the celestial equator. This event occurs two times each year: **Vernal** is around March 20 and **Autumnal** is around September 22.

Evening Star: A planet that is above the western horizon at sunset and less than 180° east of the Sun in right ascension.

Golden Number: A number in the 19-year cycle of the Moon, used in calculations for determining the date of Easter. (Approximately every 19 years, the Moon's phases occur on the same dates.) Add 1 to any given year and divide by 19; the remainder is the Golden Number. If there is no remainder, use 19.

Magnitude: A measure of a celestial object's brightness. **Apparent magnitude** measures the brightness of an object as seen from Earth. Objects with an apparent magnitude of 6 or less are observable to the naked eye. The lower the magnitude, the greater the

Astronomical Glossary

brightness. An object with a magnitude of –1, for example, is brighter than an object with a magnitude of +1.

Midnight: Astronomically, the time when the Sun is opposite its highest point in the sky. Both 12 hours before and after noon (so, technically, both A.M. and P.M.), midnight in civil time is usually treated as the beginning of the day, rather than the end. It is typically displayed as 12:00 A.M. on 12-hour digital clocks. On a 24-hour time cycle, 00:00, rather than 24:00, usually indicates midnight.

Moon on Equator: The Moon is on the celestial equator.

Moon Rides High/Runs Low: The Moon is highest above or farthest below the celestial equator.

Moonrise/Moonset: When the Moon rises above or sets below the horizon.

Moon's Phases: The changing appearance of the Moon, caused by the different angles at which it is illuminated by the Sun. **First Quarter:** Right half of the Moon is illuminated. **Full:** The Sun and the Moon are in opposition; the entire disk of the Moon is illuminated. **Last Quarter:** Left half of the Moon is illuminated. **New:** The Sun and the Moon are in conjunction; the Moon is darkened because it lines up between Earth and the Sun.

Moon's Place, Astronomical: The position of the Moon within the constellations on the celestial sphere at midnight. **Astrological:** The position of the Moon within the tropical zodiac, whose twelve 30° segments (signs) along the ecliptic were named more than 2,000 years ago after constellations within each area. Because of precession and other factors, the zodiac signs no longer match actual constellation positions.

Morning Star: A planet that is above the eastern horizon at sunrise and less than 180° west of the Sun in right ascension.

Node: Either of the two points where a celestial body's orbit intersects the ecliptic. **Ascending:** When the body is moving from south to north of the ecliptic. **Descending:** When the body is moving from north to south of the ecliptic.

Occultation (Occn.): The eclipse of a star or planet by the Moon or another celestial object.

Opposition: The Moon or a planet appears on the opposite side of the sky from the Sun (elongation 180°).

Perigee (Perig.): The point in the Moon's orbit that is closest to Earth.

Perihelion (Perih.): The point in a planet's orbit that is closest to the Sun.

Precession: The slowly changing position of the stars and equinoxes in the sky caused by a slight wobble as Earth rotates around its axis.

Right Ascension (R.A.): The celestial longitude of an object in the sky, measured eastward along the celestial equator in hours of time from the vernal equinox; analogous to longitude on Earth.

Solar Cycle: In the Julian calendar, a period of 28 years, at the end of which the days of the month return to the same days of the week.

Solstice, Summer: When the Sun reaches its greatest declination (23½°) north of the celestial equator, around June 21. **Winter:** When the Sun reaches its greatest declination (23½°) south of the celestial equator, around December 21.

Stationary (Stat.): The brief period of apparent halted movement of a planet against the background of the stars shortly before it appears to move backward/westward (retrograde motion) or forward/eastward (direct motion).

Sun Fast/Slow: When a sundial reading is ahead of (fast) or behind (slow) clock time.

Sunrise/Sunset: The visible rising and setting of the upper edge of the Sun's disk across the unobstructed horizon of an observer whose eyes are 15 feet above ground level.

Twilight: For definitions of civil, nautical, and astronomical twilight, **see page 122.** ■

2017's Greatest Spectacle

THE FIRST TOTAL SOLAR ECLIPSE OVER THE U.S. MAINLAND IN 38 YEARS WILL BE TOTALLY COOL—ESPECIALLY IN ITS SHADOW.

By Bob Berman

TO THE NAKED EYE, the sky is an inverted bowl hosting thousands of glowing points and two disks. The points—stars and planets—exhibit no size because of their immense distance from Earth. The two disks are the Sun and Moon. By amazing coincidence, these disks appear exactly the same size. Why?

The Sun is 400 times larger than the Moon but also 400 times farther from Earth than the Moon. These facts allow the Moon to fit perfectly over the Sun's face to create a total eclipse. Yet, it's not so big that it blocks out the Sun's dramatic hot-pink corona or atmosphere and not so small that it leaves the Sun's blinding gas surface (photosphere) uncovered. This bizarre alignment does not hold for any other planet and will not last forever: The Moon is spiraling away from Earth like a skyrocket and gradually increasing its separation.

The perfect lineup of these two disks (Sun and Moon) to form a total solar eclipse does not happen often—just once every 360 years, on average, for any one point on Earth. (This is one reason why relatively few people have ever seen one.) The U.S. mainland

Photo: NASA

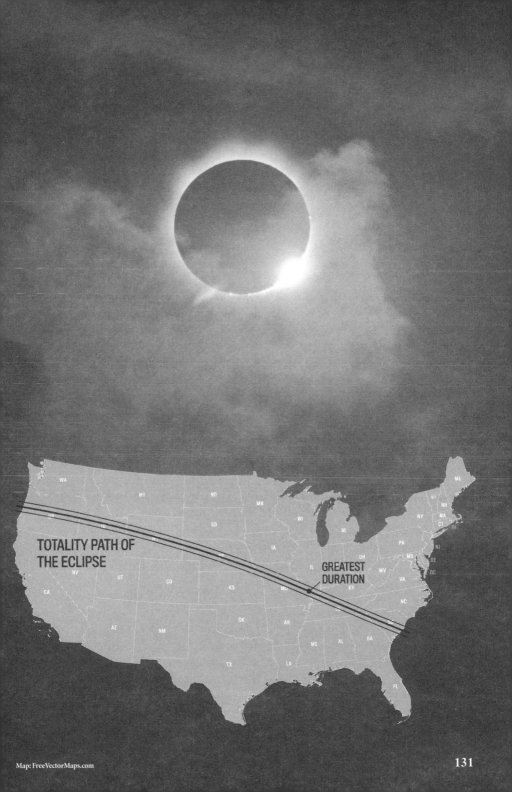

TOTALITY PATH OF THE ECLIPSE

GREATEST DURATION

Map: FreeVectorMaps.com

is currently experiencing its longest totality drought in history. The last total solar eclipse occurred on February 26, 1979, over northwestern states and south central Canada.

This cycle of paucity finally ends on August 21, 2017.

Eerie Events Within the Ribbon of Darkness

FOR SHEER VISCERAL impact, a total solar eclipse is not even remotely comparable to a lunar eclipse or partial solar eclipse. Or even major auroral displays. A solar totality stands alone. If you are in the right place, it creates darkness in daytime along a 140-mile-wide ribbon of Earth. The brightest stars come out in midday but not as you might presume: During totality, they appear in seasonal reverse. In summer, the winter constellations emerge; during a winter solar totality, summer's stars appear.

And that's not all.

An uncommon mind-set takes over people when the Sun, Moon, and your spot on Earth form a perfectly straight line in space. Many observers shout and babble. Some weep. Afterward, everyone proclaims it to be the greatest spectacle they have ever beheld. Beyond that, many are speechless. (Animals also exhibit odd behavior, such as falling strangely silent.)

The experience surpasses all expectations and imaginings:

- The eye sees the transition of the Moon over the Sun differently from photographs; because of under- or overexposure, a camera lens can not capture the same range of brightness as human vision.

Eclipse Equipment

The cost to watch this wondrous event is affordable for most people. For about $5, purchase "eclipse glasses" online or buy welding goggles at the nearest welding supply store. Choose shade number 12 or 14 filters (even numbers are the most common). Number 12 makes the solar image a bit brighter, but since the Sun will be high for this eclipse, 14 is probably ideal—but either will work. Do not use any other number.

Use the filtered shades during the hourlong partial phase before totality and then again afterward for an hour. Once totality begins, you can watch the event for the duration of totality (between 2 and 2½ minutes) with naked eyes or through binoculars. The moment the first speck of sunlight returns at the edge of the Moon, look away and use the filter again.

- The delicate tendrils of the Sun's corona splay into the surrounding sky in a manner wholly different from the way they appear in photos.
- During the 10 minutes before and after totality, when the Sun is more than 80 percent eclipsed and its light arrives only from its edge, or limb, earthly colors turn richer and more saturated, while shadows become stark and oddly crisp—as if a different type of star is illuminating Earth.
- As the Moon slides over the Sun, not only is light blocked in the ribbon of space, but solar heat is, too. The steady

drop in temperature usually results in a haunting eclipse wind.

• At 1 minute before and after totality, all white and light-color ground surfaces underfoot (sidewalks, sand, the like) suddenly exhibit shimmering shadow bands everywhere. (Think of black lines on the bottom of a swimming pool that appear to wiggle.) This eerie phenomenon can make your hair stand on end, yet it can not be captured on film. (Try it!) Recent research suggests that shadow bands are the edges of atmospheric temperature cells (air pockets) made visible by the remaining tiny point of Sun. Their motion catches the eye despite their extremely low contrast.

To witness these extraordinary phenomena, you need to be in totality's path (see map, page 131). This year, you can drive into it and watch from a roadside! Totality lasts longest—over 2 minutes—within the centerline of the ribbon. A partial eclipse will be visible outside of that ribbon, and the phenomena described above will not occur there.

The Ribbon's Route

THE ECLIPSE'S path starts over the Pacific Ocean and first touches land in Oregon.

• The Moon's shadow then traverses southern portions of Idaho; passes directly over both Jackson and Casper, Wyoming; and continues eastward over Nebraska in late morning.

• The path continues east and south, eventually passing over St. Joseph, Missouri, before continuing on to southwestern Illinois, where it reaches its maximum duration of totality and where the Sun will be highest in the sky. (Each town has a different clock time for totality. It happens during the morning over the Pacific Northwest, midday over southern Illinois, and afternoon over the southeastern states.)

• The eclipse shadow continues east and south in the midafternoon and concludes its track over Nashville, Tennessee; Columbia, South Carolina; and a lot of smaller communities.

If possible, travel to where the forecast is for clear weather.

For viewers outside of the ribbon of darkness (virtually the entire continent), this will be a partial eclipse, a fairly frequent sight (which does require eye protection) that is interesting, yes—but nothing like solar totality. ■

Lucky Seven

Total solar eclipses can be addictive. Fortunately, fanatics—and anyone who misses this year's event—won't need to wait 38 more years for the next U.S. and Canadian one—only 7. On April 8, 2024, solar totality will unfold over the continent in a path that curves north from Texas; passes over Cleveland, Ohio, and Buffalo and Rochester, New York; sweeps over Burlington, Vermont; and then continues across central Maine and eastern Canada.

But why wait? Circle August 21 on your calendar and plan a rendezvous with the Moon's shadow this summer!

Bob Berman, *Old Farmer's Almanac* astronomy editor, has led many eclipse and aurora expeditions, venturing as far as the Arctic and Antarctic.

2016

January

S	M	T	W	T	F	S
					1	2
3	4	5	6	7	8	9
10	11	12	13	14	15	16
17	18	19	20	21	22	23
24	25	26	27	28	29	30
31						

February

S	M	T	W	T	F	S
	1	2	3	4	5	6
7	8	9	10	11	12	13
14	15	16	17	18	19	20
21	22	23	24	25	26	27
28	29					

March

S	M	T	W	T	F	S
		1	2	3	4	5
6	7	8	9	10	11	12
13	14	15	16	17	18	19
20	21	22	23	24	25	26
27	28	29	30	31		

April

S	M	T	W	T	F	S
					1	2
3	4	5	6	7	8	9
10	11	12	13	14	15	16
17	18	19	20	21	22	23
24	25	26	27	28	29	30

May

S	M	T	W	T	F	S
1	2	3	4	5	6	7
8	9	10	11	12	13	14
15	16	17	18	19	20	21
22	23	24	25	26	27	28
29	30	31				

June

S	M	T	W	T	F	S
			1	2	3	4
5	6	7	8	9	10	11
12	13	14	15	16	17	18
19	20	21	22	23	24	25
26	27	28	29	30		

July

S	M	T	W	T	F	S
					1	2
3	4	5	6	7	8	9
10	11	12	13	14	15	16
17	18	19	20	21	22	23
24	25	26	27	28	29	30
31						

August

S	M	T	W	T	F	S
	1	2	3	4	5	6
7	8	9	10	11	12	13
14	15	16	17	18	19	20
21	22	23	24	25	26	27
28	29	30	31			

September

S	M	T	W	T	F	S
				1	2	3
4	5	6	7	8	9	10
11	12	13	14	15	16	17
18	19	20	21	22	23	24
25	26	27	28	29	30	

October

S	M	T	W	T	F	S
						1
2	3	4	5	6	7	8
9	10	11	12	13	14	15
16	17	18	19	20	21	22
23	24	25	26	27	28	29
30	31					

November

S	M	T	W	T	F	S
		1	2	3	4	5
6	7	8	9	10	11	12
13	14	15	16	17	18	19
20	21	22	23	24	25	26
27	28	29	30			

December

S	M	T	W	T	F	S
				1	2	3
4	5	6	7	8	9	10
11	12	13	14	15	16	17
18	19	20	21	22	23	24
25	26	27	28	29	30	31

2017

January

S	M	T	W	T	F	S
1	2	3	4	5	6	7
8	9	10	11	12	13	14
15	16	17	18	19	20	21
22	23	24	25	26	27	28
29	30	31				

February

S	M	T	W	T	F	S
			1	2	3	4
5	6	7	8	9	10	11
12	13	14	15	16	17	18
19	20	21	22	23	24	25
26	27	28				

March

S	M	T	W	T	F	S
			1	2	3	4
5	6	7	8	9	10	11
12	13	14	15	16	17	18
19	20	21	22	23	24	25
26	27	28	29	30	31	

April

S	M	T	W	T	F	S
						1
2	3	4	5	6	7	8
9	10	11	12	13	14	15
16	17	18	19	20	21	22
23	24	25	26	27	28	29
30						

May

S	M	T	W	T	F	S
	1	2	3	4	5	6
7	8	9	10	11	12	13
14	15	16	17	18	19	20
21	22	23	24	25	26	27
28	29	30	31			

June

S	M	T	W	T	F	S
				1	2	3
4	5	6	7	8	9	10
11	12	13	14	15	16	17
18	19	20	21	22	23	24
25	26	27	28	29	30	

July

S	M	T	W	T	F	S
						1
2	3	4	5	6	7	8
9	10	11	12	13	14	15
16	17	18	19	20	21	22
23	24	25	26	27	28	29
30	31					

August

S	M	T	W	T	F	S
		1	2	3	4	5
6	7	8	9	10	11	12
13	14	15	16	17	18	19
20	21	22	23	24	25	26
27	28	29	30	31		

September

S	M	T	W	T	F	S
					1	2
3	4	5	6	7	8	9
10	11	12	13	14	15	16
17	18	19	20	21	22	23
24	25	26	27	28	29	30

October

S	M	T	W	T	F	S
1	2	3	4	5	6	7
8	9	10	11	12	13	14
15	16	17	18	19	20	21
22	23	24	25	26	27	28
29	30	31				

November

S	M	T	W	T	F	S
			1	2	3	4
5	6	7	8	9	10	11
12	13	14	15	16	17	18
19	20	21	22	23	24	25
26	27	28	29	30		

December

S	M	T	W	T	F	S
					1	2
3	4	5	6	7	8	9
10	11	12	13	14	15	16
17	18	19	20	21	22	23
24	25	26	27	28	29	30
31						

2018

January

S	M	T	W	T	F	S
	1	2	3	4	5	6
7	8	9	10	11	12	13
14	15	16	17	18	19	20
21	22	23	24	25	26	27
28	29	30	31			

February

S	M	T	W	T	F	S
				1	2	3
4	5	6	7	8	9	10
11	12	13	14	15	16	17
18	19	20	21	22	23	24
25	26	27	28			

March

S	M	T	W	T	F	S
				1	2	3
4	5	6	7	8	9	10
11	12	13	14	15	16	17
18	19	20	21	22	23	24
25	26	27	28	29	30	31

April

S	M	T	W	T	F	S
1	2	3	4	5	6	7
8	9	10	11	12	13	14
15	16	17	18	19	20	21
22	23	24	25	26	27	28
29	30					

May

S	M	T	W	T	F	S
		1	2	3	4	5
6	7	8	9	10	11	12
13	14	15	16	17	18	19
20	21	22	23	24	25	26
27	28	29	30	31		

June

S	M	T	W	T	F	S
					1	2
3	4	5	6	7	8	9
10	11	12	13	14	15	16
17	18	19	20	21	22	23
24	25	26	27	28	29	30

July

S	M	T	W	T	F	S
1	2	3	4	5	6	7
8	9	10	11	12	13	14
15	16	17	18	19	20	21
22	23	24	25	26	27	28
29	30	31				

August

S	M	T	W	T	F	S
			1	2	3	4
5	6	7	8	9	10	11
12	13	14	15	16	17	18
19	20	21	22	23	24	25
26	27	28	29	30	31	

September

S	M	T	W	T	F	S
						1
2	3	4	5	6	7	8
9	10	11	12	13	14	15
16	17	18	19	20	21	22
23	24	25	26	27	28	29
30						

October

S	M	T	W	T	F	S
	1	2	3	4	5	6
7	8	9	10	11	12	13
14	15	16	17	18	19	20
21	22	23	24	25	26	27
28	29	30	31			

November

S	M	T	W	T	F	S
				1	2	3
4	5	6	7	8	9	10
11	12	13	14	15	16	17
18	19	20	21	22	23	24
25	26	27	28	29	30	

December

S	M	T	W	T	F	S
						1
2	3	4	5	6	7	8
9	10	11	12	13	14	15
16	17	18	19	20	21	22
23	24	25	26	27	28	29
30	31					

How to Use This Almanac

–Beth Krommes

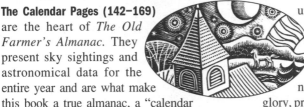

The Calendar Pages (142–169) are the heart of *The Old Farmer's Almanac.* They present sky sightings and astronomical data for the entire year and are what make this book a true almanac, a "calendar of the heavens." In essence, these pages are unchanged since 1792, when Robert B. Thomas published his first edition. The long columns of numbers and symbols reveal all of nature's precision, rhythm, and glory, providing an astronomical look at the year 2017.

Why We Have Seasons

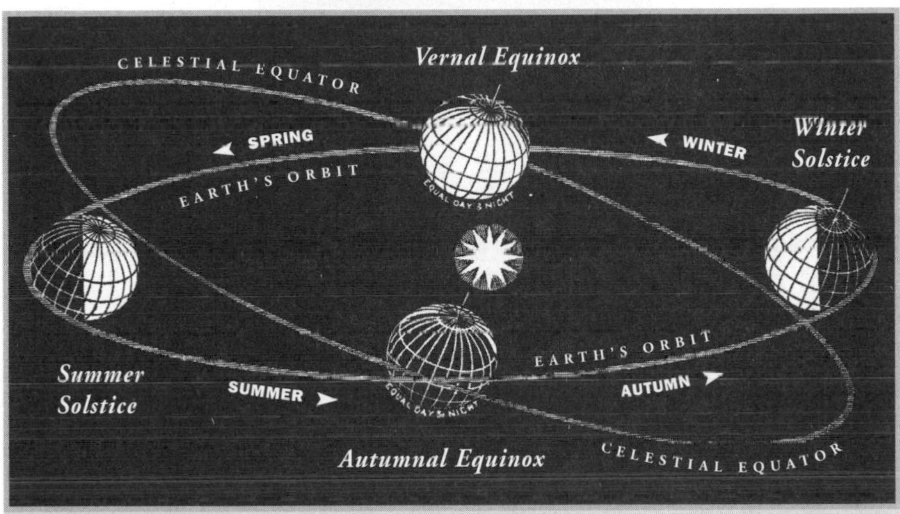

THE SEASONS OF 2017

Vernal equinox . . . March 20, 6:29 A.M. EDT	**Autumnal equinox . . . . Sept. 22, 4:02 P.M. EDT**
Summer solstice . . June 21, 12:24 A.M. EDT	**Winter solstice. . . . . . . Dec. 21, 11:28 A.M. EST**

■ The seasons occur because as Earth revolves around the Sun, its axis remains tilted at 23.5 degrees from the perpendicular. This tilt causes different latitudes on Earth to receive varying amounts of sunlight throughout the year.

In the Northern Hemisphere, the summer solstice marks the beginning of summer and occurs when the North Pole is tilted toward the Sun. The winter solstice marks the beginning of winter and occurs when the North Pole is tilted away from the Sun.

The equinoxes occur when the hemispheres equally face the Sun. At this time, the Sun rises due east and sets due west. The vernal equinox marks the beginning of spring; the autumnal equinox marks the beginning of autumn.

In the Southern Hemisphere, the seasons are the reverse of those in the Northern Hemisphere.

(continued)

The Left-Hand Calendar Pages • 142–168

The **Left-Hand Calendar Pages** contain sky highlights, daily Sun and Moon rise and set times, the length of day, high tide times, the Moon's astronomical place and age, and more for Boston. Examples of how to calculate astronomical times for your location are shown below.

A SAMPLE MONTH

SKY WATCH ☆ *The box at the top of each Left-Hand Calendar Page describes the best times to view celestial highlights, including conjunctions, meteor showers, and planets. The dates on which select astronomical events occur appear on the Right-Hand Calendar Pages.*

Get these pages with times set to your zip code at Almanac.com/Access.

Day of Year	Day of Month	Day of Week	☼ Rises h. m.	Rise Key	☼ Sets h. m.	Set Key	Length of Day h. m.	Sun Fast m.	Declination of Sun ° '	High Tide Times Boston		☾ Rises h. m.	Rise Key	☾ Sets h. m.	Set Key	☾ Astron. Place	☾ Age
1	1	**A**	7:13	E	**4:23**	A	9 10	12	22s.56	1	**1**	9:16	E	**7:59**	C	CAP	3
2	2	M.	7:13	E	**4:24**	A	9 11	12	22 50	$1\frac{3}{4}$	$\mathbf{1\frac{3}{4}}$	9:52	E	**9:02**	C	AQU	4
3	3	Tu.	7:13	E	**4:24**	A	9 11	11	22 44	$2\frac{1}{2}$	$\mathbf{2\frac{1}{2}}$	10:25	D	**10:07**	D	AQU	5

1 To calculate the sunrise time for your locale: Note the Sun Rise Key Letter on the chosen day. In the **Time Corrections** table on **page 252**, find your city or the city nearest you. Add or subtract the minutes that correspond to the Sun Rise Key Letter to/from the sunrise time given for Boston.

EXAMPLE:

■ To calculate the time of sunrise in Denver, Colorado, on the first day of the month:

Sunrise, Boston, with Key Letter E (above)	**7:13 A.M. EST**
Value of Key Letter E for Denver (p. 252)	**+ 7 minutes**
Sunrise, Denver	**7:20 A.M. MST**

Use the same procedure with Boston's sunset time and the Sun Set Key Letter value to calculate the time of sunset in your locale.

2 To calculate the length of day for your locale: Note the Sun Rise and Sun Set Key Letters on the chosen day. In the **Time Corrections** table on **page 252**, find your city. Add or subtract the minutes that correspond to the Sun Set Key Letter to/from Boston's length of day. *Reverse* the sign (minus to plus, or plus to minus) of the Sun Rise Key Letter minutes. Add or subtract it to/from the first result.

EXAMPLE:

■ To calculate the length of day in Richmond, Virginia, on the first day of the month:

Length of day, Boston (above)	**9h. 10m.**
Sunset Key Letter A for Richmond (p. 256)	**+ 41m.**
	9h. 51m.
Reverse sunrise Key Letter E for Richmond (p. 256, +11 to −11)	**− 11m.**
Length of day, Richmond	**9h. 40m.**

3 Use the Sun Fast column to change sundial time to clock time. A sundial reads natural, or Sun, time, which is neither Standard nor Daylight time. To calculate clock time on a sundial in Boston, subtract the minutes given in this column; add the minutes when preceded by an asterisk [*]. To convert the time to your city, use Key Letter C in the table on **page 252**.

ATTENTION, READERS: *All times given in this edition of the Almanac are for Boston, Massachusetts, and are in Eastern Standard Time (EST), except from 2:00 A.M., March 12, until 2:00 A.M., November 5, when Eastern Daylight Time (EDT) is given.*

EXAMPLE:

■ To change sundial time to clock time in Boston, or, for example, in Salem, Oregon:

Sundial reading (Boston or Salem)	**12:00 noon**
Subtract Sun Fast (p. 138)	**– 12 minutes**
Clock time, Boston	**11:48 A.M. EST**
Use Key Letter C for Salem (p. 255)	**+ 27 minutes**
Clock time, Salem	**12:15 P.M. PST**

4 This column gives the degrees and minutes of the Sun from the celestial equator at noon EST or EDT.

5 This column gives the approximate times of high tides in Boston. For example, the first high tide occurs at 1:00 A.M. and the second occurs at 1:00 P.M. the same day. (A dash indicates that high tide occurs on or after midnight and is recorded on the next day.) Figures for calculating high tide times and heights for localities other than Boston are given in the **Tide Corrections** table on **page 250**.

6 To calculate the moonrise time for your locale: Note the Moon Rise Key Letter on the chosen day. Find your city on **page 252**. Add or subtract the minutes that correspond to the Moon Rise Key Letter to/from the moonrise time given for Boston. (A dash indicates that the moonrise occurs on or after midnight and is recorded on the next day.) Find the longitude of your city on **page 252**. Add a correction in minutes for your city's longitude (see table, above right).

–Beth Krommes

➡ Get the Left-Hand Calendar Pages with times set to your zip code at **Almanac.com/Access.**

Longitude of city	**Correction minutes**
58°–76°	0
77°–89°	+1
90°–102°	+2
103°–115°	+3
116°–127°	+4
128°–141°	+5
142°–155°	+6

Use the same procedure with Boston's moonset time and the Moon Set Key Letter value to calculate the time of moonset in your locale.

EXAMPLE:

■ To calculate the time of moonset in Lansing, Michigan, on the first day of the month:

Moonset, Boston, with Key Letter C (p. 138)	**7:59 P.M. EST**
Value of Key Letter C for Lansing (p. 254)	**+ 53 minutes**
Correction for Lansing longitude, 84° 33'	**+ 1 minute**
Moonset, Lansing	**8:53 P.M. EST**

7 The Moon's Place is its *astronomical* position among the constellations (not the zodiac) at midnight. For *astrological* data, see **pages 244–246.**

Constellations have irregular borders; on successive nights, the midnight Moon may enter one, cross into another, then move to a new area of the previous. It visits the 12 zodiacal constellations, as well as Auriga **(AUR)**, a northern constellation between Perseus and Gemini; Cetus **(CET)**, which lies south of the zodiac, just south of Pisces and Aries; Ophiuchus **(OPH)**, a constellation primarily north of the zodiac but with a small corner between Scorpius and Sagittarius; Orion **(ORI)**, a constellation whose northern limit first reaches the zodiac between Taurus and Gemini; and Sextans **(SEX)**, which lies south of the zodiac except for a corner that just touches it near Leo.

8 The last column gives the Moon's Age, which is the number of days since the previous new Moon. (The average length of the lunar month is 29.53 days.) **(continued)**

The Right-Hand Calendar Pages • 143–169

A SAMPLE MONTH

- Weather prediction rhyme.
- Symbols for notable celestial events. (See opposite page for explanations.)
- The bold letter is the Dominical Letter (from A to G), a traditional ecclesiastical designation for Sunday determined by the date on which the first Sunday falls. For 2017, the Dominical Letter is **A**.
- Sundays and special holy days generally appear in this font.
- Proverbs, poems, and adages generally appear in this font.
- Civil holidays and astronomical events appear in this font.
- Noteworthy historical events, folklore, and legends appear in this font.
- Religious feasts generally appear in this font. A ᵀ indicates a major feast that the church has this year temporarily transferred to a date other than its usual one.
- High tide heights, in feet, at Boston, Massachusetts.

Day of Month	Day of Week	Dates, Feasts, Fasts, Aspects, Tide Heights	Weather
1	W.	Ash Wednesday • ☌♂☾ • ☌♅☾ • ☌♆☉	*It's*
2	Th.	St. Chad • ♀ STAT. • Puerto Ricans granted U.S. citizenship, 1917 • Tides { 10.9 / 10.7	*brisk,*
3	Fr.	☾ AT PERIG. • Inventor Alexander Graham Bell born, 1847 • Tides { 10.9 / 10.3	*but*
4	Sa.	☌☿♆ • James Monroe inaugurated as 5th U.S. president, 1817 • Tides { 10.8 / 9.8	*travel's*
5	**A**	1st S. in Lent • 6.96" rain, Butlerville, Ind., 1897 • Tides { 10.6 / 9.4	*no*
6	M.	☾ RIDES HIGH • ☿ IN SUP. ☌ • *A March sun sticks like a lock of wool.* • { 10.4 / 9.2	*risk.*
7	Tu.	St. Perpetua • Astronomer Henry Draper born, 1837 • Tides { 10.3 / 9.1	*Occasional*
8	W.	Ember Day • Whirlwind I's Director, precursor to computer operating systems, demonstrated, 1955	*spates*
9	Th.	Hummingbirds migrate north now. • Tides { 10.5 / 9.6	*for*
10	Fr.	Ember Day • ☾ AT ☊ • Professional bicycle racer Lyne Bessette born, 1975 • { 10.7 / 9.9	*town*
11	Sa.	Ember Day • Florida panther added to endangered species list, 1967 • { 10.8 / 10.2	*meeting*
12	**A**	2nd S. in Lent • **Daylight Saving Time begins, 2:00 A.M.** • **Full Worm** ○	*debates.*
13	M.	☾ ON EQ. • UFOs seen over Ariz., Nev., and Sonora, Mexico, 1997 • Tides { 10.3 / 10.7	*A*
14	Tu.	☌♃☾ • Shirley Temple added sidewalk prints, Grauman's Chinese Theatre, Hollywood, Calif., 1935	*little*
15	W.	Beware the ides of March. • First escalator patented by Jesse W. Reno, 1892 • Tides { 10.3 / 10.1	*snow,*
16	Th.	☌☿♀ • United States Military Academy at West Point established, 1802 • Tides { 10.1 / 9.7	*a*
17	Fr.	**St. Patrick's Day** • *Care and diligence bring luck.* • Tides { 9.8 / 9.2	*little*
18	Sa.	☾ AT APO. • Haboob storm brought 1,000'-high wall of dust, western Tex. and N.Mex., 2014 • { 9.5 / 8.8	*rain;*
19	**A**	3rd S. in Lent • Actress Glenn Close born, 1947 • Tides { 9.2 / 8.4	*this*
20	M.	St. Josephᵀ • **Vernal Equinox** • ☌♄☾ • Tides { 9.0 / 8.2	*month*
21	Tu.	☾ RUNS LOW • Funeral for Pocahontas (aka Rebecca Rolfe) took place, 1617 • { 8.9 / 8.1	*has*
22	W.	☌♇☾ • 7.0-magnitude earthquake, Fox Islands, Alaska, 1957 • Tides { 8.9 / 8.2	*water*
23	Th.	Culinary expert Fannie Farmer born, 1857 • 65°F, Montreal, Que., 1979 • { 9.1 / 8.6	*on*
24	Fr.	Chipmunks emerge from hiberation now. • Tides { 9.5 / 9.1	*the*
25	Sa.	Annunciation • ☾ AT ☋ • ♀ IN INF. ☌ • 4" hailstones, Fla., 1992	*brain!*
26	**A**	4th S. in Lent • ☌♆☾ • Deadly dynamite explosion in quarry, Sandts Eddy, Pa., 1942	*Note*

☞ **For explanations of Almanac terms, see the glossaries on pages 126 and 171.**

Predicting Earthquakes

■ Note the dates in the **Right-Hand Calendar Pages** when the Moon rides high or runs low. The date of the high begins the most likely 5-day period of earthquakes in the Northern Hemisphere; the date of the low indicates a similar 5-day period in the Southern Hemisphere. Also noted are the 2 days each month when the Moon is on the celestial equator, indicating the most likely time for earthquakes in either hemisphere.

–Beth Krommes

■ Throughout the **Right-Hand Calendar Pages** are groups of symbols that represent notable celestial events. The symbols and names of the principal planets and aspects are:

☉	**Sun**	♆	**Neptune**
○●☾	**Moon**	♇	**Pluto**
☿	**Mercury**	☌	**Conjunction (on the same celestial longitude)**
♀	**Venus**		
⊕	**Earth**		
♂	**Mars**	☊	**Ascending node**
♃	**Jupiter**	☋	**Descending node**
♄	**Saturn**	☍	**Opposition (180 degrees from Sun)**
♅	**Uranus**		

EXAMPLE:

☌♂☾ on the 1st day of the month (see opposite page) means that on that date a conjunction (☌) of Mars (♂) and the Moon (☾) occurs: They are aligned along the same celestial longitude and appear to be closest together in the sky.

EARTH AT PERIHELION AND APHELION

■ Perihelion: January 4, 2017. Earth will be 91,404,401 miles from the Sun. Aphelion: July 3, 2017. Earth will be 94,505,982 miles from the Sun.

2017 Calendar Highlights

MOVABLE RELIGIOUS OBSERVANCES

Septuagesima Sunday	**Feb. 12**
Shrove Tuesday	**Feb. 28**
Ash Wednesday	**March 1**
Palm Sunday	**April 9**
Passover begins at sundown	**April 10**
Good Friday	**April 14**
Easter	**April 16**
Orthodox Easter	**April 16**
Rogation Sunday	**May 21**
Ascension Day	**May 25**
Ramadan begins at sundown	**May 26**
Whitsunday–Pentecost	**June 4**
Trinity Sunday	**June 11**
Corpus Christi	**June 18**
Rosh Hashanah begins at sundown	**Sept. 20**
Yom Kippur begins at sundown	**Sept. 29**
First Sunday of Advent	**Dec. 3**
Chanukah begins at sundown	**Dec. 12**

CHRONOLOGICAL CYCLES

Dominical Letter	**A**
Epact	**2**
Golden Number (Lunar Cycle)	**4**
Roman Indiction	**10**
Solar Cycle	**10**
Year of Julian Period	**6730**

–Beth Krommes

ERAS

Era	Year	Begins
Byzantine	**7526**	September 14
Jewish (A.M.)*	**5778**	September 20
Chinese (Lunar) [Year of the Rooster]	**4715**	January 28
Roman (A.U.C.)	**2770**	January 14
Nabonassar	**2766**	April 19
Japanese	**2677**	January 1
Grecian (Seleucidae)	**2329**	September 14 (or October 14)
Indian (Saka)	**1939**	March 22
Diocletian	**1734**	September 11
Islamic (Hegira)*	**1439**	September 20

**Year begins at sundown.*

THE ELEVENTH MONTH • 2016

SKY WATCH ☆ *The Moon floats above Saturn and Venus on the 2nd, 45 minutes after sunset. Returning Venus moves higher this month and will be widely noticed; it is no longer a challenge. The Moon stands high above Mars on the 6th, due south at nightfall. An extraordinary "Supermoon" occurs on the 14th as the Moon comes its nearest to Earth since January 26, 1948. For most people, this is the largest and brightest full Moon of their lives. The effect on the tides, especially on the 15th, will be dramatic. A bright waning gibbous Moon will spoil the medium-strength Leonid meteor shower on the 18th. On the 25th, the Moon dangles below returning Jupiter in its new home of Virgo. Jupiter rises at around 4:00 A.M.*

◐	**First Quarter**	7th day	14th hour	51st minute
○	**Full Moon**	14th day	8th hour	52nd minute
◑	**Last Quarter**	21st day	3rd hour	34th minute
●	**New Moon**	29th day	7th hour	19th minute

After 2:00 A.M. on November 6, Eastern Standard Time is given.

Get these pages with times set to your zip code at Almanac.com/Access.

Day of Year	Day of Month	Day of Week	☼ Rises h. m.	Rise Key	☼ Sets h. m.	Set Key	Length of Day h.	m.	Sun Fast m.	Declination of Sun °	'	High Tide Times Boston		☾ Rises h. m.	Rise Key	☾ Sets h. m.	Set Key	☾ Astron. Place	☾ Age
306	1	Tu.	7:18	D	**5:37**	B	10	19	32	14 s.	43	12¾	**1**	8:48	E	**7:08**	B	LIB	2
307	2	W.	7:19	D	**5:36**	B	10	17	32	15	01	1½	**1½**	9:43	E	**7:48**	B	OPH	3
308	3	Th.	7:21	D	**5:34**	B	10	13	32	15	20	2	**2¼**	10:35	E	**8:31**	B	OPH	4
309	4	Fr.	7:22	D	**5:33**	B	10	11	32	15	38	2¾	**3**	11:25	E	**9:20**	B	SAG	5
310	5	Sa.	7:23	E	**5:32**	B	10	09	32	15	57	3½	**3¾**	**12:12**	E	**10:13**	B	SAG	6
311	6	**B**	6:24	E	**4:31**	B	10	07	32	16	14	3¼	**3½**	11:55	E	**10:11**	C	SAG	7
312	7	M.	6:26	E	**4:30**	B	10	04	32	16	32	4¼	**4¼**	**12:35**	E	**11:12**	C	CAP	8
313	8	Tu.	6:27	E	**4:29**	B	10	02	32	16	49	5	**5¼**	**1:12**	E	—	–	CAP	9
314	9	W.	6:28	E	**4:28**	B	10	00	32	17	06	6	**6¼**	**1:47**	D	12:16	C	AQU	10
315	10	Th.	6:29	E	**4:27**	B	9	58	32	17	23	6¾	**7¼**	**2:21**	D	1:24	D	AQU	11
316	11	Fr.	6:31	E	**4:26**	B	9	55	32	17	40	7¾	**8¼**	**2:56**	C	2:34	D	PSC	12
317	12	Sa.	6:32	E	**4:25**	B	9	53	32	17	56	8½	**9**	**3:33**	C	3:46	E	PSC	13
318	13	**B**	6:33	E	**4:24**	B	9	51	31	18	11	9½	**10**	**4:13**	C	5:01	E	PSC	14
319	14	M.	6:34	E	**4:23**	B	9	49	31	18	27	10¼	**10¾**	**4:58**	C	6:16	E	ARI	15
320	15	Tu.	6:36	E	**4:22**	B	9	46	31	18	42	11¼	**11¾**	**5:48**	B	7:30	E	TAU	16
321	16	W.	6:37	E	**4:21**	B	9	44	31	18	57	**12**	—	**6:44**	B	8:40	E	TAU	17
322	17	Th.	6:38	E	**4:20**	B	9	42	31	19	11	12¾	**1**	**7:44**	B	9:42	E	ORI	18
323	18	Fr.	6:39	E	**4:19**	B	9	40	30	19	26	1½	**1¾**	**8:47**	C	10:37	E	GEM	19
324	19	Sa.	6:40	E	**4:19**	B	9	39	30	19	39	2½	**2¾**	**9:51**	C	11:23	E	CAN	20
325	20	**B**	6:42	E	**4:18**	B	9	36	30	19	53	3½	**3¾**	**10:54**	C	**12:03**	E	CAN	21
326	21	M.	6:43	E	**4:17**	B	9	34	30	20	06	4½	**4¾**	**11:56**	D	**12:38**	D	LEO	22
327	22	Tu.	6:44	E	**4:17**	A	9	33	29	20	19	5½	**5¾**	—	–	**1:09**	D	LEO	23
328	23	W.	6:45	E	**4:16**	A	9	31	29	20	31	6½	**6¾**	12:56	D	**1:38**	D	LEO	24
329	24	Th.	6:46	E	**4:15**	A	9	29	29	20	43	7½	**7¾**	1:54	D	**2:06**	C	VIR	25
330	25	Fr.	6:48	E	**4:15**	A	9	27	29	20	55	8¼	**8¾**	2:52	D	**2:34**	C	VIR	26
331	26	Sa.	6:49	E	**4:14**	A	9	25	28	21	06	9	**9½**	3:49	E	**3:04**	C	VIR	27
332	27	**B**	6:50	E	**4:14**	A	9	24	28	21	17	9½	**10**	4:46	E	**3:35**	C	LIB	28
333	28	M.	6:51	E	**4:13**	A	9	22	28	21	27	10¼	**10¾**	5:42	E	**4:09**	B	LIB	29
334	29	Tu.	6:52	E	**4:13**	A	9	21	27	21	37	10¾	**11½**	6:38	E	**4:47**	B	SCO	0
335	30	W.	6:53	E	**4:13**	A	9	20	27	21 s.	46	11½	—	7:32	E	**5:29**	B	OPH	1

 To use this page, see p. 138; for Key Letters, see p. 252. ☞ **Bold = P.M.** ☞ Light = A.M.

November hath 30 days • 2016

The soft November days are here,
The aftermath of blossom's year. –Sara Louisa (Vickers) Oberholtzer

Day of Month	Day of Week	Dates, Feasts, Fasts, Aspects, Tide Heights	Weather
1	Tu.	**All Saints'** • Rainbow Bridge, connecting Niagara Falls of New York and Ontario, opened to public, 1941	*Fields*
2	W.	**All Souls'** • ☌♄☾ • *Sesame Street* character Cookie Monster born (no year)	*whitening,*
3	Th.	☌♀☾ • 96°F, Los Angeles, Calif., 1890 • {9.2 / 9.9	*cold*
4	Fr.	☾ runs low • Newscaster Walter Cronkite born, 1916 • Tides {9.0 / 9.8	*tightening:*
5	Sa.	Sadie Hawkins Day • ☌♇☾ • Actor Fred MacMurray died, 1991 • {8.8 / 9.6	*This*
6	**B**	**25th S. af. P.** • **Daylight Saving Time ends, 2:00 A.M.** • ☌♂☾ • {8.7 / 9.4	*is*
7	M.	Elston Howard won American League's Most Valuable Player award, 1963 • {8.7 / 9.4	*frightening!*
8	Tu.	**Election Day** • Black bears head to winter dens now. • Tides {8.9 / 9.5	*Lawns*
9	W.	☾ at ☋ • ☌♆☾ • Maj. Robert White flew X-15 rocket plane at Mach 6.04, 1961	*are*
10	Th.	*The aurora, when very bright, indicates approaching storm.*	*lakes,*
11	Fr.	**St. Martin of Tours** • **Veterans Day** • ☾ on Eq. • Tides {10.5 / 10.4	*floured*
12	Sa.	Indian Summer • ☌♅☾ • Ellis Island federal immigration station closed, N.Y./N.J., 1954	*with*
13	**B**	**26th S. af. P.** • Lobsters move to offshore waters now. • {11.8 / 11.1	*flakes.*
14	M.	**Full Beaver** ○ • ☾ at perig. • Tides {12.2 / 11.2	*Miserable?*
15	Tu.	Elvis Presley's first movie, *Love Me Tender,* premiered, 1956 • Tides {12.5 / 11.2	*Worse!*
16	W.	Poet Louis-Honoré Fréchette born, 1839 • Tides {12.4 / —	*It's*
17	Th.	**St. Hugh of Lincoln** • ☾ rides high • {11.0 / 12.1	*blizzard-able!*
18	Fr.	**St. Hilda of Whitby** • Crab apples are ripe now. • Tides {10.7 / 11.7	*Everything*
19	Sa.	U.S. president James Garfield born, 1831 • {10.3 / 11.0	*squishes—*
20	**B**	**27th S. af. P.** • ♆ stat. • J. Haven & C. Hettrich patented a whirligig (yo-yo), 1866	*even*
21	M.	☾ at ☊ • Snowflakes fell in central Fla., 2006 • {9.6 / 9.9	*your*
22	Tu.	Entrepreneur Mary Kay Ash died, 2001 • Tides {9.4 / 9.4	*favorite*
23	W.	**St. Clement** • ☌☿♄ • *A feast is not made of mushrooms only.*	*Thanksgiving*
24	Th.	**Thanksgiving Day** • ☾ on Eq. • ☌♀♇ • ☌♃☾ • {9.5 / 9.1	*dishes!*
25	Fr.	First YMCA in North America opened, Montreal, Que., 1851	*As*
26	Sa.	First lion exhibited in U.S., Boston, Mass., 1716 • {9.8 / 9.2	*the*
27	**B**	**1st S. of Advent** • ☾ at apo. • Astronomer Anders Celsius born, 1701	*inches*
28	M.	Thomas Jefferson: ". . . the freezing of the ink on the point of my pen renders it difficult to write."	*accumulate,*
29	Tu.	**New** ● • *Better do it than wish it done.* • {10.2 / 9.2	*spirits*
30	W.	**St. Andrew** • ☌☿☾ • ☌♄☾ • Tides {10.2 / —	*agloomulate.*

Sweet words butter no parsnips. –English proverb

Farmer's Calendar

■ The town moderator is responsible for running the elections. It's not a big chore. The town clerk, the supervisors of the checklist, and the ballot clerks do all the work; the moderator is a figurehead. In this town, I've been the figurehead for 12 years.

The moderator opens the polls at 8:00 A.M., stands at the checkout table, takes everyone's ballots from their hands (as state law requires), and puts them in the box.

The ballots are made of paper, and it's a wooden box, made in 1883, the same year that our Victorian town hall was built. The voters mark their ballots with pencils in little booths with red-white-and-blue curtains.

The polls close at 7:00 P.M. and we start counting the votes by hand. The only sounds are the shuffle of the ballots, the scratching of pencils, and the murmur of the clerks. We're usually finished by 10:00, although in a presidential election, we've stayed as late as 1:00 in the morning.

After announcing the results, I thank the workers for participating in this civic sacrament. That's when I get choked up; the weight of what we've been doing hits me hard. This is democracy—marking pieces of paper, putting them in a wooden box, and then counting them one by one.

SKY WATCH ☆ *Venus finally makes its run to prominence, getting even higher and brighter as it meets the Moon on the 2nd and 3rd. Mercury lurks far lower as it starts a mediocre 3-week evening star apparition. Mars, just one-tenth as bright as it was in June, moves through Capricornus and into Aquarius, steadily sinking toward Venus. The solstice falls on the 21st at 5:44* A.M.*, inaugurating winter. On the predawn stage, the Moon floats above brilliant Jupiter early on the 22nd, with Virgo's famous blue star Spica just beneath them both after 3:00* A.M. *Much more challenging is dim returning Saturn meeting a hair-thin Moon very low in morning twilight on the 27th.*

◐	**First Quarter**	7th day	4th hour	3rd minute
○	**Full Moon**	13th day	19th hour	6th minute
◑	**Last Quarter**	20th day	20th hour	56th minute
●	**New Moon**	29th day	1st hour	54th minute

All times are given in Eastern Standard Time.

Get these pages with times set to your zip code at Almanac.com/Access.

Day of Year	Day of Month	Day of Week	☼ Rises h. m.	Rise Key	☼ Sets h. m.	Set Key	Length of Day h. m.	Sun Fast m.	Declination of Sun ° '	High Tide Times Boston		☾ Rises h. m.	Rise Key	☾ Sets h. m.	Set Key	☾ Astron. Place	☾ Age
336	1	Th.	6:54	E	**4:12**	A	9 18	26	21 s. 56	12	**12¼**	8:23	E	**6:16**	B	SAG	2
337	2	Fr.	6:55	E	**4:12**	A	9 17	26	22 04	12¾	**12¾**	9:11	E	**7:08**	B	SAG	3
338	3	Sa.	6:56	E	**4:12**	A	9 16	26	22 13	1½	**1½**	9:55	E	**8:04**	C	SAG	4
339	4	**B**	6:57	E	**4:12**	A	9 15	25	22 21	2	**2¼**	10:36	E	**9:03**	C	CAP	5
340	5	M.	6:58	E	**4:12**	A	9 14	25	22 28	2¾	**3**	11:13	E	**10:05**	C	AQU	6
341	6	Tu.	6:59	E	**4:12**	A	9 13	24	22 35	3½	**3¾**	11:48	D	**11:09**	C	AQU	7
342	7	W.	7:00	E	**4:12**	A	9 12	24	22 42	4½	**4¾**	**12:21**	D	—	–	AQU	8
343	8	Th.	7:01	E	**4:12**	A	9 11	24	22 48	5½	**5¾**	**12:54**	D	12:16	D	PSC	9
344	9	Fr.	7:02	E	**4:12**	A	9 10	23	22 53	6¼	**6¾**	**1:28**	C	1:24	D	CET	10
345	10	Sa.	7:03	E	**4:12**	A	9 09	23	22 59	7¼	**7¾**	**2:05**	C	2:35	E	PSC	11
346	11	**B**	7:04	E	**4:12**	A	9 08	22	23 03	8¼	**8¾**	**2:45**	C	3:48	E	ARI	12
347	12	M.	7:04	E	**4:12**	A	9 08	22	23 08	9	**9¾**	**3:31**	B	5:02	E	TAU	13
348	13	Tu.	7:05	E	**4:12**	A	9 07	21	23 12	10	**10½**	**4:24**	B	6:14	E	TAU	14
349	14	W.	7:06	E	**4:12**	A	9 06	21	23 15	10¾	**11½**	**5:23**	B	7:21	E	TAU	15
350	15	Th.	7:07	E	**4:13**	A	9 06	20	23 18	11¾	—	**6:26**	B	8:22	E	GEM	16
351	16	Fr.	7:07	E	**4:13**	A	9 06	20	23 20	12¼	**12½**	**7:32**	C	9:14	E	GEM	17
352	17	Sa.	7:08	E	**4:13**	A	9 05	19	23 22	1¼	**1½**	**8:38**	C	9:59	E	CAN	18
353	18	**B**	7:09	E	**4:14**	A	9 05	19	23 24	2¼	**2¼**	**9:43**	C	10:37	E	LEO	19
354	19	M.	7:09	E	**4:14**	A	9 05	18	23 25	3	**3¼**	**10:45**	D	11:11	D	LEO	20
355	20	Tu.	7:10	E	**4:15**	A	9 05	18	23 25	4	**4¼**	**11:45**	D	11:41	D	LEO	21
356	21	W.	7:10	E	**4:15**	A	9 05	17	23 26	4¾	**5¼**	—	–	**12:10**	D	VIR	22
357	22	Th.	7:11	E	**4:16**	A	9 05	17	23 25	5¾	**6¼**	12:44	D	**12:38**	C	VIR	23
358	23	Fr.	7:11	E	**4:16**	A	9 05	16	23 24	6¾	**7¼**	1:41	E	**1:07**	C	VIR	24
359	24	Sa.	7:12	E	**4:17**	A	9 05	16	23 23	7½	**8**	2:38	E	**1:37**	C	LIB	25
360	25	**B**	7:12	E	**4:17**	A	9 05	15	23 21	8¼	**9**	3:35	E	**2:10**	B	LIB	26
361	26	M.	7:12	E	**4:18**	A	9 06	15	23 19	9	**9¾**	4:31	E	**2:46**	B	LIB	27
362	27	Tu.	7:13	E	**4:19**	A	9 06	14	23 16	9¾	**10¼**	5:26	E	**3:27**	B	OPH	28
363	28	W.	7:13	E	**4:19**	A	9 06	14	23 13	10½	**11**	6:19	E	**4:12**	B	OPH	29
364	29	Th.	7:13	E	**4:20**	A	9 07	13	23 10	11	**11¾**	7:09	E	**5:03**	B	SAG	0
365	30	Fr.	7:13	E	**4:21**	A	9 08	13	23 05	11¾	—	7:55	E	**5:58**	B	SAG	1
366	31	Sa.	7:13	E	**4:22**	A	9 09	13	23 s. 01	12¼	**12½**	8:37	E	**6:57**	C	CAP	2

 To use this page, see p. 138 for Key Letters, see p. 252. ☞ **Bold = P.M.** ☞ Light = A.M.

DECEMBER HATH 31 DAYS • 2016

Heart-warm against the stormy white,
The Rose of Joy burns warmer yet. –Thomas Gold Appleton

Day of Month	Day of Week	Dates, Feasts, Fasts, Aspects, Tide Heights	Weather
1	Th.	☾ RUNS LOW • First flight of helium-filled blimp (C-7), between Va. and D.C., 1921 • Tides {9.2 / 10.2	*Snow,*
2	Fr.	St. Viviana • ☌♇☾ • Former U.S. First Lady Jane Pierce died, 1863 • Tides {9.1 / 10.1	*then*
3	Sa.	☌♀☾ • Commonwealth Pacific Cable (COMPAC) opened, 1963 • Tides {9.1 / 10.0	*rain,*
4	**B**	2nd S. of Advent • Matisse's *Le Bateau* rehung after being upside down 47 days, MoMA, N.Y.C., 1961	*then*
5	M.	☌♂☾ • *A blustering night, a fair day.* • Tides {9.0 / 9.7	*temps*
6	Tu.	St. Nicholas • ☾ AT ☋ • ☌♆☾ • Winterberry fruit especially showy now.	*easing.*
7	W.	St. Ambrose • **Nat'l Pearl Harbor Remembrance Day** • Tides {9.3 / 9.6	*Déjà vu:*
8	Th.	☾ ON EQ. • After FDR's "a date which will live in infamy" speech, U.S. declared war on Japan, WWII, 1941	*one*
9	Fr.	☌♅☾ • Actor Kirk Douglas born, 1916 • Tides {10.1 / 9.8	*dump*
10	Sa.	St. Eulalia • ☌♄☉ • ☿ GR. ELONG. (21° EAST) • Tides {10.7 / 10.0	*or*
11	**B**	**3rd S. of Advent** • Ind. admitted to Union as 19th state, 1816 • {11.3 / 10.3	*two?*
12	M.	**Our Lady of Guadalupe** • ☾ AT PERIG. • George Grant received patent for improved golf tee, 1899	*Frosty's*
13	Tu.	St. Lucia • **Full Cold** ○ • *Love rules his kingdom without a sword.* • {12.1 / 10.7	*freezing!*
14	W.	Ember Day • Halcyon Days begin. • ☾ RIDES HIGH • Tides {12.3 / 10.8	*No*
15	Th.	U.S. Bill of Rights ratified, 1791 • Beware the Pogonip. • Tides {12.2 / —	*relief*
16	Fr.	Ember Day • Beatrix Potter's *The Tale of Peter Rabbit* first published, 1901 • Tides {10.7 / 12.0	*to be*
17	Sa.	Ember Day • Bob Fisher made 2,371 basketball free throws in 1 hour, Centralia, Kans., 2011	*seen—*
18	**B**	**4th S. of Advent** • ☾ AT ☊ • Tides {10.2 / 10.9	*is*
19	M.	☿ STAT. • La. Purchase explorer Wm. Dunbar: ". . . the e[a]ves of our cabin hang with beautiful icicles," 1804	*that*
20	Tu.	$1 bachelor tax imposed, Mo., 1820 • Tides {9.6 / 9.6	*Santa*
21	W.	St. Thomas • **Winter Solstice** • ☾ ON EQ. • Vladimir Horowitz wed Wanda Toscanini, 1933	*riding*
22	Th.	☌♃☾ • Pirate Bluebeard died, 1440 • Tides {9.2 / 8.7	*on a*
23	Fr.	–50°F, Almont and Williston, N.Dak., 1983 • Tides {9.2 / 8.5	*snow*
24	Sa.	**Chanukah begins at sundown** • CONAD (later, NORAD) began to track Santa Claus, 1955	*machine?*
25	**B**	**Christmas** • ☾ AT APO. • Pansy blossoms picked, Manhattan, Mont., 1896	*Please:*
26	M.	St. Stephen • **Boxing Day (Canada)** • **First day of Kwanzaa** • Tides {9.7 / 8.7	*more*
27	Tu.	St. John • ☌♄☾ • *Man's best candle is his understanding.* • Tides {9.9 / 8.9	*green,*
28	W.	Holy Innocents • ☾ RUNS LOW • ☌☿☾ • ☿ IN INF. ☌ • {10.1 / 9.0	*less*
29	Th.	New ● • ☌♇☾ • ♅ STAT. • Chemist Charles Macintosh born, 1766	*spleen*
30	Fr.	1.3" snow, Las Vegas, Nev., 2003 • Tides {10.3 / —	*in*
31	Sa.	St. Sylvester • Guy Lombardo and His Royal Canadians first played "Auld Lang Syne" at midnight, 1929	*'17!*

Farmer's Calendar

■ A few weeks before Christmas, I found a dead star-nosed mole near our pond. A little bigger than an ordinary mole, it has an uncanny star-shaped nose. Circling the tip are 22 hairless tentacles that serve as the mole's primary sensory organ.

Like other moles, it has weak eyesight, which is not much use belowground. Its nose, though, is covered with 25,000 sensory receptors called Eimer's organs, which make it six times more sensitive than the human hand. Underground, the tentacles whirl around, touching objects near the mole with astounding swiftness: 12 objects per second. In a quarter of a second, the mole can identify an object, decide if it's prey (worms, mostly), and eat it. Half the mole's brain is devoted to processing this information; it literally thinks with its nose.

This mole also hunts underwater by smell. Its stellar nostrils emit tiny bubbles—5 to 10 per second—that pick up scent molecules. These the mole inhales. Not until this was discovered did scientists believe that mammals could smell underwater.

I walked home that day contemplating the magnificent weirdness of nature and the Magi, those ancient astronomers who also found their way through the darkness by following a star.

THE FIRST MONTH • 2017

SKY WATCH ☆ *An eventful celestial year begins splendidly, with dazzling Venus in Aquarius, high in the west at nightfall. The crescent Moon dangles below it on the 1st. On the 2nd, the Moon hovers between Venus and much less brilliant, first-magnitude Mars. Earth reaches its annual closest approach to the Sun on the 4th. Mercury begins a mediocre morning star apparition on the 6th; it's best viewed in midmonth. Jupiter, in Virgo, rises at around midnight and is highest before dawn. Saturn, in Ophiuchus, starts 2017 in the low predawn east. It hangs below the crescent Moon on the 24th. The Moon stands below Venus on the 30th and forms a lovely triangle with Venus and Mars on the 31st.*

◐	**First Quarter**	5th day	14th hour	47th minute
○	**Full Moon**	12th day	6th hour	34th minute
◑	**Last Quarter**	19th day	17th hour	13th minute
●	**New Moon**	27th day	19th hour	7th minute

All times are given in Eastern Standard Time.

Get these pages with times set to your zip code at Almanac.com/Access.

Day of Year	Day of Month	Day of Week	☼ Rises h. m.	Rise Key	☼ Sets h. m.	Set Key	Length of Day h. m.	Sun Fast m.	Declination of Sun ° '	High Tide Times Boston		☾ Rises h. m.	Rise Key	☾ Sets h. m.	Set Key	☾ Astron. Place	☾ Age
1	1	**A**	7:13	E	**4:23**	A	9 10	12	22s.56	1	**1**	9:16	E	**7:59**	C	CAP	3
2	2	M.	7:13	E	**4:24**	A	9 11	12	22 50	1¾	**1¾**	9:52	E	**9:02**	C	AQU	4
3	3	Tu.	7:13	E	**4:24**	A	9 11	11	22 44	2½	**2½**	10:25	D	**10:07**	D	AQU	5
4	4	W.	7:13	E	**4:25**	A	9 12	11	22 38	3¼	**3½**	10:57	D	**11:13**	D	AQU	6
5	5	Th.	7:13	E	**4:26**	A	9 13	10	22 31	4	**4¼**	11:30	C	—	–	CET	7
6	6	Fr.	7:13	E	**4:27**	A	9 14	10	22 24	5	**5¼**	**12:04**	C	12:21	E	PSC	8
7	7	Sa.	7:13	E	**4:28**	A	9 15	9	22 16	5¾	**6½**	**12:41**	C	1:31	E	CET	9
8	8	**A**	7:13	E	**4:29**	A	9 16	9	22 08	6¾	**7½**	**1:22**	C	2:41	E	ARI	10
9	9	M.	7:13	E	**4:30**	A	9 17	9	21 59	7¾	**8½**	**2:10**	B	3:52	E	TAU	11
10	10	Tu.	7:12	E	**4:32**	A	9 20	8	21 50	8¾	**9½**	**3:04**	B	5:00	E	TAU	12
11	11	W.	7:12	E	**4:33**	A	9 21	8	21 41	9¾	**10½**	**4:04**	B	6:03	E	ORI	13
12	12	Th.	7:12	E	**4:34**	A	9 22	7	21 31	10½	**11¼**	**5:09**	C	7:00	E	GEM	14
13	13	Fr.	7:11	E	**4:35**	A	9 24	7	21 21	11½	—	**6:16**	C	7:49	E	CAN	15
14	14	Sa.	7:11	E	**4:36**	A	9 25	7	21 10	12	**12¼**	**7:23**	C	8:32	E	CAN	16
15	15	**A**	7:11	E	**4:37**	B	9 26	6	20 59	1	**1¼**	**8:28**	C	9:08	E	LEO	17
16	16	M.	7:10	E	**4:38**	B	9 28	6	20 48	1¾	**2**	**9:31**	D	9:41	D	LEO	18
17	17	Tu.	7:10	E	**4:40**	B	9 30	6	20 36	2½	**2¾**	**10:32**	D	10:11	D	VIR	19
18	18	W.	7:09	E	**4:41**	B	9 32	5	20 23	3¼	**3¾**	**11:31**	D	10:40	C	VIR	20
19	19	Th.	7:08	E	**4:42**	B	9 34	5	20 11	4¼	**4½**	—	–	11:09	C	VIR	21
20	20	Fr.	7:08	E	**4:43**	B	9 35	5	19 58	5	**5½**	12:29	E	11:39	C	VIR	22
21	21	Sa.	7:07	E	**4:45**	B	9 38	4	19 44	6	**6½**	1:26	E	**12:10**	C	LIB	23
22	22	**A**	7:06	E	**4:46**	B	9 40	4	19 30	6¾	**7½**	2:22	E	**12:45**	B	LIB	24
23	23	M.	7:06	E	**4:47**	B	9 41	4	19 16	7¾	**8¼**	3:17	E	**1:24**	B	OPH	25
24	24	Tu.	7:05	E	**4:48**	B	9 43	4	19 02	8½	**9**	4:11	E	**2:07**	B	OPH	26
25	25	W.	7:04	E	**4:50**	B	9 46	3	18 47	9¼	**9¾**	5:02	E	**2:56**	B	SAG	27
26	26	Th.	7:03	E	**4:51**	B	9 48	3	18 32	10	**10½**	5:50	E	**3:49**	B	SAG	28
27	27	Fr.	7:02	E	**4:52**	B	9 50	3	18 16	10¾	**11¼**	6:35	E	**4:48**	B	SAG	0
28	28	Sa.	7:01	E	**4:53**	B	9 52	3	18 00	11¼	12	7:16	E	**5:49**	C	CAP	1
29	29	**A**	7:00	E	**4:55**	B	9 55	3	17 44	**12**	—	7:53	E	**6:53**	C	CAP	2
30	30	M.	6:59	E	**4:56**	B	9 57	3	17 27	12½	**12¾**	8:28	D	**7:59**	D	AQU	3
31	31	Tu.	6:58	E	**4:57**	B	9 59	2	17s.11	1¼	**1½**	9:01	D	**9:06**	D	AQU	4

 To use this page, see p. 138; for Key Letters, see p. 252. ☞ **Bold = P.M.** ☞ Light = A.M.

JANUARY HATH 31 DAYS • 2017

The fresh New Year, the bright New Year
That telleth of hope and joy, my dear! –Bryan Waller Procter

Day of Month	Day of Week	Dates, Feasts, Fasts, Aspects, Tide Heights	Weather
1	**A**	**New Year's Day** • **Holy Name** • ☌♂♆ • *One minute of patience, ten years of peace.*	*An*
2	M.	☾ AT ☋ • ☌♀☾ • ☌♆☾ • Tides {9.4 / 10.3	*inkling*
3	Tu.	☌♂☾ • Writer J.R.R. Tolkien born, 1892 • Tides {9.5 / 10.1	*of*
4	W.	**St. Elizabeth Ann Seton** • ☾ ON EQ. • ⊕ AT PERIHELION	*sprinkling;*
5	Th.	Twelfth Night • ☌♅☾ • First Trans-Pacific (Calif. to Hawaii) cable opened to public use, 1903	*warmer*
6	Fr.	**Epiphany** • Clarence King, founder of the U.S. Geological Survey, born, 1842 • {10.0 / 9.5	*than*
7	Sa.	Distaff Day • ☌♇☉ • Tom Seaver elected to Baseball Hall of Fame, 1992 • {10.3 / 9.5	*you'd*
8	**A**	**1st S. af. Ep.** • ☿ STAT. • Astronomer Galileo died, 1642	*guess.*
9	M.	Plough Monday • 5.7 earthquake struck Miramichi, N.B., 1982 • Tides {11.0 / 9.8	*Flurrier—*
10	Tu.	☾ AT PERIG. • Frontiersman Buffalo Bill Cody died, 1917 • Tides {11.4 / 10.0	*visit a*
11	W.	☾ RIDES HIGH • U.S. statesman Alexander Hamilton born, 1757 • Tides {11.7 / 10.2	*furrier!*
12	Th.	**Full Wolf** ○ • ☌♀♆ • ♀ GR. ELONG. (47° EAST) • Tides {11.8 / 10.4	*Sunny*
13	Fr.	**St. Hilary** • *The road to success is lined with many tempting parking spaces.* • {11.8 / —	*skies.*
14	Sa.	Astronomer Edmond Halley died, 1742 • {10.4 / 11.6	*What*
15	**A**	**2nd S. af. Ep.** • ☾ AT ☊ • 2" snow, Los Angeles, Calif., 1932	*a*
16	M.	**Martin Luther King Jr.'s Birthday, observed** • Ivan the Terrible crowned first Russian czar, 1547	*mess!*
17	Tu.	☾ ON EQ. • U.S. statesman Benjamin Franklin born, 1706 • St. Elmo's fire, Conn. River Valley, 1817	*Milder,*
18	W.	Poet Rubén Darío born, 1867 • Yellowknife became capital of N.W.T., 1967 • Tides {9.6 / 9.4	*then*
19	Th.	☌♃☾ • ☿ GR. ELONG. (24° WEST) • *Wind from the north, cold and snow.* • {9.3 / 8.8	*turning*
20	Fr.	74-lb. striped bass caught near Cape Henry, Va., 2012	*wilder,*
21	Sa.	☾ AT APO. • First commerical extraction of magnesium from seawater began, Freeport, Tex., 1941	*with*
22	**A**	**3rd S. af. Ep.** • –4°F to 45°F in 2 minutes due to chinook, Spearfish, S.Dak., 1943	*hours*
23	M.	Charles Curtis first of Native American descent to be elected as U.S. senator, 1907 • {9.2 / 8.2	*of*
24	Tu.	☌♄☾ • January thaw traditionally begins about now. • Tides {9.4 / 8.4	*snow*
25	W.	**Conversion of Paul** • ☾ RUNS LOW • ☌☿☾ • Tides {9.7 / 8.7	*showers.*
26	Th.	**Sts. Timothy & Titus** • ☌♇☾ • Tides {10.0 / 9.0	*Tapering*
27	Fr.	**New** ● • Writer Lewis Carroll born, 1832 • {10.3 / 9.3	*off*
28	Sa.	**St. Thomas Aquinas** • **Chinese New Year (Rooster)** • {10.5 / 9.5	*while*
29	**A**	**4th S. af. Ep.** • ☾ AT ☋ • ☌☿♇ • Tides {10.7 / —	*kids*
30	M.	☌♆☾ • *No snowflake ever falls in the wrong place.* • {9.8 / 10.7	*are*
31	Tu.	☌♀☾ • ☌♂☾ • Raccoons mate now. • {10.0 / 10.6	*capering.*

Farmer's Calendar

■ Winter often brings out the best in small towns. Our dog Echo disappeared in the last big snowstorm. We checked with the neighbors, called the police, and walked up and down the road rattling her food dish and shouting her name.

The next morning, friends and neighbors, even some we barely knew, called to find out if she'd come home or if they could help look for her. My wife, May, got to her elementary school and told her students that Echo was missing. They offered to buy her a new dog.

A friend of ours was on the state highway about 5 miles from our house that morning. He was on his way to pick up a friend when he saw a black dog running back and forth across the road, dodging cars and trucks. He didn't know it was our dog; he just knew that the dog was in trouble. He stopped to try to pick her up, but she wouldn't come close. He called his friend to say he'd be late. As Echo headed west, toward the center of town, our friend followed, creeping in the breakdown lane. Several more cars fell in behind them. At the Town Hall, Echo stopped and the escorts halted. Our friend, helped by people from the other cars, managed to herd her to the police station just across the street. May got the news when the chief called to say, "I think I've got your dog."

THE SECOND MONTH • 2017

SKY WATCH ☆ *On the 1st, at nightfall, Venus, Mars, and the crescent Moon stand in a straight line in Pisces. Venus retains its shadow-casting, magnitude –4.8 brilliance and 30 degree elevation throughout this month, with dimmer Mars staying to its upper left. The Moon returns to form a triangle with them on the 28th. Jupiter, now rising by 10:30* P.M.*, hovers above Virgo's blue star, Spica; the Moon stands above the pair on the 14th and to their left the next night. In the predawn southeastern sky, the Moon sits above Saturn on the morning of the 20th and to its left on the 21st; by month's end, the Ringed World rises almost 4 hours ahead of the Sun.*

◐	**First Quarter**	3rd day	23rd hour	19th minute
○	**Full Moon**	10th day	19th hour	33rd minute
◑	**Last Quarter**	18th day	14th hour	33rd minute
●	**New Moon**	26th day	9th hour	58th minute

All times are given in Eastern Standard Time.

Get these pages with times set to your zip code at Almanac.com/Access.

Day of Year	Day of Month	Day of Week	☼ Rises h. m.	Rise Key	☼ Sets h. m.	Set Key	Length of Day h. m.	Sun Fast m.	Declination of Sun ° '	High Tide Times Boston		☾ Rises h. m.	Rise Key	☾ Sets h. m.	Set Key	☾ Astron. Place	☾ Age
32	1	W.	6:57	E	**4:59**	B	10 02	2	16 s. 54	2	**2¼**	9:34	C	**10:13**	E	PSC	5
33	2	Th.	6:56	E	**5:00**	B	10 04	2	16 36	2¾	**3**	10:07	C	**11:21**	E	PSC	6
34	3	Fr.	6:55	E	**5:01**	B	10 06	2	16 18	3½	**4**	10:42	C	—	–	CET	7
35	4	Sa.	6:54	E	**5:03**	B	10 09	2	16 00	4½	**5**	11:21	C	12:30	E	ARI	8
36	5	**A**	6:53	D	**5:04**	B	10 11	2	15 42	5½	**6**	**12:05**	B	1:39	E	TAU	9
37	6	M.	6:52	D	**5:05**	B	10 13	2	15 24	6½	**7¼**	**12:54**	B	2:46	E	TAU	10
38	7	Tu.	6:51	D	**5:07**	B	10 16	2	15 05	7½	**8¼**	**1:50**	B	3:49	E	ORI	11
39	8	W.	6:49	D	**5:08**	B	10 19	2	14 46	8½	**9¼**	**2:51**	B	4:47	E	GEM	12
40	9	Th.	6:48	D	**5:09**	B	10 21	2	14 27	9½	**10¼**	**3:56**	C	5:39	E	CAN	13
41	10	Fr.	6:47	D	**5:10**	B	10 23	2	14 07	10½	**11**	**5:02**	C	6:24	E	CAN	14
42	11	Sa.	6:46	D	**5:12**	B	10 26	2	13 47	11¼	**11¾**	**6:08**	C	7:03	E	LEO	15
43	12	**A**	6:44	D	**5:13**	B	10 29	2	13 27	**12**	—	**7:13**	D	7:38	D	LEO	16
44	13	M.	6:43	D	**5:14**	B	10 31	2	13 07	12½	**12¾**	**8:16**	D	8:10	D	LEO	17
45	14	Tu.	6:42	D	**5:16**	B	10 34	2	12 47	1¼	**1½**	**9:16**	D	8:40	C	VIR	18
46	15	W.	6:40	D	**5:17**	B	10 37	2	12 26	2	**2¼**	**10:16**	E	9:09	C	VIR	19
47	16	Th.	6:39	D	**5:18**	B	10 39	2	12 05	2¾	**3**	**11:14**	E	9:39	C	VIR	20
48	17	Fr.	6:37	D	**5:19**	B	10 42	2	11 44	3½	**3¾**	—	–	10:10	B	LIB	21
49	18	Sa.	6:36	D	**5:21**	B	10 45	2	11 23	4¼	**4¾**	12:11	E	10:43	B	LIB	22
50	19	**A**	6:35	D	**5:22**	B	10 47	2	11 01	5	**5¾**	1:06	E	11:20	B	SCO	23
51	20	M.	6:33	D	**5:23**	B	10 50	2	10 40	6	**6¾**	2:01	E	**12:01**	B	OPH	24
52	21	Tu.	6:32	D	**5:24**	B	10 52	2	10 18	7	**7½**	2:53	E	**12:46**	B	SAG	25
53	22	W.	6:30	D	**5:26**	B	10 56	2	9 56	7¾	**8½**	3:42	E	**1:38**	B	SAG	26
54	23	Th.	6:29	D	**5:27**	B	10 58	3	9 34	8¾	**9¼**	4:28	E	**2:34**	B	SAG	27
55	24	Fr.	6:27	D	**5:28**	B	11 01	3	9 12	9½	**10**	5:10	E	**3:34**	C	CAP	28
56	25	Sa.	6:25	D	**5:29**	B	11 04	3	8 50	10¼	**10¾**	5:50	E	**4:38**	C	CAP	29
57	26	**A**	6:24	D	**5:31**	B	11 07	3	8 27	11	**11½**	6:26	E	**5:45**	C	AQU	0
58	27	M.	6:22	D	**5:32**	C	11 10	3	8 05	11¾	—	7:01	D	**6:53**	D	AQU	1
59	28	Tu.	6:21	D	**5:33**	C	11 12	3	7 s. 42	12	**12¼**	7:34	D	**8:02**	D	PSC	2

 To use this page, see p. 138; for Key Letters, see p. 252. ☞ **Bold = P.M.** ☞ Light = A.M.

FEBRUARY HATH 28 DAYS • 2017

The true redde letter *day* [Feb. 14] *returns,*
When summer time in winter burns. –James Henry Leigh Hunt

Day of Month	Day of Week	Dates, Feasts, Fasts, Aspects, Tide Heights	Weather
1	W.	**St. Brigid** • ☾ ON EQ. • "Battle Hymn of the Republic" published, 1862	*Groundhogs*
2	Th.	**Candlemas** • Groundhog Day • ☌⛢☾ • Tides {10.2 10.1	*stock*
3	Fr.	105°F, Montezuma, Ariz., 1963 • Tides {10.3 9.7	*up on*
4	Sa.	Dennis Conner and crew of *Stars & Stripes* recaptured America's Cup, 1987 • {10.3 9.4	*sunblock.*
5	**A**	**5th S. af. Ep.** • HESSI launched to study solar flares, 2002	*Melting:*
6	M.	☾ AT PERIG. • ♃ STAT. • Elizabeth Alexandra Mary Windsor proclaimed Queen of Canada, 1952	*Get*
7	Tu.	☾ RIDES HIGH • *He who knows his heart, mistrusts his eyes.* • Tides {10.7 9.4	*ready*
8	W.	Debi Thomas won Women's Singles, U.S. National Figure Skating Championship, 1986 • {10.9 9.7	*for*
9	Th.	Pathologist Howard Taylor Ricketts born, 1871 • –52°F, Butte, Mont., 1933 • {11.2 10.0	*a*
10	Fr.	**Full Snow** ○ • **Eclipse** ☾ • "Chattanooga Choo Choo" first to earn gold record, 1942	*belting!*
11	Sa.	☾ AT ☊ • Inventor Thomas Alva Edison born, 1847 • Writer Sidney Sheldon born, 1917	*Blizzards*
12	**A**	**Septuagesima** • U.S. president Abraham Lincoln born, 1809	*confound*
13	M.	Novocain (procaine) patented, 1906 • –72°F, Shepherd Bay, Nunavut, 1973 • {10.3 10.8	*weather*
14	Tu.	**Sts. Cyril & Methodius** • **Valentine's Day** • ☾ ON EQ. • Tides {10.2 10.4	*wizards.*
15	W.	☌♃☾ • Susan B. Anthony born, 1820 • *Ocean Ranger* drilling rig sank in storm off Nfld., 1982	*Bright*
16	Th.	Winter's back breaks. • Future Canadian prime minister (Sir) John A. Macdonald married Susan A. Bernard, 1867	*but*
17	Fr.	National Congress of Mothers, later known as PTA, founded, 1897 • Tides {9.4 8.8	*bitter*
18	Sa.	☾ AT APO. • Pluto discovered by astronomer Clyde W. Tombaugh, 1930 • Tides {9.1 8.3	*as*
19	**A**	**Sexagesima** • Prizes first added to boxes of Cracker Jack, 1912 • {8.9 8.0	*flakes*
20	M.	**Presidents' Day** • ☌♄☾ • Actor Dick York died, 1992 • Tides {8.8 8.0	*flitter.*
21	Tu.	☾ RUNS LOW • 21–23: Destructive ice storm, Wis., 1922 • Tides {8.9 8.1	*Better,*
22	W.	☌♇☾ • U.S. president George Washington born, 1732 • Poet Edna St. Vincent Millay born, 1892	*then*
23	Th.	Artist George Frederic Watts born, 1817 • Tides {9.6 8.7	*wetter.*
24	Fr.	**St. Matthias** • Skunks mate now. • Tides {10.0 9.2	*Good*
25	Sa.	☌☿☾ • *A little pot is soon hot.* • Tides {10.4 9.7	*news*
26	**A**	**Quinquagesima** • **New** ● • **Eclipse** ☉ • ☾ AT ☋ • ☌♆☾	*for*
27	M.	**Clean Monday** • ☌♂⛢ • Loyalists defeated in Battle of Moores Creek Bridge, N.C., 1776	*the*
28	Tu.	**Shrove Tuesday** • **St. Romanus** • ☾ ON EQ. • ☌♀☾	*sledder!*

The stars are the jewels of the night, and perchance surpass anything which day has to show.
–Henry David Thoreau

Farmer's Calendar

■ The coldest day in the recorded history of North America (outside of Greenland) was 70 years ago this month, when a Canadian weather station at Snag, Yukon Territory, hit –81.4°F. How cold is that? So cold that your spit freezes before it hits the ground. So cold that your nostrils ice up. So cold that you can hear your breath freeze—"a tinkling sound," according to witnesses. So cold that the four weather observers present could hear laughter and conversations in an aboriginal village 3 miles away. "A spoken word remained in the air as a tiny, motionless mist for 3 to 4 minutes," one reported.

The Greek philosopher Antisthenes spoke of a faraway land where words froze as they were spoken and could not be heard until summer, when they thawed.

The deepest cold I've ever experienced was on a winter camping trip in the White Mountains. It was 30° below zero. The water in our canteens froze solid, as did a jar of chunky peanut butter.

Hiking out, we began showing symptoms of hypothermia—slurred speech, difficulty walking, an almost drunken hilarity. We laughed all the way back to our cars, trailing little clouds behind us. If Antisthenes was right, some June hikers must have been startled when they passed by.

THE THIRD MONTH • 2017

SKY WATCH ☆ *The year's highest and most dramatic Moon for small telescopes can be seen at nightfall during the first-quarter period of the 4th through 6th. It nearly touches the orange star Aldebaran on the 4th. Venus starts the month still brilliant and moderately high but appears much lower each evening and reaches conjunction with the Sun on the 25th, ending its apparition as an evening star. Jupiter now rises before 9:00* P.M.*; the planet forms a lovely triangle with the Moon and the star Spica on the 14th. Spring begins with the equinox on the 20th at 6:29* A.M. *Mercury appears low in evening twilight during the end of March, sitting to the right of the thin crescent Moon on the 29th.*

◐	**First Quarter**	5th day	6th hour	32nd minute
○	**Full Moon**	12th day	10th hour	54th minute
◑	**Last Quarter**	20th day	11th hour	58th minute
●	**New Moon**	27th day	22nd hour	57th minute

After 2:00 A.M. *on March 12, Eastern Daylight Time is given.*

Get these pages with times set to your zip code at Almanac.com/Access.

Day of Year	Day of Month	Day of Week	☼ Rises h. m.	Rise Key	☼ Sets h. m.	Set Key	Length of Day h.	m.	Sun Fast m.	Declination of Sun °	'	High Tide Times Boston		☾ Rises h. m.	Rise Key	☾ Sets h. m.	Set Key	☾ Astron. Place	☾ Age
60	1	W.	6:19	D	**5:34**	C	11	15	4	7 s.	19	12¾	**1¼**	8:08	C	**9:12**	E	CET	3
61	2	Th.	6:18	D	**5:36**	C	11	18	4	6	56	1½	**2**	8:44	C	**10:22**	E	PSC	4
62	3	Fr.	6:16	D	**5:37**	C	11	21	4	6	33	2¼	**2¾**	9:22	C	**11:31**	E	ARI	5
63	4	Sa.	6:14	D	**5:38**	C	11	24	4	6	10	3¼	**3¾**	10:04	B	—	–	TAU	6
64	5	**A**	6:13	D	**5:39**	C	11	26	5	5	47	4	**4¾**	10:51	B	12:39	E	TAU	7
65	6	M.	6:11	D	**5:40**	C	11	29	5	5	24	5¼	**5¾**	11:44	B	1:43	E	TAU	8
66	7	Tu.	6:09	D	**5:42**	C	11	33	5	5	00	6¼	**7**	**12:42**	B	2:41	E	GEM	9
67	8	W.	6:08	C	**5:43**	C	11	35	5	4	37	7¼	**8**	**1:44**	B	3:33	E	GEM	10
68	9	Th.	6:06	C	**5:44**	C	11	38	5	4	13	8½	**9**	**2:48**	C	4:19	E	CAN	11
69	10	Fr.	6:04	C	**5:45**	C	11	41	6	3	50	9¼	**10**	**3:53**	C	5:00	E	LEO	12
70	11	Sa.	6:03	C	**5:46**	C	11	43	6	3	26	10¼	**10¾**	**4:57**	D	5:36	D	LEO	13
71	12	**A**	7:01	C	**6:48**	C	11	47	6	3	03	**12**	—	**7:00**	D	7:08	D	LEO	14
72	13	M.	6:59	C	**6:49**	C	11	50	7	2	39	12½	**12¾**	**8:02**	D	7:39	D	VIR	15
73	14	Tu.	6:57	C	**6:50**	C	11	53	7	2	15	1	**1½**	**9:02**	E	8:08	C	VIR	16
74	15	W.	6:56	C	**6:51**	C	11	55	7	1	52	1¾	**2**	**10:01**	E	8:38	C	VIR	17
75	16	Th.	6:54	C	**6:52**	C	11	58	7	1	28	2½	**2¾**	**10:59**	E	9:08	C	LIB	18
76	17	Fr.	6:52	C	**6:53**	C	12	01	8	1	04	3	**3½**	**11:56**	E	9:41	B	LIB	19
77	18	Sa.	6:50	C	**6:54**	C	12	04	8	0	40	3¾	**4¼**	—	–	10:16	B	SCO	20
78	19	**A**	6:49	C	**6:56**	C	12	07	8	0 s.	17	4½	**5**	12:51	E	10:55	B	OPH	21
79	20	M.	6:47	C	**6:57**	C	12	10	9	0 n.	06	5¼	**6**	1:43	E	11:38	B	OPH	22
80	21	Tu.	6:45	C	**6:58**	C	12	13	9	0	30	6¼	**7**	2:33	E	**12:27**	B	SAG	23
81	22	W.	6:44	C	**6:59**	C	12	15	9	0	53	7¼	**8**	3:20	E	**1:20**	B	SAG	24
82	23	Th.	6:42	C	**7:00**	C	12	18	9	1	17	8¼	**8¾**	4:04	E	**2:18**	B	CAP	25
83	24	Fr.	6:40	C	**7:01**	C	12	21	10	1	41	9	**9½**	4:44	E	**3:20**	C	CAP	26
84	25	Sa.	6:38	C	**7:02**	C	12	24	10	2	04	10	**10½**	5:21	E	**4:25**	C	AQU	27
85	26	**A**	6:37	C	**7:04**	C	12	27	10	2	28	10¾	**11¼**	5:56	D	**5:32**	D	AQU	28
86	27	M.	6:35	C	**7:05**	C	12	30	11	2	51	11½	**11¾**	6:31	D	**6:42**	D	AQU	0
87	28	Tu.	6:33	C	**7:06**	C	12	33	11	3	15	**12¼**	—	7:05	D	**7:54**	E	CET	1
88	29	W.	6:31	C	**7:07**	D	12	36	11	3	38	12½	**1**	7:41	C	**9:06**	E	PSC	2
89	30	Th.	6:30	C	**7:08**	D	12	38	12	4	01	1¼	**1¾**	8:19	C	**10:19**	E	CET	3
90	31	Fr.	6:28	C	**7:09**	D	12	41	12	4 n.	25	2	**2¾**	9:00	C	**11:29**	E	TAU	4

 To use this page, see p. 138; for Key Letters, see p. 252. ☞ **Bold = P.M.** ☞ Light = A.M.

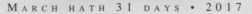

MARCH HATH 31 DAYS • 2017

Shout and sing for the Spring is here!
Laugh and dance for Winter's away! –Agnes Mary Frances Robinson

Day of Month	Day of Week	Dates, Feasts, Fasts, Aspects, Tide Heights	Weather
1	W.	**Ash Wednesday** • ☌♂☾ • ☌♅☾ • ☌♆☉	*It's*
2	Th.	**St. Chad** • ♀ STAT. • Puerto Ricans granted U.S. citizenship, 1917 • Tides { 10.9 / 10.7	*brisk,*
3	Fr.	☾ AT PERIG. • Inventor Alexander Graham Bell born, 1847 • Tides { 10.9 / 10.3	*but*
4	Sa.	☌☿♆ • James Monroe inaugurated as 5th U.S. president, 1817 • Tides { 10.8 / 9.8	*travel's*
5	**A**	**1st S. in Lent** • 6.96" rain, Butlerville, Ind., 1897 • Tides { 10.6 / 9.4	*no*
6	M.	☾ RIDES HIGH • ☿ IN SUP. ☌ • *A March sun sticks like a lock of wool.* • { 10.4 / 9.2	*risk.*
7	Tu.	**St. Perpetua** • Astronomer Henry Draper born, 1837 • Tides { 10.3 / 9.1	*Occasional*
8	W.	Ember Day • Whirlwind I's Director, precursor to computer operating systems, demonstrated, 1955	*spates*
9	Th.	Hummingbirds migrate north now. • Tides { 10.3 / 9.6	*for*
10	Fr.	Ember Day • ☾ AT ☊ • Professional bicycle racer Lyne Bessette born, 1975 • { 10.7 / 9.9	*town*
11	Sa.	Ember Day • Florida panther added to endangered species list, 1967 • { 10.8 / 10.2	*meeting*
12	**A**	**2nd S. in Lent** • **Daylight Saving Time begins, 2:00 A.M.** • **Full Worm** ○	*debates.*
13	M.	☾ ON EQ. • UFOs seen over Ariz., Nev., and Sonora, Mexico, 1997 • Tides { 10.3 / 10.7	*A*
14	Tu.	☌♃☾ • Shirley Temple added sidewalk prints, Grauman's Chinese Theatre, Hollywood, Calif., 1935	*little*
15	W.	Beware the ides of March. • First escalator patented by Jesse W. Reno, 1892 • Tides { 10.3 / 10.1	*snow,*
16	Th.	☌☿♀ • United States Military Academy at West Point established, 1802 • Tides { 10.1 / 9.7	*a*
17	Fr.	**St. Patrick's Day** • *Care and diligence bring luck.* • Tides { 9.8 / 9.2	*little*
18	Sa.	☾ AT APO. • Haboob storm brought 1,000'-high wall of dust, western Tex. and N.Mex., 2014 • { 9.5 / 8.8	*rain;*
19	**A**	**3rd S. in Lent** • Actress Glenn Close born, 1947 • Tides { 9.2 / 8.4	*this*
20	M.	**St. Joseph**[T] • **Vernal Equinox** • ☌♄☾ • Tides { 9.0 / 8.2	*month*
21	Tu.	☾ RUNS LOW • Funeral for Pocahontas (aka Rebecca Rolfe) took place, 1617 • { 8.9 / 8.1	*has*
22	W.	☌♇☾ • 7.0-magnitude earthquake, Fox Islands, Alaska, 1957 • Tides { 8.9 / 8.2	*water*
23	Th.	Culinary expert Fannie Farmer born, 1857 • 65°F, Montreal, Que., 1979 • { 9.1 / 8.6	*on*
24	Fr.	Chipmunks emerge from hiberation now. • Tides { 9.5 / 9.1	*the*
25	Sa.	**Annunciation** • ☾ AT ☋ • ♀ IN INF. ☌ • 4" hailstones, Fla., 1992	*brain!*
26	**A**	**4th S. in Lent** • ☌♆☾ • Deadly dynamite explosion in quarry, Sandts Eddy, Pa., 1942	*Note*
27	M.	**New** ● • ☾ ON EQ. • ☌☿♅ • ☌♀☾ • Tides { 10.9 / 10.8	*to*
28	Tu.	☌♅☾ • Zoologist Marlin Perkins born, 1905 • Tides { 11.2 / —	*self:*
29	W.	☌☿☾ • *Friendships multiply joys and divide griefs.* • { 11.3 / 11.3	*Clear*
30	Th.	☾ AT PERIG. • ☌♂☾ • "Seward's folly" purchase (Alaska) took place, 1867 • { 11.6 / 11.2	*storm*
31	Fr.	U.S. took formal possession of Virgin Islands from Denmark, 1917 • Tides { 11.6 / 10.9	*drain!*

Farmer's Calendar

■ While out walking yesterday, the dogs froze and stared into some scrub pines at a round brown bird with a long straight bill walking in the snow.

I'd never seen a woodcock walking. Dancing, yes. In mating season, normally mid-March to mid-May, male woodcocks appear at dawn or dusk in scrubby open meadows and announce their presence with a loud, buzzing *peent*.

After four or five such calls, the male launches himself vertically into the sky, climbing as high as 100 yards before spiraling back down to the ground, singing a liquid trill while the wind in its stubby wings twitters eerily.

If this display attracts a female, the male dances for her, hopping and bowing and *peenting* lustily. It's a comical sight, which may have inspired one of the bird's nicknames—the timberdoodle. If nature takes its course, the female will nest on the ground and raise four chicks. This is usually an unfailing harbinger of spring.

But we've had a brutal winter, with record cold and late snowfall. The woodcocks can't dig earthworms and insects out of the frozen ground with their tubelike bills. They are walking because they're starving.

It's not exactly a silent spring: I heard the *conk-la-ree* of red-winged blackbirds this week—but no *peenting*.

THE FOURTH MONTH • 2017

SKY WATCH ☆ *Mercury is low in the western sky from the 1st to the 6th, in Aries. Mars, above it, moves into Taurus and drops lower at nightfall; at only magnitude 1.5, the Red Planet does not command attention. Brilliant Jupiter comes closest to Earth on the 7th, still floating above the blue star Spica. The planet rises at sunset and is out all night. This most distant opposition of its 12-year orbit lets it shine at magnitude –2.3. Jupiter stands strikingly close to the full Moon on the 10th. Saturn rises at midnight in midmonth and dangles below the Moon on the 16th. Venus begins its morning star apparition and sits to the left of the Moon on the 23rd, before becoming its brightest on the 30th.*

◐	**First Quarter**	3rd day	14th hour	39th minute
○	**Full Moon**	11th day	2nd hour	8th minute
◑	**Last Quarter**	19th day	5th hour	57th minute
●	**New Moon**	26th day	8th hour	16th minute

All times are given in Eastern Daylight Time.

Get these pages with times set to your zip code at Almanac.com/Access.

Day of Year	Day of Month	Day of Week	☼ Rises h. m.	Rise Key	☼ Sets h. m.	Set Key	Length of Day h. m.	Sun Fast m.	Declination of Sun ° '	High Tide Times Boston		☾ Rises h. m.	Rise Key	☾ Sets h. m.	Set Key	☾ Astron. Place	☾ Age
91	1	Sa.	6:26	C	**7:10**	D	12 44	12	4 N. 48	3	**3½**	9:47	B	—	–	TAU	5
92	2	**A**	6:25	C	**7:12**	D	12 47	12	5 11	3¾	**4½**	10:39	B	12:36	E	TAU	6
93	3	M.	6:23	C	**7:13**	D	12 50	13	5 34	4¾	**5½**	11:36	B	1:37	E	GEM	7
94	4	Tu.	6:21	C	**7:14**	D	12 53	13	5 57	6	**6¾**	**12:37**	B	2:32	E	GEM	8
95	5	W.	6:19	C	**7:15**	D	12 56	13	6 19	7	**7¾**	**1:40**	C	3:19	E	CAN	9
96	6	Th.	6:18	B	**7:16**	D	12 58	14	6 42	8	**8¾**	**2:44**	C	4:01	E	CAN	10
97	7	Fr.	6:16	B	**7:17**	D	13 01	14	7 04	9¼	**9¾**	**3:48**	C	4:37	E	LEO	11
98	8	Sa.	6:14	B	**7:18**	D	13 04	14	7 27	10	**10½**	**4:50**	D	5:10	D	LEO	12
99	9	**A**	6:13	B	**7:19**	D	13 06	14	7 49	11	**11¼**	**5:51**	D	5:40	D	VIR	13
100	10	M.	6:11	B	**7:21**	D	13 10	15	8 11	11¾	—	**6:52**	D	6:09	C	VIR	14
101	11	Tu.	6:09	B	**7:22**	D	13 13	15	8 33	12	**12½**	**7:51**	E	6:38	C	VIR	15
102	12	W.	6:08	B	**7:23**	D	13 15	15	8 55	12½	**1**	**8:50**	E	7:08	C	VIR	16
103	13	Th.	6:06	B	**7:24**	D	13 18	15	9 17	1¼	**1¾**	**9:47**	E	7:40	B	LIB	17
104	14	Fr.	6:04	B	**7:25**	D	13 21	16	9 39	1¾	**2¼**	**10:43**	E	8:14	B	LIB	18
105	15	Sa.	6:03	B	**7:26**	D	13 23	16	10 00	2½	**3**	**11:36**	E	8:51	B	OPH	19
106	16	**A**	6:01	B	**7:27**	D	13 26	16	10 21	3¼	**3¾**	—	–	9:32	B	OPH	20
107	17	M.	6:00	B	**7:28**	D	13 28	16	10 42	4	**4½**	12:27	E	10:18	B	SAG	21
108	18	Tu.	5:58	B	**7:30**	D	13 32	17	11 03	4¾	**5½**	1:15	E	11:09	B	SAG	22
109	19	W.	5:57	B	**7:31**	D	13 34	17	11 24	5½	**6¼**	1:59	E	**12:04**	B	SAG	23
110	20	Th.	5:55	B	**7:32**	D	13 37	17	11 44	6½	**7¼**	2:39	E	**1:03**	C	CAP	24
111	21	Fr.	5:53	B	**7:33**	D	13 40	17	12 05	7½	**8**	3:17	E	**2:05**	C	CAP	25
112	22	Sa.	5:52	B	**7:34**	D	13 42	17	12 25	8½	**9**	3:52	E	**3:10**	D	AQU	26
113	23	**A**	5:50	B	**7:35**	D	13 45	17	12 45	9¼	**9¾**	4:26	D	**4:19**	D	AQU	27
114	24	M.	5:49	B	**7:36**	D	13 47	18	13 05	10¼	**10½**	5:00	D	**5:29**	D	PSC	28
115	25	Tu.	5:47	B	**7:37**	D	13 50	18	13 24	11	**11¼**	5:34	C	**6:42**	E	PSC	29
116	26	W.	5:46	B	**7:39**	D	13 53	18	13 43	11¾	—	6:11	C	**7:56**	E	CET	0
117	27	Th.	5:45	B	**7:40**	D	13 55	18	14 02	12	**12¾**	6:52	C	**9:10**	E	ARI	1
118	28	Fr.	5:43	B	**7:41**	D	13 58	18	14 21	1	**1½**	7:38	B	**10:22**	E	TAU	2
119	29	Sa.	5:42	B	**7:42**	E	14 00	18	14 40	1¾	**2½**	8:29	B	**11:28**	E	TAU	3
120	30	**A**	5:40	B	**7:43**	E	14 03	19	14 N. 58	2¾	**3¼**	9:26	B	—	–	ORI	4

 To use this page, see p. 138; for Key Letters, see p. 252. ☞ **Bold = P.M.** ☞ Light = A.M.

April hath 30 days • 2017

Light comes upon the earth in radiant showers,
And mingling rainbows play among the flowers. –Ludwig Tieck

Day of Month	Day of Week	Dates, Feasts, Fasts, Aspects, Tide Heights	Weather
1	Sa.	**All Fools'** • ☿ GR. ELONG. (19° EAST) • 27°F, Atlanta, Ga., 1987 • {11.5 10.4}	*Foolish*
2	A	**5th S. in Lent** • U.S. Mint established, 1792 • {11.2 10.0}	*and*
3	M.	**St. Richard of Chichester** • ☽ RIDES HIGH • Singer Wayne Newton born, 1942	*coolish.*
4	Tu.	First one-way radio telephone communication, N.Y. to Del., 1915 • Tides {10.4 9.3}	*Spring*
5	W.	*When April shall shrilly sound his horn, On Earth there will be plenty of hay and corn.* • {10.1 9.3}	*is*
6	Th.	♄ STAT. • U.S. declared war on Germany, thus entering WWI, 1917 • {10.1 9.5}	*cruelish.*
7	Fr.	☽ AT ☊ • ♃ AT ☍ • First baseball game of Toronto Blue Jays, 1977 • {10.1 9.8}	*Hardly*
8	Sa.	Mouseketeer Annette Funicello died, 2013 • {10.2 10.0}	*pleasant;*
9	A	**Palm Sunday** • ☽ ON EQ. • ☿ STAT. • Tides {10.3 10.2}	*rain*
10	M.	**Passover begins at sundown** • ☌♃☽ • Naturalist Jack Miner born, 1865 • {10.3 —}	*and*
11	Tu.	**Full Pink** ○ • *Apollo 13* launched; returned on 17th safely after major difficulties, 1970 • {10.4 10.2}	*snow's*
12	W.	♀ STAT. • John George Lambdon, governor-general of British North America, born, 1792	*incessant.*
13	Th.	**Maundy Thursday** • U.S. president Thomas Jefferson born, 1743 • Tides {10.3 9.8}	*The*
14	Fr.	**Good Friday** • ☌♅☉ • J. Kellogg patented process to make cornflakes, 1896	*yard's*
15	Sa.	☽ AT APO. • General Electric Co. incorporated, 1892 • {10.0 9.2}	*a*
16	A	**Easter** • **Orthodox Easter** • ☌♄☽ • Aviator Wilbur Wright born, 1867	*marsh—*
17	M.	**Easter Monday** • ☽ RUNS LOW • Columbus's trip financed by Spain, 1492 • {9.5 8.6}	*this*
18	Tu.	☌♇☽ • *Fairest gems lie deepest.* • Tides {9.2 8.4}	*is*
19	W.	Tom Longboat won Boston Marathon in 2 hrs., 24 min., 24 sec., 1907 • Tides {9.1 8.4}	*harsh!*
20	Th.	☿ IN INF. ☌ • ♇ STAT. • Comedian Benny Hill died, 1992 • {9.1 8.6}	*A*
21	Fr.	☽ AT ☋ • Waterspout formed off Isle of Palms, S.C., 2010	*ray*
22	Sa.	☌♆☽ • Jacques Cousteau granted patent for diving apparatus, 1952 • Tides {9.6 9.6}	*of*
23	A	**2nd S. of Easter** • ☌♀☽ • Canadian prime minister Lester Pearson born, 1897	*hope?*
24	M.	**St. George**[T] • ☽ ON EQ. • *Old Farmer's Almanac* founder Robert B. Thomas born, 1766	*Nope:*
25	Tu.	**St. Mark** • ☌☿☽ • ☌♅☽ • First circus telecast, 1940 • Tides {10.9 11.5}	*Even*
26	W.	**New** ● • Landscape architect Frederick Law Olmsted born, 1822 • Tides {11.1 —}	*the*
27	Th.	☽ AT PERIG. • 100°F, Pahala, Hawaii, 1931 • Tides {11.9 11.2}	*peepers*
28	Fr.	☌☿♅ • ☌♂☽ • *The greatest oaks have been little acorns.* • {12.1 11.2}	*are*
29	Sa.	Poplars leaf out about now. • Film director Alfred Hitchcock died, 1980 • Tides {12.1 10.9}	*saying,*
30	A	☽ RIDES HIGH • USS *Peto* first sub to be launched sideways, Manitowoc, Wisc., 1942 • {11.9 10.6}	*"Jeepers!"*

Fools grow without watering. –Italian proverb

Farmer's Calendar

■ Go out around midnight on a clear New Moon night and look straight up. See that faint oval-shape smudge of light? That's the Andromeda Galaxy, which may contain a trillion stars. It's the most distant object visible to the naked eye—more than two million light-years away.

Astronomers know it as M31. The M is for Charles Messier, a French astronomer who died 200 years ago this month. Over his long life and career—he lived to be 86—he discovered 13 comets. King Louis XV nicknamed him "the ferret of comets."

Ironically, Messier is best known for his eponymous Catalog, a list of 110 objects in deep space—some that he discovered, some discovered by others. He didn't know exactly what they were, but they were not comets and thus "not to be looked for." He called them "nebulae," the Greek word for clouds.

Indeed, many of them are clouds of gases, some the remnants of supernovae, the colossal explosions of dying stars. M1, the first on the list, is just that—the debris of a supernova that appeared in 1054.

The Messier Catalog is a curiosity now, but it raises an interesting question: How many other marvels, then and now, are dismissed as "not to be looked for"?

MAY

THE FIFTH MONTH • 2017

SKY WATCH ☆ *Mars, just to the right of Aldebaran in Taurus from the 1st to the 4th, sinks lower and is hard to see by month's end. Jupiter is brilliant and hovers dramatically close to the Moon on the 7th. Saturn, now rising before midnight, stands to the right of the Moon on the 13th. On the 18th, Mercury begins a rather poor morning star apparition that lasts the rest of the month. Also in the predawn eastern sky, Venus rises by 3:30 and shines brilliantly, standing strikingly to the left of the crescent Moon on the 22nd. Three days later, while new, the Moon reaches its closest approach to Earth of the entire year. Expect strong tides from the 25th to the 27th.*

◐	**First Quarter**	2nd day	22nd hour	47th minute
○	**Full Moon**	10th day	17th hour	42nd minute
◑	**Last Quarter**	18th day	20th hour	33rd minute
●	**New Moon**	25th day	15th hour	44th minute

All times are given in Eastern Daylight Time.

Get these pages with times set to your zip code at Almanac.com/Access.

Day of Year	Day of Month	Day of Week	☼ Rises h. m.	Rise Key	☼ Sets h. m.	Set Key	Length of Day h. m.	Sun Fast m.	Declination of Sun ° '	High Tide Times Boston		☾ Rises h. m.	Rise Key	☾ Sets h. m.	Set Key	☾ Astron. Place	☾ Age
121	1	M.	5:39	B	**7:44**	E	14 05	19	15 N. 16	3½	**4¼**	10:28	B	12:27	E	GEM	5
122	2	Tu.	5:38	B	**7:45**	E	14 07	19	15 34	4½	**5¼**	11:32	C	1:18	E	CAN	6
123	3	W.	5:36	B	**7:46**	E	14 10	19	15 52	5½	**6½**	**12:37**	C	2:02	E	CAN	7
124	4	Th.	5:35	B	**7:47**	E	14 12	19	16 09	6¾	**7½**	**1:41**	C	2:40	E	LEO	8
125	5	Fr.	5:34	B	**7:49**	E	14 15	19	16 26	7¾	**8½**	**2:43**	D	3:14	D	LEO	9
126	6	Sa.	5:33	B	**7:50**	E	14 17	19	16 43	8¾	**9¼**	**3:45**	D	3:44	D	VIR	10
127	7	**A**	5:31	B	**7:51**	E	14 20	19	16 59	9¾	**10¼**	**4:45**	D	4:13	D	VIR	11
128	8	M.	5:30	B	**7:52**	E	14 22	19	17 16	10½	**10¾**	**5:44**	E	4:42	C	VIR	12
129	9	Tu.	5:29	B	**7:53**	E	14 24	19	17 32	11¼	**11½**	**6:42**	E	5:10	C	VIR	13
130	10	W.	5:28	B	**7:54**	E	14 26	19	17 47	**12**	—	**7:40**	E	5:41	C	LIB	14
131	11	Th.	5:27	B	**7:55**	E	14 28	19	18 03	12¼	**12¾**	**8:36**	E	6:14	B	LIB	15
132	12	Fr.	5:26	B	**7:56**	E	14 30	19	18 18	12¾	**1¼**	**9:31**	E	6:49	B	SCO	16
133	13	Sa.	5:25	A	**7:57**	E	14 32	19	18 32	1¼	**2**	**10:23**	E	7:29	B	OPH	17
134	14	**A**	5:23	A	**7:58**	E	14 35	19	18 47	2	**2½**	**11:12**	E	8:13	B	SAG	18
135	15	M.	5:22	A	**7:59**	E	14 37	19	19 01	2¾	**3¼**	**11:57**	E	9:02	B	SAG	19
136	16	Tu.	5:21	A	**8:00**	E	14 39	19	19 15	3½	**4**	—	–	9:55	B	SAG	20
137	17	W.	5:20	A	**8:01**	E	14 41	19	19 28	4¼	**4¾**	12:38	E	10:52	B	CAP	21
138	18	Th.	5:20	A	**8:02**	E	14 42	19	19 41	5	**5¾**	1:16	E	11:51	C	CAP	22
139	19	Fr.	5:19	A	**8:03**	E	14 44	19	19 54	6	**6½**	1:51	E	**12:54**	C	AQU	23
140	20	Sa.	5:18	A	**8:04**	E	14 46	19	20 06	6¾	**7½**	2:24	D	**1:59**	D	AQU	24
141	21	**A**	5:17	A	**8:05**	E	14 48	19	20 19	7¾	**8¼**	2:57	D	**3:06**	D	AQU	25
142	22	M.	5:16	A	**8:06**	E	14 50	19	20 30	8¾	**9¼**	3:29	C	**4:16**	E	CET	26
143	23	Tu.	5:15	A	**8:07**	E	14 52	19	20 42	9¾	**10**	4:04	C	**5:29**	E	PSC	27
144	24	W.	5:15	A	**8:08**	E	14 53	19	20 53	10½	**10¾**	4:42	C	**6:43**	E	CET	28
145	25	Th.	5:14	A	**8:09**	E	14 55	19	21 04	11½	**11¾**	5:25	B	**7:58**	E	TAU	0
146	26	Fr.	5:13	A	**8:10**	E	14 57	19	21 14	**12¼**	—	6:14	B	**9:09**	E	TAU	1
147	27	Sa.	5:13	A	**8:11**	E	14 58	18	21 24	12½	**1¼**	7:10	B	**10:14**	E	TAU	2
148	28	**A**	5:12	A	**8:12**	E	15 00	18	21 33	1½	**2¼**	8:12	B	**11:11**	E	GEM	3
149	29	M.	5:11	A	**8:12**	E	15 01	18	21 43	2¼	**3**	9:17	C	**11:59**	E	GEM	4
150	30	Tu.	5:11	A	**8:13**	E	15 02	18	21 51	3¼	**4**	10:24	C	—	–	CAN	5
151	31	W.	5:10	A	**8:14**	E	15 04	18	22 N. 00	4¼	**5**	11:31	C	12:41	E	LEO	6

 To use this page, see p. 138; for Key Letters, see p. 252. ☞ **Bold = P.M.** ☞ Light = A.M.

MAY HATH 31 DAYS • 2017

Sing me a song of idle days,
When Spring is queen over woods and ways! –Francis W. Bourdillon

Day of Month	Day of Week	Dates, Feasts, Fasts, Aspects, Tide Heights	Weather
1	M.	**Sts. Philip & James** • **May Day** • Elvis Presley married Priscilla Beaulieu, 1967	*Drizzling*
2	Tu.	**St. Athanasius** • ☿ STAT. • Fire caused deadly Sunshine Mine disaster, Kellogg, Idaho, 1972	*and*
3	W.	Red River flood crested, Winnipeg, Man., 1997 • Tides {10.4 9.6}	*far*
4	Th.	☾ AT ☊ • 12" snow near Keene, N.H., 1812 • {10.0 9.6}	*from*
5	Fr.	*Adversity often leads to prosperity.* • Tides {9.8 9.7}	*sizzling.*
6	Sa.	Actress Marlene Dietrich died, 1992 • Tides {9.7 9.9}	*Thunder-*
7	**A**	**4th S. of Easter** • ☾ ON EQ. • ☌☿♅ • ☌♃☾ • {9.7 10.1}	*storms*
8	M.	**St. Julian of Norwich** • Children's book author Maurice Sendak died, 2012	*kabooming.*
9	Tu.	**St. Gregory of Nazianzus** • William F. Ford issued patent for stethoscope, 1882	*Wow!*
10	W.	**Vesak** • **Full Flower** ○ • *Garden flowers larger, field flowers stronger.*	*Everything's*
11	Th.	First known dated printed book, Wang Jie's copy of the *Diamond Sutra,* "published," 868 • **Three**	*blooming!*
12	Fr.	☾ AT APO. • Adler Planetarium opened, Chicago, Ill., 1930 • **Chilly** • {10.3 9.4}	*It's*
13	Sa.	☌♄☾ • Inventor Cyrus McCormick died, 1884 • Cranberries in bud now. • **Saints**	*warm*
14	**A**	**5th S. of Easter** • **Mother's Day** • ☾ RUNS LOW • {10.1 9.1}	*enough*
15	M.	☌♇☾ • 85°F, Olympia and Seattle, Wash., 2007 • {9.9 9.0}	*to*
16	Tu.	Neuroscientist Theodore Holmes Bullock born, 1915 • {9.7 8.8}	*wear*
17	W.	☿ GR. ELONG. (26° WEST) • New York Stock Exchange established, 1792 • Tides {9.5 8.8}	*short*
18	Th.	☾ AT ☋ • Montreal, Que., founded, 1642 • {9.4 8.9}	*sleeves,*
19	Fr.	**St. Dunstan** • Philanthropist Johns Hopkins born, 1795 • Tides {9.4 9.1}	*and*
20	Sa.	☌♆☾ • Charles Lindbergh began first nonstop solo flight across Atlantic, 1927	*blossoms*
21	**A**	**Rogation S.** • ☾ ON EQ. • Explorer Hernando de Soto died, 1542	*dapple*
22	M.	**Victoria Day (Canada)** • ☌♀☾ • Athlete Rick Hansen completed Man in Motion World Tour, 1987	*apple*
23	Tu.	☌☿☾ • ☌♅☾ • Botanist Carl Linnaeus born, 1707 • {10.3 11.4}	*leaves.*
24	W.	Peace Tower clock stopped ticking, Ottawa, Ont., 2006 • Tides {10.7 11.9}	*Honor*
25	Th.	**Ascension** • **Orthodox Ascension** • **New** ● • ☾ AT PERIG.	*the*
26	Fr.	**Ramadan begins at sundown** • ☌♂☾ • *A May flood Never did good.* • {11.0 —}	*brave*
27	Sa.	☾ RIDES HIGH • Conservationist Rachel Carson born, 1907 • Tides {12.4 11.0}	*by*
28	**A**	**1st S. af. Asc.** • Sierra Club founded, 1892 • {12.3 10.9}	*decorating*
29	M.	**Memorial Day, observed** • U.S. president John F. Kennedy born, 1917 • Tides {12.0 10.6}	*a*
30	Tu.	**Shavuot begins at sundown** • Arvind Mahankali won Scripps National Spelling Bee, 2013 • {11.5 10.3}	*hero's*
31	W.	**Visit. of Mary** • ☾ AT ☊ • 1,376-lb. Pacific blue marlin caught, Kaiwi Point, Kona, Hawaii, 1982	*grave.*

Farmer's Calendar

■ The black flies showed up right on schedule this year—the first week of May. Melting snows provide just the kind of rushing streams they prefer for breeding; in April, after the fourth- and fifth-grade classes had visited the stream nearest our house and collected water samples, they found thousands of black fly larvae wriggling in their microscopes.

Black fly season lasts about 3 weeks here. The most obvious sign is the outlandish way in which people dress to go out to work in their gardens or around the house. Long sleeves and ankle-length pants are a must, and mosquito nets adorn every head. The town looks like it has been invaded by aliens.

Tough guys (and girls) rely instead on a variety of noisome unguents and goos rubbed into the skin. They look better but smell worse.

We try not to talk about this annual plague. It's considered citified to complain. What's more, we've just finished whining about the cold and the snow that lingers in the shade.

When we first moved to the country from the city, we tolerated the cold by anticipating the pleasures of a rural spring and summer. After a fortnight of the flies, I asked a neighbor how people who've always lived here stand it.

"It makes us look forward to winter," he explained.

CALENDAR

JUNE

THE SIXTH MONTH • 2017

SKY WATCH ☆ *Brilliant Jupiter is dramatically close to the Moon on the 3rd. Having retrograded into western Virgo, it is no longer above blue Spica. The Moon stands to the left of Saturn on the 9th. The planet, its rings maximally wide open, comes its closest to Earth and makes its largest and brightest appearance of the year on the 15th. It has retrograded back into Ophiuchus, where it will remain until it vanishes in late autumn. Summer begins with the solstice on the 21st at 12:24 A.M. In the predawn sky, the Moon is to the right of Venus on the 20th and below the planet on the 21st. The Moon then again meets Jupiter on the 30th.*

◐	**First Quarter**	1st day	8th hour	42nd minute
○	**Full Moon**	9th day	9th hour	10th minute
◑	**Last Quarter**	17th day	7th hour	33rd minute
●	**New Moon**	23rd day	22nd hour	31st minute
◐	**First Quarter**	30th day	20th hour	51st minute

All times are given in Eastern Daylight Time.

Get these pages with times set to your zip code at Almanac.com/Access.

Day of Year	Day of Month	Day of Week	☼ Rises h. m.	Rise Key	☼ Sets h. m.	Set Key	Length of Day h. m.	Sun Fast m.	Declination of Sun ° '	High Tide Times Boston		☾ Rises h. m.	Rise Key	☾ Sets h. m.	Set Key	☾ Astron. Place	☾ Age
152	1	Th.	5:10	A	**8:15**	E	15 05	18	22 N.08	5¼	**6**	**12:35**	D	1:17	E	LEO	7
153	2	Fr.	5:09	A	**8:16**	E	15 07	18	22 16	6¼	**7**	**1:38**	D	1:48	D	LEO	8
154	3	Sa.	5:09	A	**8:16**	E	15 07	17	22 23	7¼	**8**	**2:38**	D	2:18	D	VIR	9
155	4	**A**	5:09	A	**8:17**	E	15 08	17	22 30	8¼	**8¾**	**3:38**	D	2:46	C	VIR	10
156	5	M.	5:08	A	**8:18**	E	15 10	17	22 36	9¼	**9½**	**4:36**	E	3:15	C	VIR	11
157	6	Tu.	5:08	A	**8:18**	E	15 10	17	22 43	10	**10¼**	**5:34**	E	3:44	C	LIB	12
158	7	W.	5:08	A	**8:19**	E	15 11	17	22 48	11	**11**	**6:31**	E	4:16	C	LIB	13
159	8	Th.	5:07	A	**8:20**	E	15 13	17	22 54	11½	**11¾**	**7:26**	E	4:50	B	SCO	14
160	9	Fr.	5:07	A	**8:20**	E	15 13	16	22 58	**12¼**	—	**8:20**	E	5:28	B	OPH	15
161	10	Sa.	5:07	A	**8:21**	E	15 14	16	23 03	12¼	**1**	**9:10**	E	6:11	B	SAG	16
162	11	**A**	5:07	A	**8:21**	E	15 14	16	23 07	1	**1½**	**9:57**	E	6:58	B	SAG	17
163	12	M.	5:07	A	**8:22**	E	15 15	16	23 11	1½	**2¼**	**10:39**	E	7:50	B	SAG	18
164	13	Tu.	5:07	A	**8:22**	E	15 15	16	23 14	2¼	**3**	**11:18**	E	8:45	B	CAP	19
165	14	W.	5:07	A	**8:23**	E	15 16	15	23 17	3	**3½**	**11:53**	E	9:43	C	CAP	20
166	15	Th.	5:07	A	**8:23**	E	15 16	15	23 19	3¾	**4¼**	—	–	10:44	C	AQU	21
167	16	Fr.	5:07	A	**8:23**	E	15 16	15	23 21	4½	**5¼**	12:26	D	11:46	D	AQU	22
168	17	Sa.	5:07	A	**8:24**	E	15 17	15	23 23	5¼	**6**	12:58	D	**12:51**	D	AQU	23
169	18	**A**	5:07	A	**8:24**	E	15 17	14	23 24	6¼	**6¾**	1:29	D	**1:58**	D	CET	24
170	19	M.	5:07	A	**8:24**	E	15 17	14	23 25	7¼	**7¾**	2:01	C	**3:07**	E	PSC	25
171	20	Tu.	5:07	A	**8:24**	E	15 17	14	23 26	8¼	**8¾**	2:36	C	**4:18**	E	CET	26
172	21	W.	5:07	A	**8:25**	E	15 18	14	23 26	9¼	**9½**	3:15	C	**5:32**	E	ARI	27
173	22	Th.	5:08	A	**8:25**	E	15 17	14	23 25	10¼	**10½**	4:00	B	**6:44**	E	TAU	28
174	23	Fr.	5:08	A	**8:25**	E	15 17	13	23 24	11	**11¼**	4:51	B	**7:53**	E	TAU	0
175	24	Sa.	5:08	A	**8:25**	E	15 17	13	23 23	**12**	—	5:51	B	**8:55**	E	GEM	1
176	25	**A**	5:09	A	**8:25**	E	15 16	13	23 21	12¼	**1**	6:56	B	**9:50**	E	GEM	2
177	26	M.	5:09	A	**8:25**	E	15 16	13	23 19	1¼	**1¾**	8:04	C	**10:36**	E	CAN	3
178	27	Tu.	5:09	A	**8:25**	E	15 16	13	23 17	2	**2¾**	9:13	C	**11:15**	E	LEO	4
179	28	W.	5:10	A	**8:25**	E	15 15	12	23 14	3	**3¾**	10:21	C	**11:50**	D	LEO	5
180	29	Th.	5:10	A	**8:25**	E	15 15	12	23 11	4	**4½**	11:26	D	—	–	LEO	6
181	30	Fr.	5:11	A	**8:25**	E	15 14	12	23 N.07	4¾	**5½**	**12:29**	D	12:21	D	VIR	7

 To use this page, see p. 138; for Key Letters, see p. 252. ☞ **Bold = P.M.** ☞ Light = A.M.

JUNE

JUNE HATH 30 DAYS • 2017

O fields in June's fair verdure drest,
And vocal now with birds and bees! –Henry Stevenson Washburn

Day of Month	Day of Week	Dates, Feasts, Fasts, Aspects, Tide Heights	Weather
1	Th.	Ky. became 15th U.S. state, 1792 • Tides {10.4 / 9.9	*Flashes*
2	Fr.	☌♀♅ • Geochemist Clair Cameron Patterson born, 1922 • Tides {9.9 / 9.8	*gild*
3	Sa.	☾ ON EQ. • ☌♃☾ • ♀ GR. ELONG. (46° WEST) • Tides {9.5 / 9.8	*the*
4	**A**	**Whit S. • Pentecost • Orthodox Pentecost** • *Strawberries at Whitsuntide indicate good wine.*	*sky;*
5	M.	**St. Boniface** • N.Y. first U.S. state to pass legislation on oleomargarine, 1877 • {9.2 / 10.0	*cool,*
6	Tu.	D-Day, 1944 • First U.S. drive-in movie theater opened, Camden, N.J., 1933 • Tides {9.2 / 10.1	*dry.*
7	W.	Ember Day • Fashion leader Beau Brummel born, 1778 • {9.2 / 10.2	*Hot*
8	Th.	☾ AT APO. • Architect Frank Lloyd Wright born, 1867 • Tides {9.2 / 10.2	*as*
9	Fr.	Ember Day • **Full Strawberry** ○ • ☌♄☾ • {9.2 / —	*blazes,*
10	Sa.	Ember Day • ☾ RUNS LOW • ♃ STAT. • Tides {10.2 / 9.2	*thunderstorms*
11	**A**	**Trinity • Orthodox All Saints'** • ☌♇☾ • {10.2 / 9.2	*amaze*
12	M.	**St. Barnabas**[T] • 113°F, Tribune, Kans., 2013 • {10.2 / 9.1	*us.*
13	Tu.	Thurgood Marshall nominated to U.S. Supreme Court, 1967 • Miranda rights established in U.S., 1966	*Warm,*
14	W.	**St. Basil** • ☾ AT ☋ • Congress adopted Stars and Stripes as U.S. flag, 1777 • {9.9 / 9.1	*then*
15	Th.	♄ AT ☍ • Richard Weber and Mikhail Malakhov first to walk from Can. to North Pole and back unaided, 1995	*cool*
16	Fr.	☌♆☾ • ♆ STAT. • *Wisdom is easy to carry but difficult to gather.* • {9.7 / 9.4	*as*
17	Sa.	Army weekly magazine *Yank* coined term "G.I. Joe" in comic strip drawn by Dave Breger, 1942 • {9.6 / 9.7	*kids*
18	**A**	**Corpus Christi • Father's Day** • ☾ ON EQ. • Tides {9.6 / 10.1	*leave*
19	M.	☌♅☾ • Slavery abolished in U.S. territories, 1862 • Tides {9.7 / 10.5	*school.*
20	Tu.	☌♀☾ • New National Library of Canada building officially opened, Ottawa, Ont., 1967	*Rumbling,*
21	W.	**Summer Solstice** • ☿ IN SUP. ☌ • 99°F, Washington, D.C., 2012 • {10.1 / 11.6	*grumbling,*
22	Th.	**St. Alban** • *Love thy neighbor, but pull not down thy hedge.* • {10.4 / 12.0	*temperatures*
23	Fr.	**New** ● • ☾ AT PERIG. • "Mercedes" lodged as trade name, 1902 • {10.6 / 12.3	*tumbling.*
24	Sa.	**Nativ. John the Baptist • Midsummer Day** • ☾ RIDES HIGH • ☌☿☾ • ☌♂☾	
25	**A**	**3rd S. af. P.** • Golfer attacked by alligator, Venice, Fla., 2007	*Forecasters*
26	M.	U.S. statesman Arthur Middleton born, 1742 • Humanitarian Pearl S. Buck born, 1892 • Tides {12.2 / 10.8	*find*
27	Tu.	☾ AT ☊ • Hundreds of fish fell during heavy rain, Tiller's Ferry, S.C., 1901 • Tides {11.9 / 10.6	*their*
28	W.	**St. Irenaeus** • ☌☿♂ • 7.3 earthquake struck Landers, Calif., 1992 • {11.4 / 10.4	*jobs*
29	Th.	**Sts. Peter & Paul** • Britain's Townshend Revenue Act passed, taxing colonists, 1767	*are oft*
30	Fr.	☾ ON EQ. • Singer Lena Horne born, 1917 • Tides {10.2 / 10.0	*humbling.*

Vision is the art of seeing what is invisible to others. –Jonathan Swift

Farmer's Calendar

■ The animal flashed across the road so suddenly that I had to slam on my brakes to avoid hitting it. In that frozen instant, I identified it as a bobcat with a rabbit hanging from its jaws.

It was only the third bobcat I'd seen in 40 years of living in southwestern New Hampshire. It was the first to bolt out of the woods at midday at a busy small town intersection between a Mexican restaurant and a shopping center.

In colonial times, bobcats were common here, but their numbers diminished to the verge of extinction. When New Hampshire ended the legal hunt in 1989, experts estimated that only 150 of the reclusive creatures were left in the state.

By 2015, aided by the successful reintroduction of wild turkeys, one of the bobcat's favorite foods, there were 10 times as many. The state decided to consider permitting hunting and trapping again.

While hunters applauded, environmentalists and some wildlife scientists howled. It was far too early, they said, to revive the hunt.

The debate was overfamiliar. But the sight of that magnificent predator was not. It was an eruption of pure wildness in the most ordinary of settings, as weird and exhilarating as a band of Cheyenne warriors pursuing a buffalo down Main Street.

THE SEVENTH MONTH • 2017

SKY WATCH ☆ *Mercury may be glimpsed as an evening star all month, but it's very low. Saturn, its outermost ring telescopically seen completely around the planet, is below the Moon on the 6th, superbly placed for viewing. The dwarf planet Pluto is at opposition on the 10th. At magnitude 14.2, it's over a thousand times fainter than the dimmest naked-eye stars. From the 9th to the 13th, Venus hovers above orange Aldebaran in Taurus. The Moon forms a striking triangle with Venus and Aldebaran on the morning of the 20th and then stands closely above Jupiter on the 28th, a dramatic sight. Jupiter is now getting lower at nightfall, as it moves eastward in Virgo back toward Spica.*

○	**Full Moon**	9th day	0 hour	7th minute
◑	**Last Quarter**	16th day	15th hour	26th minute
●	**New Moon**	23rd day	5th hour	46th minute
◐	**First Quarter**	30th day	11th hour	23rd minute

All times are given in Eastern Daylight Time.

Get these pages with times set to your zip code at Almanac.com/Access.

Day of Year	Day of Month	Day of Week	☼ Rises h. m.	Rise Key	☼ Sets h. m.	Set Key	Length of Day h. m.	Sun Fast m.	Declination of Sun ° '	High Tide Times Boston		☾ Rises h. m.	Rise Key	☾ Sets h. m.	Set Key	☾ Astron. Place	☾ Age
182	1	Sa.	5:11	A	**8:25**	E	15 14	12	23 N. 03	5¾	**6½**	**1:30**	D	12:50	C	VIR	8
183	2	**A**	5:12	A	**8:25**	E	15 13	12	22 58	6¾	**7¼**	**2:29**	E	1:18	C	VIR	9
184	3	M.	5:12	A	**8:24**	E	15 12	11	22 53	7¾	**8¼**	**3:27**	E	1:47	C	LIB	10
185	4	Tu.	5:13	A	**8:24**	E	15 11	11	22 48	8¾	**9**	**4:24**	E	2:18	C	LIB	11
186	5	W.	5:14	A	**8:24**	E	15 10	11	22 42	9½	**9¾**	**5:20**	E	2:51	B	LIB	12
187	6	Th.	5:14	A	**8:24**	E	15 10	11	22 36	10½	**10½**	**6:14**	E	3:28	B	OPH	13
188	7	Fr.	5:15	A	**8:23**	E	15 08	11	22 30	11	**11¼**	**7:06**	E	4:09	B	OPH	14
189	8	Sa.	5:16	A	**8:23**	E	15 07	11	22 23	11¾	12	**7:55**	E	4:55	B	SAG	15
190	9	**A**	5:16	A	**8:22**	E	15 06	10	22 16	**12½**	—	**8:39**	E	5:45	B	SAG	16
191	10	M.	5:17	A	**8:22**	E	15 05	10	22 08	12½	**1¼**	**9:19**	E	6:39	B	CAP	17
192	11	Tu.	5:18	A	**8:21**	E	15 03	10	22 00	1¼	**1¾**	**9:56**	E	7:37	C	CAP	18
193	12	W.	5:18	A	**8:21**	E	15 03	10	21 52	1¾	**2½**	**10:30**	D	8:37	C	CAP	19
194	13	Th.	5:19	A	**8:20**	E	15 01	10	21 43	2½	**3**	**11:01**	D	9:39	C	AQU	20
195	14	Fr.	5:20	A	**8:20**	E	15 00	10	21 34	3¼	**3¾**	**11:32**	D	10:43	D	AQU	21
196	15	Sa.	5:21	A	**8:19**	E	14 58	10	21 24	4	**4½**	—	–	11:47	D	PSC	22
197	16	**A**	5:22	A	**8:18**	E	14 56	10	21 14	5	**5½**	12:03	C	**12:54**	E	CET	23
198	17	M.	5:23	A	**8:18**	E	14 55	10	21 04	5¾	**6¼**	12:36	C	**2:02**	E	PSC	24
199	18	Tu.	5:23	A	**8:17**	E	14 54	9	20 53	6¾	**7¼**	1:12	C	**3:12**	E	ARI	25
200	19	W.	5:24	A	**8:16**	E	14 52	9	20 42	7¾	**8¼**	1:52	B	**4:23**	E	TAU	26
201	20	Th.	5:25	A	**8:15**	E	14 50	9	20 31	8¾	**9¼**	2:39	B	**5:32**	E	TAU	27
202	21	Fr.	5:26	A	**8:15**	E	14 49	9	20 19	9¾	**10¼**	3:33	B	**6:37**	E	ORI	28
203	22	Sa.	5:27	A	**8:14**	E	14 47	9	20 07	10¾	**11**	4:34	B	**7:35**	E	GEM	29
204	23	**A**	5:28	A	**8:13**	E	14 45	9	19 55	11¾	—	5:41	B	**8:26**	E	CAN	0
205	24	M.	5:29	A	**8:12**	E	14 43	9	19 42	12	**12¾**	6:50	C	**9:09**	E	CAN	1
206	25	Tu.	5:30	A	**8:11**	E	14 41	9	19 29	1	**1½**	8:00	C	**9:46**	E	LEO	2
207	26	W.	5:31	B	**8:10**	E	14 39	9	19 16	1¾	**2¼**	9:08	D	**10:20**	D	LEO	3
208	27	Th.	5:32	B	**8:09**	E	14 37	9	19 02	2¾	**3¼**	10:14	D	**10:51**	D	VIR	4
209	28	Fr.	5:33	B	**8:08**	E	14 35	9	18 49	3½	**4**	11:17	D	**11:20**	C	VIR	5
210	29	Sa.	5:34	B	**8:07**	E	14 33	9	18 34	4¼	**4¾**	**12:18**	E	**11:49**	C	VIR	6
211	30	**A**	5:35	B	**8:06**	E	14 31	9	18 20	5¼	**5¾**	**1:17**	E	—	–	VIR	7
212	31	M.	5:36	B	**8:05**	E	14 29	9	18 N. 05	6¼	**6½**	**2:16**	E	12:20	C	LIB	8

 To use this page, see p. 138; for Key Letters, see p. 252. ☞ **Bold = P.M.** ☞ Light = A.M.

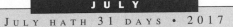

JULY HATH 31 DAYS • 2017

"Come up! come up! for the world is fair
Where the merry leaves dance in the summer air." –Mary Howitt

Day of Month	Day of Week	Dates, Feasts, Fasts, Aspects, Tide Heights	Weather
1	Sa.	**Canada Day** • ☌♃☾ • Dominion of Canada created, 1867 • 9.6 / 9.8	*Breezes*
2	**A**	**4th S. af. P.** • Steve Fossett first to circumnavigate world solo in balloon, 2002	*are*
3	M.	Dog days begin. • ⊕ AT APHELION • *As dog days commence, so they end.* • 8.9 / 9.7	*cool,*
4	Tu.	**Independence Day** • Construction of Erie Canal began, 1817 • 103°F, Portland, Maine, 1911	*barbecue's*
5	W.	Physicist Isaac Newton's *Philosophiae Naturalis Principia Mathematica* published, 1687 • 8.7 / 9.8	*hot!*
6	Th.	☾ AT APO. • ☌♄☾ • Armadillos mate now. • 8.8 / 10.0	*Beaches*
7	Fr.	Cornerstone laid for first Catholic cathedral in U.S. (Baltimore Basilica), Baltimore, Md., 1806 • 8.9 / 10.1	*are*
8	Sa.	☾ RUNS LOW • Group of Seven artist Tom Thomson last seen alive, Canoe Lake, Algonquin Park, Ont., 1917	*peaches:*
9	**A**	**5th S. af. P.** • Full Buck ○ • ☌♇☾ • Journalist Eric Sevareid died, 1992	*Find a*
10	M.	♇ AT ☍ • Cornscateous air is everywhere. • Tides 10.3 / 9.2	*good*
11	Tu.	U.S. president John Quincy Adams born, 1767 • 10.3 / 9.3	*spot!*
12	W.	☾ AT ☋ • Writer Henry David Thoreau born, 1817 • Tides 10.3 / 9.4	*Feeling*
13	Th.	☌♆☾ • Tornado touched down near Pikes Peak, Colo., 2013 • Tides 10.2 / 9.5	*no*
14	Fr.	Bastille Day • Gold discovered, Last Chance Gulch (Helena), Mont., 1864 • Tides 10.1 / 9.7	*pain—*
15	Sa.	**St. Swithin** • ☾ ON EQ. • *A good maxim is never out of season.* • 10.0 / 9.9	*who'd*
16	**A**	**6th S. af. P.** • ☌♅☾ • Former U.S. First Lady Mary Todd Lincoln died, 1882	*complain?*
17	M.	Contact with *Surveyor 4* lost 2.5 minutes before Moon touchdown, 1967 • Tides 9.7 / 10.4	*This*
18	Tu.	U.S. naval commander John Paul Jones died, 1792 • 9.6 / 10.7	*air's*
19	W.	Saguenay flood began, Que., 1996 • Tides 9.7 / 11.1	*like*
20	Th.	☌♀☾ • Legion of Merit established, 1942 • Tides 9.8 / 11.5	*champagne,*
21	Fr.	☾ RIDES HIGH • ☾ AT PERIG. • Black-eyed Susans in bloom now. • 10.0 / 11.8	*dry*
22	Sa.	**St. Mary Magdalene** • Frank Zybach's "self-propelled sprinkling irrigating apparatus" patented, 1952	*and*
23	**A**	**7th S. af. P.** • New ● • ☌♂☾	*bubblesome.*
24	M.	☾ AT ☊ • Mary, Queen of Scots, deposed, 1567 • Tides 12.0 / 10.7	*Showers*
25	Tu.	**St. James** • ☌☿☾ • *24 to 25:* 43" rain, Alvin, Tex., 1979 • 11.9 / 10.7	*are*
26	W.	**St. Anne** • ☌♂☉ • Actor Jason Robards born, 1922	*troublesome.*
27	Th.	Adult gypsy moths emerge. • Architect Cyrus Eidlitz born, 1853 • Tides 11.1 / 10.5	*Stormy,*
28	Fr.	☾ ON EQ. • ☌♃☾ • *Step after step, the ladder is ascended.* • Tides 10.6 / 10.2	*not*
29	Sa.	**St. Martha** • First "Chicken Wing Day," Buffalo, N.Y., 1977 • Tides 10.0 / 9.9	*too*
30	**A**	**8th S. af. P.** • ☿ GR. ELONG. (27° EAST) • Governor Arnold Schwarzenegger born, 1947	*warmy.*
31	M.	**St. Ignatius of Loyola** • 5-lb. 3-oz. white crappie caught, Enid Dam, Miss., 1957	*Normy.*

Farmer's Calendar

■ In the July twilight, bats flicker between trees, zigging and zagging in a relentless pursuit of mosquitoes. A single Little Brown Bat can eat 1,000 mosquitoes per hour—the equivalent of an average man eating eight large pizzas in the same period.

The Little Browns have had a tough time recently, due to a fungal disease called white-nose syndrome, first discovered in New York State in 2006. Bats were dying by the millions in the caves where they hibernate over winter. The diseased bats had a white fungus on their noses.

Scientists identified the fungus as *Pseudogymnoascus destructans,* which also happens to be found on bananas. Fruit growers had learned that it could be controlled with a common bacterium called *Rhodococcus rhodochrous.* A grad student studying white-nose syndrome at Georgia State University wondered if *R. rhodochrous* might work on bats as well as bananas.

The test results are promising, and in May 2015, 75 previously infected bats were released in the Mark Twain Cave Complex in Hannibal, Missouri.

With luck—and a little help from bananas—we may enjoy many more violet twilights watching bats skitter across the sky.

THE EIGHTH MONTH • 2017

SKY WATCH ☆ *On the 2nd, the Moon hovers above Saturn. The Perseid meteors arrive on the 12th, but a bright Moon will interfere with good viewing. On the 19th, the Moon is just below Venus, which adequately maintains its elevation in the morning sky, in Gemini. The first total solar eclipse in the United States in 38 years unfolds on the 21st. (See page 130.) Hopefully, many will travel to be within the narrow ribbon of totality, rather than view the mere partial eclipse seen throughout the continent. (Warning: Eye protection required, such as welder's goggles with shade number 12 or 14.) The Moon is to the right of ever-lower Jupiter on the 24th, above Jupiter on the 25th, and to the upper left of Saturn on the 30th.*

○	**Full Moon**	7th day	14th hour	11th minute
◑	**Last Quarter**	14th day	21st hour	15th minute
●	**New Moon**	21st day	14th hour	30th minute
◐	**First Quarter**	29th day	4th hour	13th minute

All times are given in Eastern Daylight Time.

Get these pages with times set to your zip code at Almanac.com/Access.

Day of Year	Day of Month	Day of Week	☼ Rises h. m.	Rise Key	☼ Sets h. m.	Set Key	Length of Day h. m.	Sun Fast m.	Declination of Sun ° '	High Tide Times Boston		☾ Rises h. m.	Rise Key	☾ Sets h. m.	Set Key	☾ Astron. Place	☾ Age
213	1	Tu.	5:37	B	**8:03**	E	14 26	9	17 N.50	7¼	**7½**	**3:12**	E	12:52	B	LIB	9
214	2	W.	5:38	B	**8:02**	E	14 24	10	17 34	8	**8¼**	**4:07**	E	1:27	B	OPH	10
215	3	Th.	5:39	B	**8:01**	E	14 22	10	17 19	9	**9¼**	**5:00**	E	2:06	B	OPH	11
216	4	Fr.	5:40	B	**8:00**	E	14 20	10	17 03	9¾	**10**	**5:50**	E	2:50	B	SAG	12
217	5	Sa.	5:41	B	**7:59**	E	14 18	10	16 46	10½	**10¾**	**6:36**	E	3:39	B	SAG	13
218	6	**A**	5:42	B	**7:57**	E	14 15	10	16 30	11¼	**11½**	**7:18**	E	4:32	B	SAG	14
219	7	M.	5:43	B	**7:56**	E	14 13	10	16 13	**12**	—	**7:57**	E	5:29	C	CAP	15
220	8	Tu.	5:44	B	**7:55**	E	14 11	10	15 56	12	**12¾**	**8:32**	E	6:30	C	CAP	16
221	9	W.	5:45	B	**7:53**	E	14 08	10	15 39	12¾	**1¼**	**9:05**	D	7:32	C	AQU	17
222	10	Th.	5:46	B	**7:52**	E	14 06	11	15 21	1½	**2**	**9:36**	D	8:35	D	AQU	18
223	11	Fr.	5:47	B	**7:51**	D	14 04	11	15 03	2¼	**2½**	**10:07**	D	9:40	D	PSC	19
224	12	Sa.	5:48	B	**7:49**	D	14 01	11	14 45	3	**3¼**	**10:39**	C	10:46	E	CET	20
225	13	**A**	5:49	B	**7:48**	D	13 59	11	14 27	3¾	**4¼**	**11:13**	C	11:53	E	PSC	21
226	14	M.	5:50	B	**7:46**	D	13 56	11	14 08	4½	**5**	**11:51**	B	**1:02**	E	CET	22
227	15	Tu.	5:52	B	**7:45**	D	13 53	11	13 49	5½	**6**	—	–	**2:10**	E	TAU	23
228	16	W.	5:53	B	**7:43**	D	13 50	12	13 30	6½	**7**	12:33	B	**3:18**	E	TAU	24
229	17	Th.	5:54	B	**7:42**	D	13 48	12	13 11	7½	**8**	1:23	B	**4:23**	E	TAU	25
230	18	Fr.	5:55	B	**7:40**	D	13 45	12	12 52	8½	**9**	2:19	B	**5:22**	E	GEM	26
231	19	Sa.	5:56	B	**7:39**	D	13 43	12	12 32	9¾	**10**	3:22	B	**6:15**	E	GEM	27
232	20	**A**	5:57	B	**7:37**	D	13 40	13	12 12	10½	**11**	4:29	C	**7:01**	E	CAN	28
233	21	M.	5:58	B	**7:36**	D	13 38	13	11 52	11½	**11¾**	5:38	C	**7:41**	E	LEO	0
234	22	Tu.	5:59	B	**7:34**	D	13 35	13	11 32	**12¼**	—	6:47	C	**8:16**	D	LEO	1
235	23	W.	6:00	B	**7:33**	D	13 33	13	11 12	12½	**1¼**	7:55	D	**8:48**	D	LEO	2
236	24	Th.	6:01	B	**7:31**	D	13 30	14	10 51	1½	**2**	9:00	D	**9:19**	C	VIR	3
237	25	Fr.	6:02	B	**7:29**	D	13 27	14	10 31	2¼	**2¾**	10:03	E	**9:49**	C	VIR	4
238	26	Sa.	6:03	B	**7:28**	D	13 25	14	10 10	3	**3½**	11:05	E	**10:19**	C	VIR	5
239	27	**A**	6:04	B	**7:26**	D	13 22	14	9 49	3¾	**4¼**	**12:04**	E	**10:51**	B	LIB	6
240	28	M.	6:05	B	**7:24**	D	13 19	15	9 27	4¾	**5**	**1:02**	E	**11:25**	B	LIB	7
241	29	Tu.	6:06	B	**7:23**	D	13 17	15	9 06	5½	**5¾**	**1:58**	E	—	–	SCO	8
242	30	W.	6:07	B	**7:21**	D	13 14	15	8 45	6½	**6¾**	**2:52**	E	12:03	B	OPH	9
243	31	Th.	6:09	B	**7:19**	D	13 10	16	8 N.23	7½	**7¾**	**3:43**	E	12:45	B	SAG	10

 To use this page, see p. 138; for Key Letters, see p. 252. ☞ **Bold = P.M.** ☞ Light = A.M.

AUGUST HATH 31 DAYS • 2017

A cloud lay cradled near the setting Sun;
A gleam of crimson tinged its braided snow. –John Wilson

Day of Month	Day of Week	Dates, Feasts, Fasts, Aspects, Tide Heights	Weather
1	Tu.	Lammas Day • Diamonds found near Murfreesboro, Ark., 1906 • Tides { 8.6 / 9.4	*It's*
2	W.	☾ AT APO. • Offshore hurricane battered fishing fleet and lightship near Nantucket, Mass., 1867 • { 8.4 / 9.4	*hard*
3	Th.	☌♄☾ • ♅ STAT. • Football player Tom Brady born, 1977 • { 8.4 / 9.6	*to*
4	Fr.	☾ RUNS LOW • *Phoenix* Mars Lander launched, Cape Canaveral, Fla., 2007 • { 8.6 / 9.8	*judge*
5	Sa.	☌♇☾ • Gray squirrels have second litters now. • { 8.8 / 10.0	*the*
6	**A**	**Transfiguration** • "Little Boy" A-bomb released over Hiroshima, Japan, WWII, 1945 • { 9.0 / 10.2	*sweeter*
7	M.	**Civic Holiday (Canada)** • **Full Sturgeon** ○ • **Eclipse** ☾ • { 9.2 / —	*sight:*
8	Tu.	**St. Dominic** • ☾ AT ☋ • U.S. president Richard Nixon announced resignation, 1974 • { 10.4 / 9.5	*a*
9	W.	☌♆☾ • Webster-Ashburton Treaty signed, concerning British N.A. colonies/U.S. borders, 1842	*lightning*
10	Th.	**St. Lawrence** • *Happy are the fields that receive summer rain.* • { 10.5 / 9.9	*bolt*
11	Fr.	**St. Clare** • Dog Days end. • ☾ ON EQ. • Tides { 10.5 / 10.1	*or*
12	Sa.	☿ STAT. • David McKibben granted patent for therapeutic horseshoe, 1986 • Tides { 10.4 / 10.3	*a*
13	**A**	**10th S. af. P.** • ☌♅☾ • Walt Disney's *Bambi* premiered, N.Y.C., 1942	*Perseids*
14	M.	Actress Hilary Duff wed ice hockey player Mike Comrie, 2010 • Tides { 9.9 / 10.5	*meteorite!*
15	Tu.	**Assumption** • Thomas Edison suggested using "Hello" when answering phones, 1877	*Come*
16	W.	5-lb. 15-oz. Arctic grayling caught, Katseyedie River, N.W.T., 1967 • Tides { 9.5 / 10.7	*in*
17	Th.	Cat Nights commence. • *In the eyes of the mouse, the cat is a lion.*	*from*
18	Fr.	☾ RIDES HIGH • ☾ AT PERIG. • Virginia Dare became first child of English parents born in America (Va. colony), 1587	*the*
19	Sa.	☌♀☾ • USS *Constitution* earned nickname "Old Ironsides" in battle with HMS *Guerrière,* 1812	*fairways*
20	**A**	**11th S. af. P.** • Ragweed in bloom. • Tides { 10.2 / 11.6	*while*
21	M.	**New** ● • **Eclipse** ☉ • ☾ AT ☊ • ☌♂☾ • Tides { 10.5 / 11.6	*Zeus*
22	Tu.	☌☿☾ • Theodore Roosevelt first U.S. president to take public automobile ride, 1902 • { 10.7 / —	*and*
23	W.	*It is not want, but abundance, that makes avarice.* • { 11.5 / 10.7	*Thor*
24	Th.	**St. Bartholomew** • ☾ ON EQ. • Basketball player Reggie Miller born, 1965	*contest*
25	Fr.	☌♃☾ • ♄ STAT. • Astronaut Neil Armstrong died, 2012 • { 10.8 / 10.4	*the*
26	Sa.	☿ IN INF. ☌ • Hummingbirds migrate south. • { 10.2 / 10.2	*airways.*
27	**A**	**12th S. af. P.** • "Sea Islands Hurricane" hit near Savannah, Ga., 1893 • { 9.7 / 9.8	*Cooling*
28	M.	**St. Augustine of Hippo** • Sen. Strom Thurmond (S.C.) began 24-hr., 18-min. filibuster speech, 1957	*trend*
29	Tu.	**St. John the Baptist** • Military Service Act became law, Canada, 1917 • { 8.7 / 9.3	*at*
30	W.	☾ AT APO. • ☌♄☾ • Ellen Arthur, wife of future U.S. president Chester Arthur, born, 1837	*summer's*
31	Th.	☾ RUNS LOW • *Better an egg this year than a chicken next year.*	*end.*

Farmer's Calendar

■ The pastor of our little church takes the month of August off. So does much of his congregation. It's not a big group to begin with; on an ordinary Sunday in October or May, we'll have 50 or so present. In mid-August, we seldom see more than 25. So, rather than pay some retired minister to "supply the pulpit," we supply ourselves. Four lay persons, all volunteers, read Bible verses and say a few words in lieu of a sermon.

It's part Chautauqua and part Amateur Hour. Last August, one of the deacons talked about the *Amistad* case, in which a group of Africans who had been kidnapped by slavers rose up and took control of the ship. On the second Sunday, a gentleman talked about the Bahá'í faith, which has a landmark in our town. The next week, a woman who had lost two siblings in childhood spoke movingly about the best ways to "be there" for people who have suffered such losses. At month's end, a choir member revealed funny details of rehearsal shenanigans.

Amateur Hour makes us appreciate each other a little more. We share our experiences, our joys and griefs. We discover unexpected depths and eloquence in our midst. We learn that certain people may be paying close attention to what we say and do—and maybe even taking notes.

SEPTEMBER

THE NINTH MONTH • 2017

SKY WATCH ☆ *Neptune comes to opposition on the 5th in Aquarius, but a telescope is needed to see its disk and blue color. On the 10th, Mercury at magnitude zero closely meets Leo's main star, Regulus, with Venus far above. Also in the predawn sky, Mercury and Mars almost touch on the 16th, but the pair is only 8 degrees high in twilight. The morning of the 18th brings a super lineup some 40 minutes before sunrise, with Mercury lowest; dim, orange Mars to its upper right; the crescent Moon; Regulus; and finally Venus at the highest point of the quintet. The next morning, the Moon is below Mercury. Autumn starts with the equinox on the 22nd at 4:02 P.M.*

○	**Full Moon**	6th day	3rd hour	3rd minute
◑	**Last Quarter**	13th day	2nd hour	25th minute
●	**New Moon**	20th day	1st hour	30th minute
◐	**First Quarter**	27th day	22nd hour	54th minute

All times are given in Eastern Daylight Time.

Get these pages with times set to your zip code at Almanac.com/Access.

Day of Year	Day of Month	Day of Week	☼ Rises h. m.	Rise Key	☼ Sets h. m.	Set Key	Length of Day h.	m.	Sun Fast m.	Declination of Sun °	'	High Tide Times Boston		☾ Rises h. m.	Rise Key	☾ Sets h. m.	Set Key	☾ Astron. Place	☾ Age
244	1	Fr.	6:10	B	**7:18**	D	13	08	16	8	N. 01	8¼	**8½**	**4:30**	E	1:31	B	SAG	11
245	2	Sa.	6:11	B	**7:16**	D	13	05	16	7	39	9¼	**9½**	**5:14**	E	2:23	B	SAG	12
246	3	**A**	6:12	B	**7:14**	D	13	02	17	7	17	10	**10¼**	**5:54**	E	3:18	B	CAP	13
247	4	M.	6:13	B	**7:13**	D	13	00	17	6	55	10¾	**11**	**6:31**	E	4:18	C	CAP	14
248	5	Tu.	6:14	C	**7:11**	D	12	57	17	6	33	11½	**11¾**	**7:05**	D	5:20	C	AQU	15
249	6	W.	6:15	C	**7:09**	D	12	54	18	6	10	**12**	—	**7:37**	D	6:24	C	AQU	16
250	7	Th.	6:16	C	**7:07**	D	12	51	18	5	48	12¼	**12¾**	**8:09**	D	7:30	D	AQU	17
251	8	Fr.	6:17	C	**7:06**	D	12	49	18	5	25	1	**1½**	**8:41**	C	8:37	D	CET	18
252	9	Sa.	6:18	C	**7:04**	D	12	46	19	5	03	1¾	**2¼**	**9:14**	C	9:45	E	PSC	19
253	10	**A**	6:19	C	**7:02**	D	12	43	19	4	40	2½	**3**	**9:51**	C	10:54	E	CET	20
254	11	M.	6:20	C	**7:00**	D	12	40	19	4	17	3¼	**3¾**	**10:32**	B	**12:03**	E	TAU	21
255	12	Tu.	6:21	C	**6:59**	D	12	38	20	3	54	4¼	**4½**	**11:19**	B	**1:10**	E	TAU	22
256	13	W.	6:22	C	**6:57**	C	12	35	20	3	31	5¼	**5½**	—	–	**2:15**	E	TAU	23
257	14	Th.	6:23	C	**6:55**	C	12	32	20	3	08	6¼	**6¾**	12:12	B	**3:15**	E	ORI	24
258	15	Fr.	6:24	C	**6:53**	C	12	29	21	2	45	7¼	**7¾**	1:11	B	**4:09**	E	GEM	25
259	16	Sa.	6:25	C	**6:52**	C	12	27	21	2	22	8½	**8¾**	2:15	C	**4:56**	E	CAN	26
260	17	**A**	6:26	C	**6:50**	C	12	24	21	1	59	9½	**9¾**	3:22	C	**5:37**	E	CAN	27
261	18	M.	6:27	C	**6:48**	C	12	21	22	1	36	10¼	**10¾**	4:30	C	**6:13**	D	LEO	28
262	19	Tu.	6:29	C	**6:46**	C	12	17	22	1	12	11¼	**11½**	5:37	D	**6:46**	D	LEO	29
263	20	W.	6:30	C	**6:45**	C	12	15	23	0	49	**12**	—	6:43	D	**7:17**	D	VIR	0
264	21	Th.	6:31	C	**6:43**	C	12	12	23	0	26	12¼	**12¾**	7:47	D	**7:47**	C	VIR	1
265	22	Fr.	6:32	C	**6:41**	C	12	09	23	0	N. 02	1	**1½**	8:50	E	**8:17**	C	VIR	2
266	23	Sa.	6:33	C	**6:39**	C	12	06	24	0	S. 20	1¾	**2**	9:51	E	**8:49**	B	LIB	3
267	24	**A**	6:34	C	**6:38**	C	12	04	24	0	43	2½	**2¾**	10:50	E	**9:22**	B	LIB	4
268	25	M.	6:35	C	**6:36**	C	12	01	24	1	07	3¼	**3½**	11:48	E	**9:58**	B	LIB	5
269	26	Tu.	6:36	C	**6:34**	C	11	58	25	1	30	4	**4¼**	**12:43**	E	**10:38**	B	OPH	6
270	27	W.	6:37	C	**6:32**	C	11	55	25	1	53	5	**5¼**	**1:35**	E	**11:23**	B	OPH	7
271	28	Th.	6:38	C	**6:30**	C	11	52	25	2	17	5¾	**6**	**2:24**	E	—	–	SAG	8
272	29	Fr.	6:39	C	**6:29**	C	11	50	26	2	40	6¾	**7**	**3:08**	E	12:12	B	SAG	9
273	30	Sa.	6:40	C	**6:27**	C	11	47	26	3	S. 03	7¾	**8**	**3:49**	E	1:05	B	CAP	10

 To use this page, see p. 138; for Key Letters, see p. 252. ☞ **Bold = P.M.** ☞ Light = A.M.

SEPTEMBER HATH 30 DAYS • 2017

And the red leaves by the roadside
Fell and floated one by one. –Hattie Tyng Griswold

Day of Month	Day of Week	Dates, Feasts, Fasts, Aspects, Tide Heights	Weather
1	Fr.	☌☿♂ • ☌♇☾ • Portrait painter Chester Harding born, 1792 • Tides { 8.3 / 9.3	*Pitter-*
2	Sa.	Writer Cleveland Amory born, 1917 • Tides { 8.6 / 9.6	*pattering,*
3	**A**	**13th S. af. P.** • "Father of Oregon," John McLoughlin, died, 1857 • { 8.9 / 9.9	*of*
4	M.	**Labor Day** • ☾ AT ☋ • ☿ STAT. • Tides { 9.2 / 10.2	*showers*
5	Tu.	♆ AT ☍ • 112°F, Centreville, Ala., 1925 • { 9.6 / 10.5	*a scattering.*
6	W.	**Full Corn** ○ • ☌♆☾ • *When the Moon's in the full, then wit's in the wane.* • { 10.0 / —	*Brief*
7	Th.	☾ ON EQ. • Financier J. P. Morgan Jr. born, 1867 • Tides { 10.7 / 10.3	*repeat*
8	Fr.	Francis Bellamy's Pledge of Allegiance first published, in *The Youth's Companion*, 1892 • Tides { 10.8 / 10.6	*of*
9	Sa.	☌♅☾ • Cranberry bog harvest begins, Cape Cod, Mass. • Tides { 10.7 / 10.8	*the*
10	**A**	**14th S. af. P.** • Faneuil Hall given to town of Boston, Mass., 1742 • { 10.6 / 10.9	*summer*
11	M.	**Patriot Day** • Hurricane Iniki made landfall, Kauai, Hawaii, 1992 • Tides { 10.3 / 10.9	*heat.*
12	Tu.	☿ GR. ELONG. (18° WEST) • U.S. president Kennedy delivered Moon speech, Rice U., Houston, Tex., 1962	*Boomier,*
13	W.	☾ AT PERIG. • Producer Leland Hayward born, 1902 • Tides { 9.7 / 10.7	*then*
14	Th.	**Holy Cross** • ☾ RIDES HIGH • Princess Grace of Monaco (Grace Kelly) died, 1982	*gloomier—*
15	Fr.	113 lb. 1-oz. black drum caught, Lewes, Del., 1975 • Tides { 9.4 / 10.6	*thrills*
16	Sa.	☌☿♂ • Supreme Court of Saskatchewan established, Regina, Sask., 1907 • Tides { 9.6 / 10.8	*and*
17	**A**	**15th S. af. P.** • ☾ AT ☊ • ☌♀☾ • Tides { 9.9 / 10.9	*chills!*
18	M.	☌☿☾ • ☌♂☾ • Central Intelligence Agency (CIA) founded, 1947 • { 10.3 / 11.0	*In*
19	Tu.	*Small fish are better than no fish.* • Tides { 10.5 / 11.1	*fall*
20	W.	Ember Day • **Rosh Hashanah begins at sundown** • **First of Muharram begins at sundown** • **New** ● • ☾ ON EQ.	
21	Th.	**St. Matthew** • New York *Sun*'s Francis Church replied, "Yes, Virginia, there is a Santa Claus," 1897	*sloshes,*
22	Fr.	Ember Day • Harvest Home • **Autumnal Equinox** • ☌♃☾ • { 10.7 / 10.6	*wearing*
23	Sa.	Ember Day • Astronomer Urbain Le Verrier died, 1877	*galoshes.*
24	**A**	**16th S. af. P.** • *Pigeons wash before rain.* • { 9.9 / 10.1	*Time to*
25	M.	3.4-magnitude earthquake occurred, near Concord, N.H., 2010	*start*
26	Tu.	☌♄☾ • Woodchucks hibernate now. • Tides { 9.0 / 9.5	*picking*
27	W.	**St. Vincent de Paul** • ☾ AT APO. • *Dawn* spacecraft launched, Cape Canaveral, Fla., 2007	*those*
28	Th.	☾ RUNS LOW • ☌♇☾ • ♇ STAT. • Tides { 8.4 / 9.0	*Cortlands*
29	Fr.	**St. Michael** • **Yom Kippur begins at sundown** • { 8.3 / 9.0	*and*
30	Sa.	**St. Gregory the Illuminator** • *Alouette 1* satellite ceased activity, 1972	*McIntoshes!*

Wonder is the seed of knowledge. –Francis Bacon

Farmer's Calendar

■ The arborist came today, accompanied by five sturdy young men, an enormous crane, and a chipper. They've been charged with taking down four very large trees that were threatening the house.

This threat did not occur overnight, of course. The land under and around the house was cleared almost 40 years ago. At the time, none of these very large trees hung over the roof. It was clearing all the trees around them that set off a growth spurt.

Under a magnifying glass, the stump of one of the fallen trees, a 60-foot-tall red oak, revealed some 80 growth rings. The first 40 or so were narrow—just a millimeter or two in width. Crowded by other trees, it got little sun. But the lens showed that in ensuing years, after space was cleared for the house, the rings expanded rapidly. Ring number 41 was half a centimeter, and the outermost ring was almost 4 centimeters wide. When that tree was no longer competing with others, it grew much faster.

That oak's seedling set its roots soon after the Great Hurricane of 1938 roared up the Connecticut River Valley, scything down millions of trees. But it left open space for millions more. Now that the big oak is gone, the Milky Way is visible above the house for the first time in decades.

SKY WATCH ☆ *From the 4th to the 6th, Venus at magnitude –4 and Mars at 2 are very close together (extremely so on the 5th); point binoculars quite low in the east 1 hour before sunrise. Venus is 250 times brighter than Mars. Uranus comes to opposition from the 18th to the 19th; the Green Planet can be glimpsed in binoculars in easternmost Pisces. The Moon will hover just to the left of Mars on the 17th and below Venus on the 18th. Venus is now starting to get low, and its long morning star apparition is winding down. The moderate-strength Orionid meteor shower from the 21st to the 22nd has no competition, as the Moon is a thin crescent.*

○	**Full Moon**	5th day	14th hour	40th minute
◑	**Last Quarter**	12th day	8th hour	25th minute
●	**New Moon**	19th day	15th hour	12th minute
◐	**First Quarter**	27th day	18th hour	22nd minute

All times are given in Eastern Daylight Time.

Get these pages with times set to your zip code at Almanac.com/Access.

Day of Year	Day of Month	Day of Week	☼ Rises h. m.	Rise Key	☼ Sets h. m.	Set Key	Length of Day h.	m.	Sun Fast m.	Declination of Sun °	'	High Tide Times Boston		☾ Rises h. m.	Rise Key	☾ Sets h. m.	Set Key	☾ Astron. Place	☾ Age
274	1	**A**	6:41	C	**6:25**	C	11	44	26	3 s.	27	8½	**8¾**	**4:27**	E	2:03	C	CAP	11
275	2	M.	6:43	C	**6:24**	C	11	41	27	3	50	9¼	**9½**	**5:02**	E	3:04	C	CAP	12
276	3	Tu.	6:44	C	**6:22**	C	11	38	27	4	13	10	**10¼**	**5:35**	D	4:07	C	AQU	13
277	4	W.	6:45	C	**6:20**	C	11	35	27	4	36	10¾	**11**	**6:07**	D	5:13	D	AQU	14
278	5	Th.	6:46	D	**6:18**	C	11	32	28	4	59	11½	**11¾**	**6:39**	D	6:20	D	PSC	15
279	6	Fr.	6:47	D	**6:17**	C	11	30	28	5	22	**12¼**	—	**7:13**	C	7:30	E	PSC	16
280	7	Sa.	6:48	D	**6:15**	C	11	27	28	5	45	12½	**1**	**7:49**	C	8:40	E	CET	17
281	8	**A**	6:49	D	**6:13**	C	11	24	28	6	08	1½	**1¾**	**8:30**	B	9:52	E	ARI	18
282	9	M.	6:50	D	**6:12**	C	11	22	29	6	31	2¼	**2½**	**9:15**	B	11:02	E	TAU	19
283	10	Tu.	6:52	D	**6:10**	C	11	18	29	6	53	3	**3¼**	**10:07**	B	**12:09**	E	TAU	20
284	11	W.	6:53	D	**6:08**	C	11	15	29	7	16	4	**4¼**	**11:05**	B	**1:11**	E	ORI	21
285	12	Th.	6:54	D	**6:07**	B	11	13	29	7	39	5	**5¼**	—	–	**2:07**	E	GEM	22
286	13	Fr.	6:55	D	**6:05**	B	11	10	30	8	01	6	**6½**	12:07	B	**2:55**	E	CAN	23
287	14	Sa.	6:56	D	**6:03**	B	11	07	30	8	23	7¼	**7½**	1:13	C	**3:37**	E	CAN	24
288	15	**A**	6:57	D	**6:02**	B	11	05	30	8	45	8¼	**8½**	2:19	C	**4:14**	E	LEO	25
289	16	M.	6:58	D	**6:00**	B	11	02	30	9	07	9¼	**9½**	3:25	C	**4:47**	D	LEO	26
290	17	Tu.	7:00	D	**5:59**	B	10	59	31	9	29	10	**10½**	4:30	D	**5:18**	D	VIR	27
291	18	W.	7:01	D	**5:57**	B	10	56	31	9	51	11	**11¼**	5:34	D	**5:47**	C	VIR	28
292	19	Th.	7:02	D	**5:56**	B	10	54	31	10	13	11½	—	6:37	E	**6:17**	C	VIR	0
293	20	Fr.	7:03	D	**5:54**	B	10	51	31	10	34	12	**12¼**	7:39	E	**6:47**	C	VIR	1
294	21	Sa.	7:04	D	**5:53**	B	10	49	31	10	56	12¾	**1**	8:39	E	**7:20**	B	LIB	2
295	22	**A**	7:06	D	**5:51**	B	10	45	31	11	17	1½	**1½**	9:37	E	**7:55**	B	LIB	3
296	23	M.	7:07	D	**5:50**	B	10	43	32	11	38	2	**2¼**	10:34	E	**8:33**	B	OPH	4
297	24	Tu.	7:08	D	**5:48**	B	10	40	32	11	59	2¾	**3**	11:28	E	**9:16**	B	OPH	5
298	25	W.	7:09	D	**5:47**	B	10	38	32	12	19	3½	**3¾**	**12:18**	E	**10:03**	B	SAG	6
299	26	Th.	7:10	D	**5:45**	B	10	35	32	12	40	4¼	**4½**	**1:04**	E	**10:54**	B	SAG	7
300	27	Fr.	7:12	D	**5:44**	B	10	32	32	13	00	5¼	**5¼**	**1:46**	E	**11:49**	B	SAG	8
301	28	Sa.	7:13	D	**5:43**	B	10	30	32	13	20	6	**6¼**	**2:24**	E	—	–	CAP	9
302	29	**A**	7:14	D	**5:41**	B	10	27	32	13	40	7	**7¼**	**2:59**	E	12:47	C	CAP	10
303	30	M.	7:15	D	**5:40**	B	10	25	32	13	59	7¾	**8**	**3:32**	D	1:49	C	AQU	11
304	31	Tu.	7:17	D	**5:39**	B	10	22	32	14 s.	19	8¾	**9**	**4:04**	D	2:52	D	AQU	12

 To use this page, see p. 138; for Key Letters, see p. 252. ☞ **Bold = P.M.** ☞ Light = A.M.

OCTOBER HATH 31 DAYS • 2017

And night with her dusky pinions
Swept down in stormy glee. –Nathan Haskell Dole

Day of Month	Day of Week	Dates, Feasts, Fasts, Aspects, Tide Heights	Weather
1	**A**	**17th S. af. P.** • ☾ AT ☋ • Maria Mitchell discovered comet Mitchell 1847VI, 1847	*Leaf-*
2	M.	Watch for banded woolly bear caterpillars now • { 9.1 / 9.8	*lovers*
3	Tu.	☌♆☾ • 767-day dry spell began, Bagdad, Calif., 1912 • Tides { 9.6 / 10.2	*harken*
4	W.	**St. Francis of Assisi** • **Sukkoth begins at sundown** • U.S.S.R.'s *Sputnik 1* launched, 1957	*as*
5	Th.	**Full Harvest** ○ • ☾ ON EQ. • ☌♀♂ • Tides { 10.6 / 10.8	*skies*
6	Fr.	☌⛢☾ • 19.26" rain in 24 hours, Ucluelet Brynnor Mines, B.C., 1967 • { 11.1 / —	*darken.*
7	Sa.	Actress June Allyson born, 1917 • Tides { 10.9 / 11.4	*Blue*
8	**A**	**18th S. af. P.** • ☿ IN SUP. ☌ • *Gather thistles, expect prickles.* • { 10.9 / 11.5	*skies*
9	M.	**Columbus Day, observed** • **Thanksgiving Day (Canada)** • ☾ AT PERIG. • { 10.7 / 11.5	*over*
10	Tu.	Actor Christopher Reeve died, 2004 • Tides { 10.4 / 11.3	*hills*
11	W.	☾ RIDES HIGH • Businessman Henry John Heinz born, 1844 • Tides { 10.0 / 11.0	*where*
12	Th.	Columbus first saw New World, 1492 • Tides { 9.7 / 10.7	*red*
13	Fr.	Cornerstone of White House laid, 1792 • Project Cirrus: 80 lbs. dry ice released onto hurricane, 1947 • { 9.5 / 10.4	*and*
14	Sa.	☾ AT ☊ • First contingent of Canadian Expeditionary Force arrived in England, WWI, 1914	*gold*
15	**A**	**19th S. af. P.** • Gregorian calendar first used (certain countries), 1582	*abound;*
16	M.	*When the wind is in the south, It blows the bait in the fishes' mouth.* • Tides { 10.0 / 10.4	*keep*
17	Tu.	**St. Ignatius of Antioch** • ☌♂☾ • ☌♀☾ • { 10.3 / 10.5	*umbrellas*
18	W.	**St. Luke** • ☾ ON EQ. • ☌☿♃ • St. Luke's little summer.	*handy*
19	Th.	**New** ● • ☌♃☾ • ⛢ AT ☍ • Parrot mimicked smoke alarm, saved family, 2007	*while*
20	Fr.	☌☿☾ • John Bardeen first to win second Nobel Prize in physics, 1972 • { 10.3 / 10.7	*watching*
21	Sa.	Poet Samuel Taylor Coleridge born, 1772 • Tides { 10.1 / 10.6	*the*
22	**A**	**20th S. af. P.** • Julian, Meyer, and Krause received patent for cortisone, 1940	*glory*
23	M.	**St. James of Jerusalem** • Little brown bats hibernate now. • Tides { 9.5 / 10.1	*unfold*
24	Tu.	☾ AT APO. • ☌♄☾ • Astronomer William Lassell discovered Uranus moons Ariel and Umbriel, 1851	*all*
25	W.	☾ RUNS LOW • Carlsbad Caverns National Monument established, N.Mex., 1923 • { 8.9 / 9.5	*around.*
26	Th.	☌♇☾ • ☌♃☉ • Pony Express service ended, 1861 • Tides { 8.6 / 9.2	*Trick-*
27	Fr.	Timber rattlesnakes move to winter dens. • Tides { 8.4 / 9.0	*or-*
28	Sa.	**Sts. Simon & Jude** • Statue of Liberty dedicated, N.Y. Harbor, 1886 • { 8.4 / 9.0	*treaters*
29	**A**	**21st S. af. P.** • ☾ AT ☋ • Deadly tornado struck Berryville, Ark., 1942	*need*
30	M.	☌♆☾ • *Night is the mother of thoughts.* • { 8.9 / 9.3	*space*
31	Tu.	**All Hallows' Eve** • **Reformation Day** • Architect Richard Morris Hunt born, 1827	*heaters!*

Farmer's Calendar

■ It's hard to believe how much noise something smaller than a thimble makes when it falls 60 or 70 feet. On warm autumn nights, if the windows are open, we hear acorns ripping through leaves and thudding onto the roof of the toolshed. When there was an aluminum canoe out there, turned upside down, the cascade sounded like a Jamaican steel band.

Most of what's inside an acorn is protein to nourish an infant tree, producing more oaks. But squirrels and other inhabitants of the wood—chipmunks, deer, rodents, even birds—also eat acorns. In the old days, farmers used to drive their pigs into the woods to fatten on heaps of fallen acorns.

Oaks produce more nuts than all other trees put together. In a good year, an acre of red oaks can produce 500 pounds of acorns. Not all years are good for oaks, though; scientists think the oaks have abundant acorn years at irregular intervals so that the creatures that eat acorns can't consume the entire crop in one year. There's a theory that the oaks "choose" when to produce a supercrop, communicating with each other by emitting chemical signals through their roots.

All those thudding, ripping, and clanging sounds that keep us awake are oak trees talking to each other, planning a sophisticated strategy for survival.

NOVEMBER

The Eleventh Month • 2017

SKY WATCH ☆ *No planet remains high or conspicuous this month. Saturn has become low in the southwest at nightfall. In the predawn east, Venus, now near blue Spica, is also getting very low. From the 12th to the 14th (especially on the 13th), the planet has an extremely close conjunction with Jupiter but will be only a few degrees above the horizon. On the 14th, the Moon forms a straight line with Mars and Spica, then hovers above Venus on the 16th and to the left of Venus on the 17th. On the 20th, the crescent Moon stands to the right of Saturn and above Mercury. The innermost planet, Mercury, is quite bright but just 8 degrees high at dusk.*

○	**Full Moon**	4th day	1st hour	23rd minute
◑	**Last Quarter**	10th day	15th hour	36th minute
●	**New Moon**	18th day	6th hour	42nd minute
◐	**First Quarter**	26th day	12th hour	3rd minute

After 2:00 A.M. on November 5, Eastern Standard Time is given.

Get these pages with times set to your zip code at Almanac.com/Access.

Day of Year	Day of Month	Day of Week	☼ Rises h. m.	Rise Key	☼ Sets h. m.	Set Key	Length of Day h.	m.	Sun Fast m.	Declination of Sun °	'	High Tide Times Boston		☾ Rises h. m.	Rise Key	☾ Sets h. m.	Set Key	☾ Astron. Place	☾ Age
305	1	W.	7:18	D	**5:37**	B	10	19	32	14 s.	38	9½	**9¾**	**4:36**	D	3:58	D	PSC	13
306	2	Th.	7:19	D	**5:36**	B	10	17	32	14	57	10¼	**10½**	**5:08**	C	5:07	D	CET	14
307	3	Fr.	7:20	D	**5:35**	B	10	15	32	15	16	11	**11½**	**5:43**	C	6:18	E	PSC	15
308	4	Sa.	7:22	D	**5:34**	B	10	12	32	15	34	11¾	—	**6:22**	B	7:31	E	ARI	16
309	5	**A**	6:23	D	**4:32**	B	10	09	32	15	52	12¼	11½	**6:07**	B	7:44	E	TAU	17
310	6	M.	6:24	E	**4:31**	B	10	07	32	16	10	12	**12¼**	**6:58**	B	8:56	E	TAU	18
311	7	Tu.	6:25	E	**4:30**	B	10	05	32	16	28	1	**1¼**	**7:55**	B	10:03	E	TAU	19
312	8	W.	6:27	E	**4:29**	B	10	02	32	16	45	1¾	**2**	**8:58**	B	11:03	E	GEM	20
313	9	Th.	6:28	E	**4:28**	B	10	00	32	17	02	2¾	**3**	**10:04**	C	11:55	E	GEM	21
314	10	Fr.	6:29	E	**4:27**	B	9	58	32	17	19	3¾	**4**	**11:11**	C	**12:39**	E	CAN	22
315	11	Sa.	6:30	E	**4:26**	B	9	56	32	17	36	4¾	**5¼**	—	–	**1:17**	E	LEO	23
316	12	**A**	6:32	E	**4:25**	B	9	53	32	17	52	6	**6¼**	12:18	C	**1:51**	D	LEO	24
317	13	M.	6:33	E	**4:24**	B	9	51	31	18	08	7	**7¼**	1:23	D	**2:22**	D	LEO	25
318	14	Tu.	6:34	E	**4:23**	B	9	49	31	18	23	8	**8¼**	2:26	D	**2:51**	C	VIR	26
319	15	W.	6:35	E	**4:22**	B	9	47	31	18	38	8¾	**9¼**	3:28	D	**3:19**	C	VIR	27
320	16	Th.	6:36	E	**4:21**	B	9	45	31	18	53	9½	**10**	4:29	E	**3:49**	C	VIR	28
321	17	Fr.	6:38	E	**4:20**	B	9	42	31	19	08	10¼	**10¾**	5:30	E	**4:20**	B	LIB	29
322	18	Sa.	6:39	E	**4:20**	B	9	41	31	19	22	10¾	**11¼**	6:29	E	**4:53**	B	LIB	0
323	19	**A**	6:40	E	**4:19**	B	9	39	30	19	36	11½	—	7:26	E	**5:30**	B	SCO	1
324	20	M.	6:41	E	**4:18**	B	9	37	30	19	50	12	**12**	8:21	E	**6:11**	B	OPH	2
325	21	Tu.	6:43	E	**4:17**	B	9	34	30	20	03	12¾	**12¾**	9:13	E	**6:57**	B	SAG	3
326	22	W.	6:44	E	**4:17**	B	9	33	30	20	16	1¼	**1½**	10:01	E	**7:46**	B	SAG	4
327	23	Th.	6:45	E	**4:16**	B	9	31	29	20	28	2	**2¼**	10:44	E	**8:39**	B	SAG	5
328	24	Fr.	6:46	E	**4:16**	B	9	30	29	20	40	2¾	**3**	11:23	E	**9:36**	B	CAP	6
329	25	Sa.	6:47	E	**4:15**	A	9	28	29	20	52	3½	**3¾**	11:59	E	**10:34**	C	CAP	7
330	26	**A**	6:48	E	**4:14**	A	9	26	28	21	03	4½	**4½**	**12:32**	E	**11:35**	C	AQU	8
331	27	M.	6:50	E	**4:14**	A	9	24	28	21	14	5¼	**5½**	**1:03**	D	—	–	AQU	9
332	28	Tu.	6:51	E	**4:14**	A	9	23	28	21	25	6	**6½**	**1:33**	D	12:38	D	AQU	10
333	29	W.	6:52	E	**4:13**	A	9	21	27	21	35	7	**7¼**	**2:04**	C	1:44	D	CET	11
334	30	Th.	6:53	E	**4:13**	A	9	20	27	21 s.	44	7¾	**8¼**	**2:37**	C	2:52	E	PSC	12

 To use this page, see p. 138; for Key Letters, see p. 252. ☞ **Bold = P.M.** ☞ Light = A.M.

NOVEMBER HATH 30 DAYS • 2017

The wind one morning sprang up from sleep,
Saying, "Now for a frolic! Now for a leap!" –William Howitt

Day of Month	Day of Week	Dates, Feasts, Fasts, Aspects, Tide Heights	Weather
1	W.	**All Saints'** • ☾ ON EQ. • Sculptor Antonio Canova born, 1757 • Tides {10.0 10.1}	*Hocus-*
2	Th.	**All Souls'** • ☌⛢☾ • *Ice in November Brings mud in December.* • {10.6 10.4}	*pocus,*
3	Fr.	Canada's first bank, Bank of Montreal, opened, Que., 1817 • Tides {11.2 10.7}	*drizzles*
4	Sa.	Sadie Hawkins Day • **Full Beaver** ○ • Future U.S. president Abraham Lincoln wed Mary Todd, 1842	*will*
5	**A**	**22nd S. af. P.** • **Daylight Saving Time ends, 2:00 A.M.** • ☾ AT PERIG.	*soak*
6	M.	First recorded sightings of supernova in Cassiopeia, 1572 • 87°F, Charleston, S.C., 2003 • {10.9 12.0}	*us.*
7	Tu.	**Election Day** • ☾ RIDES HIGH • Chemist Marie Curie born, 1867 • Tides {10.8 11.9}	*Flaky*
8	W.	Black bears head to winter dens now. • Tides {10.5 11.6}	*flurries*
9	Th.	First issue of *Rolling Stone* magazine, 1967 • Tides {10.2 11.1}	*and*
10	Fr.	☾ AT ☊ • SS *Edmund Fitzgerald,* with 29 aboard, sank during storm, Lake Superior, 1975 • {9.9 10.6}	*cold*
11	Sa.	**St. Martin of Tours** • **Veterans Day** • Actress Demi Moore born, 1962 • {9.7 10.2}	*that's*
12	**A**	**23rd S. af. P.** • Indian Summer • Tides {9.7 10.0}	*biting—*
13	M.	☌♀♃ • Lobsters move to offshore waters. • {9.9 9.8}	*anyone*
14	Tu.	☾ ON EQ. • ☌♂☾ • First caboose-less Canadian Pacific train left Winnipeg, Man., for Thunder Bay, Ont., 1989	*had*
15	W.	*Nothing is a man's truly, but what he came by duly.* • {10.3 9.8}	*a*
16	Th.	☌♃☾ • Napoleon E. Guerin granted patent for cork life preserver, 1841 • Tides {10.4 9.7}	*Sun*
17	Fr.	**St. Hugh of Lincoln** • ☌♀☾ • Capt. Nathaniel B. Palmer sighted Antarctica, 1820	*sighting?*
18	Sa.	**St. Hilda of Whitby** • **New** ● • First commercial push-button telephone introduced, Pa., 1963	*Warm*
19	**A**	**24th S. af. P.** • Crab apples are ripe now. • {10.4 —}	*hiatus*
20	M.	☌☿☾ • ☌♄☾ • U.S. suffragette Harriot Stanton Blatch died, 1940 • {9.4 10.3}	*lets*
21	Tu.	☾ RUNS LOW • ☾ AT APO. • Writer Voltaire born, 1694 • Tides {9.2 10.1}	*a*
22	W.	☌♇☾ • ♆ STAT. • Actress Lillian Russell debuted at Tony Pastor's Theatre, N.Y.C., 1880	*storm*
23	Th.	**St. Clement** • **Thanksgiving Day** • ☿ GR. ELONG. (22° EAST) • {8.9 9.6}	*deflate*
24	Fr.	239-lb. yellowfin tuna caught off Catalina Island, Calif., 1984 • Tides {8.7 9.4}	*us!*
25	Sa.	☾ AT ☋ • American College of Surgeons incorporated, 1912 • Tides {8.6 9.2}	*How*
26	**A**	**25th S. af. P.** • Movie *Casablanca* premiered, N.Y.C., 1942 • {8.6 9.1}	*long*
27	M.	☌♆☾ • *Howdy Doody* host Buffalo Bob Smith born, 1917 • Tides {8.8 9.1}	*till*
28	Tu.	☌☿♄ • Drag racer Dale Armstrong died, 2014 • {9.2 9.2}	*they*
29	W.	☾ ON EQ. • *If today will not, tomorrow may.* • Tides {9.7 9.5}	*excavate*
30	Th.	**St. Andrew** • ☌⛢☾ • Writer Jonathan Swift born, 1667 • Tides {10.3 9.8}	*us?*

Food is an important part of a balanced diet. –Fran Lebowitz

Farmer's Calendar

■ Wild turkeys are such a familiar sight now that they are as likely to inspire annoyance as awe. When we see two hens bringing a couple dozen poults across a road—one hen on each side of the crossing, herding the little ones on, gently correcting the slow learners who are bumbling off in the wrong direction—we may honk the horn to hurry them up.

Biologists call such a group a brood flock. A hen lays 10 to 12 eggs, and there's no evolutionary advantage in an unrelated hen looking after the young. They apparently find some efficiency, or increased safety, or sheer pleasure in combining forces with another mother. Maybe it's as simple as having one adult on each side of the roads that must be crossed.

In the brood flock that hangs out in our neighborhood, the poults are adult-size now. They likely hatched in June. The two other brood flocks farther up the road have smaller poults, probably mothered by hens that renested in late summer and brought off a second brood.

By winter, the young turkeys will have separated by age and sex into larger flocks, stalking through the snowy woods, leaving four-toed tracks like the dinosaurs that were their ancestors. Watching them now, it seems amazing it took so long to see the resemblance.

DECEMBER

THE TWELFTH MONTH • 2017

SKY WATCH ☆ *A strange configuration rules the sky after Saturn and Mercury vanish on the 7th. Not a single naked-eye planet can be seen virtually all night, from nightfall until Mars and Jupiter finally rise before dawn. But 2017's best meteor shower, the Geminids, delivers a superb show on the 13th, starting at around 9:00 P.M. A thin crescent Moon will not interfere. Jupiter has a close meeting with the Moon on the 14th. The year's most distant Moon is the new Moon on the 18th. Winter arrives with the solstice on the 21st at 11:28 A.M. At month's end, Jupiter rises about 3 hours before the Sun. Looking ahead: Jupiter, now in Libra, approaches Mars and will very closely meet the Red Planet on January 6 and 7, 2018.*

○	**Full Moon**	3rd day	10th hour	47th minute
◑	**Last Quarter**	10th day	2nd hour	51st minute
●	**New Moon**	18th day	1st hour	30th minute
◐	**First Quarter**	26th day	4th hour	20th minute

All times are given in Eastern Standard Time.

Get these pages with times set to your zip code at Almanac.com/Access.

Day of Year	Day of Month	Day of Week	☼ Rises h. m.	Rise Key	☼ Sets h. m.	Set Key	Length of Day h. m.	Sun Fast m.	Declination of Sun ° '	High Tide Times Boston		☾ Rises h. m.	Rise Key	☾ Sets h. m.	Set Key	☾ Astron. Place	☾ Age
335	1	Fr.	6:54	E	**4:13**	A	9 19	27	21 s. 54	8½	**9¼**	**3:13**	C	4:03	E	CET	13
336	2	Sa.	6:55	E	**4:12**	A	9 17	26	22 02	9½	**10**	**3:54**	C	5:17	E	ARI	14
337	3	**A**	6:56	E	**4:12**	A	9 16	26	22 11	10¼	**11**	**4:43**	B	6:31	E	TAU	15
338	4	M.	6:57	E	**4:12**	A	9 15	25	22 19	11	**11¾**	**5:38**	B	7:43	E	TAU	16
339	5	Tu.	6:58	E	**4:12**	A	9 14	25	22 26	**12**	—	**6:41**	B	8:49	E	GEM	17
340	6	W.	6:59	E	**4:12**	A	9 13	25	22 33	12¾	**12¾**	**7:49**	B	9:47	E	GEM	18
341	7	Th.	7:00	E	**4:12**	A	9 12	24	22 40	1½	**1¾**	**8:58**	C	10:36	E	CAN	19
342	8	Fr.	7:01	E	**4:11**	A	9 10	24	22 46	2½	**2¾**	**10:07**	C	11:18	E	LEO	20
343	9	Sa.	7:02	E	**4:12**	A	9 10	23	22 52	3½	**3¾**	**11:14**	D	11:54	E	LEO	21
344	10	**A**	7:03	E	**4:12**	A	9 09	23	22 57	4½	**4¾**	—	–	**12:26**	D	LEO	22
345	11	M.	7:03	E	**4:12**	A	9 09	22	23 02	5½	**6**	12:19	D	**12:56**	D	VIR	23
346	12	Tu.	7:04	E	**4:12**	A	9 08	22	23 07	6½	**7**	1:22	D	**1:24**	C	VIR	24
347	13	W.	7:05	E	**4:12**	A	9 07	21	23 11	7½	**8**	2:23	E	**1:53**	C	VIR	25
348	14	Th.	7:06	E	**4:12**	A	9 06	21	23 14	8¼	**8¾**	3:23	E	**2:23**	C	LIB	26
349	15	Fr.	7:06	E	**4:12**	A	9 06	20	23 17	9	**9¾**	4:22	E	**2:55**	B	LIB	27
350	16	Sa.	7:07	E	**4:13**	A	9 06	20	23 20	9¾	**10¼**	5:20	E	**3:30**	B	SCO	28
351	17	**A**	7:08	E	**4:13**	A	9 05	19	23 22	10½	**11**	6:16	E	**4:09**	B	OPH	29
352	18	M.	7:08	E	**4:13**	A	9 05	19	23 23	11	**11¾**	7:09	E	**4:53**	B	SAG	0
353	19	Tu.	7:09	E	**4:14**	A	9 05	19	23 25	11¾	—	7:58	E	**5:41**	B	SAG	1
354	20	W.	7:10	E	**4:15**	A	9 05	18	23 25	12¼	**12¼**	8:43	E	**6:33**	B	SAG	2
355	21	Th.	7:10	E	**4:15**	A	9 05	18	23 26	1	**1**	9:24	E	**7:28**	B	CAP	3
356	22	Fr.	7:11	E	**4:16**	A	9 05	17	23 25	1½	**1¾**	10:01	E	**8:26**	C	CAP	4
357	23	Sa.	7:11	E	**4:16**	A	9 05	17	23 25	2¼	**2½**	10:34	E	**9:25**	C	CAP	5
358	24	**A**	7:11	E	**4:16**	A	9 05	16	23 23	3	**3¼**	11:05	D	**10:26**	D	AQU	6
359	25	M.	7:12	E	**4:17**	A	9 05	16	23 22	3¾	**4**	11:35	D	**11:29**	D	AQU	7
360	26	Tu.	7:12	E	**4:18**	A	9 06	15	23 20	4½	**4¾**	**12:04**	D	—	–	PSC	8
361	27	W.	7:12	E	**4:18**	A	9 06	15	23 17	5½	**5¾**	**12:34**	C	12:33	D	CET	9
362	28	Th.	7:13	E	**4:19**	A	9 06	14	23 14	6¼	**6¾**	**1:07**	C	1:40	E	PSC	10
363	29	Fr.	7:13	E	**4:20**	A	9 07	14	23 10	7¼	**7¾**	**1:44**	C	2:50	E	ARI	11
364	30	Sa.	7:13	E	**4:21**	A	9 08	13	23 06	8	**8¾**	**2:27**	B	4:02	E	TAU	12
365	31	**A**	7:13	E	**4:22**	A	9 09	13	23 s. 02	9	**9¾**	**3:18**	B	5:15	E	TAU	13

 To use this page, see p. 138 for Key Letters, see p. 252. ☞ **Bold = P.M.** ☞ Light = A.M.

DECEMBER HATH 31 DAYS • 2017

For a welcome guest is expected soon,
And he comes on the crest of the rising Moon. –J. T. Burton Wollaston

Day of Month	Day of Week	Dates, Feasts, Fasts, Aspects, Tide Heights	Weather
1	Fr.	National gas rationing began in U.S., 1942 • Tides {10.9 10.2	*So*
2	Sa.	**St. Viviana** • First televised human birth, Denver, Colo., 1952 • Tides {11.5 10.5	*many*
3	**A**	**1st S. of Advent** • **Full Cold** ○ • ☿ STAT. • Last run of *20th Century Limited* train, 1967	*feathers*
4	M.	☾ AT PERIG. • National Grange of the Order of Patrons of Husbandry founded, 1867 • {12.3 10.8	*in*
5	Tu.	☾ RIDES HIGH • *If wind rises at night, It will fall at daylight.* • Tides {12.3	*the*
6	W.	**St. Nicholas** • ☌☿♄ • Ship explosion devastated Halifax, N.S., 1917 • {10.8 12.1	*sky,*
7	Th.	**St. Ambrose** • **Nat'l Pearl Harbor Remembrance Day** • ☾ AT ☊ • {10.6 11.7	*there*
8	Fr.	Winterberry fruit especially showy now. • Tides {10.4 11.2	*must*
9	Sa.	Numismatic Society of Montreal formed, 1862 • {10.1 10.6	*be a*
10	**A**	**2nd S. of Advent** • Mississippi admitted to Union as 20th state, 1817	*pillow*
11	M.	☾ ON EQ. • British King Edward VIII abdicated throne to marry Wallis Simpson, 1936 • Tides {9.8 9.6	*fight*
12	Tu.	**Our Lady of Guadalupe** • **Chanukah begins at sundown** • ☿ IN INF. ☌ • {9.8 9.3	*going*
13	W.	**St. Lucia** • ☌♂☾ • *What has been, may be.* • {9.8 9.1	*on high!*
14	Th.	Halcyon Days begin. • ☌♃☾ • First recorded meteorite in New World fell, Weston, Conn., 1807	*Not*
15	Fr.	☌☿♀ • First rendezvous of two manned spacecraft, *Gemini 6* and *Gemini 7*, 1965 • {10.1 9.1	*much*
16	Sa.	Ice jam closed Ohio R. from Warsaw, Ky., to Rising Sun, Ind., 1917 • Tides {10.1 9.1	*of*
17	**A**	**3rd S. of Advent** • ☌☿☾ • ☌♀☾ • Tides {10.2 9.1	*a*
18	M.	**New** ● • ☾ AT APO. • ☌♄☾ • Film director Steven Spielberg born, 1946	*crowd*
19	Tu.	☾ RUNS LOW • ☌♇☾ • Beware the Pogonip. • Tides {10.2 —	*out—*
20	W.	Ember Day • 40° to 0°F drop froze chickens in their tracks, central Ill., 1836 • {9.1 10.1	*nobody's*
21	Th.	**St. Thomas** • **Winter Solstice** • ☌♄☉ • Tides {9.0 10.0	*plowed*
22	Fr.	Ember Day • ☾ AT ☋ • ☿ STAT. • Tides {9.0 9.8	*out!*
23	Sa.	Ember Day • Saturn moon Rhea discovered, 1672 • Transistor first demonstrated, 1947 • {8.9 9.6	*We're*
24	**A**	**4th S. of Advent** • ☌♆☾ • Actor Jack Klugman died, 2012	*asking*
25	M.	**Christmas** • ☌♀♄ • *A gift with a kind countenance is a double present.*	*Santa*
26	Tu.	**St. Stephen** • **Boxing Day (Canada)** • **First day of Kwanzaa** • ☾ ON EQ. • {9.2 9.1	*for*
27	W.	**St. John** • ☌♅☾ • Radio City Music Hall opened, N.Y.C., 1932 • Tides {9.5 9.1	*a*
28	Th.	**Holy Innocents** • U.S. vice president John C. Calhoun resigned, 1832 • Tides {9.9 9.3	*great*
29	Fr.	William Lyon Mackenzie King became prime minister of Canada, 1921 • Tides {10.4 9.5	*scene*
30	Sa.	Figure skater David Pelletier wed skating partner Jamie Salé, 2005	*in*
31	**A**	**1st S. af. Ch.** • Explorer Jacques Cartier born, 1491 • Tides {11.5 10.1	*2018!*

Farmer's Calendar

■ Temperatures falling, skies threatening, the dogs and I started our afternoon walk a little before 3:00, heading uphill. The plan was to follow the road all the way to the top.

It climbs sharply at the end, and the prospect is magnificent there. In addition to a broad view of the Wapack Range and a few buildings in Peterborough, there was light glinting off the waters of Thorndike Pond and steam rising from the match factory in Jaffrey.

By 4:00, we were in a field just beyond the last two houses on the road—summer places, to judge from the absence of cars and the window shades pulled down. Not surprising, really; the winter heating bills must be as spectacular as the view. Generally speaking, in this town the houses with the best views are unoccupied in December.

When we started home, we flushed a massive buck that bounded farther up the wooded hill, headed north. The dogs didn't see him—their vision is surprisingly poor—but they got wildly excited when they caught his scent at the point where he began his flight and started to tug frantically on their leashes. The dogs wanted to follow him into the forest.

So did I, but it was getting dark. There will be other opportunities to track deer when the light comes back.

Holidays and Observances

Federal holidays are listed in bold. **For Movable Religious Observances, see page 141.**

CALENDAR

Jan. 1	**New Year's Day**
Jan. 16	**Martin Luther King Jr.'s Birthday, observed**
Jan. 19	Robert E. Lee Day *(Fla., Ky.)*
Jan. 20	Inauguration Day
Feb. 2	Groundhog Day
Feb. 12	Abraham Lincoln's Birthday
Feb. 14	Valentine's Day
Feb. 15	Susan B. Anthony's Birthday *(Fla.)*
Feb. 20	**Presidents' Day**
Feb. 22	George Washington's Birthday
Feb. 28	Mardi Gras *(Baldwin & Mobile counties, Ala.; La.)*
Mar. 2	Texas Independence Day
Mar. 7	Town Meeting Day *(Vt.)*
Mar. 17	St. Patrick's Day Evacuation Day *(Suffolk Co., Mass.)*
Mar. 27	Seward's Day *(Alaska)*
Mar. 31	César Chávez Day
Apr. 3	Pascua Florida Day, observed
Apr. 17	Patriots Day *(Maine, Mass.)*
Apr. 21	San Jacinto Day *(Tex.)*
Apr. 22	Earth Day
Apr. 28	National Arbor Day
May 5	Cinco de Mayo
May 8	Truman Day *(Mo.)*
May 14	Mother's Day
May 20	Armed Forces Day
May 22	National Maritime Day Victoria Day *(Canada)*
May 29	**Memorial Day, observed**
June 5	World Environment Day
June 11	King Kamehameha I Day *(Hawaii)*
June 14	Flag Day
June 17	Bunker Hill Day *(Suffolk Co., Mass.)*
June 18	Father's Day
June 19	Emancipation Day *(Tex.)*
June 20	West Virginia Day
July 1	Canada Day
July 4	**Independence Day**
July 24	Pioneer Day *(Utah)*
Aug. 1	Colorado Day
Aug. 7	Civic Holiday *(parts of Canada)*
Aug. 16	Bennington Battle Day *(Vt.)*
Aug. 19	National Aviation Day
Aug. 26	Women's Equality Day
Sept. 4	**Labor Day**
Sept. 9	Admission Day *(Calif.)*
Sept. 10	Grandparents Day
Sept. 11	Patriot Day
Sept. 17	Constitution Day
Sept. 21	International Day of Peace
Oct. 2	Child Health Day
Oct. 9	**Columbus Day, observed** Native Americans' Day *(S.Dak.)* Leif Eriksson Day Thanksgiving Day *(Canada)*
Oct. 18	Alaska Day
Oct. 24	United Nations Day
Oct. 27	Nevada Day
Oct. 31	Halloween
Nov. 4	Will Rogers Day *(Okla.)*
Nov. 7	Election Day
Nov. 11	**Veterans Day** Remembrance Day *(Canada)*
Nov. 19	Discovery of Puerto Rico Day
Nov. 23	**Thanksgiving Day**
Nov. 24	Acadian Day *(La.)*
Dec. 7	National Pearl Harbor Remembrance Day
Dec. 15	Bill of Rights Day
Dec. 17	Wright Brothers Day
Dec. 25	**Christmas Day**
Dec. 26	Boxing Day *(Canada)* First day of Kwanzaa

Tidal Glossary

Apogean Tide: A monthly tide of decreased range that occurs when the Moon is at apogee (farthest from Earth).

Diurnal Tide: A tide with one high water and one low water in a tidal day of approximately 24 hours.

Mean Lower Low Water: The arithmetic mean of the lesser of a daily pair of low waters, observed over a specific 19-year cycle called the National Tidal Datum Epoch.

Neap Tide: A tide of decreased range that occurs twice a month, when the Moon is in quadrature (during its first and last quarters, when the Sun and the Moon are at right angles to each other relative to Earth).

Perigean Tide: A monthly tide of increased range that occurs when the Moon is at perigee (closest to Earth).

Semidiurnal Tide: A tide with one high water and one low water every half day. East Coast tides, for example, are semidiurnal, with two highs and two lows during a tidal day of approximately 24 hours.

Spring Tide: A tide of increased range that occurs at times of syzygy each month. Named not for the season of spring but from the German *springen* ("to leap up"), a spring tide also brings a lower low water.

Syzygy: The nearly straight-line configuration that occurs twice a month, when the Sun and the Moon are in conjunction (on the same side of Earth, at the new Moon) and when they are in opposition (on opposite sides of Earth, at the full Moon). In both cases, the gravitational effects of the Sun and the Moon reinforce each other, and tidal range is increased.

Vanishing Tide: A mixed tide of considerable inequality in the two highs and two lows, so that the lower high (or higher low) may appear to vanish. ■

Best Fishing Days and Times

The best times to fish are when the fish are naturally most active. The Sun, Moon, tides, and weather all influence fish activity. For example, fish tend to feed more at sunrise and sunset, and also during a full Moon (when tides are higher than average). However, most of us go fishing when we can get the time off, not because it is the best time. But there *are* best times, according to fishing lore:

The Best Fishing Days for 2017, when the Moon is between new and full:

- January 1–12
- January 27–February 10
- February 26–March 12
- March 27–April 11
- April 26–May 10
- May 25–June 9
- June 23–July 9
- July 23–August 7
- August 21–September 6
- September 20–October 5
- October 19–November 4
- November 18–December 3
- December 18–31

- **One hour before and one hour after high tides, and one hour before and one hour after low tides. (The times of high tides for Boston are given on pages 142–168; also see pages 250–251. Inland, the times for high tides correspond with the times when the Moon is due south. Low tides are halfway between high tides.)**
- During the "morning rise" (after sunup for a spell) and the "evening rise" (just before sundown and the hour or so after).
- **During the rise and set of the Moon.**
- When the barometer is steady or on the rise. (But even during stormy periods, the fish aren't going to give up feeding. The smart fisherman will find just the right bait.)
- **When there is a hatch of flies—caddis flies or mayflies, commonly.**
- When the breeze is from a westerly quarter, rather than from the north or east.
- **When the water is still or slightly rippled, rather than during a wind.**

How to Estimate the Weight of a Fish

Measure the fish from the tip of its nose to the tip of its tail. Then measure its girth at the thickest portion of its midsection.

The weight of a fat-bodied fish (bass, salmon) = (length x girth x girth)/800

The weight of a slender fish (trout, northern pike) = (length x girth x girth)/900

Example: If a fish is 20 inches long and has a 12-inch girth, its estimated weight is (20 x 12 x 12)/900 = 2,880/900 = 3.2 pounds

IN HIS OWN WORDS . . .

The Life and Times of Robert B. Thomas

In the 1833 Almanac, founder Robert Bailey Thomas began this "Concise Memoir of the Author and Editor of The (Old) Farmer's Almanac,*" installments of which were published over a span of 5 years.*

My grandfather, William Thomas, was a native of Wales (Eng.) and born there of an opulent family, and received a liberal education, at Christ's College, Cambridge. He emigrated to this country about 1718. He with other brothers came first to Stonington, Conn., then to Marlborough (Mass.) about the year 1720. He married Lydia Eager, a daughter of a respectable farmer of Shrewsbury, and resided in Marlborough until he died in 1733. Two years after which my grandmother died. He had two sons and four daughters.

My father, William, was the eldest son, born in Marlborough, March 1725. After his mother's death, my father went to Shrewsbury to live with his grandmother Eager, where he resided some years. He attended the town school in the winter, and being studious and fond of reading, purchased many books, and soon became quite a scholar for those days. In 1744, he commenced school keeping at Brookfield, at the age of 19 years, which he followed winters, for upward of 40 years.

In April 1747, he left for England to obtain a patrimony belonging to his father in Wales. On May 8th, he was taken by a French privateer out of Dunkirk and stripped of everything. He was ransomed, and arrived at Boston in October. In August 1749, he made another voyage to London and visited Wales, with the expectation of obtaining his right of inheritance. He was unsuccessful, due to the lapse of time since my grandfather left Wales.

In 1764, my father bought a small farm in Shrewsbury. In 1765, he married Azubah Goodale, daughter of Joseph Goodale, a farmer in Grafton, at whose house, the subject of these memoirs was born, April 24th, 1766.

I removed with my parents, while quite an infant, from Grafton to the farm in Shrewsbury, now West Boylston. The farm was in a district then known as Shrewsbury-leg. (It

I HAVE RESIDED IN FOUR TOWNS, TWO PARISHES, AND ONE PRECINCT, YET NEVER MOVED FROM THE SAME FARM.

is rather paradoxical, but no less a fact, that I have resided in four incorporated towns and two distinct parishes, and one precinct, yet never moved from the same farm.)

I had one brother only, born June 1768, named Aaron. In our youth, we were brought up to farming. Our father, who was thought to be quite a scholar for those days, instructed us at home and sent us to the winter school. In 1781, I lost my mother, who died in an apoplectic fit. My father married Esther Whitney, a maiden lady, in 1782, but had no issue.

In the winter of 1783–4, my father sent me to Spencer to improve my penmanship with Dr. I. Allen, who wrote the most beautiful and superior copy hand of any person in the country, and I much improved my handwriting. The succeeding winter, I was agreeably and closely occupied in the study of arithmetic, under my father's inspection, who was well versed in this science.

My father was a great reader and possessed a larger miscellaneous library than usually found in a country town. I spent most of my leisure hours in reading. Among many scientific works, no one engrossed more of my attention than *Ferguson's Astronomy*. From the study of this work, I first acquired

Illustration: *The Old Farmer's Almanac*, 1837

the idea of calculating an Almanack [sic]. Previously, I had made a number of calculations of new and full Moons, projected several eclipses, but found it impracticable to make all the necessary calculations for an Almanack. In 1786, I had an application to keep school in my native town. I returned home in April and worked on the farm through the summer.

In the fall of 1787, I had an invitation to keep school in Princeton. This I continued until the first of April 1788, when I returned to my father's in Sterling and continued on the farm through the summer. In the fall, I kept school in Sterling, where I spent one of the pleasantest winters of my life.

In April 1789, I returned to my father's and pursued my favourite study of astronomy, occasionally laboring on the farm, and busying myself with bookbinding—manuscripts, account books, and neighbors' old books.

I found, with all my reading, the want of practical knowledge of the calculations of an Almanack, which I could not obtain by reading—this was my hobby. In September, I journeyed into Vermont to see the then famous Dr. S. Sternes, who for many years calculated Isaiah Thomas's Massachusetts, Connecticut, Rhode Island, New Hampshire and Vermont Almanack, but failed to see him.

The next winter, I agreed to keep school in West Boylston but left it when I agreed to open a school in Sterling. It enjoyed the full tide of success for a few weeks, when all at once the whole school was taken down with the measles and [I] was dismissed.

I pursued my avocations through the summer. I arranged for a printer in Boston to print 1,000 of *Perry's Spelling Book,* which I bound, and other school books, and commenced [a] Bookseller business. There being few books in the country, I found good sales to the storekeepers, schoolmasters, etc.

Some time in the fall, I called on Isaiah Thomas of Worcester (no relation, as I know of) to purchase 100 of his Almanacks in sheets, but he refused to let me have them, saying he did not sell in sheets, only to those of the trade. I confess I was mortified and came home with a determination to have an Almanack of my own. I well knew that there were many things in his that were not generally approved of and which I knew I could remedy.

In the fall of 1790, I had a pressing invitation to keep school again in Boylston. I commenced my school in

I WELL KNEW THAT THERE WERE MANY THINGS IN HIS [ALMANAC] THAT WERE NOT GENERALLY APPROVED OF AND WHICH I KNEW I COULD REMEDY.

STILL I COULD NOT RELINQUISH THE IDEA OF PUBLISHING AN ALMANACK OF MY OWN.

the month of December and continued it through the winter.

In the spring of 1791, I returned home to my father's and pursued bookbinding, except a few weeks when I assisted in hay-making. Early in the fall, I had several applications to keep school, but I gave no encouragement to any applicant till at last one of the school committee in Princeton agreed to postpone the school until January 1, 1792. At which time I commenced my school and boarded with Capt. Allen and his family. While there, I formed an acquaintance in a family of which, some years afterwards, I married one of the daughters.

After finishing my school, I returned to my father's in April, with a full determination never to resume it again. The business never was very congenial to my feelings; I had pursued it for want of some better employment. I had now made up my mind to follow the binding business. My brother, whose health was not good, concluded to go into business with me. We contracted a carpenter to build us a bindery and store adjoining my father's house. Still I could not relinquish the idea of publishing an Almanack of my own.

The last of June or the first of July 1792, I went to Boston and arranged with Osgood Carlton, then a teacher of mathematics, to instruct me in astronomy as related to calculating an Almanack. This he readily consented to do, for a stipulated consideration.

I continued at Mr. Carlton's school till the latter part of August, and made all the calculations for an Almanack for the year 1793. Before I left town, I disposed of my copy to two young printers for a certain percentage on all those that should be sold.

In justice to myself, I ought to state that my likeness is inserted in this number of the Almanack at the special desire of my publishers.

–R.B.T.

AFTERWORD

The Farmer's Almanac by Robert B. Thomas, a book of 48 pages, was an immediate success. Circulation of its second edition tripled from 3,000 to 9,000 copies. Thomas remained the editor until his death at age 80 in 1846, supposedly while reading proofs for the 1847 edition.

By then, his was the oldest almanac in the country. This fact inspired Thomas's successor, John H. Jenks, to add the word "Old" to the title, forever distinguishing this publication from common forms of the genre. Today, *The Old Farmer's Almanac* stands as the oldest continuously published periodical in North America. ■

[N°. I.]

THE

FARMER's ALMANAC,

CALCULATED ON A NEW AND IMPROVED PLAN,

FOR THE YEAR OF OUR LORD

1793:

Being the first after Leap Year, and seventeenth of the Independence *of* America.

Fitted to the town of BOSTON, but will serve for any of the adjoining States.

Containing, besides the large number of ASTRONOMICAL CALCULATIONS and FARMER'S CALENDAR for every month in the year, as great a variety as are to be found in any other Almanac, *Of* NEW, USEFUL, *and* ENTERTAINING MATTER.

BY ROBERT B. THOMAS.

"While the bright radient sun in centre glows,
The earth, in annual motion round it goes;
At the same time on its own axis reels,
And gives us change of seasons as it wheels."

Published according to Act of Congress.

PRINTED AT THE Apollo Press, IN BOSTON,
BY BELKNAP AND HALL,
Sold at their Office, State Street; also, by the *Author* and *M. Smith*, *Sterling*.
[*Sixpence single*, 4*s*. *per dozen*, 40*s*. *per groce.*]

P R E F A C E.

FRIENDLY READER,

HAD it not been the prevailing cuſtom to uſher theſe periodical pieces into the world by a preface, I would have excuſed myſelf the trouble of writing, and you of reading one to this: for if it be well executed, a preface will add nothing to its merit; if otherwiſe, it will be far from ſupplying its defects.

Having, for ſeveral years paſt, paid ſome attention to that divine ſcience, *Aſtronomy*, the ſtudy of which muſt afford infinite pleaſure and ſatisfaction to every contemplative mind, it is this, with the repeated ſolicitations of my friends, that have induced me to preſent you with theſe Aſtronomical Calculations for the year 1793; which I have thought proper to entitle the *Famer's Almanac*, as I have made it my principal aim to make it as uſeful as poſſible to that claſs of people: Therefore, ſhould there be any thing in it that may appear of ſmall moment, it is hoped the *Literati* will excuſe it.

The arrangement of this Almanac is novel, though I have the vanity to believe it will be found to be as uſeful and convenient as any other almanac either of a double or ſingle calendar. I have taken peculiar care to make the calculations accurate in every reſpect; and beſide the more than uſual aſtronomical calculations, I have added the riſing, ſetting, or ſouthing of the ſeven ſtars, for every evening through the year. As to my judgment of the weather, I need ſay but little; for you will in one year's time, without any aſſiſtance of mine, very eaſily diſcover how near I have come to the truth. And now, friendly reader, this being only an eſſay, which, ſhould it meet the Public's unprejudiced approbation, you may expect to hear again from your's, and the Public's

Moſt obedient humble ſervant,

Sterling, Sept. 15. ROBERT B. THOMAS.

R E C I P E S.

To cure a pimpled FACE, *and ſweeten the* BLOOD.

TAKE jena, one ounce; put it in a ſmall ſtone pot, and pour a quart or more of boiling water on it; then put as many prunes as you can get in, cover it with paper and ſet it in the oven with houſehold bread; and take of this every day, one, two, three or more of the prunes and liquor, according as it operates; continue this at leaſt half a year.

For CORNS *on the Feet.*

TAKE the yeaſt of beer, and ſpread it on a linen rag, and apply it to the part affected ; renew it once a day for three or four weeks ; it will cure.

To cure the TOOTH-ACHE.

LET the perſon that is troubled with the tooth-ache, lay on the contrary ſide, drop three drops of the juice of rue into the ear, on that ſide the teeth acheth ; let it remain an hour or two, and it will remove the pain.

To take off FRECKLES.

TAKE bean flower-water, or elder flower-water, or May dew, gathered from corn, of either, the quantity of four ſpoonfuls, and add to it one ſpoonful of oil of tartar ; mix it well together, and often waſh the face with it, and let it dry on.

To take out Spots of the SMALL POX.

TAKE half an ounce of the oil of tartar, and as much oil of bitter almonds ; mix them together, and with a fine rag apply it often to the face and hands, before the air penetrates into the ſkin.

FRIENDS' ANNUAL MEETINGS.

THE yearly meetings at Rhode-Iſland, beginning at Portſmouth, is on the 5th day before the 2d, 6th day of the 6th month ; compoſed of three quarterly meetings, which go by the name of Rhode-Iſland, Salem and Sandwich. Rhode-Iſland quarter is held on the 5th day before the 2d, 6th day of the 1ſt month, at Providence. In the 4th month, at Eaſt Greenwich. In the 7th month, at Dartmonth. Salem quarterly meeting is held at Seabrook, on on the 7th day, before the 4th, 1ſt day of the 1ſt month. At Salem, the 1ſt, 6th day of the 6th month. At Falmouth, on the 7th day before the 4th, 1ſt day of the 9th month. And at Dover, the 7th day before the 4th, 1ſt day of the 10th month. Sandwich quarter is held at Falmouth on the 2d, 6th day of the 12th month. At Sandwich, the 6th day before the laſt, firſt day in the 3d month. At Nantucket, the 3d day after the 4th, 6th day in the 6th month. And at Long Plain, the 7th day before 2d, 6th day in the 10th month.

1793. JANUARY hath 31 Days.

ASTRONOMICAL CALCULATIONS.

	Days.	☉	Days.	☉	Days.	☉
☉ place.	1	♑ 11 39	13	♑ 23 53	25	♒ 6 6
	3	13 41	15	25 55	27	8 7
	5	15 44	17	27 57	29	10 9
	7	17 46	19	♒ 0 0	31	12 11
	9	19 48	21	2 2		
	11	21 51	23	4 4		

☾ Last quarter 5 day, 8h. 14m. morning.
○ New moon 12 day, 4h. 15m. morning.
☽ First quarter 18 day, 9h. 45m. evening.
● Full moon 26 day, 10h. 50m. evening.

M. D.	W. D.	☉ rises & sets	L. D.	☉ S	● A	F. sea.	● place	● rise & set.	● so. H. M.	7*s sout.
1	Tues.	7 31 5	8 58	4	19	2 12	belly	8 57	2 57	8 40
2	Wedn.	7 31 5	8 58	4	20	2 55	belly	9 54	3 40	8 36
3	Thurs.	7 30 5	9 0	5	21	3 38	belly	10 52	4 23	8 31
4	Friday	7 30 5	9 0	5	22	4 21	reins	11 52	5 6	8 27
5	Satur.	7 29 5	9 2	6	23	5 6	reins	morn.	5 51	8 23
6	SUN.	7 28 5	9 4	6	24	5 52	secrets	0 54	6 37	8 18
7	Mond.	7 28 5	9 4	7	25	6 40	secrets	1 57	7 25	8 14
8	Tues.	7 27 5	9 6	7	26	7 32	secrets	3 3	8 17	8 10
9	Wedn.	7 26 5	9 8	8	27	8 28	thighs	4 8	9 13	8 5
10	Thurs.	7 26 5	9 8	8	28	9 27	thighs	5 13	10 12	8 1
11	Friday	7 25 5	9 10	8	29	10 28	knees	6 14	11 13	7 56
12	Satur.	7 24 5	9 12	9	○	even.	knees	☽ sets	even.	7 52
13	SUN.	7 23 5	9 14	9	1	0 31	legs	6 33	1 16	7 48
14	Mond.	7 23 5	9 14	10	2	1 29	legs	7 47	2 14	7 43
15	Tues.	7 22 5	9 16	10	3	2 24	feet	8 58	3 9	7 39
16	Wedn.	7 21 5	9 18	10	4	3 17	feet	10 4	4 2	7 35
17	Thurs.	7 20 5	9 20	11	5	4 7	head	11 16	4 52	7 31
18	Friday	7 19 5	9 22	11	6	4 55	head	morn.	5 40	7 26
19	Satur.	7 18 5	9 24	11	7	5 43	neck	0 20	6 28	7 22
20	SUN.	7 17 5	9 26	12	8	6 31	neck	1 22	7 16	7 18
21	Mond.	7 16 5	9 28	12	9	7 18	arms	2 21	8 3	7 14
22	Tues.	7 15 5	9 30	12	10	8 6	arms	3 19	8 51	7 10
23	Wedn.	7 14 5	9 32	12	11	8 54	arms	4 14	9 39	7 5
24	Thurs.	7 13 5	9 34	13	12	9 42	breast	5 4	10 27	7 1
25	Friday	7 12 5	9 36	13	13	10 29	breast	5 52	11 14	6 57
26	Satur.	7 11 5	9 38	13	●	11 15	heart	● rise	12 0	6 53
27	SUN.	7 10 5	9 40	13	15	12 0	heart	5 48	morn.	6 49
28	Mond.	7 9 5	9 42	13	16	morn.	heart	6 42	0 45	6 45
29	Tues.	7 8 5	9 44	14	17	0 45	belly	7 38	1 30	6 41
30	Wedn.	7 7 5	9 46	14	18	1 28	belly	8 38	2 13	6 37
31	Thurs.	7 5 5	9 50	14	19	2 11	reins	9 35	2 56	6 33

1793. JANUARY, firſt Month.

The new year opens—old is paſt,
Stern winter comes with its rough blaſt :
See the farmer ſhivering with cold,
Driving his flocks and herds to fold.

	Days of the Month.				
Tueſday	1	8	15	22	29
Wedneſday	2	9	16	23	30
Thurſday	3	10	17	24	31
Friday	4	11	18	25	
Saturday	5	12	19	26	
SUNDAY	6	13	20	27	
Monday	7	14	21	28	

M. D.	Calendar, Courts, Aſpects, Weather, &c.	FARMER'S CALENDAR.
1	Circumciſion. CP. Boſton,	Look to your barns and ſee that
2	*Cold* [Newglouc. Lenox	your cattle are well ſerved.
3	Lions H. riſes 8, 6 *and froſty*	See that your fattening cattle
4	Sir I. Newt. b. 1643. *weather*	have not too much given them
5	Low tides. *Cold winds.*	at once.
6	2d paſt Chriſtmas. Epiph.	Cut timber, if you wiſh to have
7	*Looks like*	it laſt long, it being the beſt
8	Lucin. CP. Hallowell.	time in the year.
9	*ſnow.*	Improve ſledding, while it is
10	*Bluſtering weather.*	good, and get your ſupply of
11	High tides.	wood for the ſummer, for it is a
12	*Moderate* ☿ Stat. ☽ Perigee.	chance if you have a better time
13	1ſt paſt Epiph. *weather.*	this winter.
14	Peace ratif. by Con. 1784.	Viſit your corn barns and gra-
15	CP. Springf. ✱ ☉ ♃ □ ☉ ♄	neries ; ſee that rats and mice
16	*Cold but pleaſant.*	don't deſtroy your grain.
17	Dr. Frankl. b. in Boſt. 1706.	Look well to your cattle, and
18	Low tides. ✱ ♄ ♂	ſee that they are kept clean.
19	*Cold and clear.*	Remember your bees, and if
20	2d paſt Epi. K. Spain b. 1716	weak, feed them with cakes made
21	*Windy*	of malt flour, mixed up with
22	*weather.*	ſweet wort ; or give them brown
23	*Clear*	ſugar ; and once and a while ſalt
24	Middling tides. *and cold.*	and water, to keep them from
25	Converſion of St. Paul.	ſcouring.
26	*Now* ☽ Apogee.	Kill your winter pork and beef,
27	Septuag. *expect*	if you wiſh to have it ſwell a
28	Peter the Great died, 1725.	cooking.
29	*ſnow or rain.*	Feed your doves, and ſpread
30	K. Charl. I. beheaded, 1648.	aſhes among their dung.
31	*Bluſtering weather.*	Burn or ſweep your chimnies.

PEOPLE OFTEN ASK HOW AND WHY THIS ALMANAC HAS LASTED. HERE'S THE ANSWER.

225 Years of Love, Luck, and Tradition

1792: Robert Bailey Thomas publishes *The Farmer's Almanac* for 1793, "containing as great a variety as any other Almanac of new, useful, and entertaining matter."

1803: After a courtship of 13 years, Thomas marries Hannah Beaman.

1815: Thomas is ill with influenza. His Boston printers send a boy to his bedside in Sterling, Mass., for the July weather forecast. "Tell the printer to print anything he wishes," he tells the boy. Thus, the printer sets "Rain, Hail, and Snow" for July 13, 1816. When Thomas recovers, he is furious and tries to call in every single printed sheet.

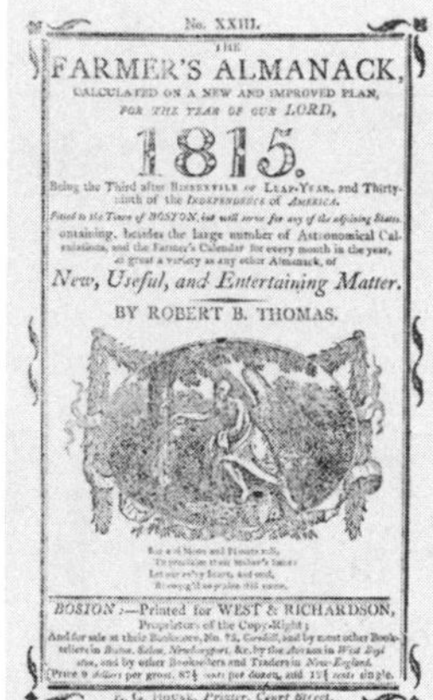

No. XXIII.

THE FARMER'S ALMANACK, CALCULATED ON A NEW AND IMPROVED PLAN, FOR THE YEAR OF OUR LORD,

1815.

Being the Third after BISSEXTILE or LEAP-YEAR, and Thirty-ninth of the INDEPENDENCE of AMERICA.

Fitted to the Town of BOSTON, but will serve for any of the adjoining States.

Containing, besides the large number of Astronomical Calculations, and the Farmer's Calendar for every month in the year, as great a variety as any other Almanack, of

New, Useful, and Entertaining Matter.

BY ROBERT B. THOMAS.

BOSTON:—Printed for WEST & RICHARDSON, Proprietors of the Copy-Right; And for sale at their Bookstore, No. 75, Cornhill, and by most other Booksellers in Boston, Salem, Newburyport, &c. by the Author in West Boylston, and by other Booksellers and Traders in New-England.

Price 9 dollars per gross, 87½ cents per dozen, and 12½ cents single.

E. G. HOUSE, Printer, Court Street.

However, a few escape. When, in July 1816, rain, hail, and snow do fall, people experience "the year without a summer" and Thomas's Almanac moves into the supremacy it has held ever since.

1829: Thomas writes, "Our main endeavor is to be useful, with a pleasant degree of humor."

1832: "(Old)" appears in the title. "Our long and continued endeavors to be useful and to please have been crowned with unprecedented success," writes Thomas.

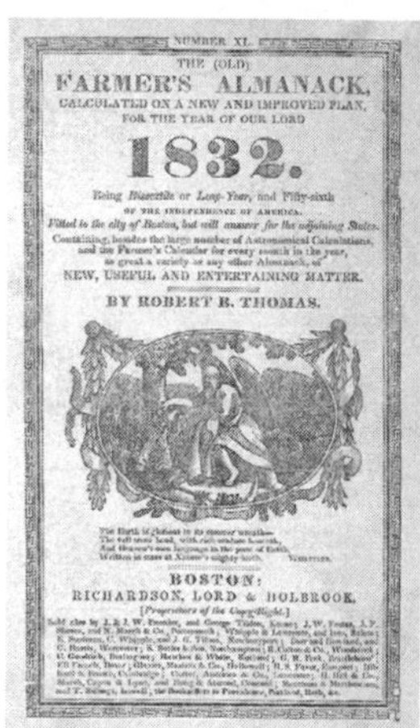

NUMBER XL.

THE (OLD) FARMER'S ALMANACK, CALCULATED ON A NEW AND IMPROVED PLAN, FOR THE YEAR OF OUR LORD

1832.

Being Bissextile or Leap-Year, and Fifty-sixth OF THE INDEPENDENCE OF AMERICA.

Fitted to the city of Boston, but will answer for the adjoining States.

Containing, besides the large number of Astronomical Calculations, and the Farmer's Calendar for every month in the year, as great a variety as any other Almanack, of

NEW, USEFUL AND ENTERTAINING MATTER.

BY ROBERT B. THOMAS.

BOSTON:

RICHARDSON, LORD & HOLBROOK.

[Proprietors of the Copy-Right.]

1836: "(Old)" disappears from the title, without comment from Thomas.

Editor's note: Most items are excerpted from an edition's "To Patrons." Others are from archives.

1847: With "deep and heartfelt regret," Almanac publishers announce the passing of Robert B. Thomas on May 19, 1846, at age 80: "Prior to Mr. T's death, arrangements were made to continue the Almanac through the present century, at least."

1848: "(Old)" is restored to the title, distinguishing it from any competition.

1851: The cover bears an image of the four seasons from a wood engraving image by Henry Nichols, with a medallion framing the portraits of Benjamin Franklin and Robert B. Thomas on a yellow background.

1853: A new engraving of Father Time appears on the frontispiece; astrological signs appear on Calendar Pages.

1858: Abraham Lincoln defends a man accused of murder. The killing, by "slungshot," allegedly occurred in the Moon's light on August 29, 1857. Citing the Almanac's Right-Hand Calendar Page for that day, Lincoln wins an acquittal by noting that his client could not have been identified because the Moon "ran low" and thus was not high enough to cast much light. The Almanac is the only one that year to indicate days on which the Moon "runs low."

1862–66: A "chronological record of events connected with the rise and progress of the rebellion against the national government [the Civil War] commencing November 1860, [appears] in the Calendar Pages" and continues through the conflict.

D. M.	D. W.	Aspects, Holidays, Events, Weather, &c.
1	Sa.	☌ ☿ ☉ Sup. L. ti. { Josi. Quincy d., '64.
2	A.	3d S. after Trin. ☌ ♄ ☾.
3	Mo.	{ 1st, 2d, and 3d. Bat. of Gettysburg, Pa., '63. *Now*
4	Tu.	{ Vicksburg surrendered, '63. *look out*
5	W.	{ Battle of Smithsburg, Va., '63. Bat. of Lebanon, Ky., '63.
6	Th.	☌ ♃ ☾. { G. P. Morris d., '64. 8th. Bat. Hagerst., Md., '63.
7	Fr.	☾ r. low. { Bat. of Williamsp., Md., and Cumberl., Ky., '63.
8	Sa.	☿ gr. hel. lat. N. { Pt. Hudson surr., '63.
9	A.	4th S. after Trin. H. tides.
10	Mo.	{ Morris Island, Charleston harbor, S. C., attacked, '63. *for*
11	Tu.	{ 10th. Bat. of Sharpsburg, Md., '63. *rain.*
12	W.	{ 13th. Riot in New York to resist draft, '63. *Warm,*
13	Th.	♆ sta. ☾ in Perigee.
14	Fr.	☌ ♆ ☾. { Confed. forces under Bragg ret. from Chattanooga, '63.
15	Sa.	□ ♄ ☉. { Jackson, Miss., evac. by rebs, '63. L. ti.
16	A.	5th S. af. Tr. ♀ gr. el. W.
17	Mo.	{ Steamer arr. at N. O. fr. St. Louis, opening trade of the Mississippi, '63.
18	Tu.	☌ ♀ ☾. { Att. on Ft. Wagner, S. C., 1863. *for*
19	W.	{ 18th. Bat. of Honey Springs In. Ter., '63. *haymaking.*
20	Th.	☌ ♅ ☾. ☾ r. hi. *Changea-*
21	Fr.	♀ gr. hel. lat. S. *ble, with*

1910: A blank page for note-taking is bound between Calendar Pages.

(continued)

1922: "An almanac is a record and reminder of the flight of time and the passage of the seasons."

1932: A hole is punched in the corner. (Until now, readers made their own hole.)

New England's Most Beloved Citizen

DURING its entire life of 142 years, THE OLD FARMER'S ALMANAC has never before published a photograph. But this year, of all years, it seems fitting that we pay a tribute to New England's most distinguished and honored son, for since our last issue he was taken from us.

The above photograph of Calvin Coolidge is the favorite photograph of his beloved wife, Grace Coolidge, who graciously selected it for this issue of The Old Farmer's Almanac.

1934: A photograph first appears in the Almanac—that of Calvin Coolidge, "New England's most distinguished and honored son," to mark his passing on January 5, 1933.

1938: Editor Roger Scaife omits weather forecasts; circulation falls below 80,000, from a peak of 450,000.

1938: President Franklin D. Roosevelt writes: "The Almanac is an invaluable friend, companion, and guide."

1939: Robb Sagendorph, founder of Yankee Publishing in Dublin, New Hampshire, and editor/publisher of *Yankee* magazine, acquires the Almanac from Little, Brown & Co. over a quick lunch and a "couple of martinis." As the Almanac's 11th editor, he sets about "reestablishing Robert B. Thomas in policy and in fact. Beginning in 1941, his original ideas shall be our guideposts."

1942: On June 12, minutes before midnight in thick fog near Amagansett, Long Island, N.Y., U.S. Coast Guardsman John C. Cullen on beach patrol comes upon German spies who had been dispatched from a submarine. Eventually, the spies are captured, and one

is found to have a copy of the 1942 Almanac in his pocket. The U.S. Office of Censorship believes that the enemy is getting weather forecasts from the Almanac—raising the possibility that it might be banned. Although Sagendorph believes that the Germans used the Almanac for

Moon phases (it was new on June 12) and tides (high on that day at 10:30 P.M.)—not weather forecasts—he agrees to change the Almanac cover line from weather "forecasts" to "indications" and publishes weather proverbs, thus maintaining the Almanac's record of continuous publication.

1942: Instead of Length of Day, Calendar Pages predict Length of Twilight, "useful for 'Dimouts' and 'Blackouts,' for telling children when to come home, and for calling in the cattle." Readers, left to calculate day length, are not pleased.

1943: Length of Day is reinstated, and a Twilight table is introduced.

1944: "With the Almanac staff at present in the armed forces or in war service, this edition [was] born in the all too few hours of evenings and Sundays . . . in candlelight."

1946: The Almanac cover reads: "God speed you home soldier." "To Patrons" offers "prayers of thanks" to our armed forces.

1950: "During the past year, the Almanac's headquarters were moved from rented space on the so-called Democratic side of Dublin's village street to its own permanent building on the Republican side."

1951: A Weather Table advises on using Calendar Page forecasts "as a rough rule of thumb": "subtract one day for each time zone west of the Hudson [River] to compensate for the easterly path of continental storms. For every 100 miles north or south of 42 degrees latitude, add a 5 degree temperature (colder if north, warmer if south) differential, and for every 1,000 feet above sea level, consider your locality as 5 degrees cooler than the weather as given."

1956: A woodcut image of Father Time created for the 1809 edition by Abel Bowen, "Boston's first professional woodcut artist," appears on page 1. Bowen's "work in the OFA antedates all other woodcuts revealed in any other almanac today."

1957: "Last year's edition again enjoyed the largest paid almanac newsstand sales in the world."

(continued)

1962: "Original portraits of the founder and his wife, painted by an itinerant artist about 1825, are now on display in an annex to these offices, which has been restored as a museum pertaining to this Almanac. It is open to visitors and for a 'potluck' luncheon on any working day."

1963: The November Farmer's Calendar essay reads "Night is coming on—and murder, perhaps" adjacent to day 22. At the bottom of the page appears "Two full moons this month—Guard against crime." John F. Kennedy is assassinated on the 22nd. Lee Harvey Oswald is killed on the 24th.

1964: "A gift [is] made by us, and accepted by Mrs. Jacqueline Kennedy, of this Almanack's [sic] issues from 1793 through 1808 for the White House library. As the first issue of the Almanac was published in 1792 for the year 1793, and the White House was built in 1792, the two may be said to be of exact age."

1967: Weather forecasts appear for five U.S. climatic regions: New England, Eastern States, Midwestern States, Western and Mountain States, Southern States.

1969: Solar scientist Dr. Richard Head, former chief scientist for NASA, begins making Almanac weather predictions.

1970: Editor Robb Sagendorph passes away on July 4, after completing the 1971 Left- and Right-Hand Calendar Pages. Jud Hale becomes editor of the Almanac and *Yankee* magazine.

1973: Weather forecast regions increase to 16, pages increase to 176, and price increases from 50¢ to 60¢.

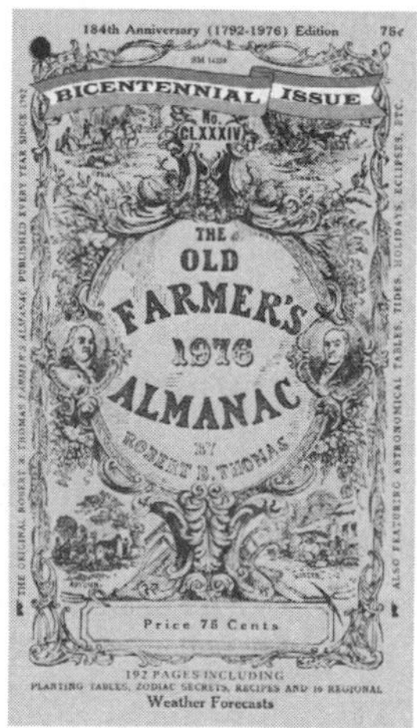

1976: For the U.S. bicentennial, the cover boasts a red, white, and blue banner.

1977: The Gardening Calendar begins its run as the (still) longest-selling retail

calendar in North America. A variety of Almanac-theme calendars follow.

1980: The Almanac page size increases to its current dimensions.

1981: *CBS Morning News* host Charles Kuralt salutes the 1982 edition on air: "Some people read it for its weather forecasts, planting tables, recipes, secrets of the zodiac, phases of the Moon. I like the ads, myself. These ads speak to the real America. The one that is worried about its false teeth falling out or its pants falling down. *The Old Farmer's Almanac* offers remedies for aching feet. That's why it's lasted for 190 years."

1982: A Canadian edition is launched, with astronomical and tide times set to Ottawa and national weather forecasts and feature stories.

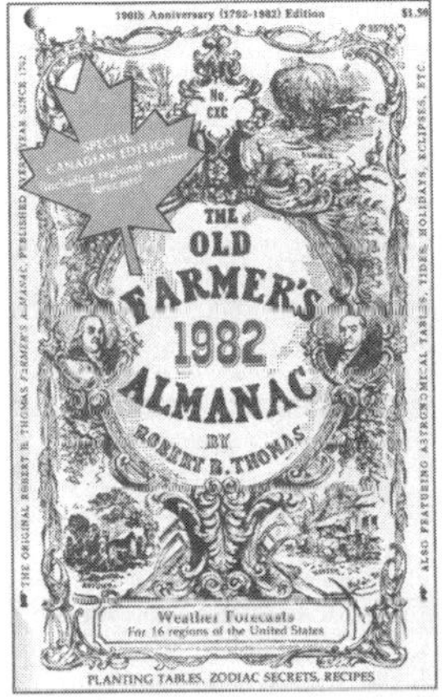

1984: "Careful observation of Nature's ways, on which many of this Almanac's predictions are based, is no longer considered a foolish method for looking ahead in time."

1985: "With the help of a few 'rooster pills' from time to time, we hope to go on forever . . ."

1986: *Good Morning America* host David Hartman asks editor Jud Hale on air, "Why should I put down this morning's *New York Times* and pick up *The Old Farmer's Almanac?"* and then answers himself: "It provides perspective, doesn't it? It has a way of placing this morning's news in perspective."

1987: The Almanac "contains more pages than any other"—232. "The success of this publication is a combination of good luck, a comforting sense of tradition, and continuity engendered by our very reappearance each fall."

1989: A survey says that 9 million people read the Almanac each year.

1991: A Western edition is launched, with astronomical and tide times set to San Francisco.

1992: President George H. W. Bush writes, "The Almanac could well be described as 'the journal of American tradition.' [It] is as relevant today as it was 200 years ago, underscoring the lasting value of traditional wisdom."

1993: "This edition [is] the first of our third century."

1994: A Southern edition is launched, with astronomical times set to Atlanta and southern tides.

1995: "A good number of letters received last year—and every year—are addressed to Robert B. Thomas, who has, of course, been resting peacefully in the cemetery at Sterling, Massachusetts, for almost 150 years. But no matter."

Michael Steinberg begins weather predictions.

1996: Almanac.com is launched. Today, the site has an average of 10 million page views every month.

1998: "We wish to thank John T. O'Malley of Sterling, Massachusetts, for instigating and overseeing (completely as a labor of love) the restoration of the gravestone of our founder, Robert B. Thomas."

1999: "Maybe the secret to our longevity has been that, in some ways, we have never been 'old.' "

2001: In keeping with tradition, the 2002 edition goes on sale on the second Tuesday in September: the 11th. After the tragic events of that day, on-sale dates move to August.

2005: The first edition of *The Old Farmer's Almanac Garden Guide,* a colorful annual magazine, appears.

2005: The full-color, undated, biannual *Old Farmer's Almanac for Kids* debuts, and "Kids can't put it down,

parents can't wait to pick it up." Volume 7 will go on sale in August 2017.

2009: The Almanac becomes available as a digital book.

2010: The Almanac joins Facebook; in 2016, it has 1.4 million friends. Activity on Twitter, Pinterest, Instagram, Google+, and Tumblr follows.

2015: Almanac.com goes mobile to phones and tablets.

2017: This year marks the Almanac's 225th edition, thanks to generations of fans and enthusiasts. ■

–compiled by Janice Stillman

In 2000, Janice Stillman became the 13th editor of *The Old Farmer's Almanac.*

A Colorful Collection of Candid Commentaries by 21st-Century Celebrities

Written specifically for this milestone edition of The Old Farmer's Almanac *and presented on these pages uncensored.*

Editor's note: We asked everyone the following questions . . .

1. Apart from *The Old Farmer's Almanac,* what one thing do you hope or feel will not change in the next 225 years?

2. What, in your opinion, most needs to change in the next 225 years?

3. Some people say that you can forecast the weather by checking the color of turkey bones or observing squirrels or woolly worms. Other than the app on your smartphone, what is your personal method of forecasting the weather?

4. In your opinion, what is America's greatest strength? And what is our greatest weakness?

5. What is your favorite part of *The Old Farmer's Almanac?* The most useful? Most useless?

JOHN W. BOYD JR.

Farmer, president of National Black Farmers Association

1. I hope the need for American agriculture and our ability to help feed the world will never diminish.

2. We will need more young farmers.

3. My grandfather, Thomas Boyd, said to watch the Moon. It will always tell the weather and when to plant your crops. We always plant on a full Moon.

4. Our strength is our ability to produce food at a mass volume. Political division is our weakness.

5. Most useful, the upcoming year's

Photo: Alex Brandon/AP Images

weather. Most useless, the Almanac comes out once a year. I would like to see a by-the-season Almanac.

TOM BROKAW

TV journalist and author

1. The manifest natural wonders of Mother Earth: the bountiful land, the rich variety of wildlife, the waters—salt and fresh—and clean air. Mankind has no greater obligation than to protect and wisely manage all that makes our lives possible and worthwhile.

2. The inability of nations, races, religions, and economic interests to solve differences peacefully.

3. Checking the cloud patterns.

4. Our greatest strength is that our continent is so vast and rich in natural resources that it can support a large immigrant population century after century.

5. The quirky small items that contain a large dose of practical wisdom.

DAN BROWN

Author

1. Our love of reading.

2. Our respect for planet Earth.

3. To predict the severity of the coming winter, I use the equation S = A/M, where inches of snowfall (S) is equal to the total number of buried acorns (A) divided by the month (M) during which the squirrels first start burying them.

4. Our strength is our capacity for creativity. Our weakness, our capacity for intolerance.

5. My favorite part is the puzzles section. The most useful part, "Advice: Living Naturally" is most useful. The least useful part, the zodiac.

KEN GLOSS

Proprietor, Brattle Book Shop, Boston, Massachusetts

1. Reading and the seeking out of knowledge.

2. Improved education for all.

3. Red sky at night / sailor's delight / Red sky in morning / sailor's warning. My wife saw a beautiful red sky on the morning of the blizzard of 1978. She moved her car away from the sea wall in Winthrop, Massachusetts, and got a hotel room in Boston before the storm started.

4. America's strength is its people. Prejudice against anything that is different is its weakness.

5. Folklore and advice. I enjoy looking through old issues back to the 1700s and seeing how some things are the same.

NICHOLAS KRISTOF

Journalist, author, winner of two Pulitzer Prizes

1. I hope that America's great natural beauty will be unchanged for the

Photos, clockwise from left: Wikimedia; Wikimedia; courtesy of Brattle Book Shop

next couple of centuries. Nature has a beauty that (I hope) won't fade!

2. I'd like to see a more equal society, with every kid getting more equal access to the starting line.

3. I look at the sky. And guess.

4. America's greatest strength has been its lack of classes, its willingness to accept immigrants. Its weakness today is that its education system hasn't kept pace.

5. I love the long-range weather forecasts, and they would also be the most useful part of the Almanac—if I believed them, which I don't particularly!

JOHN MCEUEN

Author, musician, a founding member of the Nitty Gritty Dirt Band

1. The effects of live music on people as it brings them together and the appreciation of art as an expression of our lives and the world's people.

2. The control of the monetary system by private banks. We need more involvement from the taxpayers to avoid senseless conflicts that are often years later determined to have been misguided and a waste of lives, and to have made some factions a lot of money.

3. I look at the weather map and try to determine into what type of weather I may be heading (I perform in 120 cities a year). At home, I watch a weather channel, and then stick my arm outside. If it is feeling cold, I look at my outside cat to see if it is in its little house yet. If it is, I grab a coat.

4. America's strength is its cultural diversity and incredible variety of natural resources. Its weakness is the corporate and personal misuse of those natural resources.

5. It always feels like I am opening a time capsule, but the Almanac is current and has so many relevant facts about weather and life, presented in an easy-to-follow fashion. In that respect, it is comforting and fun to read.

BILL MCKIBBEN

Environmentalist; Schumann Distinguished Scholar, Middlebury College

1. I badly fear that our climate will change in devastating ways. My great hope is that our nations will rise to the occasion and keep it from happening.

2. We've got to stop using fossil fuel and power our lives in other ways: sun, wind, water.

3. Forget forecasting. I can actually make it rain simply by scheduling a picnic.

4. I think it's crazy how unequal our society is, but as someone who grew up in Lexington, Massachusetts, I'm always certain that it's possible for us to (peacefully) change the existing order of things.

Photos, clockwise from top left: Wikimedia; Wikimedia; courtesy of John McEuen

5. Um, I'm a big eater. I like the recipes.

DAVID G. MUGAR

Chairman & CEO, Mugar Enterprises Inc.; philanthropist

1. I hope the United States will still be celebrating Independence Day on July Fourth. I also hope that the Boston celebration on the Esplanade with the concert and fireworks over the Charles River lives on.

2. I truly hope we are not overtaken by technology and resume human contact and face-to-face communication. Texting, tweeting, etc., must go.

3. Weather moves in many cycles. I pay close attention to some of them and always remember: Generally, things average out. Most every year, the temperature is within a couple of degrees of the prior year.

4. America's abundance of food production from farms to factories is huge. We are also blessed that we border both the Atlantic and Pacific oceans.

5. Most useful is the nail hole and certainly the Calendar Pages. Some of the General Store ads are amusing.

JODI PICOULT

Author

1. The small-town feel of New England. I travel all over the country as part of my work, and there are, well, a lot of strip malls. In New England we have town greens, a school, a Main Street, a post office. I hope we don't lose that!

2. We need equality—and equity—for all who are marginalized or who are not fortunate enough to be born with privileges of race, gender, sexuality, and wealth.

3. I stick my head outside the bedroom window. Literally.

4. America's greatest strength is its people. They have immeasurable depths of kindness and generosity for individuals they don't know, as witnessed by the outpouring of money and effort after a natural disaster. But America's greatest weakness is also its people. Sometimes rumor and fear can cause a groundswell of prejudice. We tend to be afraid of what we don't know and need to think through that inclination to find what we have in common instead of what separates us.

5. I live in New Hampshire, so I am always dying to know if I am going to have a snowy winter! I can't say I find any of the book useless. It's quaint!

HON. BILL RICHARDSON

Former U.S. ambassador to the UN, secretary of the Department of Energy, governor of New Mexico; author

1. The slow poetry and rhythm of American's national pastime—a major league baseball game. The

Photos, from left: courtesy of David G. Mugar; courtesy of Jodi Picoult

sound of a beautiful melody or an artful poem. What won't change is governments taxing their citizens and all of us trying to stay young.

2. The wastefulness of armed conflict and violence to settle disputes. The moral need to help feed the hungry.

3. Looking up at the sky at night. If I see stars glowing, tomorrow will be a nice day. If it's dark and there are no stars, I will listen to the TV weatherperson and expect the opposite.

4. America's greatest strength is the ethnic diversity, its people—its language, culture, and incredible ecological treasures. Its greatest weakness is the innate corruption of so many governments that prevent the economic well-being of the population.

5. The "Anecdotes & Pleasantries" section is quirky and irreverent. Who knew that there's such a thing as "cloud phobia" (nephophobia) or that global warming causes bitter-tasting chicken? The most useless: the jokes. They're lame.

MIKE ROWE

TV host, author, producer, actor, spokesman

1. The sound of a real cork being slowly pulled from a real bottle. I just watched a friend open an overpriced cabernet by unscrewing the metal top. I can't shake the sound of it, or what it portends.

2. Moving sidewalks. They're making us fatter, and I fear the next stage of their evolution.

3. I've noticed that my belly button attracts a surprising amount of lint just prior to a cold snap. Also, the incorrect use of "further" vs. "farther" often predates heavy rain.

4. Our greatest strength is tolerance. Our greatest weakness is acceptance.

5. I like the covers. They prove that some books can still be judged by them. The celebrity interviews, however, are tiresome.

JOEL SALATIN

Farmer, author, speaker

1. What won't change is the beauty and abundance of the earth. It will continue to convert energy into vegetation.

2. Human exploitation and destruction of the ecology most need to change. We need to implement models that heal the ecology by building soil, hydrating the landscape, and stimulating nutrient density in plants and animals.

3. High pressure and low pressure cast very different weather patterns that can be seen in cloud cover or clear sky, the way smoke rises or falls out of a chimney, and the way animals act. I don't have

Photos, clockwise from top left: Wikimedia; Wikimedia; courtesy of Mike Rowe

a smartphone or an app, which I think forces me to sharpen my observational and memory skills regarding weather patterns.

4. Our greatest strength is our freedom, founded in a Judeo-Christian ethic. This ethic holds freedom in check with a moral boundary that dares to pose the question: Just because we can, should we? Absent that ethic, we develop our greatest weakness, unbridled individualism and personal exploitation. Without a moral boundary, we're clever enough to innovate things we can't physically, spiritually, or emotionally metabolize—we can destroy our own nests. Unfettered freedom is our greatest weakness.

5. My favorite part is historical trivia and anecdotes because I love history. The most useless is probably the long-term weather forecasting since it's seldom accurate.

SEN. JEANNE SHAHEEN

U.S. senator, former governor of New Hampshire

1. The unrivaled natural beauty of

New Hampshire will continue to draw visitors from around the country and the world.

2. We need to get better at working together to address our nation's challenges. I'm very concerned about the impact climate change will have on future generations. But I'm also hopeful that together we can avoid the worst impacts of climate change.

3. I go by "red sky at night, sailors' delight; red sky at morning, sailors take warning."

4. Our greatest strength is the determination, courage, and ingenuity of our people.

5. I always enjoy the tips in the gardening section. I'm most likely to skip the astrology section.

WILL SHORTZ

Puzzle creator and editor

1. We're living in the best time in human history in terms of ease of life, level of culture, personal safety, etc. I hope things only improve.

2. Stopping wars, but good luck with that! Fighting, unfortunately,

seems to be part of our nature.

3. In my experience, a gentle start of winter means a rough end . . . and vice versa. (Is that true or just my imagination?) For the short term, I keep an eye on the sky outside my window.

4. Our greatest strength is our democracy and relative transparency of government. Our greatest weakness is (sometimes) taking these things for granted.

5. My favorite part is the puzzle section, of course. Puzzles in *The Old Farmer's Almanac* go all the way back to 1802. I actually studied these when I was in college. ■

Photos, from left: Wikimedia; courtesy of Will Shortz

FROTH OF OUR FATHERS

FROM THE EARLIEST DAYS, AMERICANS (AND THEIR PRESIDENTS) HAVE BEEN BREWING AND DRINKING BEER.

BY TIM CLARK · ILLUSTRATION BY TIM ROBINSON

The Pilgrims may have come to the New World from England in search of religious freedom, but it was beer, or a lack of it, that landed them at Plymouth Rock. According to *Mourt's Relation,* a journal kept by the Pilgrims of their voyage to America, they decided to settle in Massachusetts because they had run out of beer. It was written on board the *Mayflower,* December 19, 1620 (Old Style): "So in the morning, after we had called on God for direction, we came to this resolution: to go presently ashore again. . . . We could not now take time for further search or consideration, our victuals being much spent, especially our beer."

The first native to speak to them, Samoset, greeted them by asking for beer. He had learned the language, and about beer, over years of dealing with earlier English visitors, who had come to fish the teeming waters.

Beer drinking was not limited to New England. The earlier English colony at Jamestown, in Virginia, finding no one in its midst who knew anything about making beer, placed ads in London newspapers for brewers to join their company. The first brewery in America was actually in New Amsterdam (eventually New York). The Dutch colonists there were producing beer by 1612.

Beer, which has been brewed for thousands of years, was an essential beverage. Colonists, adults and children alike, drank "small beer," usually made at home, which contained far less alcohol than the "strong ale" produced by brewers. Small beer provided hydration and calories, and because it was boiled in the brewing process, it was free from dangerous bacteria found in water and milk.

One of the most famous early American beer recipes is George Washington's: *Take a large sifter full of bran hops to*

"BEER, IF DRUNK
IN MODERATION,
SOFTENS THE
TEMPER, CHEERS
THE SPIRIT, AND
PROMOTES HEALTH."
-THOMAS JEFFERSON, 3RD
U.S. PRESIDENT (1743-1826)

your taste—boil these 3 hours. Then strain out 30 gallons into a cooler, put in 3 gallons molasses while the beer is scalding hot or rather drain the molasses into the cooler and strain the beer on it while boiling hot. Let this stand till it is little more than blood warm. Then put in a quart of yeast if the weather is very cold, cover it over with a blanket, and let it work in the cooler 24 hours. Then put it into the cask. Leave the bung open till it is almost done working—bottle it that day, week it was brewed.

Usually it was the woman of the house who did the brewing. It's not clear whether John Adams's wife, Abigail, concocted the occasional beer that he had for breakfast, but in the early years of their marriage, Thomas Jefferson's wife, Martha, brewed 15 gallons of small beer about every 2 weeks.

After Martha's death in 1782, beer was not made at Monticello for three decades. But in 1813, the former president befriended Captain Joseph Miller, a British brewmaster stranded in the U.S. by the War of 1812, and persuaded him to teach the art to the slave Peter Hemings. In time, Hemings would make 100 gallons of ale every spring and fall.

"I have no doubt, either in moral or economical view, of the desirableness to introduce a taste for malt liquors instead of that for ardent spirits," Jefferson wrote to a friend in 1815. "The difficulty is in changing the public taste and habit. The business of brewing is now so much introduced in every state that it appears to me to need no other encouragement than to increase the number of consumers."

Jefferson was right. There were only 132 breweries in America in 1810, and the average annual per capita consumption was less than a gallon. (The chief American alcoholic beverage at that time was corn whiskey.) It wasn't until the mid–19th century that revolution in Europe brought many German brewers to the States. The oldest U.S. brewery still operating is Yuengling, of Pottstown, Pennsylvania, which was started in 1829. It was followed by familiar names like Schaefer (1842), Pabst (1844), Anheuser-Busch (1852), Miller (1855),

A SUDS-SOAKED MADISON MYTH

Some sources suggest that our fourth president, James Madison, had sought to establish a national beer brewery and add a Secretary of Beer to his cabinet but failed because Congress would have none of it.

Folks at the foundation that maintains Montpelier, Madison's home, assert that there is no record of Madison proposing any such thing. There is, however, a letter indicating that businessman Joseph Coppinger requested Madison's support and help in establishing a national brewing company in Washington. No response from Madison survives.

FACTS ON TAP

• The Moon has a crater named Beer. It was named for Wilhelm Wolff Beer (1797–1850), who produced the first exact map of the Moon in 1834–36.

• The top five states in annual per capita beer consumption: North Dakota (43.6 gallons), New Hampshire (42.2), Montana (40.5), South Dakota (38.2), Vermont (35.9).

• In Canada, Newfoundlanders rank first among the provinces' imbibers, at about 21 gallons per capita per year.

and Coors (1873). By 1914, annual per capita consumption had increased to 20 gallons, near today's level of 21.5 gallons per person.

The presidents after Jefferson and before Prohibition preferred wine, hard cider, or distilled liquors such as whiskey, if they drank alcohol. Before taking office, Abraham Lincoln, when ill, occasionally drank lager on the orders of a physician. While in his 20s, Lincoln co-owned a tavern that served liquor, beer, and cider. Honest Abe had a democratic view of imbibing; he once said, "I am a firm believer in the people. If given the truth, they can be depended upon to meet any national crisis. The great point is to bring them the real facts, and beer."

Two notable beer drinkers in the White House were James Garfield and Grover Cleveland. The story goes that Cleveland and one of his friends vowed to limit their beer intake to four glasses per day, but when their thirst proved too great, they used bigger steins. Jimmy Carter abstained, but with Congress in 1979, he made home brewing legal (again; it had been banned since Prohibition). Ronald Reagan drank beer in a pub on a visit to Ballyporeen, Ireland, in 1984. The interior of the pub was later wholly reconstructed in his presidential library.

In spite of its historic origins and popularity, beer was not brewed in the White House until the Obama Administration. (Washington and Jefferson took up beer brewing after leaving office.) Barack Obama bought a home-brewing kit in 2011, and White House chef Sam Kass created an exclusive recipe. Its secret ingredient? Honey from the White House beehive, another presidential first.

When word leaked of the presidential brew, the administration was reluctant to share the recipe. But home brewers protested (some filed Freedom of Information Act requests), the president relented, and the recipe for White House Honey Brown Ale was released in 2012. Beer aficionados pronounced it good.

If you're interested in trying a presidential brew, you don't have to make it yourself. Yards, a Philadelphia brewer, offers beers based on recipes from Washington, Jefferson, and even nonpresident Benjamin Franklin, who was known to enjoy a refreshing quaff now and then. He never said, "God created beer to make men happy"; the actual quotation referred to wine. But he probably would have appreciated the sentiment. ■

Tim Clark tries to limit his beer consumption to a cold one after mowing the lawn.

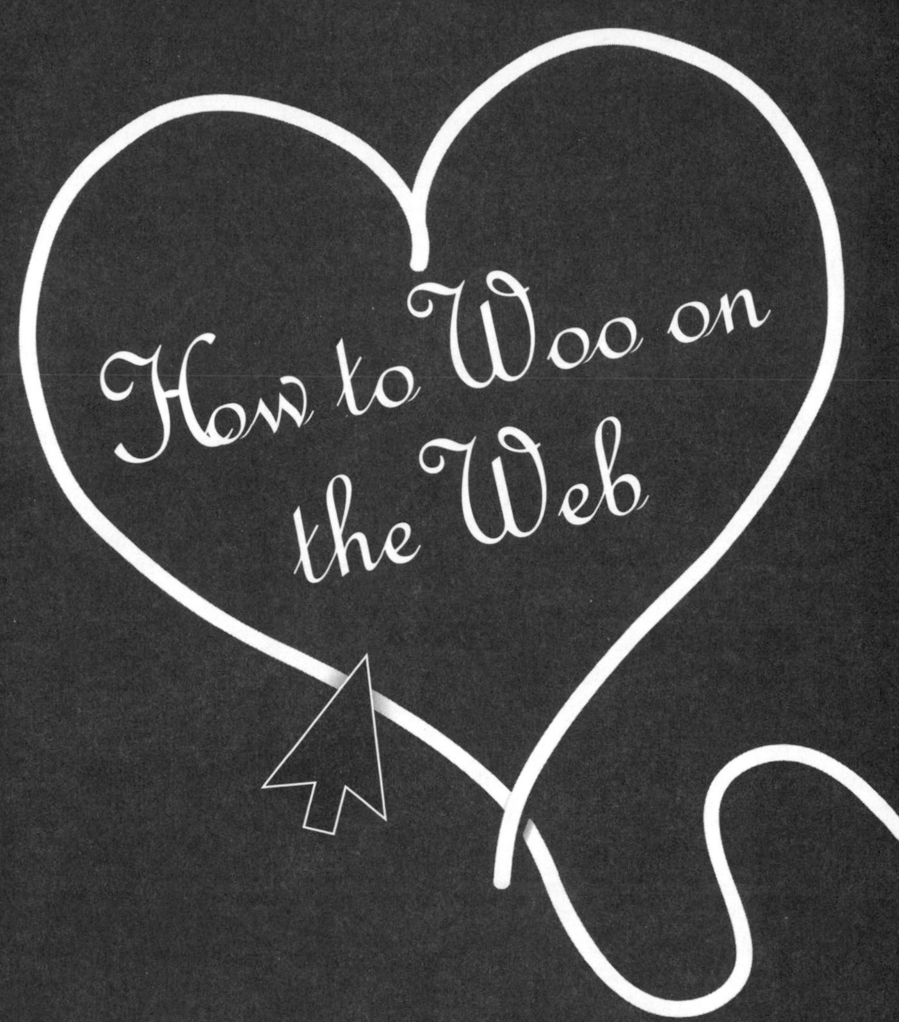

How to Woo on the Web

Or, "Pick 'em Cuter by Computer"

–computer dating slogan, c. 1966

Photo: Michele Paccione/Shutterstock

BY SUSAN SELIGSON

The desire for love—for a soul mate, companionship, romance (or, as the Greeks called it, "the madness of the gods")—is as old as time. By this measure, we may be at the dawn of computer dating.

This modern method of matchmaking began in 1959, when a Stanford University student project ("Happy Family Planning Service") paired 49 men and 49 women, based on their responses to 30 questions on punch cards that were later fed into an IBM 650. Today, by some estimates, 1 in 10 Americans (or 32 million people) uses an online dating service and 5 percent of Americans in a marriage or committed relationship say that they met their partner online.

If you're using online dating or want to, we have a few pointers for you from one of America's leading experts on love. Helen Fisher studies the brains of the infatuated, the committed, the rejected, and the rebuffed. She has written six books on relationships (most recently *Anatomy of Love*, W. W. Norton, 2016) and has been a consultant to Match.com and Chemistry.com.

To find love on the Web, Fisher says, you have to understand one thing: "These are not dating sites; they are introducing sites." Here's her advice for meeting people on the Web—or anywhere, for that matter—along with some observations from the past. *(continued)*

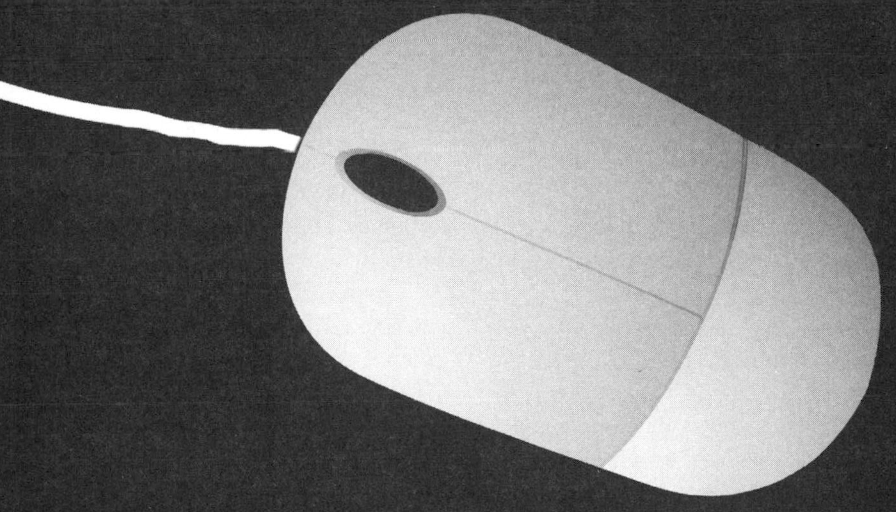

Describe the true you.

Actions, looks, words, steps form the alphabet by which you may spell characters.

–Johann Lavater, Swiss writer, in The 1793 (Old) Farmer's Almanac

Fisher's research indicates that most men and women fall in love with individuals of the same ethnic, social, religious, educational, and economic background, as well as with similar physical attractiveness, intelligence, and interests. Be honest in your profile and email exchanges.

Pick 1. Or 2. Or 3. Just pick.

Analysis kills love, as well as other things.

–John Brown, Scottish physician and writer (1810–82)

According to Fisher, the multitude of potential partners on Web sites stifles possibilities: "When you think that you've got an endless number of opportunities, you often don't choose anyone. After you've met nine people, stop using the Internet and get to know one of them better. Otherwise, chances are that you'll get to know nobody."

Give it time.

Holding hands at midnight
'Neath a starry sky . . .
Nice work if you can get it,
And you can get it , if you try.

–"Nice Work If You Can Get It," by Ira Gershwin, American songwriter/lyricist (1896–1983)

Studies show that on first dates, men decide in 15 minutes if they want a second date. Women ponder the possibility for about an hour. "Think of reasons to say 'yes,'" says Fisher. "Don't think of all the things that you don't like about the person. Focus on the positive, to get to a second or third date." In a study, Fisher found that more than a third of those polled eventually fell in love with someone they found unattractive at first.

Let faux pas pass.

Affection should not be too sharp-eyed, and love is not to be made by magnifying glasses.

–Sir Thomas Browne, English physician and writer (1605–82)

Typically, little is known about a person at the first meeting. "Someone may say something a little stupid or pick up his fork the wrong way, and it's a deal breaker," Fisher observes, "but don't put undue emphasis on minor flaws."

Succumb to silliness.

It is a common calamity;
we are all mad at some time or other.

–Johannes Baptista Montanus, Italian poet (1447–1516)

Attraction is the stage that spawns feats of poetry, prowess, and obsessive behavior bordering on the insane, says Fisher. When you fall madly in love with somebody, "the thinking parts of the brain shut down," she relates. "It's the simple ability to overlook what you don't like in a person and focus on what you do like." When this phase passes, you may be able to overlook the negatives to which you weren't paying attention.

Not sure?

1. Don't see him. Don't phone or write a letter.
2. The easy way: Get to know him better.

–"Two Cures for Love," by Wendy Cope, English poet (b. 1945)

"After the infatuation period, it can take a year and a half or more to really get to know someone and fall for that person," Fisher says. Research shows that the more we get to know someone, the more we like him or her. And, if given time, an unconscious element may surface, adds Fisher: "People gravitate toward their 'love template' or 'love map'"—an unconscious list of traits that we look for in an ideal partner. The list becomes more refined as we mature, she says.

When all else fails, get offline and go out with friends.

A friendship that, like love, is warm;
A love, like friendship, steady.

–"How Shall I Woo?," by Thomas Moore, Irish poet (1759–1852)

"Today, people go out in groups," observes Fisher. "It's an easy way to get to know each other." Or maybe *the* other. And there's more: Recent research indicates that 88 percent of couples together for less than 5 years say that they met offline, and 18- to 34-year-olds tend to meet their significant others through friends, socially, or through work. ■

Susan Seligson is a journalist and award-winning humor columnist.

Web Wooing Wisdom

"If you're computable, you're compatible."

–Robert M. Stelzer, V.P., Teens International, Inc., c. 1966

A study by Sameer Chaudhry, an internist at the University of North Texas, and Kahlid Khan, a professor of women's health and clinical epidemiology at Barts and the London School of Medicine, suggests that certain actions can yield greater responses for online daters. Their advice . . .

Create a user name that begins with a letter in the first half of the alphabet.

Men, choose a user name that suggests you are smart or clever. Ladies, pick one that hints at your appearance.

Make your profile 70 percent about you; 30 percent about whom you seek.

Be funny; don't just say that you are.

Center yourself in the photo frame, tilt your head, and smile enough to cause eye creases. Ladies, wear red.

Write messages to rhyme with the recipient's headline or user name. Note a trait about him/her from their profile.

Respond promptly.

(This worked for Chaudhry.)

Turpentine, **Tar,** & Butter

ANIMAL CARE FROM THE 1793 ALMANAC, CONTRASTED WITH 21ST-CENTURY TREATMENTS

TO CURE ANY SORT OF WOUND IN SHEEP

THEN: Mix together an equal quantity of turpentine, tar, fresh butter. Apply it plasterwise, and it will not fail but cure any sore.

NOW: For an open wound, shear the wool around the wound. Wash it with antiseptic soap, then flush with clean water. Cover area around wound with fly repellent gel. Cover the wound with a nongreasy ointment. See vet about antibiotics. Keep wound clean.

TO KILL WORMS IN HORSES

THEN: Give the horse (troubled with worms or grubs), for three mornings, a pint of strong rue tea. In it, bruise and squeeze the juice of 3 or 4 heads of garlic. Dissolve in it a handful of salt.

NOW: If possible, identify the type of parasite (fecal sample analysis helps). If necessary, employ a deworming rotation. Reduce parasite risk to pastures and facilities by picking up and disposing of manure regularly. Limit the number of horses grazing per acre and graze horses by age. Rotate horses and cattle in grazing pastures.

TO CURE A SORE OF ANY KIND ON HORSES

THEN: Put into a clean pipkin [earthenware pot] (that holds about a quart) resin the bigness of a pullet's egg. When this is melted on the fire, add the same quantity of bees' wax. When that is melted, put in 10 ounces of honey, but not till the wax is dissolved. Put in half a pound of common turpentine. Keep it gently boiling, stirring it with a stick all the time. When the turpentine is dissolved, put in 2 ounces of verdigris [copper acetate], finely powdered. But before you put in the verdigris, take the pipkin off the fire (else it will rise over into the fire in a moment), set it on again, and give it two or three stirs, and strain it through a coarse cloth into a clean vessel, and throw the dregs away.

NOW: If the wound is open, clean it with water, then disinfect with 2 tablespoons salt in 1 gallon distilled water. If the wound is very dirty, an antimicrobial wash may be necessary. Apply a nonadhesive compression bandage and contact the vet. If the wound is blisters (aka ulcers) on the mouth, avoid and/or destroy buttercup, foxtail, and sandbur in the pasture, as all are considered causes. Rinse mouth with water. ■

Dog Training for

YOU TRAINED your dog in the basic commands: "Sit!" "Come!" "Stay!" "Heel!" "Lie down!" "Roll over!" Then you moved on to the more complex commands: "Fetch!" "Dance in a circle!" "Salute!" "Beg!" "Walk backward!" "Say your prayers!" "Count to 10!"

Congratulations! You now understand that the best way to train a dog is by chaining together simple commands that your dog has already mastered. It's time to teach your dog the most challenging tricks of all, tricks that will make your busy life easier to manage.

WASH THE CAR

Most dogs love riding in cars and splashing around in water, especially on a hot summer day. This trick takes advantage of both.

Tools needed: clicker, Jumbo Box o' Treats (available from our catalog for $23.99), plastic kiddie pool filled with soapy water, hose attached to a faucet, dirty car

Skill level: 1. Your dog must be proficient in these commands: "Car!" "Bath time!" "Jump up!" "Lie Down!" "Roll over!" "Down!" "Run in a circle!"

Busy People

By Tim Clark
Illustrations by
Tim Robinson

1. Close all of your car windows.
2. Summon your dog by saying "Car!" while simultaneously clicking. When the dog comes to the car, treat.
3. Give your dog the "Bath time!" command. When the dog jumps into the pool, click and treat. Let it splash around until thoroughly wet, then use the "Jump up!" command to get it onto the car's hood.
4. When the dog jumps onto the hood, click and treat.
5. From here on, it's a simple matter of commanding the dog to lie down and roll over until the surface of the car is thoroughly wet and soapy. Don't forget to reward the dog regularly.
6. Give the dog the "Down!" command, and when it's off the car, put the nozzle of the hose between its teeth and turn the water on. Using the "Run in a circle!" command, have the dog go around the car, spraying it with the hose, until all of the suds are rinsed off. Click and treat.

Once your dog has mastered this trick, it's an easy matter to progress to similar tricks such as "Wash the dinner dishes!" or "Bathe the baby!"

CHANGE A LIGHTBULB

Here's a handy trick if you suffer from

vertigo and can't stand on a stool. It's best to use a rubber lightbulb until your dog has the trick down pat.

Tools needed: clicker, Barrel o' Treats (available from our catalog for $96.99), lightbulb, stool tall enough to enable the dog to stand on its hind legs to reach the light fixture

Skill level: 15. Your dog must be proficient in these commands: "Jump up!" Fetch!" "Lefty loosey!" "Righty tighty!" "Down!"

1. Set the stool directly under the burned-out lightbulb. Using a combination of "Jump up!" and "Fetch!," get the dog on top of the stool on its hind legs with its jaws gently grasping the old lightbulb.

2. Instruct it to dance in a clockwise circle ("Lefty loosey!") until the bulb is out. Take the old bulb away and give your dog a treat.

3. Give it a new bulb to hold in its mouth (screw threads outward), then have it dance in a counterclockwise direction ("Righty tighty!") until the bulb is secure. Give your dog the "Down!" command, then a treat.

Building on your experience with "Change a lightbulb," move on to "Change the oil in the car" and "Change the baby's diaper."

DO YOUR CHILD'S MATH HOMEWORK

Impossible? Not at all! But this trick will take patience. Don't expect your dog to get straight A's right away!

Tools needed: clicker; Freight Car o' Treats (available from our catalog for $14,999.99); calculator with paw-size buttons; quiet, well-lighted place to work without distractions (no TV or video games!)

Skill level: 35. Your dog must be proficient in these commands: "Count to 10!" "Do the multiplication tables!" "Find the least common denominator!"

1. It's a simple matter to teach your dog to read numbers. Ask it to count to 10. Treat when accomplished.

2. Next, teach it to count to each individual number. For example, when your dog starts to count to 10, stop it at each number by grasping its paw. After the first, say "One!" Click and treat. Repeat until your dog stops automatically at one to get the treat. Continue with each of the numbers up to and including 10. (Note: Don't attempt to teach your dog the concept of "zero." It will only confuse it. Even the Romans never managed it.)

3. Start slowly with addition and subtraction. Repeat lessons frequently, treating lavishly. Multiplication and division will require quite a commitment of time.

4. If your dog makes mistakes, do not spank it or shout at it! Dogs respond to love, not violence! Besides, if you use force or harsh language, your dog will never come to appreciate the beauty of pure mathematics, a problem that will come back to haunt you when your dog reaches the higher skills of calculus and quantum mechanics.

Once "Do the math homework" has been mastered, it's a logical progression to "Bring in 1 + 4 + 3 sticks of firewood!" "Do my taxes!" "Sell my house!" ■

About the inspiration for this, writer **Tim Clark** says that he gave this idea to the boys in the back room and this is what they came up with.

Frosts and Growing Seasons

■ Dates given are normal averages for a light freeze; local weather and topography may cause considerable variations. The possibility of frost occurring after the spring dates and before the fall dates is 50 percent. The classification of freeze temperatures is usually based on their effect on plants. **Light freeze:** 29° to 32°F—tender plants killed. **Moderate freeze:** 25° to 28°F—widely destructive to most vegetation. **Severe freeze:** 24°F and colder—heavy damage to most plants. *–dates below courtesy of National Climatic Data Center*

State	City	Growing Season (days)	Last Spring Frost	First Fall Frost
AK	Juneau	148	May 8	Oct. 4
AL	Mobile	273	Feb. 28	Nov. 29
AR	Pine Bluff	243	Mar. 16	Nov. 12
AZ	Phoenix	*	*	*
AZ	Tucson	332	Jan. 19	Dec. 18
CA	Eureka	322	Jan. 27	Dec. 16
CA	Sacramento	296	Feb. 10	Dec. 4
CA	San Francisco	*	*	*
CO	Denver	156	Apr. 30	Oct. 4
CT	Hartford	165	Apr. 26	Oct. 9
DE	Wilmington	202	Apr. 10	Oct. 30
FL	Miami	*	*	*
FL	Tallahassee	239	Mar. 22	Nov. 17
GA	Athens	227	Mar. 24	Nov. 7
GA	Savannah	268	Mar. 1	Nov. 25
IA	Atlantic	148	May 2	Sept. 28
IA	Cedar Rapids	163	Apr. 25	Oct. 6
ID	Boise	148	May 10	Oct. 6
IL	Chicago	186	Apr. 20	Oct. 24
IL	Springfield	182	Apr. 13	Oct. 13
IN	Indianapolis	182	Apr. 18	Oct. 18
IN	South Bend	175	Apr. 26	Oct. 19
KS	Topeka	174	Apr. 19	Oct. 11
KY	Lexington	192	Apr. 15	Oct. 25
LA	Monroe	256	Mar. 3	Nov. 15
LA	New Orleans	334	Jan. 30	Dec. 31
MA	Worcester	170	Apr. 26	Oct. 14
MD	Baltimore	200	Apr. 11	Oct. 29
ME	Portland	156	May 2	Oct. 6
MI	Lansing	145	May 10	Oct. 3
MI	Marquette	154	May 11	Oct. 13
MN	Duluth	155	May 15	Oct. 17
MN	Willmar	153	Apr. 30	Oct. 1
MO	Jefferson City	187	Apr. 13	Oct. 18
MS	Columbia	247	Mar. 13	Nov. 16
MS	Vicksburg	240	Mar. 20	Nov. 16
MT	Fort Peck	140	May 8	Sept. 26
MT	Helena	121	May 19	Sept. 18
NC	Fayetteville	221	Mar. 28	Nov. 5
ND	Bismarck	129	May 14	Sept. 21
NE	Blair	167	Apr. 25	Oct. 10
NE	North Platte	148	May 5	Oct. 1
NH	Concord	123	May 20	Sept. 21
NJ	Newark	217	Apr. 3	Nov. 7
NM	Carlsbad	213	Apr. 3	Nov. 3
NM	Los Alamos	149	May 11	Oct. 8
NV	Las Vegas	283	Feb. 16	Nov. 27
NY	Albany	153	May 2	Oct. 3
NY	Syracuse	167	Apr. 28	Oct. 13
OH	Akron	192	Apr. 18	Oct. 28
OH	Cincinnati	192	Apr. 13	Oct. 23
OK	Lawton	222	Mar. 29	Nov. 7
OK	Tulsa	224	Mar. 27	Nov. 7
OR	Pendleton	154	Apr. 19	Sept. 21
OR	Portland	236	Mar. 23	Nov. 15
PA	Franklin	170	Apr. 29	Oct. 17
PA	Williamsport	167	Apr. 30	Oct. 15
RI	Kingston	147	May 8	Oct. 3
SC	Charleston	315	Feb. 9	Dec. 22
SC	Columbia	238	Mar. 18	Nov. 12
SD	Rapid City	140	May 10	Sept. 28
TN	Memphis	235	Mar. 22	Nov. 13
TN	Nashville	204	Apr. 6	Oct. 28
TX	Amarillo	184	Apr. 18	Oct. 20
TX	Denton	242	Mar. 18	Nov. 16
TX	San Antonio	269	Feb. 28	Nov. 25
UT	Cedar City	132	May 21	Oct. 1
UT	Spanish Fork	167	May 1	Oct. 16
VA	Norfolk	247	Mar. 20	Nov. 23
VA	Richmond	206	Apr. 6	Oct. 30
VT	Burlington	147	May 8	Oct. 3
WA	Seattle	251	Mar. 10	Nov. 17
WA	Spokane	153	May 2	Oct. 3
WI	Green Bay	150	May 6	Oct. 4
WI	Sparta	133	May 13	Sept. 24
WV	Parkersburg	183	Apr. 21	Oct. 22
WY	Casper	119	May 22	Sept. 19

**Frosts do not occur every year.*

HOW WE PREDICT THE WEATHER

We derive our weather forecasts from a secret formula that was devised by the founder of this Almanac, Robert B. Thomas, in 1792. Thomas believed that weather on Earth was influenced by sunspots, which are magnetic storms on the surface of the Sun.

Over the years, we have refined and enhanced this formula with state-of-the-art technology and modern scientific calculations. We employ three scientific disciplines to make our long-range predictions: solar science, the study of sunspots and other solar activity; climatology, the study of prevailing weather patterns; and meteorology, the study of the atmosphere. We predict weather trends and events by comparing solar patterns and historical weather conditions with current solar activity.

Our forecasts emphasize temperature and precipitation deviations from averages, or normals. These are based on 30-year statistical averages prepared by government meteorological agencies and updated every 10 years. The most-recent tabulations span the period 1981 through 2010.

The 16 regions of the contiguous states (page 219) are based primarily on climatology and how weather in each tends to differ based on a particular weather pattern. For example, while the average weather in Richmond, Virginia, and Boston, Massachusetts, is very different (although both are in Region 2), both areas tend to be affected by the same storms and high-pressure centers and have similar departures from normal weather.

We believe that nothing in the universe happens haphazardly, that there is a cause-and-effect pattern to all phenomena. However, although neither we nor any other forecasters have as yet gained sufficient insight into the mysteries of the universe to predict the weather with total accuracy, our results are almost always very close to our traditional claim of 80%.

HOW ACCURATE WAS OUR FORECAST LAST WINTER?

Our accuracy rate in forecasting the direction of temperature and precipitation from normal in the 2014–15 winter was 96.3%, well above our historical average rate of 80%. This past winter, we were substantially less accurate: 55.6%. Whenever our forecasts are not correct, we seek to determine why, so we can learn and avoid similar mistakes in the future. We believe that the reason for our error was that while we correctly foresaw that most of California would have below-normal precipitation, we were incorrect in interpreting this to mean there would not be a strong El Niño. Strong El Niños usually bring heavy rainfalls to California, along with above-normal temperatures in most of the country. Because we did not expect a strong El Niño to occur, temperatures in the 2015–16 winter were warmer than we forecast nearly everywhere.

Despite our incorrect interpretation, we were still correct in 83.3% of our forecasts of the change in temperature from the 2014–15 winter to last winter, missing only in the Southeast, Upper Midwest, and Alaska regions—all of which were warmer than we forecast. How much warmer? Consider Fairbanks, Alaska. Our methodology of finding historical analogues (page 217) forecast that Fairbanks would average 8 degrees F cooler than normal this past winter season. We raised this forecast by 7.5 degrees, an adjustment due to climate change (and one of the largest adjustments we've ever made). As it turned out, we should have raised that forecast by about 20 degrees!

We were also correct in our forecast that snowfall would be above normal in portions of the Atlantic Corridor and Tennessee Valley, and below normal nearly everywhere else. As shown on the table below using one representative city from each region, we were correct in 83.3% of the regions in the direction of precipitation departure from normal. On average, our precipitation forecasts differed from actual conditions by 0.6 inches.

REGION/ CITY	Nov.-Mar. Precip. Variations From Normal (inches) PREDICTED	ACTUAL
1. Caribou, ME	+1.0	+0.6
2. Atlantic City, NJ	+0.1	+.04
3. Wilkes-Barre, PA	–0.1	–0.3
4. Savannah, GA	+0.3	+0.5
5. Jacksonville, FL	–1.1	–0.3
6. Buffalo, NY	–0.4	–0.6
7. Charleston, WV	–0.1	–0.2
8. Tupelo, MS	–0.8	+0.1
9. Marquette, MI	+0.4	+0.3

REGION/ CITY	Nov.-Mar. Precip. Variations From Normal (inches) PREDICTED	ACTUAL
10. Kansas City, KS	–0.4	+0.6
11. Houston, TX	–1.1	–0.2
12. Bismarck, ND	+0.1	+0.1
13. Boise, ID	–0.1	–0.1
14. Tucson, AZ	–0.3	–0.3
15. Portland, OR	+0.9	+2.5
16. San Francisco, CA	–0.4	–0.3
17. Fairbanks, AK	+0.0	+0.0
18. Honolulu, HI	+3.1	–1.4

WEATHER REGIONS

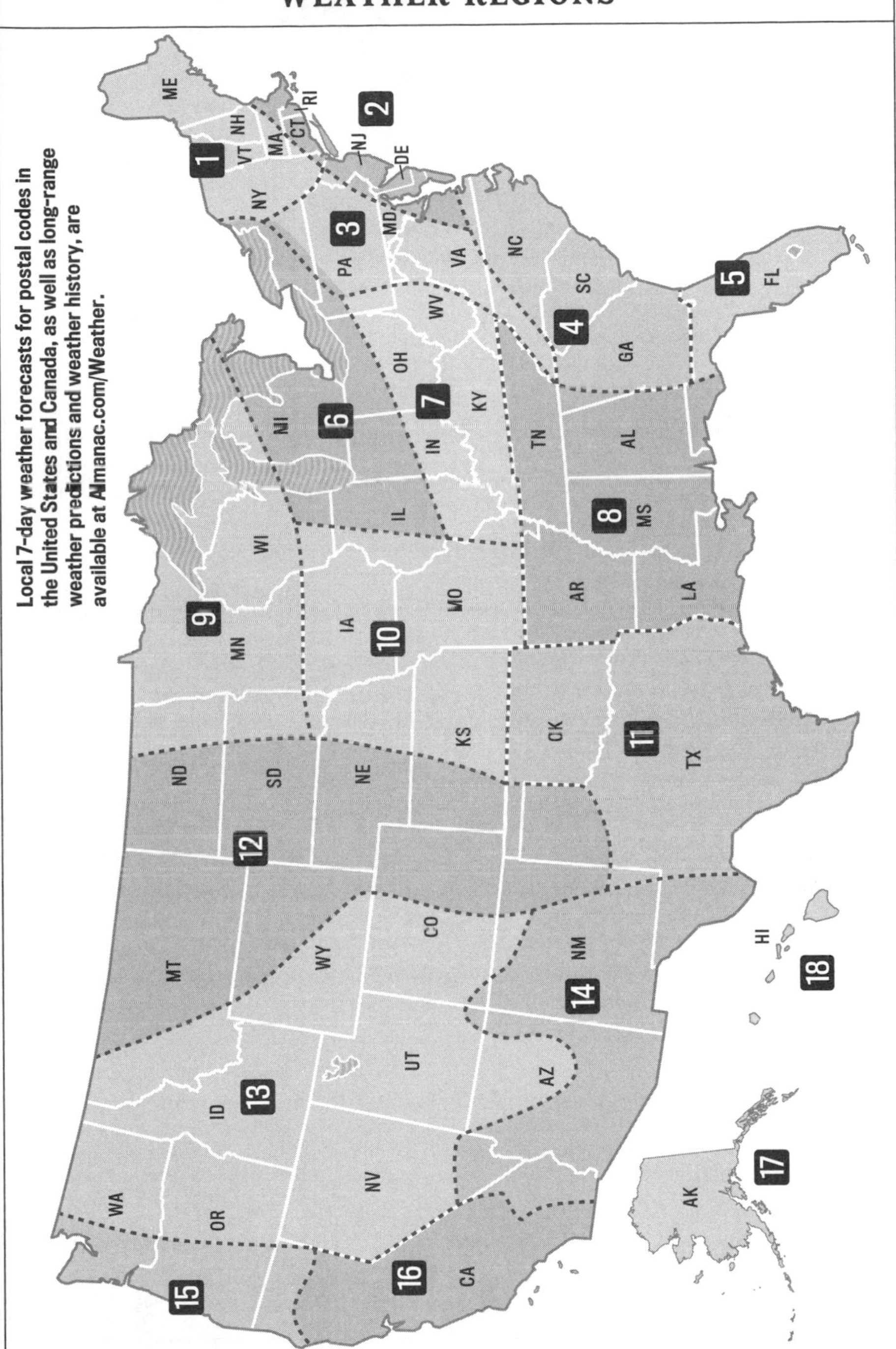
Local 7-day weather forecasts for postal codes in the United States and Canada, as well as long-range weather predictions and weather history, are available at Almanac.com/Weather.
ME
NH
VT
MA
CT
RI
NJ
DE
NY
MD
PA
VA
NC
SC
FL
GA
WV
OH
KY
MI
IN
TN
AL
IL
MS
WI
AR
LA
MO
IA
MN
KS
OK
TX
ND
SD
NE
MT
WY
CO
NM
UT
AZ
ID
NV
WA
OR
CA
AK
HI
1
2
3
4
5
6
7
8
9
10
11
12
13
14
15
16
17
18

REGION **1** FORECAST

NORTHEAST

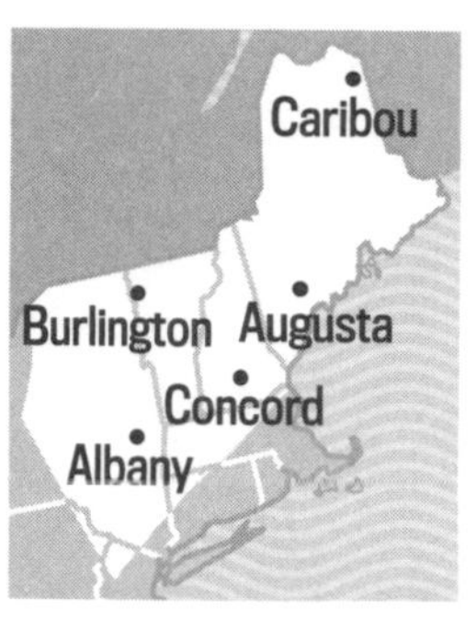

SUMMARY: Winter will be colder than normal, on average, with slightly above-normal precipitation and near-normal snowfall. The coldest periods will be in mid- and late December, mid- and late January, mid-February, and early March. The snowiest periods will be in mid-November, late January, mid- and late February, and early to mid-March. **April** and **May** will be slightly cooler than normal, with above-normal rainfall. **Summer** will be cooler than normal, despite hot periods in early to mid-July and mid- to late August. The north will have above-normal rainfall, with near-normal rainfall in the south. **September** and **October** will be cooler than normal, with near-normal rainfall.

NOV. 2016: Temp. 36° (3° below avg.); precip. 3.5" (avg.). 1–9 Snow showers, cold. 10–14 Scattered showers, mild. 15–17 Flurries, cold. 18–22 Snowstorm, then showers. 23–28 Rain to snow, then sunny, cold. 29–30 Showers, mild.

DEC. 2016: Temp. 28° (3° below avg. north, 3° above south); precip. 3" (avg.). 1–5 Showers, quite mild. 6–9 Snow showers, then sunny, mild. 10–16 Snow showers, cold. 17–22 Rain and snow showers; cold north, mild south. 23–28 Snow, then sunny, mild. 29–31 Flurries, very cold.

JAN. 2017: Temp. 25° (2° above avg.); precip. 2" (1" below avg.). 1–7 Sprinkles, quite mild. 8–10 Flurries, cold. 11–12 Sunny, mild. 13–18 Snow, then showers, mild. 19–25 Snow showers, cold. 26–31 Snow, then flurries, cold.

FEB. 2017: Temp. 20° (3° below avg.); precip. 3.5" (1" above avg.). 1–4 Sunny, cold. 5–10 Showers, mild. 11–17 Blizzard, then sunny, bitter cold. 18–21 Snow, then sunny, mild. 22–25 Snowy, cold north; showers, mild south. 26–28 Snow showers, cold.

MAR. 2017: Temp. 31° (3° below avg.); precip. 4" (1" above avg.). 1–6 Sunny, cold. 7–11 Snow, then rain, mild. 12–20 Periods of rain and snow, cold. 21–26 Showers, mild. 27–31 Wet snow, cold.

APR. 2017: Temp. 43° (3° below avg.); precip. 4" (avg. north, 2" above south). 1–5 Sunny, cool. 6–10 Rain and snow, then showers, mild. 11–17 Rainy periods, cool. 18–22 Sunny, cool. 23–26 Sunny, warm. 27–30 Showers, cool.

MAY 2017: Temp. 57° (2° above avg.); precip. 4" (0.5" above avg.). 1–6 A few showers, cool. 7–11 T-storms, warm. 12–23 Sunny, warm. 24–31 T-storms, turning cool.

JUNE 2017: Temp. 63.5° (avg. north, 3° below south); precip. 4.5" (1" above avg.). 1–5 T-storms, then sunny, cool. 6–7 Sunny, hot. 8–11 T-storms, then sunny, cool. 12–20 Scattered t-storms; warm, then cool. 21–26 A few t-storms, warm. 27–30 Sunny, cool.

JULY 2017: Temp. 69° (1° below avg.); precip. 5" (1" above avg.). 1–3 Sunny, cool. 4–10 Scattered t-storms, hot. 11–17 A few t-storms; cool north, hot south. 18–25 Sunny, cool. 26–31 T-storms, cool.

AUG. 2017: Temp. 65° (1° below avg.); precip. 4" (2" above avg. north, 2" below south). 1–6 T-storms, then sunny, cool. 7–11 Scattered t-storms, cool. 12–14 Sunny, cool. 15–21 A few t-storms, warm. 22–26 Sunny, hot. 27–31 T-storms, then sunny, cool.

SEPT. 2017: Temp. 60° (1° above avg.); precip. 4" (avg.). 1–8 Scattered showers, cool. 9–10 Sunny, warm. 11–16 T-storms, then sunny, chilly. 17–20 A few showers, mild. 21–25 Showers, cool. 26–30 T-storms, warm.

OCT. 2017: Temp. 44° (4° below avg.); precip. 3.5" (avg.). 1–9 Scattered showers, cool. 10–15 Sunny, cool. 16–25 Showers, then sunny, cool. 26–31 Rain and snow, then sunny, cool.

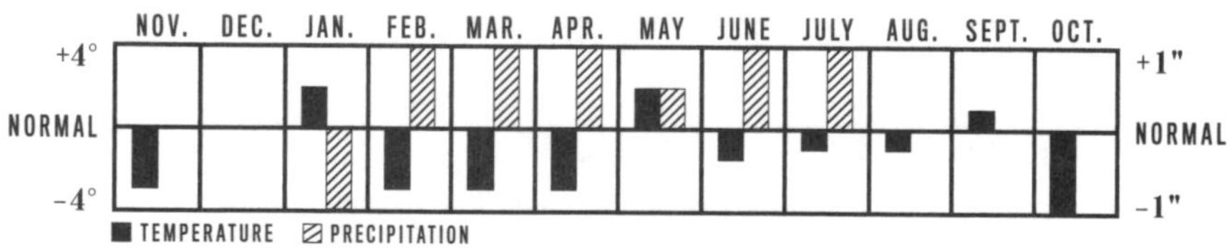

ATLANTIC CORRIDOR

SUMMARY: Winter temperatures will be above normal, on average, with the coldest periods in late December, early to mid- and mid- to late January, and early and mid-February. Precipitation will be slightly above normal in the north and below normal in the south. Snowfall will be above normal in the north, below normal in the central part of the region, and near normal in the south. The snowiest periods will occur in mid- to late January and early to mid-February. **April** and **May** will be rainier than normal, with temperatures below normal in the north and slightly above normal in the south. **Summer** will be cooler and rainier than normal, with a **hurricane threat** in mid-June and the hottest periods in early and mid-July and mid-August. **September** and **October** will be slightly warmer than normal, with near-normal rainfall.

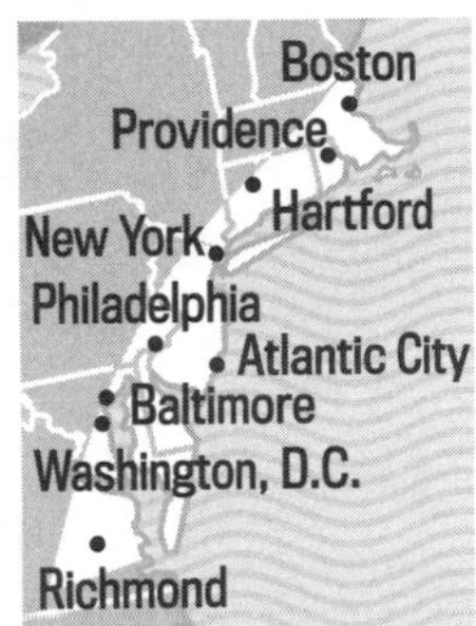

WEATHER

NOV. 2016: Temp. 44° (3° below avg.); precip. 2" (1.5" below avg.). 1–3 Sunny, cold. 4–13 A few showers, turning warmer. 14–16 Rain and wet snow. 17–22 Heavy rain, chilly. 23–28 Sunny, cold. 29–30 Snow to rain.

DEC. 2016: Temp. 45° (6° above avg.); precip. 1.5" (1.5" below avg.). 1–6 Sunny, warm. 7–10 Showers, mild. 11–14 Rain and snow, then sunny, mild. 15–21 Showers north, sunny south; turning warm. 22–29 Periods of rain and snow north, showers south. 30–31 Sunny, cold.

JAN. 2017: Temp. 38° (3° above avg.); precip. 2.5" (1" below avg.). 1–7 Rainy periods, turning warm. 8–10 Sunny, very cold. 11–18 Showers, mild. 19–25 Snow, then sunny, cold. 26–31 Periods of rain and snow.

FEB. 2017: Temp. 34° (1° below avg. north, 1° above south); precip. 5" (3" above avg. north, 1" above south). 1–4 Sunny, very cold. 5–9 Rain, then sunny. 10–15 Snowstorm, then sunny, cold. 16–19 Snow to rain. 20–23 Sunny, warm. 24–28 Rain, then sunny, cold.

MAR. 2017: Temp. 42° (2° below avg.); precip. 3" (1" below avg.). 1–4 Rain and snow showers, cold. 5–9 Rain and snow north, showers south. 10–17 A few showers, cool. 18–21 Sunny, cool. 22–28 Rainy periods, cool. 29–31 Rain and wet snow, chilly.

APR. 2017: Temp. 52.5° (1° below avg. north, 2° above south); precip. 4.5" (1" above avg.). 1–8 A few showers; cool north, turning warm south. 9–12 Showers, warm. 13–17 Rainy, cool. 18–23 Sunny, turning warm. 24–26 Heavy rain. 27–30 Sunny, turning warm.

MAY 2017: Temp. 60.5° (1.5° below avg.); precip. 5" (2" above avg.). 1–4 Rainy periods, cool. 5–6 Sunny, warm. 7–13 Rainy periods, cool. 14–22 Sunny; warm, then cooler. 23–31 Scattered t-storms, warm.

JUNE 2017: Temp. 68° (3° below avg.); precip. 7.5" (4" above avg.). 1–3 T-storms, cool. 4–8 Sunny, turning warm. 9–14 T-storms, cool. 15–18 Hurricane threat. 19–21 Sunny, cool. 22–30 A few t-storms; warm, then cool.

JULY 2017: Temp. 76.5° (0.5° above avg.); precip. 3" (1" below avg.). 1–5 Sunny; cool, then hot. 6–10 Heavy rain, then sunny, hot. 11–20 Isolated t-storms, hot. 21–31 Scattered t-storms, cool.

AUG. 2017: Temp. 73.5° (0.5° below avg.); precip. 3" (1" below avg.). 1–2 T-storms, warm. 3–11 Sunny, then t-storms, cool. 12–18 Sunny, turning hot. 19–24 Scattered t-storms, warm. 25–31 T-storms, then sunny, cool.

SEPT. 2017: Temp. 69° (2° above avg.); precip. 4.5" (1" above avg.). 1–7 A few showers; cool, then warm. 8–11 Sunny, warm. 12–17 A few showers, cool. 18–20 Sunny, warm. 21–26 T-storms, then sunny, cool. 27–30 Heavy rain arriving.

OCT. 2017: Temp. 55° (1° below avg.): precip. 2.5" (1" below avg.). 1–4 Sunny, cool. 5–15 Showers, then sunny, cold. 16–20 Sunny, warm. 21–31 Showers; cool north, mild south.

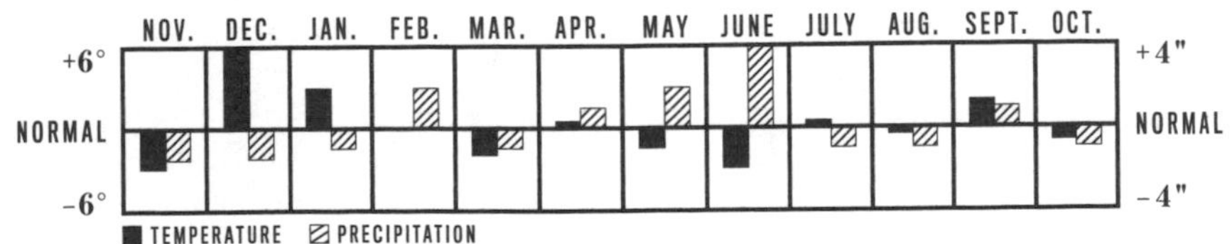

REGION **3** FORECAST

APPALACHIANS

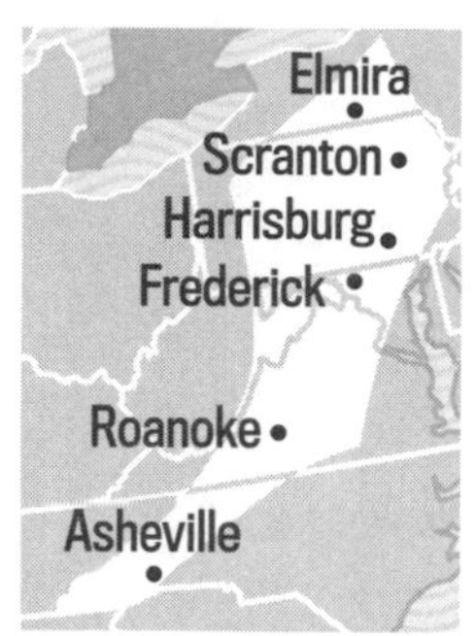

SUMMARY: Winter will be slightly warmer than normal, with near-normal precipitation and above-normal snowfall. The coldest periods will be in early to mid-January, from late January through early February, and in mid- to late February. The snowiest periods will be in mid-November, late January, and early to mid-February. **April** and **May** will be rainier than normal, with temperatures slightly cooler than normal in the north and slightly warmer than normal in the south. **Summer** will be cooler and rainier than normal, with the hottest periods in mid-July and mid-August. Tropical rains will bring a chance of flooding in mid-June. **September** and **October** will be cooler than normal, with near-normal rainfall.

NOV. 2016: Temp. 40° (4° below avg.); precip. 3.5" (avg.). 1–3 Snow showers, cold. 4–8 Sunny; cold north, mild south. 9–12 Showers, mild. 13–16 Snow showers, cold. 17–21 Snow, then flurries, cold. 22–28 Rain, then flurries, cold. 29–30 Rain.

DEC. 2016: Temp. 42° (6° above avg.); precip. 2" (1" below avg.). 1–4 Sunny, mild. 5–10 Showers, mild. 11–15 Snow showers, then sunny, mild. 16–24 Showers north, sunny south; quite mild. 25–31 Snow showers north, rain showers south.

JAN. 2017: Temp. 33° (3° above avg.); precip. 3" (avg.). 1–2 Sunny, cold. 3–6 Rainy periods, mild. 7–10 Snow showers, then sunny, cold. 11–18 Rainy periods, mild. 19–25 Snow showers, cold. 26–31 Snow, then flurries, cold.

FEB. 2017: Temp. 29° (1° below avg.); precip. 3" (0.5" above avg.). 1–4 Sunny, cold. 5–8 Rainy, mild. 9–10 Flurries, cold. 11–15 Snowstorm, then flurries, cold. 16–19 Snow showers north, snow to rain south. 20–23 Sunny, mild. 24–28 Rain to snow, then sunny, cold.

MAR. 2017: Temp. 37° (3° below avg.); precip. 3.5" (0.5" above avg.). 1–4 Snow showers north, sunny south. 5–10 Rainy periods, cool. 11–14 Sunny, cool. 15–21 Rain, then flurries, cold. 22–31 Rain and snow showers, cool.

APR. 2017: Temp. 50° (1° below avg. north, 1° above south); precip. 3.5" (1" above avg.). 1–4 Sunny, cool. 5–9 Showers; cool north, warm south. 10–17 Showers; warm, then cool. 18–22 Sunny, cool. 23–30 Showers, mild.

MAY 2017: Temp. 60° (avg.); precip. 5" (1" above avg.). 1–6 Showers, then sunny, cool. 7–14 A few showers, warm. 15–22 Sunny, warm. 23–26 T-storms, then sunny, cool. 27–31 Sunny, warm.

JUNE 2017: Temp. 63° (4° below avg.); precip. 8" (4" above avg.). 1–6 T-storms, then sunny, cool. 7–12 Scattered t-storms. 13–16 Heavy rain, chilly. 17–20 Sunny, cool. 21–30 A few t-storms; warm, then cool.

JULY 2017: Temp. 73° (avg.); precip. 2.5" (1" below avg.). 1–9 Scattered t-storms; cool, then warm. 10–17 Sunny, hot. 18–31 Scattered t-storms, cool.

AUG. 2017: Temp. 70° (1° below avg.); precip. 1.5" (2" below avg.). 1–4 Sunny, cool. 5–11 A few t-storms; warm, then cool. 12–19 Sunny, turning hot. 20–25 T-storms, then sunny, nice. 26–31 T-storms, then sunny, cool.

SEPT. 2017: Temp. 64° (avg.); precip. 4.5" (1" above avg.). 1–4 Sunny, cool. 5–11 T-storms, then sunny, warm. 12–17 A few showers, cool. 18–22 Scattered t-storms, warm. 23–26 Sunny, cool. 27–30 T-storms.

OCT. 2017: Temp. 50° (3° below avg.); precip. 2" (1" below avg.). 1–4 Sunny, chilly. 5–10 Showers; cool north, warm south. 11–19 Showers, then sunny, chilly. 20–25 Showers, cool. 26–31 Showers; cool north, mild south.

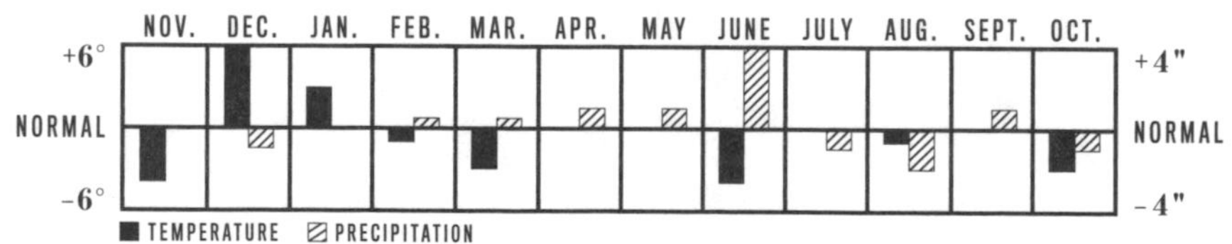

REGION 4 FORECAST

SOUTHEAST

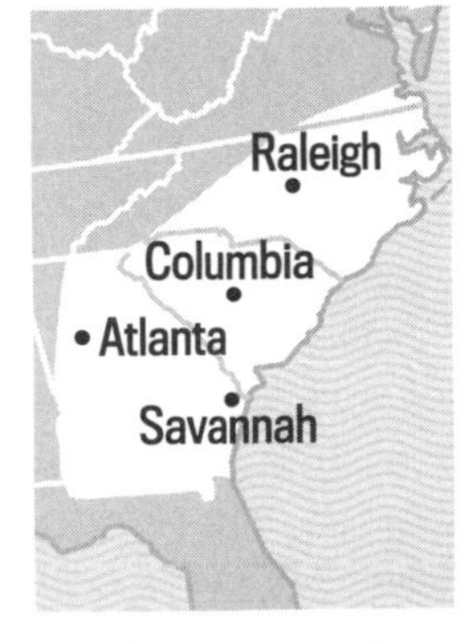

SUMMARY: Winter will be warmer than normal, with below-normal precipitation and near- to below-normal snowfall. The coldest periods will be in early to mid-January, from late January into early February, and in mid-February. The best chances for snow will be in late November, mid-February, and mid-March. **April** and **May** will be slightly cooler than normal, with rainfall below normal in the north and above normal in the south. **Summer** will be cooler than normal, on average, with rainfall above normal in the north and near normal in the south. Watch for tropical storm threats in early to mid-June and late August. The hottest periods will be in mid-July, early to mid-August, and early to mid-September. **September** and **October** will be drier than normal, with temperatures near normal in the north and above normal in the south.

NOV. 2016: Temp. 52° (3° below avg.); precip. 2.5" (0.5" below avg.). 1–5 Showers, then sunny, cool. 6–12 Sunny, warm. 13–25 Rainy periods, cool. 26–27 Snow inland, rain coast. 28–30 Showers, warm.

DEC. 2016: Temp. 55° (8° above avg.); precip. 2" (1.5" below avg.). 1–3 Sunny, warm. 4–10 A few showers, mild. 11–16 Showers, then sunny, cold. 17–22 Sunny, warm. 23–29 Showers, mild. 30–31 Sunny, cold.

JAN. 2017: Temp. 47° (4° above avg.); precip. 6" (avg. north, 3" above south). 1–7 Showers, mild. 8–13 Sunny; cold, then mild. 14–21 A few showers, mild. 22–27 Showers, some ice and wet snow inland; cold. 28–31 Sunny.

FEB. 2017: Temp. 46° (avg.); precip. 3" (1" below avg.). 1–4 Sunny, cold. 5–8 Rain, then sunny, mild. 9–12 Rainy periods, snow inland; cold. 13–18 Sunny; cold, then mild. 19–24 Rainy periods, turning mild. 25–28 Showers, cool.

MAR. 2017: Temp. 54° (1° below avg.); precip. 3.5" (1" below avg.). 1–7 Sunny, warm. 8–13 T-storms, then sunny, cool. 14–17 Rain, then sunny, cool. 18–19 Rain coast, wet snow inland. 20–28 Showers, cool. 29–31 Sunny, warm.

APR. 2017: Temp. 64° (1° above avg.); precip. 2" (1" below avg.). 1–3 Showers, then sunny, cool. 4–13 Showers, then sunny, warm. 14–18 Rainy periods, cool. 19–24 Sunny, turning warm. 25–30 T-storms, then sunny, cool.

MAY 2017: Temp. 69° (2° below avg.); precip. 4.5" (avg. north, 2" above south). 1–5 T-storms, then sunny, cool. 6–11 Scattered t-storms, cool. 12–22 A few t-storms, cool. 23–31 T-storms, then sunny, cool.

JUNE 2017: Temp. 75° (3° below avg.); precip. 5.5" (1" above avg.). 1–10 Sunny; cool, then warm. 11–14 Tropical storm threat. 15–19 Sunny, nice. 20–30 A few t-storms; warm, then cool.

JULY 2017: Temp. 82° (avg.); precip. 4.5" (2" above avg. north, 2" below south). 1–3 Sunny, cool. 4–11 A few t-storms, warm. 12–16 Sunny, hot. 17–24 T-storms inland; sunny, hot coast. 25–31 P.M. t-storms, warm.

AUG. 2017: Temp. 79° (1° below avg.); precip. 6" (1" above avg.). 1–9 Scattered t-storms, warm. 10–13 T-storms, hot. 14–18 Sunny inland, t-storms coast. 19–27 Scattered t-storms, warm. 28–31 Tropical storm threat.

SEPT. 2017: Temp. 75° (1° above avg.); precip. 2.5" (2" below avg.). 1–5 Sunny, nice. 6–12 Isolated t-storms, hot. 13–19 T-storms, then sunny, warm. 20–26 T-storms, then sunny, cool. 27–30 T-storms, then sunny, cool.

OCT. 2017: Temp. 65° (1° below avg. north, 3° above south); precip. 3" (1" below avg.). 1–5 Sunny, cool. 6–11 A few t-storms, warm. 12–15 Sunny, cool. 16–21 Showers; warm east, cool west. 22–28 Sunny, warm. 29–31 Rain.

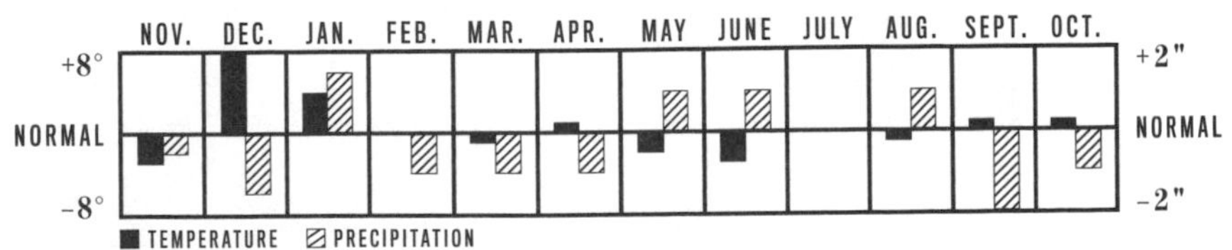

REGION **5** FORECAST

FLORIDA

SUMMARY: Winter will be much milder than normal, but coldest in early to mid-January, from late January into early February, and in mid-February. Rainfall will be above normal in the north and near normal in the south. **April** and **May** will be slightly hotter than normal, with above-normal rainfall. **Summer** will be cooler and rainier than normal, with the hottest temperatures in mid- and late June and mid- and late July. Watch for tropical storm threats in mid-May and mid-June and a **hurricane threat** in early September. **September** (especially early to mid-) and **October** will be warmer and drier than normal.

NOV. 2016: Temp. 69° (avg.); precip. 2.5" (1" above avg. north, 1" below south). 1–7 T-storms, then sunny, cool. 8–12 Sunny, warm. 13–19 Isolated showers, cool. 20–30 Scattered t-storms, turning warm.

DEC. 2016: Temp. 70° (7° above avg.); precip. 1.5" (1" below avg.). 1–9 Sunny, warm. 10–17 Scattered t-storms, warm. 18–23 Sunny, warm. 24–29 Scattered t-storms, warm. 30–31 Sunny, cool.

JAN. 2017: Temp. 65° (5° above avg.); precip. 3.5" (1" above avg.). 1–3 Sunny, turning warm. 4–7 T-storms, warm. 8–11 Scattered showers, cool. 12–22 Isolated t-storms, warm. 23–27 T-storms, mild. 28–31 Sunny, chilly.

FEB. 2017: Temp. 61° (avg.); precip. 2.5" (avg.). 1–4 Rainy periods, cool. 5–11 A few showers, seasonable. 12–18 Sunny; cool, then warm. 19–25 A few showers, mild. 26–28 Rainy periods, cool.

MAR. 2017: Temp. 67° (avg.); precip. 4" (1" above avg.). 1–6 T-storms, then sunny, cool. 7–15 Scattered t-storms, warm. 16–23 Scattered t-storms north, sunny south; cool. 24–28 T-storms, then sunny, cool. 29–31 Showers, warm.

APR. 2017: Temp. 73° (2° above avg.); precip. 2" (0.5" below avg.). 1–10 Sunny; cool, then warm. 11–22 Scattered t-storms; warm, then cool. 23–30 A few t-storms; warm north, cool south.

MAY 2017: Temp. 76° (1° below avg.); precip. 7" (3" above avg.). 1–10 Scattered t-storms, warm. 11–14 Tropical storm threat. 15–22 A few t-storms, cool. 23–29 Sunny north, t-storms south; cool. 30–31 Sunny.

JUNE 2017: Temp. 81° (1° below avg.); precip. 8" (1.5" above avg.). 1–3 Sunny. 4–10 A few t-storms, cool. 11–13 Tropical storm threat. 14–22 A few t-storms, warm. 23–27 Scattered t-storms, mainly central; hot. 28–30 T-storms, cool.

JULY 2017: Temp. 82° (1° below avg.); precip. 7.5" (1" above avg.). 1–16 Scattered t-storms, warm. 17–22 Isolated t-storms, hot. 23–31 Scattered t-storms; hot north, warm south.

AUG. 2017: Temp. 81° (1° below avg.); precip. 9.5" (2" above avg.). 1–4 T-storms north, sunny south; hot and humid. 5–10 Sunny, cooler north; scattered t-storms, humid south. 11–25 Daily t-storms, seasonable. 26–31 Sunny north, a few t-storms south; cool.

SEPT. 2017: Temp. 81° (1° above avg.); precip. 3.5" (2" below avg.). 1–4 Hurricane threat. 5–10 Sunny, hot. 11–17 A few t-storms, turning cooler. 18–22 Sunny north, a few t-storms south; warm. 23–28 T-storms, warm. 29–30 Sunny, cool.

OCT. 2017: Temp. 76.5° (3° above avg. north, avg. south); precip. 3" (1" below avg.). 1–2 Sunny, cool. 3–8 Scattered t-storms, warm. 9–12 Sunny, warm. 13–21 A few t-storms, warm. 22–31 Sunny, then scattered t-storms; warm.

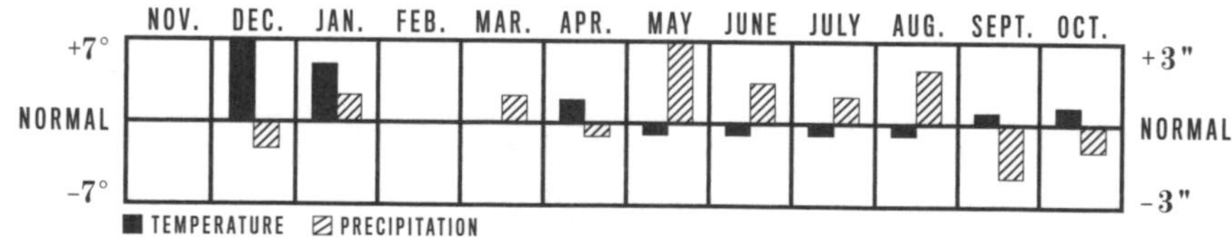

REGION **6** FORECAST

LOWER LAKES

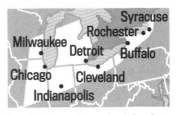

SUMMARY: Winter will be warmer than normal, with above-normal precipitation. The coldest periods will be in late December and early to mid-January and from mid-January into early February. Snowfall will be above normal in New York and Illinois and below normal elsewhere, with the snowiest periods in mid-November, late December, early and late January, mid-February, and early March. **April** and **May** will be warmer and slightly drier than normal. **Summer** will be slightly cooler and rainier than normal. The hottest period will be in mid-July, with other hot periods in early July and mid- to late August. **September** and **October** will be wetter and slightly cooler than normal.

NOV. 2016: Temp. 41° (3° below avg. east, 3° above west); precip. 2" (0.5" below avg.). 1–4 Rain and snow showers, chilly. 5–11 Showers east, sunny west; mild. 12–17 Lake snows, cold. 18–24 Rain, then snow showers, cold. 25–27 Sunny; cold east, mild west. 28–30 Rainy, mild.

DEC. 2016: Temp. 37° (5° above avg.); precip. 5" (0.5" above avg. east, 3" above west). 1–6 Rain, then sunny, mild. 7–9 Snow to rain. 10–12 Snow showers, cold. 13–19 A few rain and snow showers east, sunny west; mild. 20–22 Rain and snow showers. 23–24 Snow east, rain west. 25–31 Rain to snow, then snow showers, cold.

JAN. 2017: Temp. 26.5° (2° above avg. east, 3° below west); precip. 2" (0.5" below avg.). 1–5 Lake snows, cold east; sunny, mild west. 6–9 Rain to snow, turning bitterly cold. 10–17 Rain and snow showers, mild. 18–24 Lake snows, very cold. 25–31 Rain to snow, then lake snows, very cold.

FEB. 2017: Temp. 28° (1° above avg.); precip. 2.5" (2" above avg. east, 1" below west). 1–4 Snow showers, very cold. 5–8 Snow to rain, then showers, mild. 9–10 Flurries, cold. 11–13 Snowstorm east, flurries west; cold. 14–19 Snowy periods, cold. 20–23 Showers, mild. 24–28 Rain to snow.

MAR. 2017: Temp. 35° (3° below avg.); precip. 2.5" (0.5" below avg.). 1–3 Snow showers, cold. 4–5 Sunny, mild. 6–12 Heavy rain and snow, then rain and snow showers. 13–14 Sunny, mild. 15–21 Rain and snow showers, then sunny, cool. 22–31 Snow, then snow showers, cold.

APR. 2017: Temp. 48° (avg.); precip. 4" (0.5" above avg.). 1–3 Sunny, cool. 4–12 Rainy periods, mild. 13–20 Rain, then sunny, cool. 21–24 Showers, mild. 25–30 T-storms, then showers, cool.

MAY 2017: Temp. 61° (3° above avg.); precip. 2" (1.5" below avg.). 1–5 T-storms, then sunny. 6–8 T-storms. 9–21 Sunny, warm. 22–25 T-storms, cool. 26–27 Sunny, warm. 28–31 T-storms, then sunny, cool.

JUNE 2017: Temp. 64° (2° below avg.); precip. 5" (1.5" above avg.). 1–4 Showers, cool. 5–8 A few t-storms, warm. 9–11 Sunny, cool. 12–19 Heavy t-storms, then sunny, cool. 20–25 Scattered t-storms, warm. 26–30 Showers, cool.

JULY 2017: Temp. 71° (0.5° above avg.); precip. 3.5" (avg.). 1–2 T-storms, cool. 3–8 Scattered t-storms, hot. 9–15 Sunny; cool, then hot. 16–23 T-storms, then sunny, cool. 24–27 T-storms, warm. 28–31 Showers, cool.

AUG. 2017: Temp. 70° (1° above avg.); precip. 3.5" (0.5" below avg.). 1–4 Showers, cool. 5–10 Scattered t-storms; cool east, warm west. 11–16 Sunny, turning hot. 17–25 Scattered t-storms, warm. 26–31 Sunny; cool, then warm.

SEPT. 2017: Temp. 63.5° (1.5° above avg.); precip. 5.5" (1" above avg. east, 3" above west). 1–3 T-storms, then sunny, cool. 4–11 Scattered t-storms, warm. 12–15 Sunny, cool. 16–19 T-storms, warm. 20–25 Showers, cool. 26–30 Sunny, warm, then rainy, cool.

OCT. 2017: Temp. 50° (2° below avg.); precip. 3" (0.5" above avg.). 1–3 Sunny, cool. 4–7 Showers, cool. 8–14 Rain and snow showers, cold. 15–24 Rainy periods, cool. 25–31 Showers, mild.

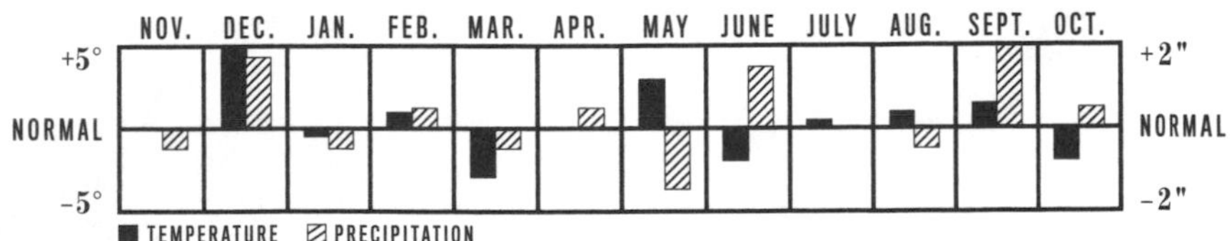

OHIO VALLEY

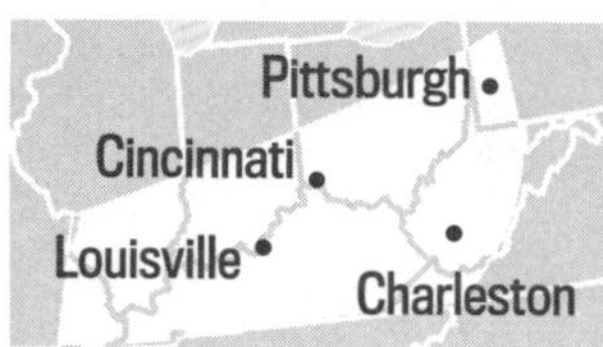

SUMMARY: **Winter** will be warmer than normal, with slightly below-normal precipitation. The coldest periods will be in early to mid-January, from late January into early February, and in late February. Snowfall will be above normal in the east and below normal in the west, with the snowiest periods in late January and early to mid-February. **April** and **May** will be warmer than normal, with rainfall below normal in the east and above normal in the west. **Summer** will be cooler and slightly drier than normal, with the hottest periods in early and mid-July and mid-August. **September** and **October** will be rainier than normal, with near-normal temperatures.

NOV. 2016: Temp. 45° (1° below avg.); precip. 3" (0.5" below avg.). 1–4 Flurries, then sunny, cold. 5–11 Sunny, turning warm. 12–14 Rainy, turning chilly. 15–23 Periods of rain and snow, cold. 24–26 Sunny, cold. 27–30 Rainy, mild.

DEC. 2016: Temp. 45° (8° above avg.); precip. 2.5" (0.5" below avg.). 1–9 Showers, quite mild. 10–12 Snow showers, cold. 13–17 Sunny, mild. 18–23 Rainy periods, mild. 24–31 Rain and snow showers, colder.

JAN. 2017: Temp. 34° (1° above avg.); precip. 2.5" (0.5" below avg.). 1–5 Rain, then sunny, mild. 6–10 Rain to snow, then sunny, bitter cold. 11–18 Rainy periods, mild. 19–25 Snow showers, cold. 26–31 Rain, then snowy periods, cold.

FEB. 2017: Temp. 33° (1° below avg.); precip. 4" (1" above avg.). 1–4 Snow showers, very cold. 5–8 Snow to rain, turning mild. 9–13 Snowstorm, then flurries, cold. 14–20 Rain and snow showers. 21–23 Sunny, warm. 24–28 Rain to snow, then snow showers, cold.

MAR. 2017: Temp. 42° (3° below avg.); precip. 4.5" (0.5" above avg.). 1–3 Snow showers, cold. 4–14 Rainy periods, mild. 15–19 Snow showers, cold. 20–31 Rainy periods, occasional wet snow, cool.

APR. 2017: Temp. 57° (2° above avg.); precip. 3.5" (avg.). 1–3 Sunny, cool. 4–12 A few t-storms, warm. 13–21 Rain, then sunny, cool. 22–30 A few showers, warm.

MAY 2017: Temp. 63° (1° above avg. east, 1° below west); precip. 3.5" (2" below avg. east, 2" above west). 1–5 Rain, then sunny, cool. 6–10 Rainy periods; warm, then cool. 11–21 Sunny, warm. 22–26 T-storms, then sunny, cool. 27–31 Scattered t-storms.

JUNE 2017: Temp. 68° (4° below avg.); precip. 4.5" (0.5" above avg.). 1–6 A few showers, cool. 7–12 T-storms, then sunny, cool. 13–18 T-storms, then showers, cool. 19–21 Sunny, nice. 22–30 A few t-storms; warm, then cool.

JULY 2017: Temp. 75° (avg.); precip. 3.5" (0.5" below avg.). 1–10 Scattered t-storms, turning warm. 11–17 Sunny, hot. 18–31 Scattered t-storms, cool.

AUG. 2017: Temp. 72° (1° below avg.); precip. 3" (1" below avg.). 1–4 Sunny, cool. 5–19 Scattered t-storms, warm. 20–24 Sunny, warm. 25–31 T-storms, then sunny, cool.

SEPT. 2017: Temp. 69° (2° above avg.); precip. 5" (2" above avg.). 1–4 T-storms, then sunny, cool. 5–11 A few t-storms, warm. 12–15 Sunny, cool. 16–22 Scattered t-storms, warm. 23–26 Sunny, cool. 27–30 Showers.

OCT. 2017: Temp. 55° (2° below avg.); precip. 4" (1.5" above avg.). 1–3 Sunny, cool. 4–11 A few showers; warm, then cool. 12–14 Sunny, cold. 15–24 A few showers, cool. 25–29 T-storms, then sunny, cool. 30–31 Rainy, mild.

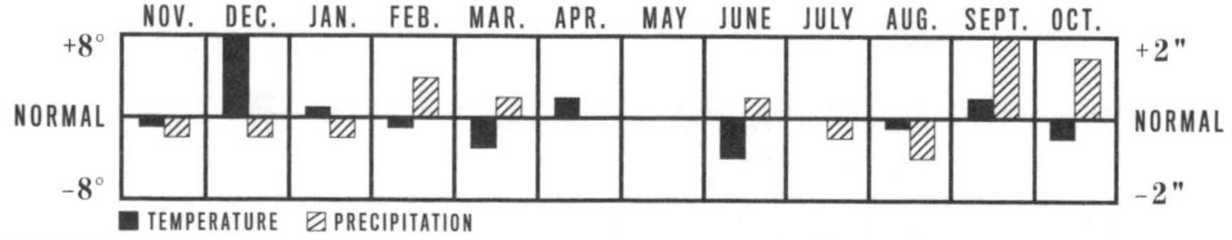

REGION 8 FORECAST

DEEP SOUTH

SUMMARY: Winter will be much milder than normal, with snowfall mostly below normal and confined to the north. The coldest periods will be in late December, early to mid-January, from late January into early February, and in late February. Rainfall will be below normal in the north and near to below normal in the south, with snowfall most likely across the north in late December and late January. **April** and **May** will be warmer and drier than normal. **Summer** will be cooler than normal, despite hot periods in late May, mid-July, mid-August, and early September. Rainfall will be slightly above normal in the north and below normal in the south. **September** and **October** will be warmer and rainier than normal.

WEATHER

NOV. 2016: Temp. 54° (1° above avg. north, 3° below south); precip. 5" (1" below avg. north, 1" above south). 1–3 Showers, cool. 4–10 Sunny, turning warm. 11–14 Showers, cool. 15–17 Snow north, rain south. 18–27 Rainy periods, cold. 28–30 Rainy, mild.

DEC. 2016: Temp. 56° (8° above avg.); precip. 5" (avg.). 1–9 A few showers, warm. 10–12 Rainy, cool. 13–19 Sunny, warm. 20–26 Showers, mild. 27–31 Snow north, rain south, then, sunny, cold.

JAN. 2017: Temp. 50° (5° above avg.); precip. 5.5" (1" below avg. north, 2" above south). 1–6 Rainy periods, mild. 7–10 Sunny, cold. 11–17 Showers, warm. 18–22 Rainy periods; colder north, warm south. 23–31 Periods of rain and snow north, showers south; cold.

FEB. 2017: Temp. 49° (2° above avg.); precip. 4" (1" below avg.). 1–3 Sunny, cold. 4–11 Rainy periods, seasonable. 12–19 Sunny, then rainy, turning warm. 20–22 Sunny, warm. 23–25 T-storms, then sunny, cold. 26–28 Showers, cold.

MAR. 2017: Temp. 56° (avg.); precip. 4" (2" below avg.). 1–5 Sunny, turning warm. 6–11 Showers, seasonable. 12–14 Sunny, warm. 15–17 T-storms, then sunny, cool. 18–22 Rainy, cool. 23–27 Sunny, cool. 28–31 T-storms, then sunny, cool.

APR. 2017: Temp. 65° (2° above avg.); precip. 2.5" (2" below avg.). 1–2 Sunny, cool. 3–9 Scattered t-storms, turning warm. 10–12 Sunny, nice. 13–20 T-storms, then sunny, cool. 21–30 Scattered t-storms, warm.

MAY 2017: Temp. 71° (1° above avg. north, 1° below south); precip. 3" (2" below avg.). 1–3 Sunny, cool. 4–12 Scattered t-storms, cool. 13–23 Isolated t-storms, warm. 24–31 Sunny; cool, then hot.

JUNE 2017: Temp. 77° (1° below avg.); precip. 5" (avg.). 1–6 Isolated t-storms, turning cooler. 7–13 A few t-storms, warm. 14–16 Sunny, cool. 17–25 Scattered t-storms, warm. 26–30 T-storms, then sunny, cool.

JULY 2017: Temp. 79° (2° below avg.); precip. 4.5" (avg.). 1–4 Sunny, cool. 5–14 Scattered t-storms, warm. 15–18 Sunny, hot. 19–31 A few t-storms, cool.

AUG. 2017: Temp. 79° (1° below avg.); precip. 4.5" (1" above avg. north, 1" below south). 1–5 T-storms, cool. 6–12 Sunny north, t-storms south. 13–19 Scattered t-storms, hot. 20–24 Sunny, nice. 25–31 Scattered t-storms; cool, then warm.

SEPT. 2017: Temp. 78° (2° above avg.); precip. 4" (0.5" above avg. north, 2" below south). 1–7 Sunny, hot. 8–10 T-storms, warm. 11–22 A few t-storms, warm. 23–30 Sunny, cool.

OCT. 2017: Temp. 67° (2° above avg.); precip. 6" (3" above avg.). 1–7 Sunny, turning warm. 8–13 A few t-storms, cool. 14–21 Scattered t-storms, cool. 22–26 T-storms, warm. 27–31 Scattered t-storms, cool.

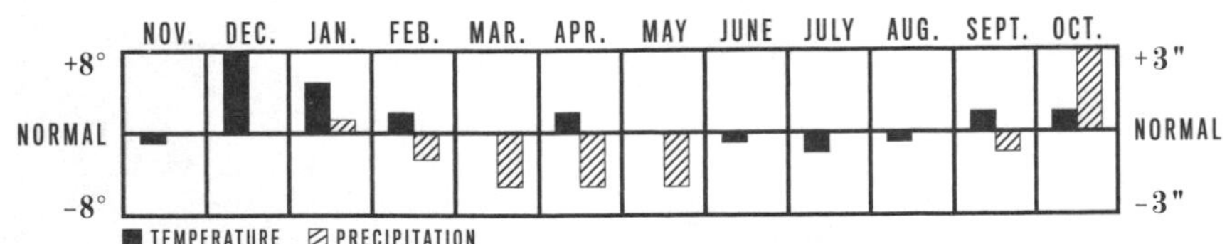

REGION **9** FORECAST

UPPER MIDWEST

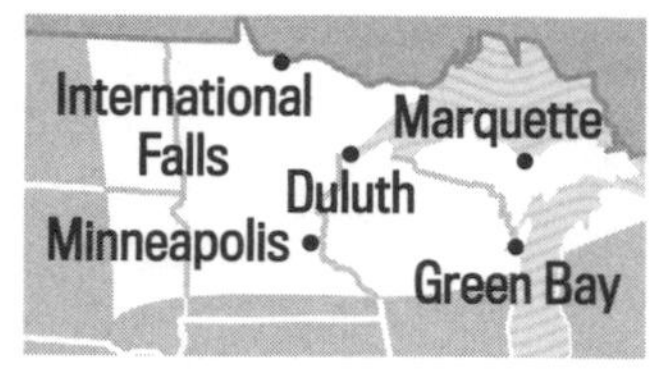

SUMMARY: Winter will be colder than normal, with the coldest periods in mid-December, through most of January, and in early and late February. Precipitation will be a bit above normal in the east and below normal in the west, with snowfall above normal from Minneapolis eastward and below normal in the west. The snowiest periods will be in early to mid- and mid- to late December, mid-January, and early to mid- and late February. **April** and **May** will be warmer than normal, with precipitation below normal in the east and near normal in the west. **Summer** will be cooler and a bit drier than normal. The hottest periods will be in mid-July and early to mid- and mid- to late August. **September** and **October** will be cooler and rainier than normal.

WEATHER

NOV. 2016: Temp. 32° (3° above avg.); precip. 2" (1" above avg. east, 1" below west). 1–6 Sunny, mild. 7–10 Rainy periods, mild. 11–15 Snow, then flurries, cold. 16–26 Snow, then flurries, cold. 27–30 Snow showers, mild.

DEC. 2016: Temp. 16° (1° above avg. east, 1° below west); precip. 1" (avg.). 1–6 Snow showers, cold. 7–9 Snowstorm east, snow showers west; mild. 10–18 Snow showers; cold, then mild. 19–25 Snowstorm, then flurries, mild. 26–31 Flurries; cold east, mild west.

JAN. 2017: Temp. 8° (5° below avg.); precip. 1" (0.5" below avg. east, 0.5" above west). 1–3 Sunny, mild. 4–8 Snow showers, turning bitterly cold. 9–11 Snow, then sunny, mild. 12–17 Snowy periods, cold. 18–22 Snow showers, frigid. 23–26 Flurries, cold. 27–31 Snow, then flurries, frigid.

FEB. 2017: Temp. 9° (3° below avg.); precip. 1.5" (0.5" above avg.). 1–6 Sunny, turning mild. 7–9 Flurries, cold. 10–20 Snow, then flurries, cold. 21–28 Snowy periods, very cold.

MAR. 2017: Temp. 26° (2° below avg.); precip. 1" (0.5" below avg.). 1–7 Sunny, turning mild. 8–13 Snow east, showers west, then sunny, mild. 14–18 Snow, then sunny, cold. 19–31 Snow, then snow showers, cold.

APR. 2017: Temp. 40° (2° below avg.); precip. 2" (avg.). 1–3 Snow showers, cold. 4–12 Showers, cool. 13–16 Periods of rain and snow. 17–22 Sunny, turning warm. 23–30 A few showers, cool.

MAY 2017: Temp. 61° (6° above avg.); precip. 2.5" (1" below avg. east, avg. west). 1–3 Sunny, cool. 4–13 Showers, then sunny, turning hot. 14–21 Sunny, hot east; a few t-storms, warm west. 22–25 T-storms, cool. 26–31 Sunny, warm.

JUNE 2017: Temp. 60° (3° below avg.); precip. 3" (1" below avg.). 1–5 T-storms, cool east; sunny, warm west. 6–15 A few t-storms, cool. 16–19 Sunny, warm. 20–23 T-storms, warm. 24–30 A few showers, cool.

JULY 2017: Temp. 65° (3° below avg.); precip. 4.5" (1" above avg.). 1–9 A few t-storms; warm, then cool. 10–16 T-storms, turning warm. 17–21 Showers, cool. 22–28 Sunny; warm, then cool. 29–31 T-storms, cool.

AUG. 2017: Temp. 67° (1° above avg.); precip. 3" (0.5" below avg.). 1–3 Showers, cool. 4–13 Isolated t-storms, turning hot. 14–18 A few t-storms, cool. 19–23 Sunny, turning hot. 24–31 A few t-storms, turning cool.

SEPT. 2017: Temp. 58° (avg.); precip. 4" (1" above avg.). 1–6 Scattered t-storms, cool. 7–12 Sunny, warm. 13–17 T-storms, then sunny, cool. 18–21 Showers, cool. 22–26 Showers east; sunny, warm west. 27–30 Showers, cool.

OCT. 2017: Temp. 44° (3° below avg.); precip. 3" (0.5" above avg.). 1–9 A few showers, cool. 10–12 Rain to snow, then sunny, cold. 13–20 Rain, then sunny, mild. 21–25 Showers east; snow, then sunny west. 26–31 Rainy periods, mild.

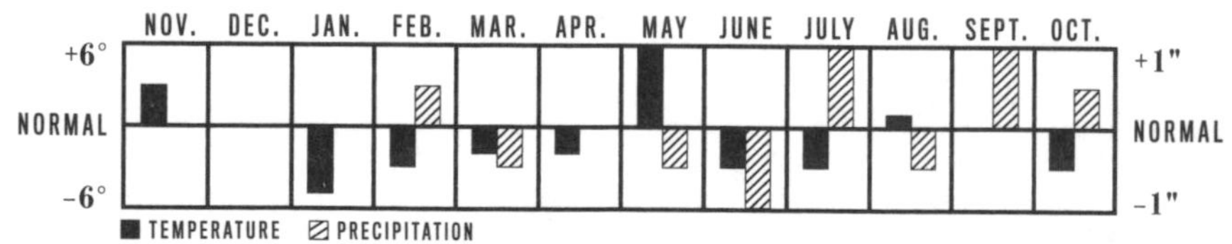

REGION **10** FORECAST

HEARTLAND

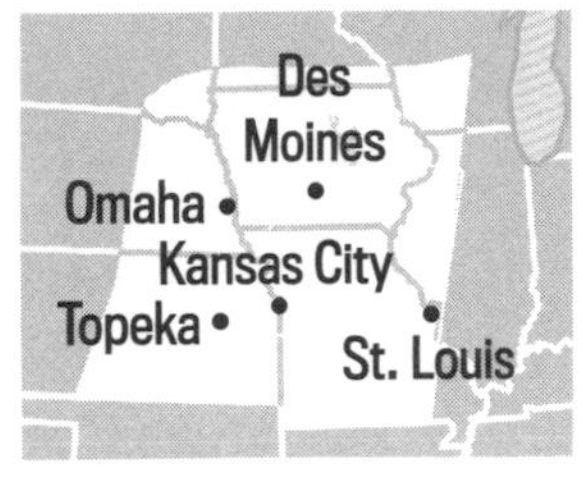

SUMMARY: Winter will be milder and drier than normal, with near- to above-normal snowfall. The coldest periods will be in early to mid- and mid- to late January and early February. The snowiest periods will be in mid- to late November, mid-January, and early February. **April** and **May** will be warmer and drier than normal. **Summer** will be cooler than normal, with the hottest periods in mid- to late June, early July, and early to mid-August. Rainfall will be below normal in the north and above normal in the south. **September** and **October** will be slightly cooler and rainier than normal.

NOV. 2016: Temp. 46° (3° above avg.); precip. 1.5" (1" below avg.). 1–8 Rain, then sunny, turning warm. 9–15 Rain, then sunny, cold. 16–19 Snow, then sunny. 20–27 Rain to snow, then sunny, cold. 28–30 Showers, mild.

DEC. 2016: Temp. 37° (5° above avg.); precip. 3" (avg. north, 3" above south). 1–8 Rainy periods, mild. 9–10 Sunny, cold. 11–19 Sunny, mild. 20–25 Occasional snow north, rain south; mild. 26–29 Snow showers, cold. 30–31 Sunny, mild.

JAN. 2017: Temp. 27° (4° below avg. north, avg. south); precip. 0.5" (0.5" below avg.). 1–4 Sunny, mild. 5–9 Rain to snow, then sunny, very cold. 10–15 Sunny, mild. 16–23 Snow, then flurries, very cold. 24–26 Snowy periods north, showers south. 27–31 Snow showers, very cold.

FEB. 2017: Temp. 31.5° (2° below avg. north, 3° above south); precip. 0.5" (1" below avg.). 1–4 Snow showers, very cold. 5–10 Snow showers north, showers south. 11–14 Sunny. 15–19 Rain and snow showers, cold. 20–22 Sunny, turning warm. 23–28 Rain to snow, then sunny, cold.

MAR. 2017: Temp. 44° (avg.); precip. 1.5" (1" below avg.). 1–4 Sunny, turning warm. 5–14 Showers, mild. 15–27 Rain and snow showers, cool. 28–31 Sunny, turning warm.

APR. 2017: Temp. 56° (2° above avg.); precip. 4.5" (1" above avg.). 1–2 Showers, cool. 3–6 Scattered t-storms, warm. 7–14 Rainy periods; cool, then warm. 15–19 Sunny, cool. 20–30 A few t-storms, seasonable.

MAY 2017: Temp. 67° (3° above avg.); precip. 2.5" (2" below avg.). 1–7 Scattered t-storms, cool. 8–15 Sunny, warm. 16–22 A few t-storms, warm. 23–27 Sunny, turning hot. 28–31 Scattered t-storms, warm.

JUNE 2017: Temp. 70° (2° below avg.); precip. 2.5" (2" below avg.). 1–6 A few t-storms; cool, then warm. 7–11 Isolated t-storms, cool. 12–16 Sunny, cool. 17–24 Scattered t-storms, turning hot. 25–30 Showers, then sunny, cool.

JULY 2017: Temp. 76° (1° below avg.); precip. 6" (2" above avg.). 1–4 Sunny, turning hot. 5–11 A few t-storms, turning cool. 12–15 Sunny, warm. 16–23 T-storms, then sunny, cool. 24–31 A few t-storms, cool.

AUG. 2017: Temp. 74° (1° below avg.); precip. 3" (2" below avg. north, 1" above south). 1–4 Showers, cool. 5–13 Sunny, hot. 14–19 T-storms, turning cool. 20–23 Sunny, warm. 24–29 T-storms, then sunny, cool. 30–31 T-storms, warm.

SEPT. 2017: Temp. 69° (2° above avg.); precip. 4.5" (1" above avg.). 1–7 A few t-storms, warm. 8–12 Sunny, hot. 13–16 T-storms, then sunny, cool. 17–23 T-storms, then sunny, cool. 24–30 Scattered t-storms; warm, then cool.

OCT. 2017: Temp. 53° (3° below avg.); precip. 4" (1" above avg.). 1–9 A few showers, cool. 10–12 Sunny, cold. 13–18 Rain, then sunny, chilly. 19–22 Sunny, mild. 23–29 Rain, then sunny, cool. 30–31 Rain.

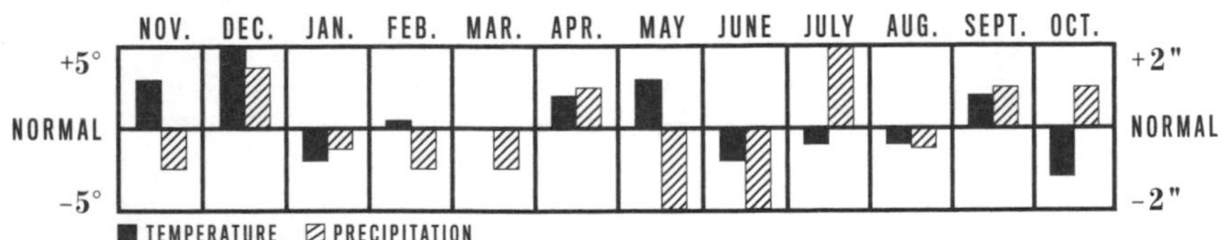

WEATHER

TEXAS–OKLAHOMA

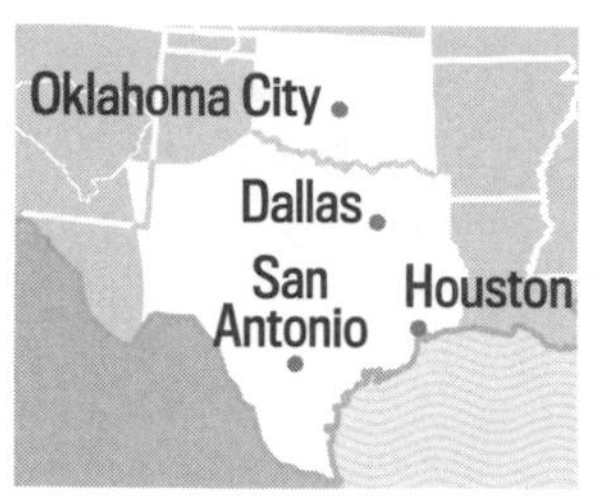

SUMMARY: Winter will be much warmer than normal, with below-normal precipitation and near-normal snowfall. The coldest periods will be in late December, early to mid- and mid- to late January, and early February. The snowiest periods in the north will be in mid- and late November, late December, and early February. **April** and **May** will be warmer than normal, with near-normal rainfall. **Summer** will be slightly cooler than normal, with rainfall below normal in the north and above normal in the south. The hottest periods will be in mid- to late June and mid- to late July. **September** (especially early) and **October** will be warmer than normal and slightly rainier than normal.

WEATHER

NOV. 2016: Temp. 56° (1° below avg.); precip. 4" (1" above avg.). 1–3 Showers, then sunny, cool. 4–8 Sunny, warm. 9–14 A few showers, mild. 15–16 Snow north, rain south. 17–21 Sunny, turning warm. 22–30 Periods of rain and snow north, rain south; chilly.

DEC. 2016: Temp. 59° (6° above avg.); precip. 1.5" (1" below avg.). 1–6 Rainy periods; cold north, warm south. 7–20 Rain, then sunny, turning warm. 21–26 Rainy periods, mild. 27–31 Snow north, rain south, then sunny, cold.

JAN. 2017: Temp. 51° (1° below avg. north, 5° above south); precip. 1" (1" below avg.). 1–5 Sunny, mild. 6–9 Flurries north, showers south, then sunny, cold. 10–17 Sunny, turning warm. 18–26 Periods of rain and snow north, rain south; turning cold. 27–31 Sunny, cool.

FEB. 2017: Temp. 53° (3° above avg.); precip. 1" (1" below avg.). 1–4 Rain to snow north, rain south; cold. 5–14 Sunny, turning warm. 15–21 Showers, then sunny, mild. 22–28 Sunny north, showers south; cool, then warm.

MAR. 2017: Temp. 63° (4° above avg.); precip. 1.5" (1" below avg.). 1–9 Sunny north, rain and drizzle south; mild. 10–12 Sunny, warm. 13–19 Scattered showers, warm. 20–28 Sunny north, showers south; turning cool. 29–31 Sunny, warm.

APR. 2017: Temp. 70° (4° above avg.); precip. 5" (2" above avg.). 1–7 Sunny, turning hot. 8–12 Scattered t-storms, warm. 13–21 A few t-storms, turning cool. 22–30 Scattered t-storms; warm, then cool.

MAY 2017: Temp. 72.5° (1° above avg. north, 2° below south); precip. 3" (2" below avg.). 1–7 Scattered t-storms, turning cool. 8–14 Sunny, warm. 15–22 A few t-storms north, sunny south; warm. 23–31 Sunny, turning hot north; a few t-storms south.

JUNE 2017: Temp. 79° (avg.); precip. 4" (avg.). 1–8 Scattered t-storms, warm. 9–13 Sunny, turning hot. 14–22 Isolated t-storms; cool, then hot. 23–30 A few t-storms, turning cool.

JULY 2017: Temp. 80° (1° below avg.); precip. 3.5" (2" below avg. north, 3" above south). 1–5 Scattered t-storms, cool. 6–15 Sunny, hot, then cool north; daily t-storms south. 16–20 Sunny, hot north; a few t-storms south. 21–31 Sunny, warm north; scattered t-storms, humid south.

AUG. 2017: Temp. 80° (1° below avg.); precip. 1.5" (avg. north, 2" below south). 1–6 Scattered t-storms, cool north; sunny south. 7–11 Sunny, turning hot. 12–21 T-storms, then sunny, cooler. 22–31 Scattered t-storms, turning hot.

SEPT. 2017: Temp. 78° (2° above avg.); precip. 2.5" (1" below avg.). 1–12 Sunny, hot north; t-storms, humid south. 13–21 A few t-storms, warm. 22–30 Sunny; cool, then warm.

OCT. 2017: Temp. 68° (1° below avg. north, 3° above south); precip. 6" (2" above avg.). 1–6 Sunny north, a few t-storms south; warm. 7–10 Sunny, warm. 11–15 Heavy t-storms, turning cool. 16–22 Scattered t-storms; cool north, warm south. 23–31 Rain, then sunny, cool.

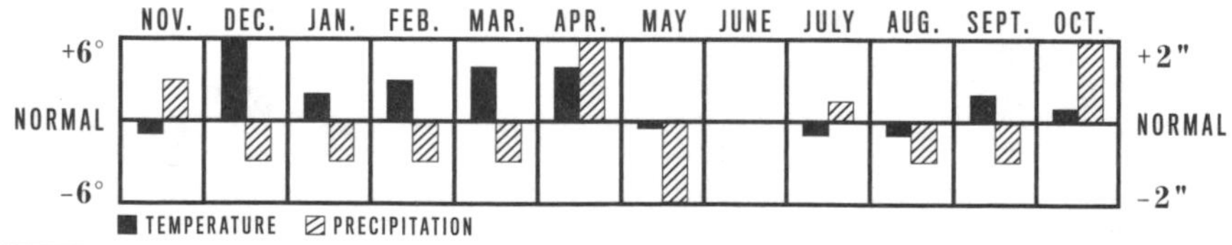

REGION 12 FORECAST

HIGH PLAINS

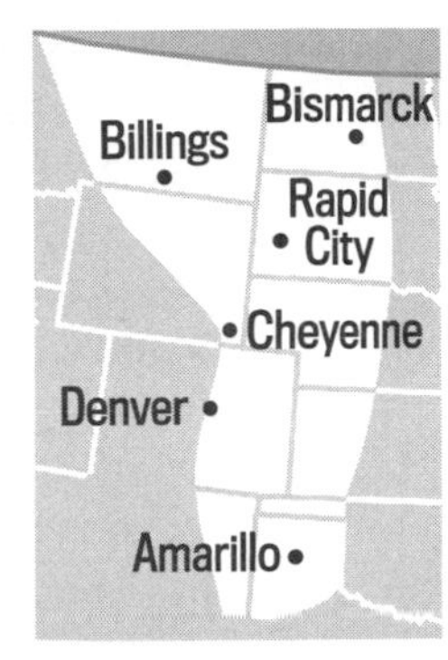

SUMMARY: Winter will be colder than normal in the north, warmer in the south. The coldest periods will be in early and late December and early and mid- to late January. Precipitation will be slightly above normal in the north and below normal in the south. Snowfall will be above normal in the north and below normal elsewhere, with the snowiest periods in late November, mid- to late December, and mid- to late February. **April** and **May** will be warmer than normal, with precipitation a bit above normal. **Summer** will be cooler than normal, with slightly below-normal rainfall. The hottest periods will be in early July and early and mid- to late August. **September** and **October** will have near-normal precipitation, with temperatures below normal in the north and near normal in the south.

NOV. 2016: Temp. 38° (2° above avg.); precip. 1.5" (0.5" above avg.). 1–7 Sunny, mild. 8–14 Rain and snow, then sunny. 15–23 Rain and snow showers, turning cold. 24–28 Snow, then flurries south, snow showers north. 29–30 Snowy, cold.

DEC. 2016: Temp. 27° (5° below avg. north, 3° below south); precip. 0.3" (0.2" below avg.). 1–7 Flurries, cold. 8–15 Snow, then sunny, milder. 16–17 Snow north, sunny south. 18–23 Sunny, turning mild. 24–28 Snowstorm, then sunny, frigid. 29–31 Sunny, mild.

JAN. 2017: Temp. 24° (8° below avg. north, avg. south); precip. 0.5" (avg.). 1–8 Flurries, then sunny, frigid. 9–16 Flurries north; sunny, mild south. 17–26 Snow showers, turning bitterly cold. 27–31 Flurries, milder.

FEB. 2017: Temp. 29.5° (2° below avg. north, 5° above south); precip. 0.5" (0.5" above avg. north, 0.5" below south). 1–6 Sunny, mild. 7–15 Flurries north, sunny south; mild. 16–22 Snow showers, cold north; sunny, mild south. 23–28 Snow, then sunny, cold.

MAR. 2017: Temp. 44° (5° above avg.); precip. 0.5" (0.5" below avg.). 1–3 Sunny, mild. 4–16 A few showers, mild. 17–23 Rain to snow, then sunny, cold. 24–26 Snow, cold. 27–31 Sunny, warm.

APR. 2017: Temp. 47° (1° below avg.); precip. 2.5" (0.5" above avg.). 1–3 Sunny; cool north, hot south. 4–9 Showers, cool. 10–18 Snow north, showers south, then sunny, cool. 19–30 Rainy periods, cool.

MAY 2017: Temp. 61° (3° above avg.); precip. 2.5" (avg.). 1–5 Showers, cool. 6–10 Sunny, turning warm. 11–19 Rainy, cool north; sunny, warm south. 20–23 Sunny north, showers south; cool. 24–31 Isolated t-storms, warm.

JUNE 2017: Temp. 65° (2° below avg.); precip. 3" (0.5" above avg.). 1–9 Showers, turning cool. 10–14 Rainy periods, cool. 15–20 A few showers; cool north, warm south. 21–23 Sunny, warm. 24–30 Scattered t-storms, cool.

JULY 2017: Temp. 69° (3° below avg.); precip. 1.5" (0.5" below avg.) 1–6 Sunny north, t-storms south; hot. 7–15 Showers, cool. 16–23 Isolated t-storms; cool, then hot. 24–27 T-storms, turning cool. 28–31 Sunny, cool.

AUG. 2017: Temp. 70° (1° below avg.); precip. 1.5" (0.5" below avg.). 1–4 Showers; hot, then cool. 5–8 T-storms north; sunny, hot south. 9–16 Scattered t-storms, turning cool. 17–21 Sunny, hot north; t-storms, cool south. 22–27 T-storms, then sunny, cool. 28–31 Showers, cool.

SEPT. 2017: Temp. 61° (2° below avg. north, 2° above south); precip. 1" (0.5" below avg.). 1–6 Showers, cool. 7–11 Sunny, warm. 12–21 Showers, cool north; sunny, warm south. 22–26 Sunny, mild. 27–30 Snow north, rain south, then sunny, cool.

OCT. 2017: Temp. 47° (2° below avg.); precip. 1.5" (0.5" above avg.). 1–6 Showers north; sunny, warm south. 7–14 Showers, cool. 15–19 Rainy north, sunny south. 20–26 Rain to snow, then sunny, cold. 27–31 Showers, mild.

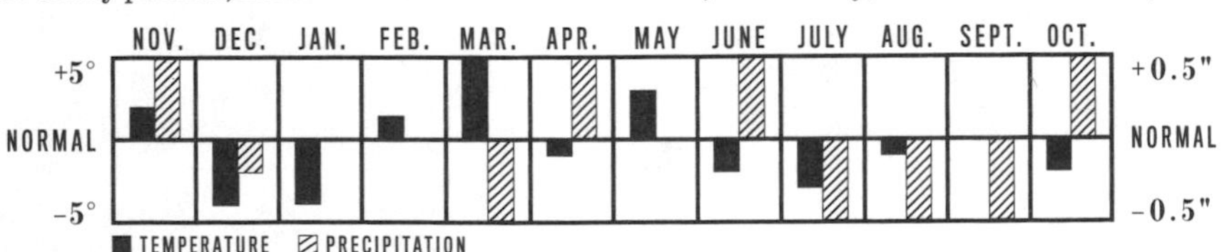

REGION **13** FORECAST

INTERMOUNTAIN

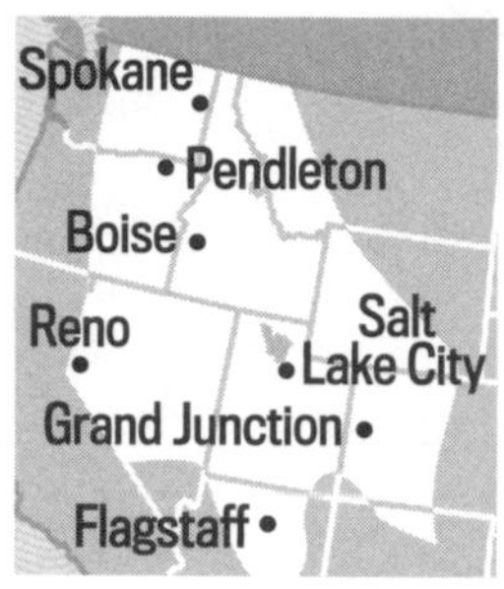

SUMMARY: Winter temperatures will be above normal, with precipitation a bit below normal. The coldest periods will be in early and mid- to late December and mid- to late January. Snowfall will be above normal in the north and below normal elsewhere, with the snowiest periods in late November, early and mid-December, and mid-January. **April** and **May** will be slightly warmer and drier than normal. **Summer** will be slightly hotter than normal, with near-normal rainfall. The hottest periods will be in late June and early to mid- and mid- to late July. **September** and **October** will be cooler than normal, with above-normal precipitation.

WEATHER

NOV. 2016: Temp. 40° (1° above avg. north, 1° below south); precip. 1.5" (avg.). 1–5 Rainy periods, mild. 6–9 Showers north, snow showers south. 10–12 Snow showers, cold. 13–15 Sunny, mild north; snow showers south. 16–20 Rain and snow showers north, sunny south. 21–27 Snowy periods, cold. 28–30 Rain to snow.

DEC. 2016: Temp. 30.5° (1° below avg. north, 4° below south); precip. 2" (0.5" above avg.). 1–4 Snowstorm north, flurries south; cold. 5–9 Snow, then flurries, cold. 10–13 Sunny, cold. 14–17 Snow, then sunny, mild. 18–20 Sunny north, snowstorm central, rainy south. 21–28 Snow showers, cold. 29–31 Sunny; mild north, cold south.

JAN. 2017: Temp. 34° (2° above avg.); precip. 1" (0.5" below avg.). 1–4 Snow showers, cold north; sunny, mild south. 5–10 Snow showers north, sunny south. 11–15 Rainy periods north, sunny south; quite mild. 16–18 Snowstorm north, flurries south. 19–27 Flurries, turning bitterly cold. 28–31 Flurries, mild.

FEB. 2017: Temp. 39° (5° above avg.); precip. 1" (0.5" below avg.). 1–3 Flurries, cold. 4–21 Rain and snow showers north, sunny south; turning mild. 22–28 Snow showers, cool north; sunny, mild south.

MAR. 2017: Temp. 47° (4° above avg.); precip. 1" (0.5" below avg.). 1–7 Rainy periods north, sunny south; mild. 8–12 Sunny, warm. 13–15 Showers north, sunny south; mild. 16–22 A few showers and flurries, cold. 23–31 Showers north, sunny south; turning mild.

APR. 2017: Temp. 47° (2° below avg.); precip. 0.5" (0.5" below avg.). 1–7 Rain and snow showers, chilly. 8–15 Sunny, cool. 16–20 Showers, mild north; sunny, cool south. 21–27 Sunny; cool, then warm. 28–30 Showers.

MAY 2017: Temp. 60° (3° above avg.); precip. 1" (avg.). 1–8 Showers, then sunny, warm. 9–18 A few showers, then sunny, cool. 19–25 Sunny, warm. 26–31 Scattered showers; warm north, cool south.

JUNE 2017: Temp. 67° (1° above avg.); precip. 0.5" (avg.). 1–8 Showers, warm. 9–13 Showers north, sunny south; cool. 14–19 T-storms, then sunny, cool. 20–30 Sunny, turning hot.

JULY 2017: Temp. 73° (avg.); precip. 0.5" (avg.). 1–4 Scattered showers, cool. 5–8 Sunny, hot. 9–15 Scattered t-storms, turning cool. 16–24 Isolated t-storms, turning hot. 25–31 Sunny; cool, then hot.

AUG. 2017: Temp. 72° (avg.); precip. 1" (avg.). 1–4 Sunny, hot. 5–16 Scattered t-storms, cool. 17–22 Sunny, hot north; scattered t-storms south. 23–31 Sunny, turning cool north; a few t-storms, warm south.

SEPT. 2017: Temp. 60° (2° below avg.); precip. 1.5" (0.5" above avg.). 1–7 T-storms, then sunny, cool. 8–14 Isolated t-storms, warm. 15–22 Sunny, cool. 23–30 Sunny north, t-storms south; warm.

OCT. 2017: Temp. 50° (1° below avg.); precip. 2" (1" above avg.). 1–8 A few showers, mild. 9–17 Sunny, nice north; rainy periods, cool south. 18–25 Rain to snow, then sunny, cold. 26–31 Rainy periods, mild north; sunny, cool south.

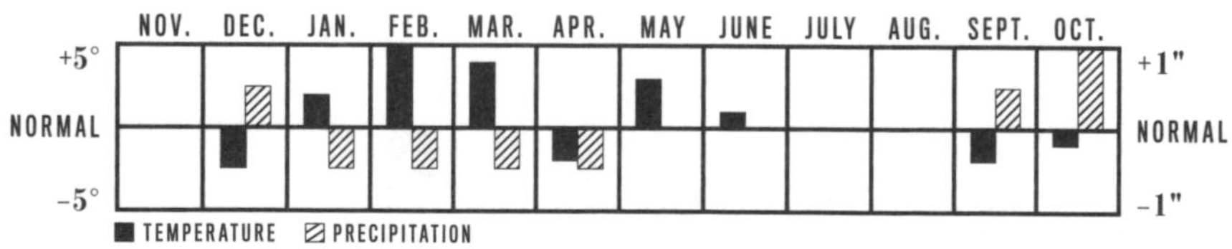

REGION **14** FORECAST

DESERT SOUTHWEST

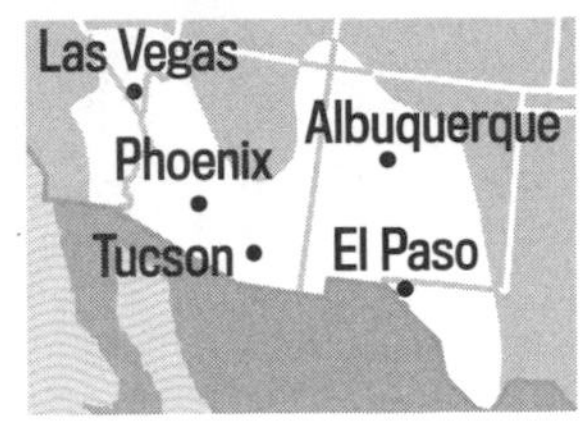

SUMMARY: Winter will be warmer and drier than normal, with below-normal snowfall. The snowiest periods will be in early and late December and mid- to late January. The coldest periods will be in early and late December and from late January into early February. **April** and **May** will be slightly rainier than normal, with below-normal temperatures. **Summer** will be slightly cooler and rainier than normal. The hottest periods will be in mid- to late June and early and mid- to late July. **September** and **October** will be cooler and rainier than normal.

NOV. 2016: Temp. 54° (2° below avg.); precip. 0.8" (0.2" below avg.). 1–7 Sunny; mild east, cool west. 8–17 Showers, then sunny, cool. 18–25 A few showers east, sunny west; cool. 26–30 Showers, chilly.

DEC. 2016: Temp. 45° (3° below avg.); precip. 0.5" (avg.). 1–5 Sunny, cold. 6–12 Rain and snow, then sunny, cold. 13–19 Sunny east, a few showers west; turning mild. 20–31 Rain and snow showers east, sunny west; cold.

JAN. 2017: Temp. 47.5° (2° above avg. east, 3° below west); precip. 0.2" (0.3" below avg.). 1–4 Sunny, cool. 5–22 Sunny; mild east, cold west. 23–31 Snow, then sunny east; sunny west; cold.

FEB. 2017: Temp. 56° (5° above avg.); precip. 0.2" (0.3" below avg.). 1–6 A few rain and snow showers east, sunny west; cold. 7–14 Sunny, turning warm. 15–28 Isolated showers, then sunny, warm.

MAR. 2017: Temp. 63° (5° above avg.); precip. 0.2" (0.3" below avg.). 1–14 Sunny, warm. 15–24 Showers, then sunny, cool. 25–31 Sunny, turning warm.

APR. 2017: Temp. 64° (1° below avg.); precip. 0.5" (avg.). 1–3 Sunny, warm. 4–9 Isolated t-storms, then sunny, cool. 10–15 Isolated t-storms, then sunny, cool. 16–26 Sunny, turning warm. 27–30 Scattered showers.

MAY 2017: Temp. 73° (1° below avg.); precip. 1" (0.5" above avg.). 1–6 Sunny, nice. 7–10 Scattered t-storms, cool east; sunny, warm west. 11–17 T-storms, then sunny, cool. 18–22 Sunny, warm. 23–31 Scattered t-storms, turning cool.

JUNE 2017: Temp. 83° (avg.); precip. 1" (0.5" above avg.). 1–3 Scattered t-storms east, sunny west; cool. 4–10 Scattered t-storms, cool east; sunny, hot west. 11–14 Sunny, hot. 15–20 T-storms, then sunny, warm. 21–26 Sunny, hot. 27–30 Scattered t-storms; cool east, hot west.

JULY 2017: Temp. 88° (1° above avg.); precip. 1" (0.5" below avg.). 1–6 T-storms, then sunny, cool east; sunny, hot west. 7–12 Scattered t-storms, warm. 13–19 Isolated t-storms, warm. 20–25 Sunny, hot. 26–31 Scattered t-storms; cool east, hot west.

AUG. 2017: Temp. 83° (2° below avg.); precip. 2.5" (1" above avg.). 1–4 Showers, cool east; sunny, hot west. 5–15 Scattered t-storms east, sunny west; warm. 16–22 A few t-storms, humid. 23–31 Scattered t-storms, seasonable.

SEPT. 2017: Temp. 77° (2° below avg.); precip. 1.5" (0.5" above avg.). 1–8 T-storms east, sunny west; cool. 9–15 T-storms, then sunny, cool. 16–25 Sunny, warm. 26–30 Scattered t-storms, cool.

OCT. 2017: Temp. 66° (2° below avg.); precip. 2.5" (1.5" above avg.). 1–8 Sunny, hot east; scattered t-storms, cool west. 9–15 T-storms, then sunny, cool. 16–22 A few showers, cool. 23–31 Scattered showers east, sunny west; cool.

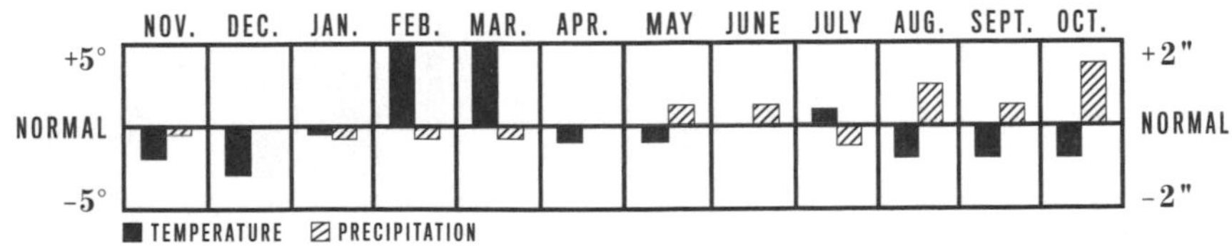

WEATHER

REGION 15 FORECAST

PACIFIC NORTHWEST

SUMMARY: Winter will be rainier than normal. Temperatures will be below normal in the north and above normal in the south, with the coldest periods in early and mid- to late December and mid- to late January. Snowfall will be above normal in the north and below normal in the south, with the snowiest periods in early December and mid-January. **April** and **May** will be slightly warmer and drier than normal. **Summer** will be warmer and rainier than normal, with the hottest temperatures in late June and early to mid-July, from late July into early August, and in mid- to late August. **September** and **October** will be cooler than normal, with near-normal rainfall.

NOV. 2016: Temp. 47.5° (0.5° above avg.); precip. 7" (2" below avg. north, 3" above south). 1–6 Rainy, mild. 7–15 Showers, cool. 16–21 Rainy, mild. 22–24 Sunny, cool. 25–30 Rain, some heavy; turning chilly.

DEC. 2016: Temp. 42° (1° below avg.); precip. 6.5" (avg.). 1–4 Rain and wet snow, cold. 5–7 Rainy, cool. 8–13 Rainy periods, cool. 14–18 Rain, some heavy; cool. 19–20 Sunny, cold. 21–22 Snow to rain. 23–31 Periods of rain and mist, turning milder.

JAN. 2017: Temp. 40° (3° below avg.); precip. 9" (3" above avg.). 1–4 Stormy, rain and wet snow. 5–8 Sprinkles, cool. 9–15 Rain, some heavy; turning mild. 16–23 Rain to snow, then sunny, very cold. 24–28 Rain and snow showers, cold. 29–31 Rainy, mild.

FEB. 2017: Temp. 44.5° (1° below avg. north, 2° above south); precip. 8" (3" above avg.). 1–12 Rainy periods, turning mild. 13–19 Showers, cool. 20–22 Heavy rain, mild. 23–28 Rainy periods, cool.

MAR. 2017: Temp. 49° (2° above avg.); precip. 6" (2" above avg.). 1–6 Rainy periods, mild. 7–13 Showers, mild. 14–18 Rain to wet snow, turning cold. 19–23 Sunny, cool. 24–31 Rainy periods, turning mild.

APR. 2017: Temp. 48° (2° below avg.); precip. 2.5" (0.5" below avg.). 1–5 Rainy, cool. 6–7 Sprinkles. 8–10 Rain and wet snow. 11–21 Rainy periods, cool. 22–30 Sunny, turning warm.

MAY 2017: Temp. 58° (3° above avg.); precip. 1.5" (0.5" below avg.). 1–7 Showers, then sunny, warm. 8–15 Rainy periods, cool. 16–21 Sunny, turning hot. 22–31 Sunny, warm.

JUNE 2017: Temp. 61° (1° above avg.); precip. 1.5" (avg.). 1–3 Rainy, cool. 4–8 Showers, cool. 9–12 Sunny, warm. 13–18 Showers, cool. 19–30 Sunny, turning warm.

JULY 2017: Temp. 68° (3° above avg.); precip. 0.5" (avg.). 1–5 Showers, cool. 6–10 Sunny, turning hot. 11–19 Isolated showers; warm, then cool. 20–31 Sunny, turning hot.

AUG. 2017: Temp. 68° (2° above avg.); precip. 1.5" (0.5" above avg.). 1–6 Sunny, turning cool. 7–15 A few showers, cool. 16–22 Sunny, turning hot. 23–28 Sunny, warm. 29–31 Showers, cool.

SEPT. 2017: Temp. 58° (3° below avg.); precip. 2.5" (1" above avg.). 1–8 Showers, then sunny, nice. 9–15 Rainy periods, turning chilly. 16–21 Showers, cold. 22–30 Sunny, cool.

OCT. 2017: Temp. 53° (1° below avg.); precip. 2" (1" below avg.). 1–6 Showers, cool. 7–12 Sunny; warm, then cool. 13–24 Rainy periods, cool. 25–31 Rain, some heavy; mild.

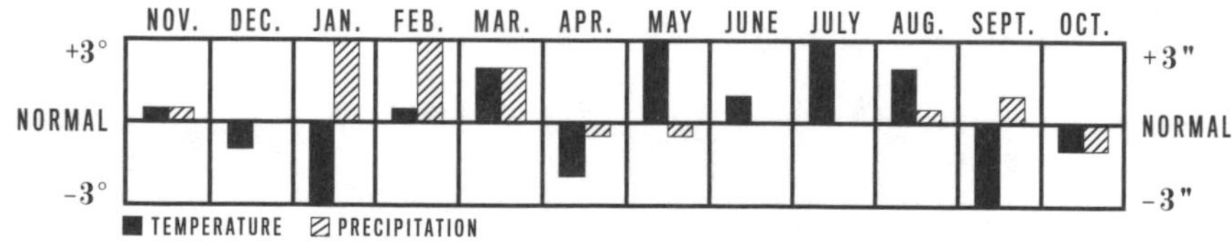

REGION **16** FORECAST

PACIFIC SOUTHWEST

SUMMARY: Winter temperatures and rainfall will be below normal, with below-normal mountain snows. The stormiest periods will be in late November, mid-December, and mid-January. The coldest temperatures will be in early and late December and mid- to late January. **April** and **May** will be warmer and slightly rainier than normal. **Summer** will be hotter than normal, with above-normal rainfall. The hottest periods will be in early and mid- to late July and mid-August. **September** and **October** will be cooler and rainier than normal.

NOV. 2016: Temp. 56° (2° below avg.); precip. 1" (0.5" below avg.). 1–3 Sunny. 4–6 Rainy, cool. 7–18 Sunny, cool. 19–30 Rainy periods, cool.

DEC. 2016: Temp. 51° (3° below avg.); precip. 2.5" (0.5" below avg. north, 2" above south). 1–6 Rainy periods, cool. 7–13 Sunny, cool. 14–16 Rainy periods, cool. 17–21 Rain, some heavy; warm, then cool. 22–31 Sunny, cold.

JAN. 2017: Temp. 51° (3° below avg.); precip. 1" (2" below avg.). 1–12 Sunny, cool. 13–20 Rainy periods, cool. 21–26 Sunny, cool. 27–31 Rainy, mild.

FEB. 2017: Temp. 57° (2° above avg.); precip. 1" (2" below avg.). 1–2 Showers north, sunny south; mild. 3–13 Sunny, seasonable. 14–24 Showers north, sunny south; seasonable. 25–28 Sunny, mild.

MAR. 2017: Temp. 59° (2° above avg.); precip. 1.5" (1" below avg.). 1–14 A few sprinkles, cool coast; sunny, warm inland. 15–17 Showers north, sunny south; seasonable. 18–23 Sunny, cool. 24–28 A few sprinkles north, sunny south; turning warm. 29–31 Showers north, sunny south.

APR. 2017: Temp. 60° (avg.); precip. 1" (avg.). 1–3 Sunny, seasonable. 4–14 Showers, then sunny, cool. 15–20 Showers, then sunny, warm. 21–27 Sunny; warm inland, cool coast. 28–30 Sprinkles, cool.

MAY 2017: Temp. 65.5° (2° above avg.); precip. 0.7" (0.2" above avg.). 1–8 Sunny, turning hot inland; A.M. clouds, P.M. sun coast. 9–13 Scattered showers, cool. 14–23 Sunny, turning hot inland; A.M. clouds and sprinkles, P.M. sun coast. 24–28 Sunny, warm. 29–31 Isolated showers, warm.

JUNE 2017: Temp. 68° (avg.); precip. 0.2" (0.1" above avg.). 1–3 Scattered showers, cool. 4–12 Sunny, turning hot inland; A.M. clouds, P.M. sun coast. 13–17 Isolated showers, turning cool. 18–25 Sunny, hot inland; A.M. clouds, P.M. sun coast. 26–30 Sunny, seasonable inland; A.M. sprinkles, P.M. sun coast.

JULY 2017: Temp. 73° (2° above avg.); precip. 0.2" (0.2" above avg.). 1–3 Sunny; cool north, warm south. 4–8 Sunny, turning hot. 9–16 Sunny, turning cool inland; A.M. clouds and sprinkles, P.M. sun coast. 17–23 Sunny, turning hot. 24–31 Sunny, warm.

AUG. 2017: Temp. 72° (1° above avg.); precip. 0.1" (avg.). 1–4 Sunny, warm. 5–11 Scattered showers, then sunny, cool. 12–15 Sunny; warm north, turning hot south. 16–21 Sunny inland; A.M. sprinkles, P.M. sun coast. 22–25 Sunny inland; A.M. sprinkles, P.M. sun coast; seasonable north, hot south. 26–31 Scattered t-storms, seasonable.

SEPT. 2017: Temp. 69° (1° below avg.); precip. 0.2" (avg.). 1–12 Sunny inland; A.M. sprinkles, P.M. sun coast; cool. 13–17 Sunny, cool. 18–25 Scattered showers north, sunny south; cool. 26–30 Sunny, quite warm.

OCT. 2017: Temp. 63° (2° below avg.); precip. 4" north, 0.5" south (2" above avg.). 1–9 Rain north, some heavy; a few showers south; cool. 10–13 Sprinkles north, rain south; cool. 14–18 Sunny, cool. 19–25 Showers, then sunny, cool. 26–31 A few showers, seasonable.

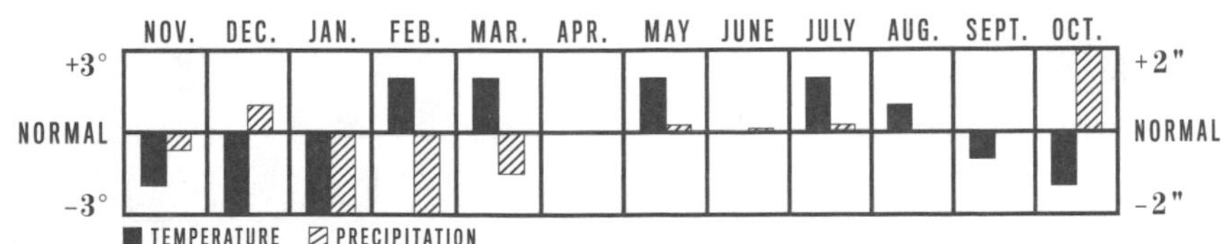

ALASKA

SUMMARY: Winter will be milder than normal, with the coldest period in early January. Precipitation will be near to below normal, with snowfall above normal in the P (see Key below) and below normal EW. The snowiest periods will be in mid-November, mid-December, and mid-January N+C; and mid-November, mid-December, late January S. **April** and **May** will be cooler than normal, with near-normal precipitation. **Summer** will be warmer and a bit drier than normal, with the hottest periods in early June, from late June into early July, and in late July. **September** and **October** precipitation will be slightly above normal, with temperatures above normal N and below normal S.

KEY: Panhandle (P), Aleutians (A), north (N), central (C), south (S), west-central (WC), east-central (EC), south-central (SC), elsewhere (EW)

WEATHER

NOV. 2016: Temp. 1° N, 35° S (1° below avg.); precip. 0.4" N, 4" S (avg. N, 1" below S). 1–7 Snow showers, turning mild. 8–13 Flurries; turning cold WC, mild EW. 14–17 Snowy periods. 18–30 Snow showers, cold.

DEC. 2016: Temp. –2° N, 30° S (5° above avg. north, 1° below south); precip. 0.2" N, 5" S (avg.). 1–8 Snow showers, cold. 9–22 Snowy periods, mild. 23–31 Flurries, turning cold N; snow showers, mild EW.

JAN. 2017: Temp. –9° N, 32° S (3° above avg.); precip. 0.2" N, 5" S (avg.). 1–9 Flurries, very cold. 10–17 Partly cloudy, cold. 18–24 Snowy periods, quite mild. 25–31 Flurries, turning colder N+C; snowy periods, mild S.

FEB. 2017: Temp. –11° N, 34° S (3° above avg.); precip. 0.2" N, 2.5" S (avg. north, 1.5" below south). 1–4 Flurries, mild. 5–11 Snow showers, cold. 12–21 Snow showers, quite mild N+C; clear, cold S. 22–28 Snow showers; cold N, mild S.

MAR. 2017: Temp. –15° N, 32° S (2° below avg.); precip. 0.5" N, 6" S (avg. north, 1" above south). 1–5 Flurries, mild. 6–11 Flurries, cold N; snowy periods, mild S. 12–16 Flurries, cold. 17–23 Snow showers; cold N, mild S. 24–31 Snow showers, cold.

APR. 2017: Temp. 0° N, 39° S (2° below avg.); precip. 0.7" N, 3" S (avg.). 1–7 Snow showers; mild N, cold S. 8–17 Flurries, mild N; snow showers, cold C; rain to snow, then sunny, cold S. 18–25 Snow showers, then sunny, turning mild. 26–30 Flurries N, showers S; mild.

MAY 2017: Temp. 20° N, 46° EW (1° below avg.); precip. 0.6" N, 3" S (avg.). 1–2 Sunny, mild. 3–10 Flurries north, sunny C+S; mild. 11–14 Showers, cool. 15–20 Sunny, warm. 21–31 Flurries and sprinkles N, a few showers C+S; cool.

JUNE 2017: Temp. 36° N, 56° EW (1° above avg.); precip. 0.4" N, 2.7" S (0.3" below avg.). 1–8 A few showers WC+S, sunny EW; turning hot EC, warm EW. 9–18 Scattered showers, cool. 19–30 A few showers, then sunny, very warm.

JULY 2017: Temp. 45° N, 60° EW (3° above avg.); precip. 0.7" N, 3.5" S (0.5" below avg.). 1–6 Isolated showers; hot EC, warm EW. 7–15 Rainy periods, cool. 16–22 A few showers, warm. 23–31 Rainy periods P+A, isolated showers EW; warm.

AUG. 2017: Temp. 42° N, 58° EW (2° above avg.); precip. 1.5" N, 4" S (0.3" above avg. north, 1" below south). 1–3 Showers, mild. 4–9 Sunny, cool N; rainy periods, warm C+S. 10–16 Showers, warm. 17–22 Showers, mild N+C; rainy, cool S. 23–31 Rainy periods, mild.

SEPT. 2017: Temp. 28° N, 50° EW (4° below avg.); precip. 1.1" N, 9" S (avg. north, 2" above south). 1–8 Rainy periods, cool. 9–17 Snow showers N, isolated showers C+S; cool. 18–23 Periods of rain and wet snow, cold. 24–30 Snow showers N+C; periods of rain and snow S; cold.

OCT. 2017: Temp. 24° N, 43° S (12° above avg. north, avg. south); precip. 1.5" N, 6" S (1" above avg. north, 1" below south). 1–4 Rainy periods, mild. 5–10 Heavy snow N, rainy periods EW; quite mild. 11–15 Flurries N, showers EW; mild. 16–20 Snow showers N, rain and snow EW; mild N+C, cold S. 21–31 Snowy periods, mild N+C; snow, then flurries, cold S.

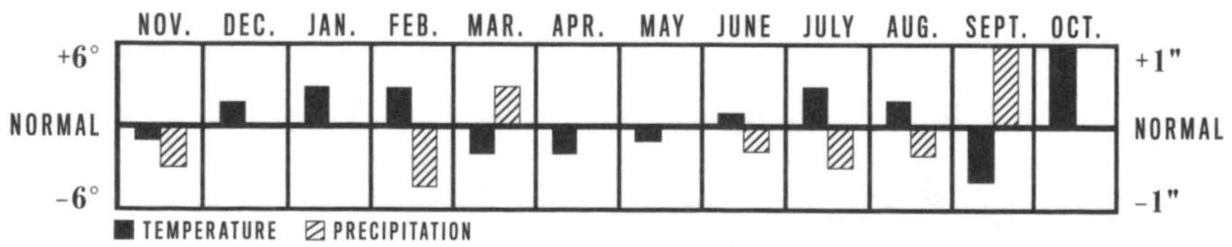

REGION **18** FORECAST

HAWAII

SUMMARY: Winter season temperatures will be below normal, on average, with the coolest periods in mid-December, early and mid- to late January, and mid- and late February. Rainfall will be below normal from Kauai eastward to Oahu and above normal farther east. **April** and **May** will be slightly warmer than normal, with rainfall a bit below normal on the Big Island and above normal elsewhere. **Summer** temperatures will be slightly cooler than normal, on average, with rainfall below normal on the Big Island and Maui and above normal elsewhere. The warmest periods will be in late July and early to mid- and mid- to late August. **September** and **October** temperatures will be slightly cooler than normal, with near-normal rainfall.

KEY: east (E), central (C), west (W) **Note:** Temperature and rainfall amounts vary substantially based upon topography and proximity to the ocean.

WEATHER

NOV. 2016: Temp. 76.5° (1° below avg.); precip. 1.5" (5" above avg. E, 7" below W). 1–16 Rain and t-storms E, daily showers C+W; cool. 17–18 T-storms, heavy E. 19–30 Rain and t-storms E, scattered showers C+W; seasonable.

DEC. 2016: Temp. 74° (1° below avg.); precip. 8.3" (15" above avg. E, avg. C+W). 1–8 Rain and t-storms E, daily showers C+W; seasonable. 9–13 Rainy periods with heavy t-storms, cool. 14–31 Rain and t-storms, cool.

JAN. 2017: Temp. 72° (1° below avg.); precip. 3.2" (avg. E+W, 2" above C). 1–9 Scattered showers, cool. 10–14 Showers E, a few sprinkles C+W; cool. 15–17 Heavy rain and t-storms. 18–27 Isolated showers, cool. 28–31 Rainy periods, seasonable.

FEB. 2017: Temp. 72° (1° below avg.); precip. 2" (avg.). 1–2 Heavy rain E, scattered showers C+W. 3–10 A few showers, cool. 11–18 A few t-storms, cool. 19–21 Sunny, cool. 22–28 Scattered showers; warm, then cool.

MAR. 2017: Temp. 75° (1° above avg.); precip. 0.5" (1.5" below avg.). 1–13 Sunny; cool, then warm. 14–20 Scattered showers; warm E, cool C+W. 21–25 Rainy E, sunny C+W; cool. 26–31 A few showers, seasonable.

APR. 2017: Temp. 76° (0.5° above avg.); precip. 3.7" (avg. E, 6" above W). 1–10 Showers and heavier t-storms, warm. 11–21 Showers and t-storms E, a few showers C+W; turning cool. 22–30 Showers E, isolated showers C+W; cool E, warm W.

MAY 2017: Temp. 77.5° (0.5° above avg.); precip. 0.3" (0.4" below avg.). 1–10 A few showers E, isolated showers C+W; warm. 11–15 Showers, cool E, sunny, warm C+W. 16–26 A few showers, warm. 27–31 Scattered showers, cool.

JUNE 2017: Temp. 80° (0.5° above avg.); precip. 0.4" (2" below avg. E, 2" above W). 1–4 Scattered showers; warm E+W, cool C. 5–12 Scattered showers, warm. 13–20 A few showers, cool. 21–30 Scattered t-storms E+W, isolated showers C; warm.

JULY 2017: Temp. 80.5° (0.5° below avg.); precip. 0.3" (2" below avg. E, 1.5" above W). 1–9 Showers and t-storms E+W, daily brief showers C; cool. 10–16 Scattered light showers, seasonable. 17–31 Showers and a few heavier t-storms E, daily brief showers C+W; cool, then warm.

AUG. 2017: Temp. 81° (0.5° below avg.); precip. 1.6" (1" above avg.). 1–13 Showers and heavier t-storms E, a few showers C+W; warm. 14–20 Isolated showers, cool. 21–31 Showers and a heavier t-storm; warm, then cool.

SEPT. 2017: Temp. 81° (0.5° below avg.); precip. 0.8" (avg.). 1–9 A few showers, warm E; sunny, cool C+W. 10–21 Showers E, a few sprinkles C+W; seasonable. 22–30 A few showers, seasonable.

OCT. 2017: Temp. 80° (avg.); precip. 1.5" (2" below avg. E, 1" above W). 1–4 A few showers, cool. 5–9 A few showers E, sunny C+W; cool. 10–18 Showers E, sunny C+W. 19–31 Showers and heavier t-storms; cool, then warm.

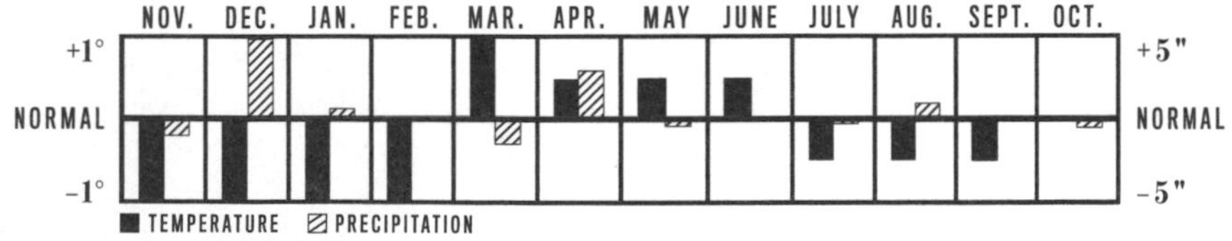

Table of Measures

LINEAR
1 hand = 4 inches
1 link = 7.92 inches
1 span = 9 inches
1 foot = 12 inches
1 yard = 3 feet
1 rod = 5½ yards
1 mile = 320 rods = 1,760 yards = 5,280 feet
1 international nautical mile = 6,076.1155 feet
1 knot = 1 nautical mile per hour
1 fathom = 2 yards = 6 feet
1 furlong = ⅛ mile = 660 feet = 220 yards
1 league = 3 miles = 24 furlongs
1 chain = 100 links = 22 yards

SQUARE
1 square foot = 144 square inches
1 square yard = 9 square feet
1 square rod = 30¼ square yards = 272¼ square feet
1 acre = 160 square rods = 43,560 square feet
1 square mile = 640 acres = 102,400 square rods
1 square rod = 625 square links
1 square chain = 16 square rods
1 acre = 10 square chains

CUBIC
1 cubic foot = 1,728 cubic inches
1 cubic yard = 27 cubic feet
1 cord = 128 cubic feet
1 U.S. liquid gallon = 4 quarts = 231 cubic inches
1 imperial gallon = 1.20 U.S. gallons = 0.16 cubic foot
1 board foot = 144 cubic inches

LIQUID
4 gills = 1 pint
63 gallons = 1 hogshead
2 hogsheads = 1 pipe or butt
2 pipes = 1 tun

DRY
2 pints = 1 quart
4 quarts = 1 gallon
2 gallons = 1 peck
4 pecks = 1 bushel

KITCHEN
3 teaspoons = 1 tablespoon
16 tablespoons = 1 cup
1 cup = 8 ounces
2 cups = 1 pint
2 pints = 1 quart
4 quarts = 1 gallon

AVOIRDUPOIS
(for general use)
1 ounce = 16 drams
1 pound = 16 ounces
1 hundredweight = 100 pounds
1 ton = 2,000 pounds
1 long ton = 2,240 pounds

APOTHECARIES'
(for pharmaceutical use)
1 scruple = 20 grains
1 dram = 3 scruples
1 ounce = 8 drams
1 pound = 12 ounces

TO CONVERT CELSIUS AND FAHRENHEIT:

°C = (°F − 32)/1.8
°F = (°C × 1.8) + 32

Metric Conversions

LINEAR
1 inch = 2.54 centimeters
1 centimeter = 0.39 inch
1 meter = 39.37 inches
1 yard = 0.914 meter
1 mile = 1.61 kilometers
1 kilometer = 0.62 mile

SQUARE
1 square inch = 6.45 square centimeters
1 square yard = 0.84 square meter
1 square mile = 2.59 square kilometers
1 square kilometer = 0.386 square mile
1 acre = 0.40 hectare
1 hectare = 2.47 acres

CUBIC
1 cubic yard = 0.76 cubic meter
1 cubic meter = 1.31 cubic yards

HOUSEHOLD
½ teaspoon = 2 mL
1 teaspoon = 5 mL
1 tablespoon = 15 mL
¼ cup = 60 mL
⅓ cup = 75 mL
½ cup = 125 mL
⅔ cup = 150 mL
¾ cup = 175 mL
1 cup = 250 mL
1 liter = 1.057 U.S. liquid quarts
1 U.S. liquid quart = 0.946 liter
1 U.S. liquid gallon = 3.78 liters
1 gram = 0.035 ounce
1 ounce = 28.349 grams
1 kilogram = 2.2 pounds
1 pound = 0.45 kilogram

The Ins and Outs of Vitamins

Getting enough vitamins and minerals isn't hard. All you really need to do is eat a healthy diet. Build it around fruit and vegetables (8 to 10 servings a day), whole-grain breads and cereals, beans, low-fat poultry and meat, nonfried fish, milk, cheese, and yogurt.

Here's what vitamins do and where they hide in your food:

VITAMIN	WHAT IT DOES	WHERE IT IS
Vitamin A	• good for your eyesight • helps you see in the dark • helps fight infections • helps bone growth	milk, cheese, eggs, liver, fish oil, yellow fruit, dark-green and yellow veggies
B Vitamins	• help make red blood cells • help make energy and release it	whole grains (wheat and oats), fish and seafood, meat, poultry, eggs, dairy products, leafy green veggies, beans and peas, citrus fruit
Vitamin C	• keeps gums and muscles healthy • helps heal cuts • helps body resist infection	citrus fruit and juices, berries, tomatoes, peppers, broccoli, potatoes, cauliflower, cantaloupe
Vitamin D	• makes strong bones and teeth	milk, egg yolks, fish
Vitamin E	• helps make red blood cells • keeps tissues in eyes, skin, and liver healthy • protects lungs from pollution	whole grains (wheat and oats), wheat germ, leafy green veggies, sardines, nuts, egg yolks
Vitamin K	• enables blood to clot	leafy green veggies, pork, liver, dairy products

Hay Fever Foods

If you experience seasonal allergies to pollen, these food compounds may help:

■ **Probiotics** (beneficial bacteria), found in dietary supplements or in yogurt containing live cultures

■ **Omega-3 fatty acids,** found in salmon, halibut, tuna, cod, sardines, fish oil, flaxseed oil, canola oil, shrimp, clams, spinach, and walnuts

■ **Quercetin,** found in citrus, apples, cranberries, grapes, olive oil, blueberries, blackberries, onions, parsley, spinach, broccoli, kale, black and green teas, and red wine. You can also buy quercetin supplements. Research has found that quercetin is more effective when combined with bromelain, an enzyme in pineapple.

■ **Vitamin C,** found in citrus, papaya, cantaloupe, kiwi, strawberries, parsley, bell peppers, broccoli, brussels sprouts, kale, cauliflower, and sweet potatoes

Caution: Some people allergic to pollen may also be allergic to certain fresh fruit, vegetables, nuts, and grains.

2016 ESSAY CONTEST WINNERS

A new U.S. holiday we need—and why

FIRST PRIZE: $250

Recently, when dropping my mother home from Bingo to her senior building, a fellow resident asked if I was going downtown. Her car was broken and she needed to get to the art store. I said, "Sorry." I wasn't. But then I saw her walking in the windy, soon-to-be-rainy weather. I thought, why not?, and offered her a ride. It wasn't that far out of my way and maybe I would enjoy the art store. I found out she was going there to pick up two screws for her friend and that she and her friend take turns every other month doing something nice for one another. She was so appreciative and couldn't believe a total stranger would drive her both ways. I said, "It was nothing compared to the nice things you do for your friend."

On the drive home, I thought, how kind that she was willing to walk in bad weather 2 miles for her friend. It should be every day, but at least one day set aside for helping others would be nice: Pay It Forward Day.

–Jill Ashcraft, Medford, Oregon

SECOND PRIZE: $150

There was a time when everyone knew how to handwrite a letter or note. Today we have college graduates who are very poor spellers with unreadable penmanship. There is nothing more personal than a handwritten note or letter. We are losing one or more of the most basic communication skills. When something is handwritten, you don't need to worry about being hacked through the Internet or if the computer or cell phone battery is low or if the electric power goes out. You will never need to remember a password. Your handwriting is unique to yourself and can show your personality. Let us celebrate our ability to show how unique we are as individuals and one of our most personal communication skills by having a National Handwritten Day.

–Keith K. Bird, Northampton, Pennsylvania

THIRD PRIZE: $100

While most of us sit down to a meal consisting of vegetables, dairy, fruit, or meat, we usually do not think about the farmers who worked hard to make such meals possible. We really should appreciate all that they do to feed the world by having National Farmers Day.

Unless you have a commercial-size farm, farming is not a high-profit job. This country really should consider creating a national holiday to thank the farmers for feeding the world. Farmers would appreciate this thanks very much. They are very deserving of such recognition.

–Michael Painter, Caledonia, Mississippi

HONORABLE MENTION

I think there should be a second Christmas because Santa could look over his naughty and nice list and be able to change his mind if boys and girls were not as bad as he may have first thought. He then could deliver toys to the good boys and girls. I also think it would allow you to visit friends and relatives that you could not see on the other Christmas holiday. Another reason why I think there should be a second Christmas is if you did not get what you wanted on the first Christmas, you might get it on the second Christmas.

–Shea X., Pennsylvania (9 years old)

EVERY DAY SHOULD BE A HOLIDAY

We received more than 200 essays on a wide range of holiday topics, all heartfelt and heartwarming. Several writers proposed especially unusual days: fishing day; sundial day; arts, hometown, and gathering days; storytelling day; heat of August day; yardsalers day; bees day; and hug day among them. A surprising number of people submitted essays on days celebrating silence (from devices); immigrants or Native People; veterans, first responders, and public service workers; sports, teams, and sporting events; pets; weather in every season, heritage and diversity; aunts, uncles, and siblings; heroes and victims of 9-11; farming and harvest; stress and health; First Ladies; historical figures (Helen Keller, George Washington Carver, Walt Disney, and Cherokee chief Wilma Mankiller, to name a few); and women in general. Election Day got many "votes," and one writer made a plea for "no politics" day.

The creativity, logic, and imagination employed by all writers made this an especially challenging contest for the judges. Thanks to everyone who took the time to conceive and submit an essay. We appreciate your enthusiasm and invite you to try your hand at this year's topic. ■

–Almanac editors

ANNOUNCING THE 2017 ESSAY CONTEST TOPIC:

The Historical Figure I Would Like to Meet and Why.

SEE CONTEST RULES ON PAGE 242.

ESSAY AND RECIPE CONTEST RULES

Cash prizes (first, $250; second, $150; third, $100) will be awarded for the best essays in 200 words or less on the subject "The Historical Figure I Would Like to Meet and Why" and the best recipes in the category "Sweet Potatoes." Entries must be yours, original, and unpublished. Amateur cooks only, please. One recipe per person. All entries become the property of Yankee Publishing, which reserves all rights to the material. The deadline for entries is Friday, January 27, 2017. Enter at Almanac.com/EssayContest or at Almanac.com/RecipeContest or label "Essay Contest" or "Recipe Contest" and mail to The Old Farmer's Almanac, P.O. Box 520, Dublin, NH 03444. Include your name, mailing address, and email address. Winners will appear in *The 2018 Old Farmer's Almanac* and on Almanac.com.

MADDENING MIND-MANGLERS

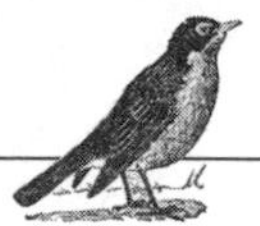

Words of a Feather

Can you flock them together? Match each bird with the mnemonic phrase that most closely describes one of its songs or calls. Answers on page 265.

–compiled by Heidi Stonehill

___ **1.** Indigo bunting

___ **2.** Northern cardinal

___ **3.** Olive-sided flycatcher

___ **4.** American goldfinch

___ **5.** Ovenbird

___ **6.** Barred owl

___ **7.** Great horned owl

___ **8.** California quail

___ **9.** King rail

___ **10.** American robin

___ **11.** White-throated sparrow

___ **12.** Tundra swan

___ **13.** Brown thrasher

___ **14.** Tufted titmouse

___ **15.** Eastern towhee

___ **16.** Red-eyed vireo

___ **17.** Black-throated blue warbler

___ **18.** Chestnut-sided warbler

___ **19.** Yellow warbler

___ **20.** Carolina wren

A. Cheer, cheer, cheer

B. Cheerily, cheer up, cheer up, cheerily, cheer up

C. Chi-CA-go!

D. Drink your tea!

E. Drop it! Drop it! Cover it up! Cover it up! Pull it up! Pull it up!

F. Here I am. Where are you?

G. Hip-hip-hurrah

H. I'm so laz-eee!

I. Old Sam Peabody, Peabody, Peabody

J. Peter, Peter, Peter

K. Pleased, pleased, pleased, pleased ta meetcha

L. Po-ta-to-chip

M. Quick! Three beers!

N. Sweet, sweet, sweet, I am so sweet

O. Tea-cher, Tea-cher, TEA-cher

P. Teakettle, teakettle, teakettle

Q. What? What? Where? Where? See it! See it!

R. Who cooks for you? Who cooks for you all?

S. Who's awake? Me, too!

T. Woo-hoo

FIND YOUR CALLING: To hear bird songs and calls, go to Almanac.com/BirdSounds.

Heidi Stonehill is a senior editor at *The Old Farmer's Almanac.* Her own particular call is "CHOC-o-late! Marvelous CHOC-o-late!"

Secrets of the Zodiac

The Man of the Signs

Ancient astrologers believed that each astrological sign influenced a specific part of the body. The first sign of the zodiac—Aries—was attributed to the head, with the rest of the signs moving down the body, ending with Pisces at the feet.

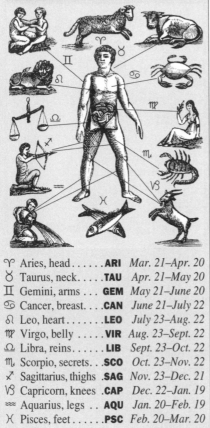

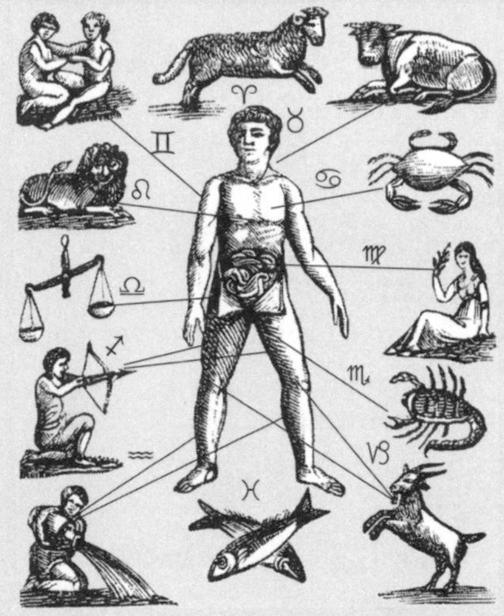

♈ Aries, head	**ARI**	*Mar. 21–Apr. 20*
♉ Taurus, neck	**TAU**	*Apr. 21–May 20*
♊ Gemini, arms	**GEM**	*May 21–June 20*
♋ Cancer, breast	**CAN**	*June 21–July 22*
♌ Leo, heart	**LEO**	*July 23–Aug. 22*
♍ Virgo, belly	**VIR**	*Aug. 23–Sept. 22*
♎ Libra, reins	**LIB**	*Sept. 23–Oct. 22*
♏ Scorpio, secrets	**SCO**	*Oct. 23–Nov. 22*
♐ Sagittarius, thighs	**SAG**	*Nov. 23–Dec. 21*
♑ Capricorn, knees	**CAP**	*Dec. 22–Jan. 19*
♒ Aquarius, legs	**AQU**	*Jan. 20–Feb. 19*
♓ Pisces, feet	**PSC**	*Feb. 20–Mar. 20*

Astrology vs. Astronomy

■ **Astrology** is a tool we use to plan events according to the placements of the Sun, the Moon, and the planets in the 12 signs of the zodiac. In astrology, the planetary movements do not cause events; rather, they explain the path, or "flow," that events tend to follow. **Astronomy** is the study of the actual placement of the known planets and constellations. *(The placement of the planets in the signs of the zodiac is not the same astrologically and astronomically.)* The Moon's astrological place is given on **page 245;** its astronomical place is given in the **Left-Hand Calendar Pages, 142–168.**

The dates in the **Best Days** table, **page 246,** are based on the astrological passage of the Moon. However, consider all indicators before making any major decisions.

When Mercury Is Retrograde

■ Sometimes the other planets appear to be traveling backward through the zodiac; this is an illusion. We call this illusion *retrograde motion.*

Mercury's retrograde periods can cause our plans to go awry. However, this is an excellent time to reflect on the past. Intuition is high during these periods, and coincidences can be extraordinary.

When Mercury is retrograde, remain flexible, allow extra time for travel, and avoid signing contracts. Review projects and plans at these times, but wait until Mercury is direct again to make any final decisions.

In 2017, Mercury will be retrograde during January 1–9, April 9–May 3, August 13–September 5, and December 3–23.

–Celeste Longacre

Gardening by the Moon's Sign

Use the chart on the next page to find the best dates for the following garden tasks:

■ **Plant, transplant, and graft:** Cancer, Scorpio, Pisces, or Taurus.

■ **Harvest:** Aries, Leo, Sagittarius, Gemini, or Aquarius.

■ **Build/fix fences or garden beds:** Capricorn.

■ **Control insect pests, plow, and weed:** Aries, Gemini, Leo, Sagittarius, or Aquarius.

■ **Prune:** Aries, Leo, or Sagittarius. During a waxing Moon, pruning encourages growth; during a waning Moon, it discourages growth.

Setting Eggs by the Moon's Sign

■ Chicks take about 21 days to hatch. Those born under a waxing Moon, in the fruitful signs of Cancer, Scorpio, and Pisces, are healthier and mature faster. To ensure that chicks are born during these times, determine the best days to "set eggs" (to place eggs in an incubator or under a hen). To calculate, find the three fruitful birth signs on the chart below. Use the **Left-Hand Calendar Pages, 142–168,** to find the dates of the new and full Moons. Using only the fruitful dates between the new and full Moons, count back 21 days to find the best days to set eggs.

EXAMPLE:

The Moon is new on March 27 and full on April 11. Between these dates, on April 2 to 4, the Moon is in the sign of Cancer. To have chicks born on April 2, count back 21 days; set eggs on March 12.

The Moon's Astrological Place, 2016–17

	Nov.	Dec.	Jan.	Feb.	Mar.	Apr.	May	June	July	Aug.	Sept.	Oct.	Nov.	Dec.
1	SAG	CAP	AQU	ARI	ARI	GEM	CAN	VIR	LIB	SAG	CAP	AQU	ARI	TAU
2	SAG	CAP	PSC	ARI	TAU	CAN	LEO	VIR	SCO	SAG	CAP	PSC	ARI	TAU
3	SAG	CAP	PSC	TAU	TAU	CAN	LEO	LIB	SCO	SAG	AQU	PSC	TAU	GEM
4	CAP	AQU	ARI	TAU	GEM	CAN	VIR	LIB	SCO	CAP	AQU	PSC	TAU	GEM
5	CAP	AQU	ARI	GEM	GEM	LEO	VIR	SCO	SAG	CAP	PSC	ARI	GEM	CAN
6	AQU	PSC	ARI	GEM	CAN	LEO	VIR	SCO	SAG	AQU	PSC	ARI	GEM	CAN
7	AQU	PSC	TAU	CAN	CAN	VIR	LIB	SCO	CAP	AQU	ARI	TAU	CAN	LEO
8	AQU	ARI	TAU	CAN	LEO	VIR	LIB	SAG	CAP	AQU	ARI	TAU	CAN	LEO
9	PSC	ARI	GEM	LEO	LEO	LIB	SCO	SAG	CAP	PSC	TAU	GEM	LEO	VIR
10	PSC	TAU	GEM	LEO	LEO	LIB	SCO	CAP	AQU	PSC	TAU	GEM	LEO	VIR
11	ARI	TAU	CAN	VIR	VIR	LIB	SAG	CAP	AQU	ARI	TAU	CAN	VIR	LIB
12	ARI	GEM	CAN	VIR	VIR	SCO	SAG	CAP	PSC	ARI	GEM	CAN	VIR	LIB
13	TAU	GEM	LEO	VIR	LIB	SCO	SAG	AQU	PSC	TAU	GEM	LEO	VIR	SCO
14	TAU	CAN	LEO	LIB	LIB	SAG	CAP	AQU	PSC	TAU	CAN	LEO	LIB	SCO
15	GEM	CAN	VIR	LIB	SCO	SAG	CAP	PSC	ARI	GEM	CAN	VIR	LIB	SCO
16	GEM	LEO	VIR	SCO	SCO	SAG	AQU	PSC	ARI	GEM	LEO	VIR	SCO	SAG
17	CAN	LEO	LIB	SCO	SCO	CAP	AQU	PSC	TAU	CAN	LEO	VIR	SCO	SAG
18	CAN	LEO	LIB	SCO	SAG	CAP	AQU	ARI	TAU	CAN	VIR	LIB	SCO	CAP
19	LEO	VIR	LIB	SAG	SAG	AQU	PSC	ARI	GEM	CAN	VIR	LIB	SAG	CAP
20	LEO	VIR	SCO	SAG	CAP	AQU	PSC	TAU	GEM	LEO	LIB	SCO	SAG	CAP
21	VIR	LIB	SCO	CAP	CAP	AQU	ARI	TAU	CAN	LEO	LIB	SCO	CAP	AQU
22	VIR	LIB	SAG	CAP	CAP	PSC	ARI	GEM	CAN	VIR	LIB	SAG	CAP	AQU
23	VIR	SCO	SAG	AQU	AQU	PSC	TAU	GEM	LEO	VIR	SCO	SAG	CAP	PSC
24	LIB	SCO	SAG	AQU	AQU	ARI	TAU	CAN	LEO	LIB	SCO	SAG	AQU	PSC
25	LIB	SCO	CAP	AQU	PSC	ARI	GEM	CAN	VIR	LIB	SAG	CAP	AQU	PSC
26	SCO	SAG	CAP	PSC	PSC	TAU	GEM	LEO	VIR	SCO	SAG	CAP	PSC	ARI
27	SCO	SAG	AQU	PSC	ARI	TAU	CAN	LEO	LIB	SCO	CAP	AQU	PSC	ARI
28	SCO	CAP	AQU	ARI	ARI	GEM	CAN	VIR	LIB	SCO	CAP	AQU	ARI	TAU
29	SAG	CAP	PSC	–	TAU	GEM	LEO	VIR	LIB	SAG	CAP	AQU	ARI	TAU
30	SAG	CAP	PSC	–	TAU	CAN	LEO	LIB	SCO	SAG	AQU	PSC	ARI	GEM
31	–	AQU	PSC	–	GEM	–	VIR	–	SCO	CAP	–	PSC	–	GEM

Best Days for 2017

This chart is based on the Moon's sign and shows the best days each month for certain activities.

–Celeste Longacre

	JAN.	FEB.	MAR.	APR.	MAY	JUNE	JULY	AUG.	SEPT.	OCT.	NOV.	DEC.
Quit smoking	16, 21	12, 17	17, 26	13, 23	20, 24	16, 21	13, 18	10, 14	10, 14, 19	7, 12, 16	8, 12	9, 14
Begin diet to lose weight	16, 21	12, 17	17, 26	13, 23	20, 24	16, 21	13, 18	10, 14	10, 14, 19	7, 12, 16	8, 12	9, 14
Begin diet to gain weight	3, 7, 30	4, 27	3, 30	3, 8	5	2, 6, 28	4, 26	22, 27	5, 23	3, 31	26, 27	1, 29
Cut hair to encourage growth	2, 3, 30, 31	3, 4, 27	2, 3, 29, 30	5, 6, 27	7, 8	3, 4, 30	1, 28, 29	24, 25	3, 21, 22	3, 4, 30, 31	3, 26, 27	1, 23–25
Cut hair to discourage growth	17–19	14, 15	13, 14	22, 23	19, 20	15–17	17, 18	13, 14	16, 17	7, 8	14, 15	11–13
Have dental care	15, 16	11–13	11, 12	7, 8	4–6	1, 2, 28, 29	25, 26	22, 23	18, 19	15–17	11–13	9, 10
Start projects	29	27	29	27	26	25	24	22	21	20	19	19
End projects	27	25	27	25	24	23	22	20	19	18	17	17
Go camping	22–24	19, 20	18, 19	14–16	11–13	8, 9	5, 6	1–3	25, 26	22–24	19, 20	16, 17
Plant aboveground crops	2, 3, 30, 31	7, 8, 26, 27	6, 7	3, 4, 30	1, 27, 28	5–7, 25	3, 4, 30, 31	26–28	5, 23, 24	3, 4, 30, 31	26, 27	23–25
Plant belowground crops	20, 21	16, 17	15–17, 25	12, 13, 22, 23	19, 20	15–17	12–14	9, 10	14, 15	11, 12	7, 8	13–15
Destroy pests and weeds	4–6	1, 2, 28	1, 27, 28	24, 25	21, 22	18, 19	15, 16	11, 12	7, 8	5, 6	1, 2, 28–30	26, 27
Graft or pollinate	11, 12	7, 8	6, 7	3, 4, 30	27, 28	24, 25	21, 22	17–19	14, 15	11, 12	7, 8	5, 6
Prune to encourage growth	4–6	1, 2, 28	1, 8–10	5, 6	2, 3, 29, 30	8, 26, 27	5, 6, 24	1–3, 29, 30	25, 26	22–24	1, 2, 28–30	26, 27
Prune to discourage growth	22–24	19, 20	18, 19	14, 15	12, 13, 21, 22	18, 19	15, 16	11, 12	16, 17	13, 14	9, 10	7, 8
Harvest aboveground crops	7, 8	3, 4	2, 3, 29, 30	7, 8	4–6	1, 2, 28, 29	8, 25, 26	4, 5, 31	1, 28, 29	25, 26	3, 21, 22	1, 2, 28, 29
Harvest belowground crops	15, 16	11–13	20–22	17, 18	23, 24	20, 21	17, 18	13, 14	18, 19	15–17	11–13	9, 10
Can, pickle, or make sauerkraut	20, 21	16–18	15–17	21–23	18–20	15–17	12–14	9, 10	14, 15	11, 12	7, 8	13–15
Cut hay	4–6	1, 2, 28	1, 27, 28	24, 25	21, 22	18, 19	15, 16	11, 12	7, 8	5, 6	1, 2, 28–30	26, 27
Begin logging	25, 26	21, 22	20–22	17, 18	14, 15	10–12	7–9	4, 5, 31	1, 2, 27–29	25, 26	21–23	18–20
Set posts or pour concrete	25, 26	21, 22	20–22	17, 18	14, 15	10–12	7–9	4, 5, 31	1, 2, 27–29	25–26	21–23	18–20
Breed animals	20, 21	16, 17	15–17	12, 13	9, 10	5–7	3, 4, 30, 31	26–28	23, 24	20, 21	16–18	13–15
Wean animals or children	16, 21	12, 17	17, 26	13, 23	20, 24	16, 21	13, 18	10, 14	10, 14, 19	7, 12, 16	8, 12	9, 14
Castrate animals	27, 28	23–25	23, 24	19–21	16–18	13, 14	10, 11	6–8	3, 4, 30	1, 27–29	24, 25	21, 22
Slaughter livestock	20, 21	16, 17	15–17	12, 13	9–10	5–7	3, 4, 30, 31	26–28	23, 24	20, 21	16–18	13–15

See what to do when at Almanac.com/BestDays.

Gestation and Mating Tables

		Proper Age or Weight for First Mating	Period of Fertility (yrs.)	Number of Females for One Male	Period of Gestation (days) AVERAGE	RANGE
CATTLE:	Cow	15–18 mos.[1]	10–14		283	279–290[2] 262–300[3]
	Bull	1 yr., well matured	10–12	50[4] / thousands[5]		
GOAT:	Doe	10 mos. or 85–90 lbs.	6		150	145–155
	Buck	well matured	5	30		
HORSE:	Mare	3 yrs.	10–12		336	310–370
	Stallion	3 yrs.	12–15	40–45[4] / record 252[5]		
PIG:	Sow	5–6 mos. or 250 lbs.	6		115	110–120
	Boar	250–300 lbs.	6	50[6] / 35–40[7]		
RABBIT:	Doe	6 mos.	5–6		31	30–32
	Buck	6 mos.	5–6	30		
SHEEP:	Ewe	1 yr. or 90 lbs.	6		147 / 151[8]	142–154
	Ram	12–14 mos., well matured	7	50–75[6] / 35–40[7]		
CAT:	Queen	12 mos.	6		63	60–68
	Tom	12 mos.	6	6–8		
DOG:	Bitch	16–18 mos.	8		63	58–67
	Male	12–16 mos.	8	8–10		

[1]Holstein and beef: 750 lbs.; Jersey: 500 lbs. [2]Beef; 8–10 days shorter for Angus. [3]Dairy. [4]Natural. [5]Artificial. [6]Hand-mated. [7]Pasture. [8]For fine wool breeds.

Incubation Period of Poultry (days)

Chicken	21
Duck	26–32
Goose	30–34
Guinea	26–28
Turkey	28

Average Life Span of Animals in Captivity (years)

Cat (domestic)	14	Goose (domestic)	20
Chicken (domestic)	8	Horse	22
Dog (domestic)	13	Pig	12
Duck (domestic)	10	Rabbit	6
Goat (domestic)	14	Turkey (domestic)	10

	Estral/Estrous Cycle (including heat period) AVERAGE	RANGE	Length of Estrus (heat) AVERAGE	RANGE	Usual Time of Ovulation	When Cycle Recurs If Not Bred
Cow	21 days	18–24 days	18 hours	10–24 hours	10–12 hours after end of estrus	21 days
Doe goat	21 days	18–24 days	2–3 days	1–4 days	Near end of estrus	21 days
Mare	21 days	10–37 days	5–6 days	2–11 days	24–48 hours before end of estrus	21 days
Sow	21 days	18–24 days	2–3 days	1–5 days	30–36 hours after start of estrus	21 days
Ewe	16½ days	14–19 days	30 hours	24–32 hours	12–24 hours before end of estrus	16½ days
Queen cat		15–21 days	3–4 days, if mated	9–10 days, in absence of male	24–56 hours after coitus	Pseudo-pregnancy
Bitch	24 days	16–30 days	7 days	5–9 days	1–3 days after first acceptance	Pseudo-pregnancy

Planting by the Moon's Phase

According to this age-old practice, cycles of the Moon affect plant growth.

■ Plant annual flowers and vegetables that bear crops above ground during the light, or waxing, of the Moon: from the day the Moon is new to the day it is full.

■ Plant flowering bulbs, biennial and perennial flowers, and vegetables that bear crops below ground during the dark, or waning, of the Moon: from the day after it is full to the day before it is new again.

The Moon Favorable columns give the best planting days based on the Moon's phases for 2017. (See the **Left-Hand Calendar Pages, 142–168,** for the exact days of the new and full Moons.) The Planting Dates columns give the safe periods for planting in areas that receive frost. See **Frosts and Growing Seasons, page 216,** for first/last frost dates and the average length of the growing season in your area.

Get local seed-sowing dates at Almanac.com/PlantingTable.

- **Aboveground crops are marked *.**
- **(E) means early; (L) means late.**
- **Map shades correspond to shades of date columns.**

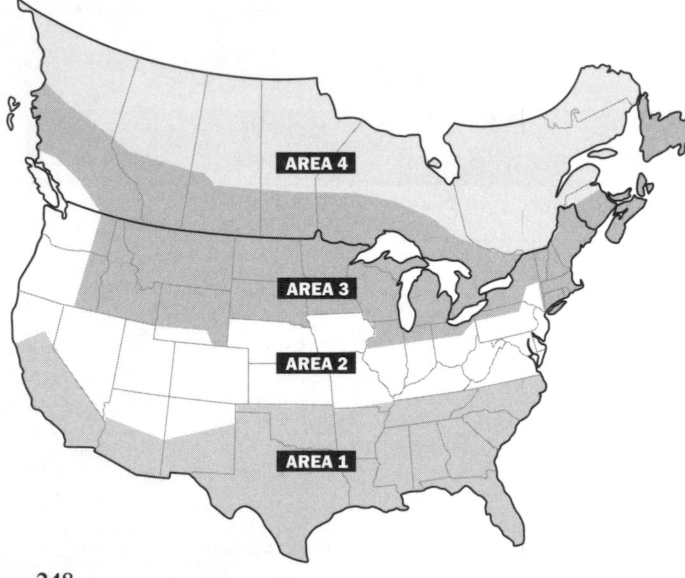

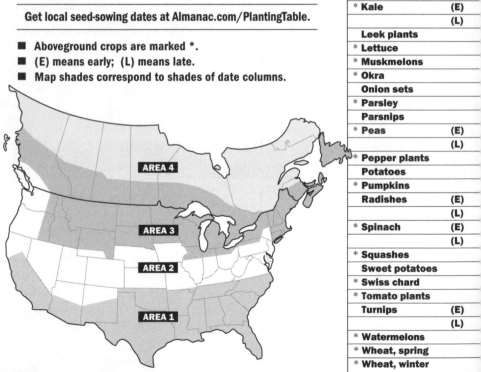

* **Barley**	
* **Beans**	**(E)**
	(L)
Beets	**(E)**
	(L)
* **Broccoli plants**	**(E)**
	(L)
* **Brussels sprouts**	
* **Cabbage plants**	
Carrots	**(E)**
	(L)
* **Cauliflower plants**	**(E)**
	(L)
* **Celery plants**	**(E)**
	(L)
* **Collards**	**(E)**
	(L)
* **Corn, sweet**	**(E)**
	(L)
* **Cucumbers**	
* **Eggplant plants**	
* **Endive**	**(E)**
	(L)
* **Kale**	**(E)**
	(L)
Leek plants	
* **Lettuce**	
* **Muskmelons**	
* **Okra**	
Onion sets	
* **Parsley**	
Parsnips	
* **Peas**	**(E)**
	(L)
* **Pepper plants**	
Potatoes	
* **Pumpkins**	
Radishes	**(E)**
	(L)
* **Spinach**	**(E)**
	(L)
* **Squashes**	
Sweet potatoes	
* **Swiss chard**	
* **Tomato plants**	
Turnips	**(E)**
	(L)
* **Watermelons**	
* **Wheat, spring**	
* **Wheat, winter**	

AREA 1		AREA 2		AREA 3		AREA 4	
lanting ates	Moon Favorable	Planting Dates	Moon Favorable	Planting Dates	Moon Favorable	Planting Dates	Moon Favorable
'15–3/7	2/26–3/7	3/15–4/7	3/27–4/7	5/15–6/21	5/25–6/9	6/1–30	6/1–9, 6/23–30
'15–4/7	3/27–4/7	4/15–30	4/26–30	5/7–6/21	5/7–10, 5/25–6/9	5/30–6/15	5/30–6/9
7–31	8/7, 8/21–31	7/1–21	7/1–9	6/15–7/15	6/23–7/9	—	—
7–28	2/11–25	3/15–4/3	3/15–26	5/1–15	5/11–15	5/25–6/10	6/10
'1–30	9/7–19	8/15–31	8/15–20	7/15–8/15	7/15–22, 8/8–15	6/15–7/8	6/15–22
'15–3/15	2/26–3/12	3/7–31	3/7–12, 3/27–31	5/15–31	5/25–31	6/1–25	6/1–9, 6/23–25
7–30	9/20–30	8/1–20	8/1–7	6/15–7/7	6/23–7/7	—	—
'11–3/20	2/26–3/12	3/7–4/15	3/7–12, 3/27–4/11	5/15–31	5/25–31	6/1–25	6/1–9, 6/23–25
'11–3/20	2/26–3/12	3/7–4/15	3/7–12, 3/27–4/11	5/15–31	5/25–31	6/1–25	6/1–9, 6/23–25
'15–3/7	2/15–25	3/7–31	3/13–26	5/15–31	5/15–24	5/25–6/10	6/10
'1–9/7	8/8–20, 9/7	7/7–31	7/10–22	6/15–7/21	6/15–22, 7/10–21	6/15–7/8	6/15–22
'15–3/7	2/26–3/7	3/15–4/7	3/27–4/7	5/15–31	5/25–31	6/1–25	6/1–9, 6/23–25
7–31	8/7, 8/21–31	7/1–8/7	7/1–9, 7/23–8/7	6/15–7/21	6/23–7/9	—	—
'15–28	2/26–28	3/7–31	3/7–12, 3/27–31	5/15–6/30	5/25–6/9, 6/23–30	6/1–30	6/1–9, 6/23–30
'15–30	9/20–30	8/15–9/7	8/21–9/6	7/15–8/15	7/23–8/7	—	—
'11–3/20	2/26–3/12	3/7–4/7	3/7–12, 3/27–4/7	5/15–31	5/25–31	6/1–25	6/1–9, 6/23–25
7–30	9/20–30	8/15–31	8/21–31	7/1–8/7	7/1–9, 7/23–8/7	—	—
'15–31	3/27–31	4/1–17	4/1–11	5/10–6/15	5/10, 5/25–6/9	5/30–6/20	5/30–6/9
7–31	8/7, 8/21–31	7/7–21	7/7–9	6/15–30	6/23–30	—	—
7–4/15	3/7–12, 3/27–4/11	4/7–5/15	4/7–11, 4/26–5/10	5/7–6/20	5/7–10, 5/25–6/9	5/30–6/15	5/30–6/9
7–4/15	3/7–12, 3/27–4/11	4/7–5/15	4/7–11, 4/26–5/10	6/1–30	6/1–9, 6/23–30	6/15–30	6/23–30
'15–3/20	2/26–3/12	4/7–5/15	4/7–11, 4/26–5/10	5/15–31	5/25–31	6/1–25	6/1–9, 6/23–25
'15–9/7	8/21–9/6	7/15–8/15	7/23–8/7	6/7–30	6/7–9, 6/23–30	—	—
'11–3/20	2/26–3/12	3/7–4/7	3/7–12, 3/27–4/7	5/15–31	5/25–31	6/1–15	6/1–9
7–30	9/20–30	8/15–31	8/21–31	7/1–8/7	7/1–9, 7/23–8/7	6/25–7/15	6/25–7/9
'15–4/15	2/15–25, 3/13–26, 4/12–15	3/7–4/7	3/13–26	5/15–31	5/15–24	6/1–25	6/10–22
'15–3/7	2/26–3/7	3/1–31	3/1–12, 3/27–31	5/15–6/30	5/25–6/9, 6/23–30	6/1–30	6/1–9, 6/23–30
'15–4/7	3/27–4/7	4/15–5/7	4/26–5/7	5/15–6/30	5/25–6/9, 6/23–30	6/1–30	6/1–9, 6/23–30
'15–6/1	4/26–5/10, 5/25–6/1	5/25–6/15	5/25–6/9	6/15–7/10	6/23–7/9	6/25–7/7	6/25–7/7
'1–28	2/11–25	3/1–31	3/13–26	5/15–6/7	5/15–24	6/1–25	6/10–22
'20–3/15	2/26–3/12	3/1–31	3/1–12, 3/27–31	5/15–31	5/25–31	6/1–15	6/1–9
'15–2/4	1/15–26	3/7–31	3/13–26	4/1–30	4/12–25	5/10–31	5/11–24
'15–2/7	1/27–2/7	3/7–31	3/7–12, 3/27–31	4/15–5/7	4/26–5/7	5/15–31	5/25–31
'15–30	9/20–30	8/7–31	8/7, 8/21–31	7/15–31	7/23–31	7/10–25	7/23–25
'1–20	3/1–12	4/1–30	4/1–11, 4/26–30	5/15–6/30	5/25–6/9, 6/23–30	6/1–30	6/1–9, 6/23–30
'10–28	2/11–25	4/1–30	4/12–25	5/1–31	5/11–24	6/1–25	6/10–22
7–20	3/7–12	4/23–5/15	4/26–5/10	5/15–31	5/25–31	6/1–30	6/1–9, 6/23–30
'21–3/1	1/21–26, 2/11–25	3/7–31	3/13–26	4/15–30	4/15–25	5/15–6/5	5/15–24
)/1–21	10/6–18	9/7–30	9/7–19	8/15–31	8/15–20	7/10–31	7/10–22
7–3/15	2/7–10, 2/26–3/12	3/15–4/20	3/27–4/11	5/15–31	5/25–31	6/1–25	6/1–9, 6/23–25
)/1–21	10/1–5, 10/19–21	8/1–9/15	8/1–7, 8/21–9/6	7/17–9/7	7/23–8/7, 8/21–9/6	7/20–8/5	7/23–8/5
'15–4/15	3/27–4/11	4/15–30	4/26–30	5/15–6/15	5/25–6/9	6/1–30	6/1–9, 6/23–30
'23–4/6	3/23–26	4/21–5/9	4/21–25	5/15–6/15	5/15–24, 6/10–15	6/1–30	6/10–22
7–3/15	2/7–10, 2/26–3/12	3/15–4/15	3/27–4/11	5/1–31	5/1–10, 5/25–31	5/15–31	5/25–31
7–20	3/7–12	4/7–30	4/7–11, 4/26–30	5/15–31	5/25–31	6/1–15	6/1–9
'20–2/15	1/20–26, 2/11–15	3/15–31	3/15–26	4/7–30	4/12–25	5/10–31	5/11–24
'1–10/15	9/7–19, 10/6–15	8/1–20	8/8–20	7/1–8/15	7/10–22, 8/8–15	—	—
'15–4/7	3/27–4/7	4/15–5/7	4/26–5/7	5/15–6/30	5/25–6/9, 6/23–30	6/1–30	6/1–9, 6/23–30
'15–28	2/26–28	3/1–20	3/1–12	4/7–30	4/7–11, 4/26–30	5/15–6/10	5/25–6/9
)/15–12/7	10/19–11/4, 11/18–12/3	9/15–10/20	9/20–10/5, 10/19–20	8/11–9/15	8/21–9/6	8/5–30	8/5–7, 8/21–30

Tide Corrections

■ Many factors affect the times and heights of the tides: the shoreline, the time of the Moon's southing (crossing the meridian), and the Moon's phase. The High Tide column on the **Left-Hand Calendar Pages, 142–168,** lists the times of high tide at Commonwealth Pier in Boston Harbor. The heights of some of these tides, reckoned from Mean Lower Low Water, are given on the **Right-Hand Calendar Pages, 143–169.** Use the table below to calculate the approximate times and heights of high tide at the places shown. Apply the time difference to the times of high tide at Boston and the height difference to the heights at Boston. A tide calculator can be found at **Almanac.com/Tides.**

EXAMPLE:

The conversion of the times and heights of the tides at Boston to those at Cape Fear, North Carolina, is given below:

High tide at Boston	**11:45 A.M.**
Correction for Cape Fear	**– 3 55**
High tide at Cape Fear	**7:50 A.M.**
Tide height at Boston	**11.6 ft.**
Correction for Cape Fear	**– 5.0 ft.**
Tide height at Cape Fear	**6.6 ft.**

Estimations derived from this table are *not* meant to be used for navigation. *The Old Farmer's Almanac* accepts no responsibility for errors or any consequences ensuing from the use of this table.

Tidal Site Difference:	Time (h. m.)	Height (ft.)
Canada		
Alberton, PE	*–5 45	–7.5
Charlottetown, PE	*–0 45	–3.5
Halifax, NS	–3 23	–4.5
North Sydney, NS	–3 15	–6.5
Saint John, NB	+0 30	+15.0
St. John's, NL	–4 00	–6.5
Yarmouth, NS	–0 40	+3.0
Maine		
Bar Harbor	–0 34	+0.9
Belfast	–0 20	+0.4
Boothbay Harbor	–0 18	–0.8
Chebeague Island	–0 16	–0.6
Eastport	–0 28	+8.4
Kennebunkport	+0 04	–1.0
Machias	–0 28	+2.8
Monhegan Island	–0 25	–0.8
Old Orchard	0 00	–0.8
Portland	–0 12	–0.6
Rockland	–0 28	+0.1
Stonington	–0 30	+0.1
York	–0 09	–1.0
New Hampshire		
Hampton	+0 02	–1.3
Portsmouth	+0 11	–1.5
Rye Beach	–0 09	–0.9
Massachusetts		
Annisquam	–0 02	–1.1
Beverly Farms	0 00	–0.5
Cape Cod Canal		
East Entrance	–0 01	–0.8
West Entrance	–2 16	–5.9
Chatham Outer Coast	+0 30	–2.8
Inside	+1 54	**0.4
Cohasset	+0 02	–0.07
Cotuit Highlands	+1 15	**0.3
Dennis Port	+1 01	**0.4
Duxbury–Gurnet Point	+0 02	–0.3
Fall River	–3 03	–5.0
Gloucester	–0 03	–0.8
Hingham	+0 07	0.0
Hull	+0 03	–0.2
Hyannis Port	+1 01	**0.3
Magnolia–Manchester	–0 02	–0.7
Marblehead	–0 02	–0.4
Marion	–3 22	–5.4
Monument Beach	–3 08	–5.4
Nahant	–0 01	–0.5
Nantasket	+0 04	–0.1
Nantucket	+0 56	**0.3
Nauset Beach	+0 30	**0.6
New Bedford	–3 24	–5.7
Newburyport	+0 19	–1.8
Oak Bluffs	+0 30	**0.2
Onset–R.R. Bridge	–2 16	–5.9
Plymouth	+0 05	0.0
Provincetown	+0 14	–0.4
Revere Beach	–0 01	–0.3
Rockport	–0 08	–1.0
Salem	0 00	–0.5
Scituate	–0 05	–0.7

Tidal Site	Difference: Time (h. m.)	Height (ft.)
Wareham	–3 09	–5.3
Wellfleet	+0 12	+0.5
West Falmouth	–3 10	–5.4
Westport Harbor	–3 22	–6.4
Woods Hole		
Little Harbor	–2 50	**0.2
Oceanographic Institute	–3 07	**0.2
Rhode Island		
Bristol	–3 24	–5.3
Narragansett Pier	–3 42	–6.2
Newport	–3 34	–5.9
Point Judith	–3 41	–6.3
Providence	–3 20	–4.8
Sakonnet	–3 44	–5.6
Watch Hill	–2 50	–6.8
Connecticut		
Bridgeport	+0 01	–2.6
Madison	–0 22	–2.3
New Haven	–0 11	–3.2
New London	–1 54	–6.7
Norwalk	+0 01	–2.2
Old Lyme		
Highway Bridge	–0 30	–6.2
Stamford	+0 01	–2.2
Stonington	–2 27	–6.6
New York		
Coney Island	–3 33	–4.9
Fire Island Light	–2 43	**0.1
Long Beach	–3 11	–5.7
Montauk Harbor	–2 19	–7.4
New York City–Battery	–2 43	–5.0
Oyster Bay	+0 04	–1.8
Port Chester	–0 09	–2.2
Port Washington	–0 01	–2.1
Sag Harbor	–0 55	–6.8
Southampton		
Shinnecock Inlet	–4 20	**0.2
Willets Point	0 00	–2.3
New Jersey		
Asbury Park	–4 04	–5.3
Atlantic City	–3 56	–5.5
Bay Head–Sea Girt	–4 04	–5.3
Beach Haven	–1 43	**0.24
Cape May	–3 28	–5.3
Ocean City	–3 06	–5.9
Sandy Hook	–3 30	–5.0
Seaside Park	–4 03	–5.4
Pennsylvania		
Philadelphia	+2 40	–3.5
Delaware		
Cape Henlopen	–2 48	–5.3
Rehoboth Beach	–3 37	–5.7
Wilmington	+1 56	–3.8
Maryland		
Annapolis	+6 23	–8.5
Baltimore	+7 59	–8.3
Cambridge	+5 05	–7.8
Havre de Grace	+11 21	–7.7
Point No Point	+2 28	–8.1
Prince Frederick		
Plum Point	+4 25	–8.5
Virginia		
Cape Charles	–2 20	–7.0
Hampton Roads	–2 02	–6.9
Norfolk	–2 06	–6.6
Virginia Beach	–4 00	–6.0
Yorktown	–2 13	–7.0
North Carolina		
Cape Fear	–3 55	–5.0
Cape Lookout	–4 28	–5.7
Currituck	–4 10	–5.8
Hatteras		
Inlet	–4 03	–7.4
Kitty Hawk	–4 14	–6.2
Ocean	–4 26	–6.0
South Carolina		
Charleston	–3 22	–4.3
Georgetown	–1 48	**0.36
Hilton Head	–3 22	–2.9
Myrtle Beach	–3 49	–4.4
St. Helena		
Harbor Entrance	–3 15	–3.4
Georgia		
Jekyll Island	–3 46	–2.9
St. Simon's Island	–2 50	–2.9
Savannah Beach		
River Entrance	–3 14	–5.5
Tybee Light	–3 22	–2.7
Florida		
Cape Canaveral	–3 59	–6.0
Daytona Beach	–3 28	–5.3
Fort Lauderdale	–2 50	–7.2
Fort Pierce Inlet	–3 32	–6.9
Jacksonville		
Railroad Bridge	–6 55	**0.1
Miami Harbor Entrance	–3 18	–7.0
St. Augustine	–2 55	–4.9

**Varies widely; accurate only to within 1½ hours. Consult local tide tables for precise times and heights.*

***Where the difference in the Height column is so marked, the height at Boston should be multiplied by this ratio.*

Time Corrections

■ Astronomical data for Boston is given on **pages 120, 124–125,** and **142–168.** Use the Key Letter shown to the right of each time on those pages with this table to find the number of minutes that you must add to or subtract from Boston time to get the correct time for your city. (Because of complex calculations for different locales, times are approximate.) For more information on the use of Key Letters and this table, **see How to Use This Almanac, page 138.**

Get times simply and specifically: Download astronomical times calculated for your zip code and presented like a Left-Hand Calendar Page at **Almanac.com/Access.**

TIME ZONES: Codes represent *standard time.* Atlantic is –1, Eastern is 0, Central is 1, Mountain is 2, Pacific is 3, Alaska is 4, and Hawaii-Aleutian is 5.

State	City	North Latitude °	North Latitude '	West Longitude °	West Longitude '	Time Zone Code	Key Letters A (min.)	B (min.)	C (min.)	D (min.)	E (min.)
AK	Anchorage	61	10	149	59	4	–46	+27	+71	+122	+171
AK	Cordova	60	33	145	45	4	–55	+13	+55	+103	+149
AK	Fairbanks	64	48	147	51	4	–127	+2	+61	+131	+205
AK	Juneau	58	18	134	25	4	–76	–23	+10	+49	+86
AK	Ketchikan	55	21	131	39	4	–62	–25	0	+29	+56
AK	Kodiak	57	47	152	24	4	0	+49	+82	+120	+154
AL	Birmingham	33	31	86	49	1	+30	+15	+3	–10	–20
AL	Decatur	34	36	86	59	1	+27	+14	+4	–7	–17
AL	Mobile	30	42	88	3	1	+42	+23	+8	–8	–22
AL	Montgomery	32	23	86	19	1	+31	+14	+1	–13	–25
AR	Fort Smith	35	23	94	25	1	+55	+43	+33	+22	+14
AR	Little Rock	34	45	92	17	1	+48	+35	+25	+13	+4
AR	Texarkana	33	26	94	3	1	+59	+44	+32	+18	+8
AZ	Flagstaff	35	12	111	39	2	+64	+52	+42	+31	+22
AZ	Phoenix	33	27	112	4	2	+71	+56	+44	+30	+20
AZ	Tucson	32	13	110	58	2	+70	+53	+40	+24	+12
AZ	Yuma	32	43	114	37	2	+83	+67	+54	+40	+28
CA	Bakersfield	35	23	119	1	3	+33	+21	+12	+1	–7
CA	Barstow	34	54	117	1	3	+27	+14	+4	–7	–16
CA	Fresno	36	44	119	47	3	+32	+22	+15	+6	0
CA	Los Angeles–Pasadena–Santa Monica	34	3	118	14	3	+34	+20	+9	–3	–13
CA	Palm Springs	33	49	116	32	3	+28	+13	+1	–12	–22
CA	Redding	40	35	122	24	3	+31	+27	+25	+22	+19
CA	Sacramento	38	35	121	30	3	+34	+27	+21	+15	+10
CA	San Diego	32	43	117	9	3	+33	+17	+4	–9	–21
CA	San Francisco–Oakland–San Jose	37	47	122	25	3	+40	+31	+25	+18	+12
CO	Craig	40	31	107	33	2	+32	+28	+25	+22	+20
CO	Denver–Boulder	39	44	104	59	2	+24	+19	+15	+11	+7
CO	Grand Junction	39	4	108	33	2	+40	+34	+29	+24	+20
CO	Pueblo	38	16	104	37	2	+27	+20	+14	+7	+2
CO	Trinidad	37	10	104	31	2	+30	+21	+13	+5	0
CT	Bridgeport	41	11	73	11	0	+12	+10	+8	+6	+4
CT	Hartford–New Britain	41	46	72	41	0	+8	+7	+6	+5	+4
CT	New Haven	41	18	72	56	0	+11	+8	+7	+5	+4
CT	New London	41	22	72	6	0	+7	+5	+4	+2	+1
CT	Norwalk–Stamford	41	7	73	22	0	+13	+10	+9	+7	+5
CT	Waterbury–Meriden	41	33	73	3	0	+10	+9	+7	+6	+5
DC	Washington	38	54	77	1	0	+35	+28	+23	+18	+13
DE	Wilmington	39	45	75	33	0	+26	+21	+18	+13	+10

State	City	North Latitude °	North Latitude '	West Longitude °	West Longitude '	Time Zone Code	Key Letters A (min.)	Key Letters B (min.)	Key Letters C (min.)	Key Letters D (min.)	Key Letters E (min.)
FL	Fort Myers	26	38	81	52	0	+87	+63	+44	+21	+4
FL	Jacksonville	30	20	81	40	0	+77	+58	+43	+25	+11
FL	Miami	25	47	80	12	0	+88	+57	+37	+14	–3
FL	Orlando	28	32	81	22	0	+80	+59	+42	+22	+6
FL	Pensacola	30	25	87	13	1	+39	+20	+5	–12	–26
FL	St. Petersburg	27	46	82	39	0	+87	+65	+47	+26	+10
FL	Tallahassee	30	27	84	17	0	+87	+68	+53	+35	+22
FL	Tampa	27	57	82	27	0	+86	+64	+46	+25	+9
FL	West Palm Beach	26	43	80	3	0	+79	+55	+36	+14	–2
GA	Atlanta	33	45	84	24	0	+79	+65	+53	+40	+30
GA	Augusta	33	28	81	58	0	+70	+55	+44	+30	+19
GA	Macon	32	50	83	38	0	+79	+63	+50	+36	+24
GA	Savannah	32	5	81	6	0	+70	+54	+40	+25	+13
HI	Hilo	19	44	155	5	5	+94	+62	+37	+7	–15
HI	Honolulu	21	18	157	52	5	+102	+72	+48	+19	–1
HI	Lanai City	20	50	156	55	5	+99	+69	+44	+15	–6
HI	Lihue	21	59	159	23	5	+107	+77	+54	+26	+5
IA	Davenport	41	32	90	35	1	+20	+19	+17	+16	+15
IA	Des Moines	41	35	93	37	1	+32	+31	+30	+28	+27
IA	Dubuque	42	30	90	41	1	+17	+18	+18	+18	+18
IA	Waterloo	42	30	92	20	1	+24	+24	+24	+25	+25
ID	Boise	43	37	116	12	2	+55	+58	+60	+62	+64
ID	Lewiston	46	25	117	1	3	–12	–3	+2	+10	+17
ID	Pocatello	42	52	112	27	2	+43	+44	+45	+46	+46
IL	Cairo	37	0	89	11	1	+29	+20	+12	+4	–2
IL	Chicago–Oak Park	41	52	87	38	1	+7	+6	+6	+5	+4
IL	Danville	40	8	87	37	1	+13	+9	+6	+2	0
IL	Decatur	39	51	88	57	1	+19	+15	+11	+7	+4
IL	Peoria	40	42	89	36	1	+19	+16	+14	+11	+9
IL	Springfield	39	48	89	39	1	+22	+18	+14	+10	+6
IN	Fort Wayne	41	4	85	9	0	+60	+58	+56	+54	+52
IN	Gary	41	36	87	20	1	+7	+6	+4	+3	+2
IN	Indianapolis	39	46	86	10	0	+69	+64	+60	+56	+52
IN	Muncie	40	12	85	23	0	+64	+60	+57	+53	+50
IN	South Bend	41	41	86	15	0	+62	+61	+60	+59	+58
IN	Terre Haute	39	28	87	24	0	+74	+69	+65	+60	+56
KS	Fort Scott	37	50	94	42	1	+49	+41	+34	+27	+21
KS	Liberal	37	3	100	55	1	+76	+66	+59	+51	+44
KS	Oakley	39	8	100	51	1	+69	+63	+59	+53	+49
KS	Salina	38	50	97	37	1	+57	+51	+46	+40	+35
KS	Topeka	39	3	95	40	1	+49	+43	+38	+32	+28
KS	Wichita	37	42	97	20	1	+60	+51	+45	+37	+31
KY	Lexington–Frankfort	38	3	84	30	0	+67	+59	+53	+46	+41
KY	Louisville	38	15	85	46	0	+72	+64	+58	+52	+46
LA	Alexandria	31	18	92	27	1	+58	+40	+26	+9	–3
LA	Baton Rouge	30	27	91	11	1	+55	+36	+21	+3	–10
LA	Lake Charles	30	14	93	13	1	+64	+44	+29	+11	–2
LA	Monroe	32	30	92	7	1	+53	+37	+24	+9	–1
LA	New Orleans	29	57	90	4	1	+52	+32	+16	–1	–15
LA	Shreveport	32	31	93	45	1	+60	+44	+31	+16	+4
MA	Brockton	42	5	71	1	0	0	0	0	0	–1
MA	Fall River–New Bedford	41	42	71	9	0	+2	+1	0	0	–1
MA	Lawrence–Lowell	42	42	71	10	0	0	0	0	0	+1
MA	Pittsfield	42	27	73	15	0	+8	+8	+8	+8	+8
MA	Springfield–Holyoke	42	6	72	36	0	+6	+6	+6	+5	+5
MA	Worcester	42	16	71	48	0	+3	+2	+2	+2	+2

(continued)

State	City	North Latitude °	'	West Longitude °	'	Time Zone Code	Key Letters A (min.)	B (min.)	C (min.)	D (min.)	E (min.)
MD	Baltimore	39	17	76	37	0	+32	+26	+22	+17	+13
MD	Hagerstown	39	39	77	43	0	+35	+30	+26	+22	+18
MD	Salisbury	38	22	75	36	0	+31	+23	+18	+11	+6
ME	Augusta	44	19	69	46	0	–12	–8	–5	–1	0
ME	Bangor	44	48	68	46	0	–18	–13	–9	–5	–1
ME	Eastport	44	54	67	0	0	–26	–20	–16	–11	–8
ME	Ellsworth	44	33	68	25	0	–18	–14	–10	–6	–3
ME	Portland	43	40	70	15	0	–8	–5	–3	–1	0
ME	Presque Isle	46	41	68	1	0	–29	–19	–12	–4	+2
MI	Cheboygan	45	39	84	29	0	+40	+47	+53	+59	+64
MI	Detroit–Dearborn	42	20	83	3	0	+47	+47	+47	+47	+47
MI	Flint	43	1	83	41	0	+47	+49	+50	+51	+52
MI	Ironwood	46	27	90	9	1	0	+9	+15	+23	+29
MI	Jackson	42	15	84	24	0	+53	+53	+53	+52	+52
MI	Kalamazoo	42	17	85	35	0	+58	+57	+57	+57	+57
MI	Lansing	42	44	84	33	0	+52	+53	+53	+54	+54
MI	St. Joseph	42	5	86	26	0	+61	+61	+60	+60	+59
MI	Traverse City	44	46	85	38	0	+49	+54	+57	+62	+65
MN	Albert Lea	43	39	93	22	1	+24	+26	+28	+31	+33
MN	Bemidji	47	28	94	53	1	+14	+26	+34	+44	+52
MN	Duluth	46	47	92	6	1	+6	+16	+23	+31	+38
MN	Minneapolis–St. Paul	44	59	93	16	1	+18	+24	+28	+33	+37
MN	Ortonville	45	19	96	27	1	+30	+36	+40	+46	+51
MO	Jefferson City	38	34	92	10	1	+36	+29	+24	+18	+13
MO	Joplin	37	6	94	30	1	+50	+41	+33	+25	+18
MO	Kansas City	39	1	94	20	1	+44	+37	+33	+27	+23
MO	Poplar Bluff	36	46	90	24	1	+35	+25	+17	+8	+1
MO	St. Joseph	39	46	94	50	1	+43	+38	+35	+30	+27
MO	St. Louis	38	37	90	12	1	+28	+21	+16	+10	+5
MO	Springfield	37	13	93	18	1	+45	+36	+29	+20	+14
MS	Biloxi	30	24	88	53	1	+46	+27	+11	–5	–19
MS	Jackson	32	18	90	11	1	+46	+30	+17	+1	–10
MS	Meridian	32	22	88	42	1	+40	+24	+11	–4	–15
MS	Tupelo	34	16	88	34	1	+35	+21	+10	–2	–11
MT	Billings	45	47	108	30	2	+16	+23	+29	+35	+40
MT	Butte	46	1	112	32	2	+31	+39	+45	+52	+57
MT	Glasgow	48	12	106	38	2	–1	+11	+21	+32	+42
MT	Great Falls	47	30	111	17	2	+20	+31	+39	+49	+58
MT	Helena	46	36	112	2	2	+27	+36	+43	+51	+57
MT	Miles City	46	25	105	51	2	+3	+11	+18	+26	+32
NC	Asheville	35	36	82	33	0	+67	+55	+46	+35	+27
NC	Charlotte	35	14	80	51	0	+61	+49	+39	+28	+19
NC	Durham	36	0	78	55	0	+51	+40	+31	+21	+13
NC	Greensboro	36	4	79	47	0	+54	+43	+35	+25	+17
NC	Raleigh	35	47	78	38	0	+51	+39	+30	+20	+12
NC	Wilmington	34	14	77	55	0	+52	+38	+27	+15	+5
ND	Bismarck	46	48	100	47	1	+41	+50	+58	+66	+73
ND	Fargo	46	53	96	47	1	+24	+34	+42	+50	+57
ND	Grand Forks	47	55	97	3	1	+21	+33	+43	+53	+62
ND	Minot	48	14	101	18	1	+36	+50	+59	+71	+81
ND	Williston	48	9	103	37	1	+46	+59	+69	+80	+90
NE	Grand Island	40	55	98	21	1	+53	+51	+49	+46	+44
NE	Lincoln	40	49	96	41	1	+47	+44	+42	+39	+37
NE	North Platte	41	8	100	46	1	+62	+60	+58	+56	+54
NE	Omaha	41	16	95	56	1	+43	+40	+39	+37	+36
NH	Berlin	44	28	71	11	0	–7	–3	0	+3	+7
NH	Keene	42	56	72	17	0	+2	+3	+4	+5	+6

State	City	North Latitude °	North Latitude '	West Longitude °	West Longitude '	Time Zone Code	Key Letters A (min.)	B (min.)	C (min.)	D (min.)	E (min.)
NH	Manchester–Concord	42	59	71	28	0	0	0	+1	+2	+3
NH	Portsmouth	43	5	70	45	0	–4	–2	–1	0	0
NJ	Atlantic City	39	22	74	26	0	+23	+17	+13	+8	+4
NJ	Camden	39	57	75	7	0	+24	+19	+16	+12	+9
NJ	Cape May	38	56	74	56	0	+26	+20	+15	+9	+5
NJ	Newark–East Orange	40	44	74	10	0	+17	+14	+12	+9	+7
NJ	Paterson	40	55	74	10	0	+17	+14	+12	+9	+7
NJ	Trenton	40	13	74	46	0	+21	+17	+14	+11	+8
NM	Albuquerque	35	5	106	39	2	+45	+32	+22	+11	+2
NM	Gallup	35	32	108	45	2	+52	+40	+31	+20	+11
NM	Las Cruces	32	19	106	47	2	+53	+36	+23	+8	–3
NM	Roswell	33	24	104	32	2	+41	+26	+14	0	–10
NM	Santa Fe	35	41	105	56	2	+40	+28	+19	+9	0
NV	Carson City–Reno	39	10	119	46	3	+25	+19	+14	+9	+5
NV	Elko	40	50	115	46	3	+3	0	–1	–3	–5
NV	Las Vegas	36	10	115	9	3	+16	+4	–3	–13	–20
NY	Albany	42	39	73	45	0	+9	+10	+10	+11	+11
NY	Binghamton	42	6	75	55	0	+20	+19	+19	+18	+18
NY	Buffalo	42	53	78	52	0	+29	+30	+30	+31	+32
NY	New York	40	45	74	0	0	+17	+14	+11	+9	+6
NY	Ogdensburg	44	42	75	30	0	+8	+13	+17	+21	+25
NY	Syracuse	43	3	76	9	0	+17	+19	+20	+21	+22
OH	Akron	41	5	81	31	0	+46	+43	+41	+39	+37
OH	Canton	40	48	81	23	0	+46	+43	+41	+38	+36
OH	Cincinnati–Hamilton	39	6	84	31	0	+64	+58	+53	+48	+44
OH	Cleveland–Lakewood	41	30	81	42	0	+45	+43	+42	+40	+39
OH	Columbus	39	57	83	1	0	+55	+51	+47	+43	+40
OH	Dayton	39	45	84	10	0	+61	+56	+52	+48	+44
OH	Toledo	41	39	83	33	0	+52	+50	+49	+48	+47
OH	Youngstown	41	6	80	39	0	+42	+40	+38	+36	+34
OK	Oklahoma City	35	28	97	31	1	+67	+55	+46	+35	+26
OK	Tulsa	36	9	95	60	1	+59	+48	+40	+30	+22
OR	Eugene	44	3	123	6	3	+21	+24	+27	+30	+33
OR	Pendleton	45	40	118	47	3	–1	+4	+10	+16	+21
OR	Portland	45	31	122	41	3	+14	+20	+25	+31	+36
OR	Salem	44	57	123	1	3	+17	+23	+27	+31	+35
PA	Allentown–Bethlehem	40	36	75	28	0	+23	+20	+17	+14	+12
PA	Erie	42	7	80	5	0	+36	+36	+35	+35	+35
PA	Harrisburg	40	16	76	53	0	+30	+26	+23	+19	+16
PA	Lancaster	40	2	76	18	0	+28	+24	+20	+17	+13
PA	Philadelphia–Chester	39	57	75	9	0	+24	+19	+16	+12	+9
PA	Pittsburgh–McKeesport	40	26	80	0	0	+42	+38	+35	+32	+29
PA	Reading	40	20	75	56	0	+26	+22	+19	+16	+13
PA	Scranton–Wilkes Barre	41	25	75	40	0	+21	+19	+18	+16	+15
PA	York	39	58	76	43	0	+30	+26	+22	+18	+15
RI	Providence	41	50	71	25	0	+3	+2	+1	0	0
SC	Charleston	32	47	79	56	0	+64	+48	+36	+21	+10
SC	Columbia	34	0	81	2	0	+65	+51	+40	+27	+17
SC	Spartanburg	34	56	81	57	0	+66	+53	+43	+32	+23
SD	Aberdeen	45	28	98	29	1	+37	+44	+49	+54	+59
SD	Pierre	44	22	100	21	1	+49	+53	+56	+60	+63
SD	Rapid City	44	5	103	14	2	+2	+5	+8	+11	+13
SD	Sioux Falls	43	33	96	44	1	+38	+40	+42	+44	+46
TN	Chattanooga	35	3	85	19	0	+79	+67	+57	+45	+36
TN	Knoxville	35	58	83	55	0	+71	+60	+51	+41	+33
TN	Memphis	35	9	90	3	1	+38	+26	+16	+5	–3
TN	Nashville	36	10	86	47	1	+22	+11	+3	–6	–14

(continued)

TIME CORRECTIONS

State/ Province	City	North Latitude °	'	West Longitude °	'	Time Zone Code	Key Letters A (min.)	B (min.)	C (min.)	D (min.)	E (min.)
TX	Amarillo	35	12	101	50	1	+85	+73	+63	+52	+43
TX	Austin	30	16	97	45	1	+82	+62	+47	+29	+15
TX	Beaumont	30	5	94	6	1	+67	+48	+32	+14	0
TX	Brownsville	25	54	97	30	1	+91	+66	+46	+23	+5
TX	Corpus Christi	27	48	97	24	1	+86	+64	+46	+25	+9
TX	Dallas–Fort Worth	32	47	96	48	1	+71	+55	+43	+28	+17
TX	El Paso	31	45	106	29	2	+53	+35	+22	+6	–6
TX	Galveston	29	18	94	48	1	+72	+52	+35	+16	+1
TX	Houston	29	45	95	22	1	+73	+53	+37	+19	+5
TX	McAllen	26	12	98	14	1	+93	+69	+49	+26	+9
TX	San Antonio	29	25	98	30	1	+87	+66	+50	+31	+16
UT	Kanab	37	3	112	32	2	+62	+53	+46	+37	+30
UT	Moab	38	35	109	33	2	+46	+39	+33	+27	+22
UT	Ogden	41	13	111	58	2	+47	+45	+43	+41	+40
UT	Salt Lake City	40	45	111	53	2	+48	+45	+43	+40	+38
UT	Vernal	40	27	109	32	2	+40	+36	+33	+30	+28
VA	Charlottesville	38	2	78	30	0	+43	+35	+29	+22	+17
VA	Danville	36	36	79	23	0	+51	+41	+33	+24	+17
VA	Norfolk	36	51	76	17	0	+38	+28	+21	+12	+5
VA	Richmond	37	32	77	26	0	+41	+32	+25	+17	+11
VA	Roanoke	37	16	79	57	0	+51	+42	+35	+27	+21
VA	Winchester	39	11	78	10	0	+38	+33	+28	+23	+19
VT	Brattleboro	42	51	72	34	0	+4	+5	+5	+6	+7
VT	Burlington	44	29	73	13	0	0	+4	+8	+12	+15
VT	Rutland	43	37	72	58	0	+2	+5	+7	+9	+11
VT	St. Johnsbury	44	25	72	1	0	–4	0	+3	+7	+10
WA	Bellingham	48	45	122	29	3	0	+13	+24	+37	+47
WA	Seattle–Tacoma–Olympia	47	37	122	20	3	+3	+15	+24	+34	+42
WA	Spokane	47	40	117	24	3	–16	–4	+4	+14	+23
WA	Walla Walla	46	4	118	20	3	–5	+2	+8	+15	+21
WI	Eau Claire	44	49	91	30	1	+12	+17	+21	+25	+29
WI	Green Bay	44	31	88	0	1	0	+3	+7	+11	+14
WI	La Crosse	43	48	91	15	1	+15	+18	+20	+22	+25
WI	Madison	43	4	89	23	1	+10	+11	+12	+14	+15
WI	Milwaukee	43	2	87	54	1	+4	+6	+7	+8	+9
WI	Oshkosh	44	1	88	33	1	+3	+6	+9	+12	+15
WI	Wausau	44	58	89	38	1	+4	+9	+13	+18	+22
WV	Charleston	38	21	81	38	0	+55	+48	+42	+35	+30
WV	Parkersburg	39	16	81	34	0	+52	+46	+42	+36	+32
WY	Casper	42	51	106	19	2	+19	+19	+20	+21	+22
WY	Cheyenne	41	8	104	49	2	+19	+16	+14	+12	+11
WY	Sheridan	44	48	106	58	2	+14	+19	+23	+27	+31
CANADA											
AB	Calgary	51	5	114	5	2	+13	+35	+50	+68	+84
AB	Edmonton	53	34	113	25	2	–3	+26	+47	+72	+93
BC	Vancouver	49	13	123	6	3	0	+15	+26	+40	+52
MB	Winnipeg	49	53	97	10	1	+12	+30	+43	+58	+71
NB	Saint John	45	16	66	3	–1	+28	+34	+39	+44	+49
NS	Halifax	44	38	63	35	–1	+21	+26	+29	+33	+37
NS	Sydney	46	10	60	10	–1	+1	+9	+15	+23	+28
ON	Ottawa	45	25	75	43	0	+6	+13	+18	+23	+28
ON	Peterborough	44	18	78	19	0	+21	+25	+28	+32	+35
ON	Thunder Bay	48	27	89	12	0	+47	+61	+71	+83	+93
ON	Toronto	43	39	79	23	0	+28	+30	+32	+35	+37
QC	Montreal	45	28	73	39	0	–1	+4	+9	+15	+20
SK	Saskatoon	52	10	106	40	1	+37	+63	+80	+101	+119

(continued from page 85)

WEATHER

SNOW PUDDING

Whether by the spoon- or shovelful, this melts in your mouth.

PUDDING:

½ cup cold water
1 envelope unflavored gelatin
1½ cups boiling water
¼ cup lemon juice
¾ cup sugar
1 pasteurized egg, separated

SAUCE:

¼ cup sugar
½ teaspoon cornstarch
1 cup milk
¼ teaspoon vanilla extract

FOR PUDDING:

1. Put cold water into a bowl and sprinkle with gelatin. Allow to set for 1 minute. Add hot water, lemon juice, and sugar. Stir until gelatin and sugar dissolve. Refrigerate until thick, but not firm (6 to 8 hours).

2. In another bowl, beat egg white until soft peaks form. Remove gelatin from refrigerator. Fold egg white into it. Return to refrigerator. Reserve egg yolk for sauce.

FOR SAUCE:

1. In a saucepan, stir together egg yolk, sugar, and cornstarch. Add milk and cook over medium heat, stirring constantly until slightly thick. Remove from heat, stir in vanilla, and set aside to cool.

2. Serve pudding with sauce.

Makes 6 servings.

NATURE

LADYBUG CUPCAKES

These scrumptious "bugs" are welcome at any party or picnic.

your favorite cupcakes
red, black, and white frosting
miniature chocolate chips
black jelly beans
black licorice cut into pieces

1. Frost cupcakes with red icing. At edge of each cupcake, make a large round area of black frosting for a "head." On it, make two white frosting "eyes." In each eye, place one chocolate chip. On red frosting, scatter jelly bean "spots." Insert six black licorice "legs" into cupcake.

CALENDAR

DAY-AFTER-THANKSGIVING HASH

Follow the national "feast day" with a leftovers dish that everyone will love.

2 tablespoons unsalted butter
1 onion, chopped
3 cups leftover stuffing, crumbled
2 cups leftover mashed potatoes
2 cups chopped leftover turkey
1 cup leftover gravy

1. Preheat oven to 400°F.

2. In an ovenproof skillet over medium heat, melt butter. Add onions and cook for 7 minutes. Add stuffing. Distribute spoonfuls of mashed potatoes on top. Repeat with turkey.

3. In a saucepan or microwave, warm gravy. Add water to thin slightly. Pour over turkey. Stir lightly. Mash the hash down gently with a fork. Bake for 20 minutes.

Makes 4 to 5 servings.

HOME REMEDIES

GRANNY'S CHICKEN SOUP

For a sure cure, cook up this centuries-old classic at the first sneeze or sniffle.

4 quarts cold water
1 chicken (4 to 5 pounds), quartered
4 to 5 stems parsley
2 carrots, peeled and chopped
2 stalks celery, chopped
2 cloves garlic, crushed
1 onion, quartered
1 bay leaf
2 teaspoons salt
½ teaspoon freshly ground black pepper

1. Put water into a stockpot. Add remaining ingredients and bring to a boil. Reduce heat and simmer for 3 hours. Using a spoon, skim soup frequently. Remove from heat and cool. Skim fat from surface. Strain soup, discarding bay leaf and parsley and reserving other solids. Wash stockpot, then return strained stock to it.

2. Mash carrots, celery, and onion. Add to stock. Skin and debone chicken. Chop meat and add to stock. Heat and season to taste with salt and pepper. **Makes 8 to 10 servings.**

HISTORY

GEORGE WASHINGTON'S EGGNOG

From the commander-in-chief at this Almanac's inception, in his own words

1 quart cream, 1 quart milk, 1 dozen tablespoons sugar, 1 pint brandy, ½ pint rye whiskey, ½ pint Jamaica rum, ¼ pint sherry—mix liquor first, then separate yolks and whites of 12 eggs, add sugar to beaten yolks, mix well. Add milk and cream, slowly beating. Beat whites of eggs until stiff and fold slowly into mixture. Let set in cool place for several days. Taste frequently.

ASTRONOMY

CINNAMON STARS

Watch eyes brighten when these heavenly confections come out.

1 pound shelled almonds or 3½ cups almond meal/flour
4 egg whites
¼ teaspoon salt
3 cups confectioners' sugar
1 tablespoon lemon juice
1½ tablespoons ground cinnamon

1. In a food processor, pulse whole almonds until finely ground.

2. In a bowl, beat egg whites until soft peaks form. Add salt and gradually beat in sugar. Set aside ½ cup for glaze. Fold ground almonds, lemon juice, and cinnamon into egg mixture. Refrigerate dough and glaze for several hours or overnight.

3. Preheat oven to 300°F.

4. Lightly sprinkle a work surface with confectioners' sugar. Roll portions of dough to a ¼-inch thickness. Cut into stars with a cookie cutter.

5. Line two baking sheets with parchment paper. Brush glaze over each cookie. Bake for 25 minutes. Cool on wire racks.

Makes about 4 dozen cookies. ■

Sarah Perreault is the food editor of *The Old Farmer's Almanac*.

The Old Farmer's General Store

A special section featuring unique mail-order products for all our readers who shop by mail.

General Store Classifieds

For advertising information, go to Almanac.com/Advertising.

ASTROLOGY

FREE SPIRITUAL CATALOG
"With POWER and FAITH, You Can Conquer All Situations. Suffer No More!"
Over 8,000 items.
Church Goods Co., Dept. OFA,
PO Box 718, Glenview IL 60025
www.LuckShop.com

MRS. KING, spiritual reader, advisor, helps in matters of life where others have failed. 912-283-0635.

REV. EVETTE answers all questions, solves life's problems. Need help desperately? Does what others claim! Call immediately, 100% guaranteed! PO Box 80322, Chattanooga TN 37414. 423-894-6699.

FREE! 40 OCCULT SECRETS
for gaining money and love you can use immediately!
Plus our super catalog!
Neuman, PO Box 1157,
Saint George UT 84771
www.solarvisionpublishing.com

GIFTED HEALER
Solves all problems, troubles, unusual sickness, bad luck, love, life. Removes evil influences, nature problems, brings back lovers to stay, good luck, money. Sister Grace, Hwy. 48, 7905 Bluff Rd., Gadsden SC 29052
803-353-0659 No calls between 9 AM & 6 PM

FREE POWER PRAYER. Rev. Angel Ann has returned from the Holy Land. Don't miss this opportunity. Call for your FREE consultation and Power Prayer. Guaranteed results with just one call! Call 850-691-2039.

MOTHER FIXER, POOR MAN'S ROOTWORKER
Spiritualist—SpellCaster.
Difficult cases. Lottery. Enemies. Love.
All problems. Guaranteed.
269-353-8717

MASTER SPIRITUALIST BROTHER DANIEL
I will end your confusion and problems for good!
Get 100% results in all life matters of love, money, success, health, employment, court cases.
50 years' experience.
772-971-2830

ROSELLA, PSYCHIC SPIRITUALIST, solves problems! Stops sadness! Reunites lovers forever! Free sample reading! Call 586-215-3838.

JENNIFER GREEN, 5th-GENERATION CELEBRITY PSYCHIC. Master astrologer reunites lovers, heals broken hearts. One free question. Call or text today: 615-944-9707. Visit: 5thGenPsychic.com.

REV. GRACE, SPIRITUAL HEALER
Removes bad luck,
evil spells.
Guaranteed help.
In the name of Jesus, call:
602-430-1762

READINGS BY ANGELA. Reunites lovers. Solves all problems. 100% guaranteed. One FREE reading. 940-612-4757.

MISS LISA. A gifted astrology reader and advisor with positive results. Will help you with all problems. Waycross, GA. 912-283-3206.

SARAH DAVIS
Helps in all problems. Removes curses, evil, voodoo, bad luck. Returns loved ones. Marriage, business, health, money.
Call for lucky numbers:
512-586-3696

AUNT JEMIMA helps in all matters in life. Specializes in reuniting lovers. Guaranteed Mississippi's finest. 662-838-8525.

WWW.AZUREGREEN.NET
Jewelry, amulets, incense,
oils, statuary, gifts,
herbs, candles, gemstones.
8,000 items. Wholesale and retail.

PSYCHIC READINGS BY MILLIE. Over 35 years. Specializing in palm tarot past & life readings plus 95% accuracy. We provide Chakra balancing. Please call 309-686-2255 or visit us online at www.peoriaspsychicshop.com.

HEALING HEART ROSE. Master psychic solves problems forever. Reunites lovers immediately, guaranteed! Call 731-333-4840 or visit online psychiclovespellsbyrose.com.

ATTENTION: SISTER LIGHT,
Spartanburg, South Carolina
One free reading when you call.
I will help in all problems.
864-576-9397

ONE FREE "WISHES COME TRUE" RITUAL. Tell us your special wish. ElizabethZenor.com. ElizabethZenor@gmail.com. Phone: 909-473-7470, Elizabeth Zenor, Box 9315b, San Bernardino CA 92427-9315.

SOPHIA GREEN: Don't tell me, I'll tell you. Help with all problems. Help reuniting lovers. You will be satisfied with results. 956-878-7053.

BEAUTY & HEALTH

FREE ESSENTIAL OIL GUIDE & NATURAL PRODUCTS CATALOG
170 pure essential oils. Large selection of blends, liniments, creams, rubs, cosmetics, diffusers, and supplies.
1-800-308-6284
www.AromaTherapeutix.com/fa

BEER & WINE MAKING

FREE ILLUSTRATED CATALOG
Fast service. Since 1967.
Kraus, PO Box 7850-YB,
Independence MO 64054
1-800-841-7404
www.eckraus.com/offers/fd.asp

BOOKS/PUBLICATIONS/CATALOGS

FREE BOOKLETS: Life, immortality, soul, pollution crisis, Judgment Day, restitution. Sample magazine. Bible Standard (OF), 1156 St. Matthews Rd., Chester Springs PA 19425. www.biblestandard.com.

FREE BOOKLET: Pro-and-con assessment of Jehovah's Witnesses teachings. Bible Standard (OFA), 1156 St. Matthews Rd., Chester Springs PA 19425. www.biblestandard.com.

BUILDING

BUILD UNDERGROUND
houses/shelters/greenhouses dirt-cheap!
Live protected. Slash energy costs. "Brilliant breakthrough thinking"–*Countryside Magazine*
Featured on HGTV. 1-800-328-8790.
www.undergroundhousing.com

BUSINESS OPPORTUNITIES

$500 WEEKLY ASSEMBLING PRODUCTS
from home. Free information; send SASE:
Home Assembly-FA,
PO Box 450,
New Britain CT 06050-0450

$800 WEEKLY POTENTIAL! Process HUD/FHA refunds from home. Free information available. Call 860-357-1599.

COINS

HIGHEST PRICES PAID
Serving dealers and collectors for over 40 years.
Will travel to home or bank.
Call 978-255-1127
or email rickbagg@hotmail.com.
www.richardbagg.com

CRAFTS

TANDY LEATHER
We have a free 188-page Buyers' Guide full of supplies for the leather craftsman.
Saddle and tack hardware, leather, tools, and more farm and ranch essentials.
Tandy Leather Factory,
Dept. 17 FA, 1900 SE Loop 820,
Ft. Worth TX 76140
www.tandyleatherfactory.com

FARM & GARDEN

OPEN-POLLINATED CORN SEED
Silage, grain, wildlife. 75-85-87-90-95-100-114-120-day. Open-pollinated Cinderella pumpkin, popcorn, sweet corn seed. Green Haven,
607-566-9253
www.openpollinated.com

Advertisements and statements contained herein are the sole responsibility of the persons or entities that post the advertisement, and The Old Farmer's Almanac does not make any warranty as to the accuracy, completeness, truthfulness, or reliability of such advertisements. The Old Farmer's Almanac has no liability whatsoever for any third-party claims arising in connection with such advertisements or any products or services mentioned therein. The postal service recommends not sending cash by mail.

ANSWERS TO MADDENING MIND-MANGLERS (FROM PAGE 243):

1. Q; **2.** A; **3.** M; **4.** L; **5.** O; **6.** R; **7.** S; **8.** C; **9.** G; **10.** B; **11.** I; **12.** T; **13.** E; **14.** J; **15.** D; **16.** F; **17.** H; **18.** K; **19.** N; **20.** P

Index to Advertisers

The Old Farmer's Almanac Products

ANECDOTES & PLEASANTRIES

A sampling from the thousands of letters, clippings, articles, and emails sent to us by Almanac readers from all over the United States and Canada during the past year.

Update: Revenge of the Beavers

Fresh on the heels—er, webbed feet—of last year's report on beavers "forced" to skydive, a new true tale

–courtesy of J.D.H., Drury, New Hampshire, from Reuters.com

In a classic "man bites dog" turnaround, a mad beaver attacked two Oregon hikers after they walked on its dam. After knocking one hiker into the river and cornering the other in a tangle of submerged logs, the crazy castor retreated. The men were rescued by authorities who had received reports of cries for help. Whether other beavers across the land are similarly on the dam warpath of revenge remains a gnawing question.

WHAT TO DO WHEN A SQUIRREL FALLS INTO YOUR SAP BUCKET

–courtesy of T. C., Dublin, New Hampshire

In Vermont, an old-time farmer checks to see if anyone is looking and then—not wanting to waste the sap and figuring he's going to boil it anyway—fishes out the squirrel, tosses it aside, and pours the sap into his gathering tank.

The old-time New Hampshire farmer, on the other hand, faced with the same dead squirrel, fishes it out of the bucket, makes sure no one is looking, and then wrings out the squirrel to save every drop of sap.

An old-time farmer from Maine would never do such a thing. He'd dump the sap and the well-marinated squirrel into a stew pot, put the burner on the stove to medium high, and head to the cellar to find a potato.

Health Notes of the Year

–courtesy of (in order) NPR, The Guardian.com, *Appetite,* CBSNews.com

CHICKEN LICKIN' SICKENS: The Centers for Disease Control and Prevention have issued a caution to people about kissing and snuggling with their fowl: It can lead to salmonella poisoning. You have been warned.

SO LONG, SUCKER: Englishman Steve Easton sneezed and out came the sucker tip of a dart the size of a penny that, unbeknownst to him, had been in his nose for 44 years. His mum said that they had taken him to the hospital when he was 7, shortly after the tip of a toy dart went missing. But doctors found nothing. No, we are not running a photo of this.

WANT SOME CREAM FOR THAT COFFEE? Austrian scientists have determined that people who prefer bitter tastes such as that of black coffee have a tendency toward Machiavellianism, psychopathy, narcissism, and everyday meanness.

FINALLY, WHY DIETS DON'T WORK: The online journal *Occupational & Environmental Medicine* has published a study linking belly fat to traffic noise.

THE EYEBROW WHISPERER

Here's how to identify the telltale traits represented by eyebrows.

–courtesy of J. P., Baltimore, Maryland, from *Amazing Face Reading,* by Mac Fulfer, J.D.

CURVED: People-oriented, doesn't want details, needs to see usefulness

STRAIGHT: Detail-oriented, factual, logical, unemotional

ANGLED: Mentally focused, gregarious, authoritative

HIGH: Discerning, selective, wait-and-see approach

LOW: Expressive, quick to take action, processes information quickly

BUSHY: Mentally active, powerful intellect, nonstop thinker

THIN (LIKE A PENCIL LINE): Single-minded, focuses on one thing at a time, can be overly self-conscious

CONTINUOUS/UNI-BROW: Thoughts are continuous and restless, trouble sleeping because can't stop thinking

TANGLED: Unconventional thinker, sees all sides of issues

SCATTERED (HAIRS OUTSIDE OF BROWS): Wide-ranging focus, curious

CHAMELEON (NEARLY INVISIBLE BROWS): Impossible to read, blends into almost any group

(continued)

A Panegyric for Presidents' Day

FEBRUARY 20

In malls today it is inhuman
Not to talk of Taft or Truman,
Nor should a shopper crack a joke
Evoking faults of Ford or Polk.
Make Roosevelts a Facebook
"like"
And generally embrace our Ike.

No matter what you may have
heard,
Toast Silent Cal—without a word.
May Andrew Johnson now receive
Our pity and a brief reprieve.
Until tomorrow, pardon Nixon
As well as every Clinton vixen.

Let food courts ring with Taylor's
praise!
Remember Rutherford B. Hayes,
Those Millard Fillmore glory days,
Ulysses S.—plus his white
horse—
Van Buren, Tyler, too, of course,
And celebrate, this chilly day,
Young JFK, then LBJ.

Let rancor fade and no one mock
Buchanan, Bushes, or Barack.
Thank Washington and James
Monroe—
And everybody, friend or foe,
Republican or Democrat:
Don't mix up Garfield with that
cat!
Avoid unfair comparisons
When speaking of the Harrisons.
Tom Jefferson and Franklin Pierce
Should be provoking pride that's
fierce.

Applaud The Great Emancipator;
Educate an Adams-hater.
Grant Madison what he is due,
Be fair regarding Harding, too,
And share what Hoover means
to you.

Wear cardigans for Carter's years
And give McKinley hearty cheers.
Spread Cleveland's fame without
dissension;
Old Hickory deserves some
mention.
Keep Woodrow Wilson jokes
suppressed;
Chester A. Arthur did his best.
Imagine them all, if you will,
On Ronald Reagan's mythic hill.

–courtesy of A. M. Juster, in The Weekly Standard *and* Sleaze and Slander *(Measure Press, 2016)*

YET ANOTHER STUDY ON SLEEP

If anyone out there tries this, please let us know how it works out.

–courtesy of C. W., Long Beach, California, from Everydayhealth.com

A recent study by dream experts at Hong Kong Shue Yan University suggested that dreams are, for better or worse, the result of how we lie in bed. Each position puts pressure on the body that sets the theme for a dream. So, if you sleep . . .

ON YOUR SIDE: You generally have more pleasant dreams; however, left-side sleepers may experience nightmares, and right-side sleepers, sensations of swallowing or burning.

ON YOUR BACK: You tend to experience more nightmares and have greater difficulty in recalling your dreams.

ON YOUR STOMACH: You may have more intense and erotic dreams; however, avoid sleeping facedown on the pillow and don't try to force the effect.

IN MULTIPLE POSITIONS: The position in which you wake up is the strongest influencer of your dreams.

Deer Quiz

–courtesy of P. R., Charlottetown, Prince Edward Island, from CampfireStories.com

True or false: A white-tailed buck can jump higher than the average five-story building.

ANSWER TO DEER QUIZ

True. The average five-story building can't jump.

Send your contribution for *The 2018 Old Farmer's Almanac* by January 27, 2017, to "A & P," The Old Farmer's Almanac, P.O. Box 520, Dublin, NH 03444, or email it to almanac@ypi.com (subject: A & P).

A Reference Compendium

CALENDAR

WEATHER

IN THE GARDEN

AROUND THE HOUSE

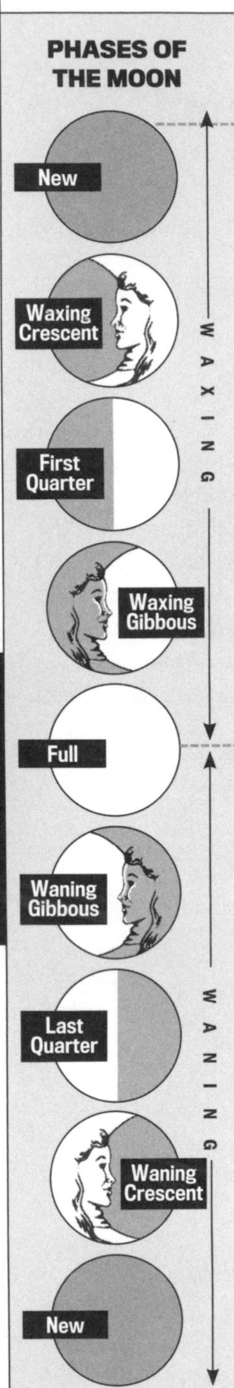

REFERENCE

WHEN WILL THE MOON RISE?

A lunar puzzle involves the timing of moonrise. If you enjoy the out-of-doors and the wonders of nature, you may wish to commit to memory the following gem:

The new Moon always rises near sunrise;

The first quarter, near noon;

The full Moon always rises near sunset;

The last quarter, near midnight.

Moonrise occurs about 50 minutes later each day.

FULL MOON NAMES

NAME	MONTH	VARIATIONS
Full Wolf Moon	JANUARY	Full Old Moon
Full Snow Moon	FEBRUARY	Full Hunger Moon
Full Worm Moon	MARCH	Full Crow Moon Full Crust Moon Full Sugar Moon Full Sap Moon
Full Pink Moon	APRIL	Full Sprouting Grass Moon Full Egg Moon Full Fish Moon
Full Flower Moon	MAY	Full Corn Planting Moon Full Milk Moon
Full Strawberry Moon	JUNE	Full Rose Moon Full Hot Moon
Full Buck Moon	JULY	Full Thunder Moon Full Hay Moon
Full Sturgeon Moon	AUGUST	Full Red Moon Full Green Corn Moon
Full Harvest Moon*	SEPTEMBER	Full Corn Moon Full Barley Moon
Full Hunter's Moon	OCTOBER	Full Travel Moon Full Dying Grass Moon
Full Beaver Moon	NOVEMBER	Full Frost Moon
Full Cold Moon	DECEMBER	Full Long Nights Moon

*The Harvest Moon is always the full Moon closest to the autumnal equinox. If the Harvest Moon occurs in October, the September full Moon is usually called the Corn Moon.

THE ORIGIN OF FULL MOON NAMES

Historically, the Native Americans who lived in the area that is now the northern and eastern United States kept track of the seasons by giving a distinctive name to each recurring full Moon. This name was applied to the entire month in which it occurred. These names, and some variations, were used by the Algonquin tribes from New England to Lake Superior.

Meanings of Full Moon Names

JANUARY'S full Moon was called the **Wolf Moon** because it appeared when wolves howled outside Native American villages.

FEBRUARY'S full Moon was called the **Snow Moon** because it was a time of heavy snow. It was also called the **Hunger Moon** because hunting was difficult and hunger often resulted.

MARCH'S full Moon was called the **Worm Moon** because, as the Sun increasingly warmed the soil, earthworms became active and their castings (excrement) began to appear.

APRIL'S full Moon was called the **Pink Moon** because it heralded the appearance of the moss pink, or wild ground phlox—one of the first spring flowers.

MAY'S full Moon was called the **Flower Moon** because blossoms were abundant everywhere at this time.

JUNE'S full Moon was called the **Strawberry Moon** because it appeared when the strawberry harvest took place.

JULY'S full Moon was called the **Buck Moon** because it arrived when male deer started growing new antlers.

AUGUST'S full Moon was called the **Sturgeon Moon** because this large fish, which is found in the Great Lakes and Lake Champlain, was caught easily at this time.

SEPTEMBER'S full Moon was called the **Corn Moon** because this was the time to harvest corn.

The **Harvest Moon** is the full Moon that occurs closest to the autumnal equinox. It can occur in either September or October. At this time, crops such as corn, pumpkins, squash, and wild rice are ready for gathering.

OCTOBER'S full Moon was called the **Hunter's Moon** because this was the time to hunt in preparation for winter.

NOVEMBER'S full Moon was called the **Beaver Moon** because it was the time to set beaver traps, before the waters froze over.

DECEMBER'S full Moon was called the **Cold Moon.** It was also called the **Long Nights Moon** because nights at this time of year were the longest.

THE ORIGIN OF MONTH NAMES

JANUARY. For the Roman god Janus, protector of gates and doorways. Janus is depicted with two faces, one looking into the past, the other into the future.

FEBRUARY. From the Latin *februa,* "to cleanse." The Roman Februalia was a festival of purification and atonement that took place during this time of year.

MARCH. For the Roman god of war, Mars. This was the time of year to resume military campaigns that had been interrupted by winter.

APRIL. From the Latin *aperio,* "to open (bud)," because plants begin to grow now.

MAY. For the Roman goddess Maia, who oversaw the growth of plants. Also from the Latin *maiores,* "elders," who were celebrated now.

JUNE. For the Roman goddess Juno, patroness of marriage and the well-being of women. Also from the Latin *juvenis,* "young people."

JULY. To honor Roman dictator Julius Caesar (100 B.C.–44 B.C.). In 46 B.C., with the help of Sosigenes, he developed the Julian calendar.

AUGUST. To honor the first Roman emperor (and grandnephew of Julius Caesar), Augustus Caesar (63 B.C.–A.D. 14).

SEPTEMBER. From the Latin *septem,* "seven," because this was the seventh month of the early Roman calendar.

OCTOBER. From the Latin *octo,* "eight," because this was the eighth month of the early Roman calendar.

NOVEMBER. From the Latin *novem,* "nine," because this was the ninth month of the early Roman calendar.

DECEMBER. From the Latin *decem,* "ten," because this was the tenth month of the early Roman calendar.

REFERENCE

Easter Dates (2017–20)

Christian churches that follow the Gregorian calendar celebrate Easter on the first Sunday after the paschal full Moon on or just after the vernal equinox.

YEAR	EASTER
2017	April 16
2018	April 1
2019	April 21
2020	April 12

The Julian calendar is used by some churches, including many Eastern Orthodox. The dates below are Julian calendar dates for Easter converted to Gregorian dates.

YEAR	EASTER
2017	April 16
2018	April 8
2019	April 28
2020	April 19

FRIGGATRISKAIDEKAPHOBIA TRIVIA

Here are a few facts about Friday the 13th:

In the 14 possible configurations for the annual calendar (see any perpetual calendar), the occurrence of Friday the 13th is this:

6 of 14 years have one Friday the 13th.
6 of 14 years have two Fridays the 13th.
2 of 14 years have three Fridays the 13th.

No year is without one Friday the 13th, and no year has more than three.

Months that have a Friday the 13th begin on a Sunday.

2017 has a Friday the 13th in January and October.

THE ORIGIN OF DAY NAMES

The days of the week were named by ancient Romans with the Latin words for the Sun, the Moon, and the five known planets. These names have survived in European languages, but English names also reflect Anglo-Saxon and Norse influences.

ENGLISH	LATIN	FRENCH	ITALIAN	SPANISH	ANGLO-SAXON AND NORSE
SUNDAY	dies Solis (Sol's day)	dimanche	domenica	domingo	Sunnandaeg (Sun's day)
		from the Latin for "Lord's day"			
MONDAY	dies Lunae (Luna's day)	lundi	lunedì	lunes	Monandaeg (Moon's day)
TUESDAY	dies Martis (Mars's day)	mardi	martedì	martes	Tiwesdaeg (Tiw's day)
WEDNESDAY	dies Mercurii (Mercury's day)	mercredi	mercoledì	miércoles	Wodnesdaeg (Woden's day)
THURSDAY	dies Jovis (Jupiter's day)	jeudi	giovedì	jueves	Thursdaeg (Thor's day)
FRIDAY	dies Veneris (Venus's day)	vendredi	venerdì	viernes	Frigedaeg (Frigga's day)
SATURDAY	dies Saturni (Saturn's day)	samedi	sabato	sábado	Saeterndaeg (Saturn's day)
		from the Latin for "Sabbath"			

How to Find the Day of the Week for Any Given Date

To compute the day of the week for any given date as far back as the mid-18th century, proceed as follows:

Add the last two digits of the year to one-quarter of the last two digits (discard any remainder), the day of the month, and the month key from the key box below. Divide the sum by 7; the remainder is the day of the week (1 is Sunday, 2 is Monday, and so on). If there is no remainder, the day is Saturday. If you're searching for a weekday prior to 1900, add 2 to the sum before dividing; prior to 1800, add 4. The formula doesn't work for days prior to 1753. From 2000 through 2099, subtract 1 from the sum before dividing.

Example:

THE DAYTON FLOOD WAS ON MARCH 25, 1913.

Last two digits of year: 13
One-quarter of these two digits: 3
Given day of month: 25
Key number for March: 4
Sum: 45

45 ÷ 7 = 6, with a remainder of 3. The flood took place on Tuesday, the third day of the week.

KEY

JANUARY	1
LEAP YEAR	0
FEBRUARY	4
LEAP YEAR	3
MARCH	4
APRIL	0
MAY	2
JUNE	5
JULY	0
AUGUST	3
SEPTEMBER	6
OCTOBER	1
NOVEMBER	4
DECEMBER	6

REFERENCE

ANIMAL SIGNS OF THE CHINESE ZODIAC

The animal designations of the Chinese zodiac follow a 12-year cycle and are always used in the same sequence. The Chinese year of 354 days begins 3 to 7 weeks into the western 365-day year, so the animal designation changes at that time, rather than on January 1. This year, the Chinese New Year starts on January 28.

RAT

Ambitious and sincere, you can be generous with your money. Compatible with the dragon and the monkey. Your opposite is the horse.

1924 1936 1948
1960 1972 1984
1996 2008 2020

OX OR BUFFALO

A leader, you are bright, patient, and cheerful. Compatible with the snake and the rooster. Your opposite is the sheep.

1925 1937 1949
1961 1973 1985
1997 2009 2021

TIGER

Forthright and sensitive, you possess great courage. Compatible with the horse and the dog. Your opposite is the monkey.

1926 1938 1950
1962 1974 1986
1998 2010 2022

RABBIT OR HARE

Talented and affectionate, you are a seeker of tranquility. Compatible with the sheep and the pig. Your opposite is the rooster.

1927 1939 1951
1963 1975 1987
1999 2011 2023

DRAGON

Robust and passionate, your life is filled with complexity. Compatible with the monkey and the rat. Your opposite is the dog.

1928 1940 1952
1964 1976 1988
2000 2012 2024

SNAKE

Strong-willed and intense, you display great wisdom. Compatible with the rooster and the ox. Your opposite is the pig.

1929 1941 1953
1965 1977 1989
2001 2013 2025

HORSE

Physically attractive and popular, you like the company of others. Compatible with the tiger and the dog. Your opposite is the rat.

1930 1942 1954
1966 1978 1990
2002 2014 2026

SHEEP OR GOAT

Aesthetic and stylish, you enjoy being a private person. Compatible with the pig and the rabbit. Your opposite is the ox.

1931 1943 1955
1967 1979 1991
2003 2015 2027

MONKEY

Persuasive, skillful, and intelligent, you strive to excel. Compatible with the dragon and the rat. Your opposite is the tiger.

1932 1944 1956
1968 1980 1992
2004 2016 2028

ROOSTER OR COCK

Seeking wisdom and truth, you have a pioneering spirit. Compatible with the snake and the ox. Your opposite is the rabbit.

1933 1945 1957
1969 1981 1993
2005 2017 2029

DOG

Generous and loyal, you have the ability to work well with others. Compatible with the horse and the tiger. Your opposite is the dragon.

1934 1946 1958
1970 1982 1994
2006 2018 2030

PIG OR BOAR

Gallant and noble, your friends will remain at your side. Compatible with the rabbit and the sheep. Your opposite is the snake.

1935 1947 1959
1971 1983 1995
2007 2019 2031

A Table Foretelling the Weather Through All the Lunations of Each Year, or Forever

This table is the result of many years of actual observation and shows what sort of weather will probably follow the Moon's entrance into any of its quarters. For example, the table shows that the week following January 5, 2017, will be fair and mild, because the Moon enters the first quarter on that day at 2:47 P.M. EST. (See the **Left-Hand Calendar Pages, 142–168,** for Moon phases.)

EDITOR'S NOTE: Although the data in this table is taken into consideration in the year-long process of compiling the annual long-range weather forecasts for *The Old Farmer's Almanac,* we rely far more on our projections of solar activity.

TIME OF CHANGE	SUMMER	WINTER
Midnight to 2 A.M.	Fair	Hard frost, unless wind is south or west
2 A.M. to 4 A.M.	Cold, with frequent showers	Snow and stormy
4 A.M. to 6 A.M.	Rain	Rain
6 A.M. to 8 A.M.	Wind and rain	Stormy
8 A.M. to 10 A.M.	Changeable	Cold rain if wind is west; snow, if east
10 A.M. to noon	Frequent showers	Cold with high winds
Noon to 2 P.M.	Very rainy	Snow or rain
2 P.M. to 4 P.M.	Changeable	Fair and mild
4 P.M. to 6 P.M.	Fair	Fair
6 P.M. to 10 P.M.	Fair if wind is northwest; rain if wind is south or southwest	Fair and frosty if wind is north or northeast; rain or snow if wind is south or southwest
10 P.M. to midnight	Fair	Fair and frosty

This table was created more than 180 years ago by Dr. Herschell for the Boston Courier; *it first appeared in* The Old Farmer's Almanac *in 1834.*

REFERENCE

SAFE ICE THICKNESS*

ICE THICKNESS	PERMISSIBLE LOAD	ICE THICKNESS	PERMISSIBLE LOAD
3 inches	Single person on foot	12 inches	Heavy truck (8-ton gross)
4 inches	Group in single file	15 inches	10 tons
7½ inches	Passenger car (2-ton gross)	20 inches	25 tons
8 inches	Light truck (2½-ton gross)	30 inches	70 tons
10 inches	Medium truck (3½-ton gross)	36 inches	110 tons

***Solid, clear, blue/black pond and lake ice**

Slush ice has only half the strength of blue ice. The strength value of river ice is 15 percent less.

HEAT INDEX °F (°C)

TEMP. °F (°C)	RELATIVE HUMIDITY (%) 40	45	50	55	60	65	70	75	80
100 (38)	109 (43)	114 (46)	118 (48)	124 (51)	129 (54)	136 (58)			
98 (37)	105 (41)	109 (43)	113 (45)	117 (47)	123 (51)	128 (53)	134 (57)		
96 (36)	101 (38)	104 (40)	108 (42)	112 (44)	116 (47)	121 (49)	126 (52)	132 (56)	
94 (34)	97 (36)	100 (38)	103 (39)	106 (41)	110 (43)	114 (46)	119 (48)	124 (51)	129 (54)
92 (33)	94 (34)	96 (36)	99 (37)	101 (38)	105 (41)	108 (42)	112 (44)	116 (47)	121 (49)
90 (32)	91 (33)	93 (34)	95 (35)	97 (36)	100 (38)	103 (39)	106 (41)	109 (43)	113 (45)
88 (31)	88 (31)	89 (32)	91 (33)	93 (34)	95 (35)	98 (37)	100 (38)	103 (39)	106 (41)
86 (30)	85 (29)	87 (31)	88 (31)	89 (32)	91 (33)	93 (34)	95 (35)	97 (36)	100 (38)
84 (29)	83 (28)	84 (29)	85 (29)	86 (30)	88 (31)	89 (32)	90 (32)	92 (33)	94 (34)
82 (28)	81 (27)	82 (28)	83 (28)	84 (29)	84 (29)	85 (29)	86 (30)	88 (31)	89 (32)
80 (27)	80 (27)	80 (27)	81 (27)	81 (27)	82 (28)	82 (28)	83 (28)	84 (29)	84 (29)

EXAMPLE: *When the temperature is 88°F (31°C) and the relative humidity is 60 percent, the heat index, or how hot it feels, is 95°F (35°C).*

REFERENCE

THE UV INDEX FOR MEASURING ULTRAVIOLET RADIATION RISK

The U.S. National Weather Service's daily forecasts of ultraviolet levels use these numbers for various exposure levels:

UV INDEX NUMBER	EXPOSURE LEVEL	TIME TO BURN	ACTIONS TO TAKE
0, 1, 2	Minimal	60 minutes	Apply SPF 15 sunscreen
3, 4	Low	45 minutes	Apply SPF 15 sunscreen; wear a hat
5, 6	Moderate	30 minutes	Apply SPF 15 sunscreen; wear a hat
7, 8, 9	High	15–25 minutes	Apply SPF 15 to 30 sunscreen; wear a hat and sunglasses; limit midday exposure
10 or higher	Very high	10 minutes	Apply SPF 30 sunscreen; wear a hat, sunglasses, and protective clothing; limit midday exposure

"Time to Burn" and "Actions to Take" apply to people with fair skin that sometimes tans but usually burns. People with lighter skin need to be more cautious. People with darker skin may be able to tolerate more exposure.

85	90	95	100
135 (57)			
126 (52)	131 (55)		
117 (47)	122 (50)	127 (53)	132 (56)
110 (43)	113 (45)	117 (47)	121 (49)
102 (39)	105 (41)	108 (42)	112 (44)
96 (36)	98 (37)	100 (38)	103 (39)
90 (32)	91 (33)	93 (34)	95 (35)
85 (29)	86 (30)	86 (30)	87 (31)

What Are Cooling/Heating Degree Days?

Each degree of a day's average temperature above 65°F is considered one cooling degree day, an attempt to measure the need for air-conditioning. If the average of the day's high and low temperatures is 75°, that's 10 cooling degree days.

Similarly, each degree of a day's average temperature below 65° is considered one heating degree and is an attempt to measure the need for fuel consumption. For example, a day with temperatures ranging from 60° to 40° results in an average of 50°, or 15 degrees less than 65°. Hence, that day would be credited as 15 heating degree days.

HOW TO MEASURE HAIL

The **TORRO HAILSTORM INTENSITY SCALE** was introduced by Jonathan Webb of Oxford, England, in 1986 as a means of categorizing hailstorms. The name derives from the private and mostly British research body named the TORnado and storm Research Organisation.

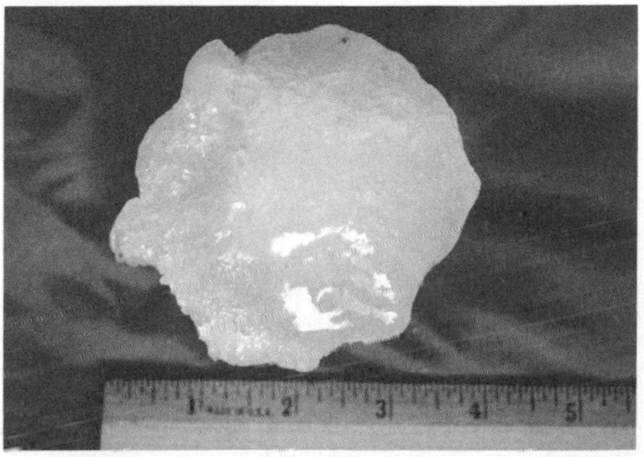

INTENSITY/DESCRIPTION OF HAIL DAMAGE	
H0	True hail of pea size causes no damage
H1	Leaves and flower petals are punctured and torn
H2	Leaves are stripped from trees and plants
H3	Panes of glass are broken; auto bodies are dented
H4	Some house windows are broken; small tree branches are broken off; birds are killed
H5	Many windows are smashed; small animals are injured; large tree branches are broken off
H6	Shingle roofs are breached; metal roofs are scored; wooden window frames are broken away
H7	Roofs are shattered to expose rafters; autos are seriously damaged
H8	Shingle and tile roofs are destroyed; small tree trunks are split; people are seriously injured
H9	Concrete roofs are broken; large tree trunks are split and knocked down; people are at risk of fatal injuries
H10	Brick houses are damaged; people are at risk of fatal injuries

REFERENCE

HOW TO MEASURE WIND SPEED

The **BEAUFORT WIND FORCE SCALE** is a common way of estimating wind speed. It was developed in 1805 by Admiral Sir Francis Beaufort of the British Navy to measure wind at sea. We can also use it to measure wind on land.

Admiral Beaufort arranged the numbers 0 to 12 to indicate the strength of the wind from calm, force 0, to hurricane, force 12. Here's a scale adapted to land.

"Used Mostly at Sea but of Help to All Who Are Interested in the Weather"

BEAUFORT FORCE	DESCRIPTION	WHEN YOU SEE OR FEEL THIS EFFECT	WIND SPEED (mph)	(km/h)
0	CALM	Smoke goes straight up	less than 1	less than 2
1	LIGHT AIR	Wind direction is shown by smoke drift but not by wind vane	1–3	2–5
2	LIGHT BREEZE	Wind is felt on the face; leaves rustle; wind vanes move	4–7	6–11
3	GENTLE BREEZE	Leaves and small twigs move steadily; wind extends small flags straight out	8–12	12–19
4	MODERATE BREEZE	Wind raises dust and loose paper; small branches move	13–18	20–29
5	FRESH BREEZE	Small trees sway; waves form on lakes	19–24	30–39
6	STRONG BREEZE	Large branches move; wires whistle; umbrellas are difficult to use	25–31	40–50
7	MODERATE GALE	Whole trees are in motion; walking against the wind is difficult	32–38	51–61
8	FRESH GALE	Twigs break from trees; walking against the wind is very difficult	39–46	62–74
9	STRONG GALE	Buildings suffer minimal damage; roof shingles are removed	47–54	75–87
10	WHOLE GALE	Trees are uprooted	55–63	88–101
11	VIOLENT STORM	Widespread damage	64–72	102–116
12	HURRICANE	Widespread destruction	73+	117+

REFERENCE

RETIRED ATLANTIC HURRICANE NAMES

These storms have been some of the most destructive and costly.

NAME	YEAR	NAME	YEAR	NAME	YEAR
Dennis	2005	Felix	2007	Tomas	2010
Katrina	2005	Noel	2007	Irene	2011
Rita	2005	Gustav	2008	Sandy	2012
Stan	2005	Ike	2008	Ingrid	2013
Wilma	2005	Paloma	2008	Erika	2015
Dean	2007	Igor	2010	Joaquin	2015

ATLANTIC TROPICAL (AND SUBTROPICAL) STORM NAMES FOR 2017

Arlene	Harvey	Ophelia
Bret	Irma	Philippe
Cindy	Jose	Rina
Don	Katia	Sean
Emily	Lee	Tammy
Franklin	Maria	Vince
Gert	Nate	Whitney

EASTERN NORTH-PACIFIC TROPICAL (AND SUBTROPICAL) STORM NAMES FOR 2017

Adrian	Irwin	Ramon
Beatriz	Jova	Selma
Calvin	Kenneth	Todd
Dora	Lidia	Veronica
Eugene	Max	Wiley
Fernanda	Norma	Xina
Greg	Otis	York
Hilary	Pilar	Zelda

How to Measure Hurricane Strength

The **SAFFIR-SIMPSON HURRICANE WIND SCALE** assigns a rating from 1 to 5 based on a hurricane's intensity. It is used to give an estimate of the potential property damage from a hurricane landfall. Wind speed is the determining factor in the scale, as storm surge values are highly dependent on the slope of the continental shelf in the landfall region. Wind speeds are measured at a height of 33 feet (10 meters) using a 1-minute average.

CATEGORY ONE. Average wind: 74–95 mph. Significant damage to mobile homes. Some damage to roofing and siding of well-built frame homes. Large tree branches snap and shallow-rooted trees may topple. Power outages may last a few to several days.

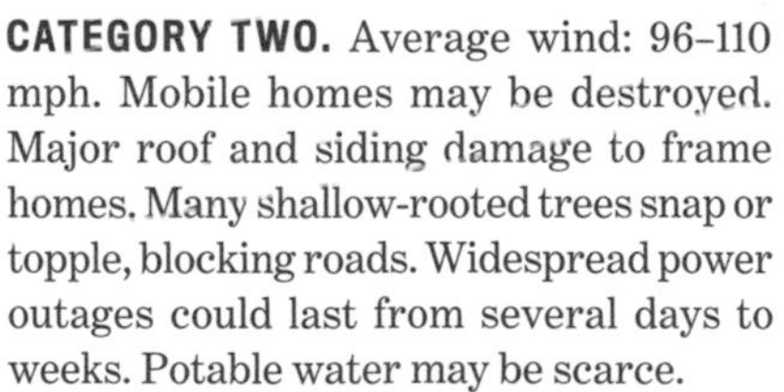

CATEGORY TWO. Average wind: 96–110 mph. Mobile homes may be destroyed. Major roof and siding damage to frame homes. Many shallow-rooted trees snap or topple, blocking roads. Widespread power outages could last from several days to weeks. Potable water may be scarce.

CATEGORY THREE. Average wind: 111–129 mph. Most mobile homes destroyed. Frame homes may sustain major roof damage. Many trees snap or topple, blocking numerous roads. Electricity and water may be unavailable for several days to weeks.

CATEGORY FOUR. Average wind: 130–156 mph. Mobile homes destroyed. Frame homes severely damaged or destroyed. Windborne debris may penetrate protected windows. Most trees snap or topple. Residential areas isolated by fallen trees and power poles. Most of the area uninhabitable for weeks to months.

CATEGORY FIVE. Average wind: 157+ mph. Most homes destroyed. Nearly all windows blown out of high-rises. Most of the area uninhabitable for weeks to months.

HOW TO MEASURE A TORNADO

The original **FUJITA SCALE** (or F Scale) was developed by Dr. Theodore Fujita to classify tornadoes based on wind damage. All tornadoes, and other severe local windstorms, were assigned a number according to the most intense damage caused by the storm. An enhanced F (EF) scale was implemented in the United States on February 1, 2007. The EF scale uses 3-second gust estimates based on a more detailed system for assessing damage, taking into account different building materials.

F SCALE		EF SCALE (U.S.)
F0 • 40–72 mph (64–116 km/h)	LIGHT DAMAGE	EF0 • 65–85 mph (105–137 km/h)
F1 • 73–112 mph (117–180 km/h)	MODERATE DAMAGE	EF1 • 86–110 mph (138–178 km/h)
F2 • 113–157 mph (181–253 km/h)	CONSIDERABLE DAMAGE	EF2 • 111–135 mph (179–218 km/h)
F3 • 158–207 mph (254–332 km/h)	SEVERE DAMAGE	EF3 • 136–165 mph (219–266 km/h)
F4 • 208–260 mph (333–419 km/h)	DEVASTATING DAMAGE	EF4 • 166–200 mph (267–322 km/h)
F5 • 261–318 mph (420–512 km/h)	INCREDIBLE DAMAGE	EF5 • over 200 mph (over 322 km/h)

Wind/Barometer Table

BAROMETER (REDUCED TO SEA LEVEL)	WIND DIRECTION	CHARACTER OF WEATHER INDICATED
30.00 to 30.20, and steady	WESTERLY	Fair, with slight changes in temperature, for one to two days
30.00 to 30.20, and rising rapidly	WESTERLY	Fair, followed within two days by warmer and rain
30.00 to 30.20, and falling rapidly	SOUTH TO EAST	Warmer, and rain within 24 hours
30.20 or above, and falling rapidly	SOUTH TO EAST	Warmer, and rain within 36 hours
30.20 or above, and falling rapidly	WEST TO NORTH	Cold and clear, quickly followed by warmer and rain
30.20 or above, and steady	VARIABLE	No early change
30.00 or below, and falling slowly	SOUTH TO EAST	Rain within 18 hours that will continue a day or two
30.00 or below, and falling rapidly	SOUTHEAST TO NORTHEAST	Rain, with high wind, followed within two days by clearing, colder
30.00 or below, and rising	SOUTH TO WEST	Clearing and colder within 12 hours
29.80 or below, and falling rapidly	SOUTH TO EAST	Severe storm of wind and rain imminent; in winter, snow or cold wave within 24 hours
29.80 or below, and falling rapidly	EAST TO NORTH	Severe northeast gales and heavy rain or snow, followed in winter by cold wave
29.80 or below, and rising rapidly	GOING TO WEST	Clearing and colder

NOTE: *A barometer should be adjusted to show equivalent sea-level pressure for the altitude at which it is to be used. A change of 100 feet in elevation will cause a decrease of 1/10 inch in the reading.*

REFERENCE

WINDCHILL TABLE

As wind speed increases, your body loses heat more rapidly, making the air feel colder than it really is. The combination of cold temperature and high wind can create a cooling effect so severe that exposed flesh can freeze.

WIND SPEED (mph)	TEMPERATURE (°F)														
Calm	**35**	**30**	**25**	**20**	**15**	**10**	**5**	**0**	**–5**	**–10**	**–15**	**–20**	**–25**	**–30**	**–35**
5	31	25	19	13	7	1	–5	–11	–16	–22	–28	–34	–40	–46	–52
10	27	21	15	9	3	–4	–10	–16	–22	–28	–35	–41	–47	–53	–59
15	25	19	13	6	0	–7	–13	–19	–26	–32	–39	–45	–51	–58	–64
20	24	17	11	4	–2	–9	–15	–22	–29	–35	–42	–48	–55	–61	–68
25	23	16	9	3	–4	–11	–17	–24	–31	–37	–44	–51	–58	–64	–71
30	22	15	8	1	–5	–12	–19	–26	–33	–39	–46	–53	–60	–67	–73
35	21	14	7	0	–7	–14	–21	–27	–34	–41	–48	–55	–62	–69	–76
40	20	13	6	–1	–8	–15	–22	–29	–36	–43	–50	–57	–64	–71	–78
45	19	12	5	–2	–9	–16	–23	–30	–37	–44	–51	–58	–65	–72	–79
50	19	12	4	–3	–10	–17	–24	–31	–38	–45	–52	–60	–67	–74	–81
55	18	11	4	–3	–11	–18	–25	–32	–39	–46	–54	–61	–68	–75	–82
60	17	10	3	–4	–11	–19	–26	–33	–40	–48	–55	–62	–69	–76	–84

FROSTBITE OCCURS IN 30 MINUTES 10 MINUTES 5 MINUTES

EXAMPLE: *When the temperature is 15°F and the wind speed is 30 miles per hour, the windchill, or how cold it feels, is –5°F. For a Celsius version of this table, visit Almanac.com/WindchillCelsius.*

–courtesy of National Weather Service

HOW TO MEASURE EARTHQUAKES

In 1979, seismologists developed a measurement of earthquake size called **MOMENT MAGNITUDE.** It is more accurate than the previously used Richter scale, which is precise only for earthquakes of a certain size and at a certain distance from a seismometer. All earthquakes can now be compared on the same scale.

MAGNITUDE	EFFECT
LESS THAN 3	MICRO
3-3.9	MINOR
4-4.9	LIGHT
5-5.9	MODERATE
6-6.9	STRONG
7-7.9	MAJOR
8 OR MORE	GREAT

REFERENCE

A GARDENER'S WORST PHOBIAS

NAME OF FEAR	OBJECT FEARED
Alliumphobia	Garlic
Anthophobia	Flowers
Apiphobia	Bees
Arachnophobia	Spiders
Batonophobia	Plants
Bufonophobia	Toads
Dendrophobia	Trees
Entomophobia	Insects
Lachanophobia	Vegetables
Melissophobia	Bees
Mottephobia	Moths
Myrmecophobia	Ants
Ornithophobia	Birds
Ranidaphobia	Frogs
Rupophobia	Dirt
Scoleciphobia	Worms
Spheksophobia	Wasps

PLANTS FOR LAWNS

Choose varieties that suit your soil and your climate. All of these can withstand mowing and considerable foot traffic.

Ajuga or bugleweed *(Ajuga reptans)*
Corsican mint *(Mentha requienii)*
Dwarf cinquefoil *(Potentilla tabernaemontani)*
English pennyroyal *(Mentha pulegium)*
Green Irish moss *(Sagina subulata)*
Pearly everlasting *(Anaphalis margaritacea)*
Roman chamomile *(Chamaemelum nobile)*
Rupturewort *(Herniaria glabra)*
Speedwell *(Veronica officinalis)*
Stonecrop *(Sedum ternatum)*
Sweet violets (*Viola odorata* or *V. tricolor*)
Thyme *(Thymus serpyllum)*
White clover *(Trifolium repens)*
Wild strawberries *(Fragaria virginiana)*
Wintergreen or partridgeberry *(Mitchella repens)*

REFERENCE

Lawn-Growing Tips

- Test your soil: The pH balance should be 7.0 or more; 6.2 to 6.7 puts your lawn at risk for fungal diseases. If the pH is too low, correct it with liming, best done in the fall.
- The best time to apply fertilizer is just before it rains.
- If you put lime and fertilizer on your lawn, spread half of it as you walk north to south, the other half as you walk east to west to cut down on missed areas.
- Any feeding of lawns in the fall should be done with a low-nitrogen, slow-acting fertilizer.
- In areas of your lawn where tree roots compete with the grass, apply some extra fertilizer to benefit both.
- Moss and sorrel in lawns usually means poor soil, poor aeration or drainage, or excessive acidity.
- Control weeds by promoting healthy lawn growth with natural fertilizers in spring and early fall.
- Raise the level of your lawn-mower blades during the hot summer days. Taller grass resists drought better than short.
- You can reduce mowing time by redesigning your lawn, reducing sharp corners and adding sweeping curves.
- During a drought, let the grass grow longer between mowings and reduce fertilizer.
- Water your lawn early in the morning or in the evening.

Flowers and Herbs That Attract Butterflies

Common name	Botanical name
Allium	*Allium*
Aster	*Aster*
Bee balm	*Monarda*
Butterfly bush	*Buddleia*
Catmint	*Nepeta*
Clove pink	*Dianthus*
Cornflower	*Centaurea*
Creeping thyme	*Thymus serpyllum*
Daylily	*Hemerocallis*
Dill	*Anethum graveolens*
False indigo	*Baptisia*
Fleabane	*Erigeron*
Floss flower	*Ageratum*
Globe thistle	*Echinops*
Goldenrod	*Solidago*
Helen's flower	*Helenium*
Hollyhock	*Alcea*
Honeysuckle	*Lonicera*
Lavender	*Lavandula*
Lilac	*Syringa*
Lupine	*Lupinus*
Lychnis	*Lychnis*
Mallow	*Malva*
Mealycup sage	*Salvia farinacea*
Milkweed	*Asclepias*
Mint	*Mentha*
Oregano	*Origanum vulgare*
Pansy	*Viola*
Parsley	*Petroselinum crispum*
Phlox	*Phlox*
Privet	*Ligustrum*
Purple coneflower	*Echinacea purpurea*
Rock cress	*Arabis*
Sea holly	*Eryngium*
Shasta daisy	*Chrysanthemum*
Snapdragon	*Antirrhinum*
Stonecrop	*Sedum*
Sweet alyssum	*Lobularia*
Sweet marjoram	*Origanum majorana*
Sweet rocket	*Hesperis*
Tickseed	*Coreopsis*
Verbena	*Verbena*
Zinnia	*Zinnia*

FLOWERS* THAT ATTRACT HUMMINGBIRDS

Common name	Botanical name
Beard tongue	*Penstemon*
Bee balm	*Monarda*
Butterfly bush	*Buddleia*
Catmint	*Nepeta*
Clove pink	*Dianthus*
Columbine	*Aquilegia*
Coral bells	*Heuchera*
Daylily	*Hemerocallis*
Desert candle	*Yucca*
Flag iris	*Iris*
Flowering tobacco	*Nicotiana alata*
Foxglove	*Digitalis*
Larkspur	*Delphinium*
Lily	*Lilium*
Lupine	*Lupinus*
Petunia	*Petunia*
Pincushion flower	*Scabiosa*
Red-hot poker	*Kniphofia*
Scarlet sage	*Salvia splendens*
Soapwort	*Saponaria*
Summer phlox	*Phlox paniculata*
Trumpet honeysuckle	*Lonicera sempervirens*
Verbena	*Verbena*
Weigela	*Weigela*

***NOTE:** *Choose varieties in red and orange shades, if available.*

REFERENCE

pH PREFERENCES OF TREES, SHRUBS, FLOWERS, AND VEGETABLES

An accurate soil test will indicate your soil pH and will specify the amount of lime or sulfur that is needed to bring it up or down to the appropriate level. A pH of 6.5 is just about right for most home gardens, since most plants thrive in the 6.0 to 7.0 (slightly acidic to neutral) range. Some plants (azaleas, blueberries) prefer more strongly acidic soil in the 4.0 to 6.0 range, while a few (asparagus, plums) do best in soil that is neutral to slightly alkaline. Acidic, or sour, soil (below 7.0) is counteracted by applying finely ground limestone, and alkaline, or sweet, soil (above 7.0) is treated with ground sulfur.

COMMON NAME	OPTIMUM pH RANGE
TREES AND SHRUBS	
Apple	5.0–6.5
Azalea	4.5–6.0
Beautybush	6.0–7.5
Birch	5.0–6.5
Blackberry	5.0–6.0
Blueberry	4.0–5.0
Boxwood	6.0–7.5
Cherry, sour	6.0–7.0
Crab apple	6.0–7.5
Dogwood	5.0–7.0
Fir, balsam	5.0–6.0
Hemlock	5.0–6.0
Hydrangea, blue-flowered	4.0–5.0
Hydrangea, pink-flowered	6.0–7.0
Juniper	5.0–6.0
Laurel, mountain	4.5–6.0
Lemon	6.0–7.5
Lilac	6.0–7.5
Maple, sugar	6.0–7.5
Oak, white	5.0–6.5
Orange	6.0–7.5
Peach	6.0–7.0
Pear	6.0–7.5
Pecan	6.4–8.0
Plum	6.0–8.0
Raspberry, red	5.5–7.0
Rhododendron	4.5–6.0
Willow	6.0–8.0
FLOWERS	
Alyssum	6.0–7.5
Aster, New England	6.0–8.0
Baby's breath	6.0–7.0
Bachelor's button	6.0–7.5
Bee balm	6.0–7.5
Begonia	5.5–7.0
Black-eyed Susan	5.5–7.0
Bleeding heart	6.0–7.5
Canna	6.0–8.0
Carnation	6.0–7.0
Chrysanthemum	6.0–7.5
Clematis	5.5–7.0
Coleus	6.0–7.0
Coneflower, purple	5.0–7.5
Cosmos	5.0–8.0
Crocus	6.0–8.0
Daffodil	6.0–6.5
Dahlia	6.0–7.5
Daisy, Shasta	6.0–8.0
Daylily	6.0–8.0
Delphinium	6.0–7.5
Foxglove	6.0–7.5
Geranium	6.0–8.0
Gladiolus	5.0–7.0
Hibiscus	6.0–8.0
Hollyhock	6.0–8.0
Hyacinth	6.5–7.5
Iris, blue flag	5.0–7.5
Lily-of-the-valley	4.5–6.0
Lupine	5.0–6.5
Marigold	5.5–7.5
Morning glory	6.0–7.5
Narcissus, trumpet	5.5–6.5
Nasturtium	5.5–7.5
Pansy	5.5–6.5
Peony	6.0–7.5
Petunia	6.0–7.5
Phlox, summer	6.0–8.0
Poppy, oriental	6.0–7.5
Rose, hybrid tea	5.5–7.0
Rose, rugosa	6.0–7.0
Snapdragon	5.5–7.0
Sunflower	6.0–7.5
Tulip	6.0–7.0
Zinnia	5.5–7.0
VEGETABLES	
Asparagus	6.0–8.0
Bean	6.0–7.5
Beet	6.0–7.5
Broccoli	6.0–7.0
Brussels sprout	6.0–7.5
Cabbage	6.0–7.5
Carrot	5.5–7.0
Cauliflower	5.5–7.5
Celery	5.8–7.0
Chive	6.0–7.0
Collard	6.5–7.5
Corn	5.5–7.0
Cucumber	5.5–7.0
Eggplant	6.0–7.0
Garlic	5.5–8.0
Kale	6.0–7.5
Leek	6.0–8.0
Lettuce	6.0–7.0
Okra	6.0–7.0
Onion	6.0–7.0
Pea	6.0–7.5
Pepper, sweet	5.5–7.0
Potato	4.8–6.5
Pumpkin	5.5–7.5
Radish	6.0–7.0
Spinach	6.0–7.5
Squash, crookneck	6.0–7.5
Squash, Hubbard	5.5–7.0
Swiss chard	6.0–7.0
Tomato	5.5–7.5
Watermelon	5.5–6.5

PRODUCE WEIGHTS AND MEASURES

VEGETABLES

ASPARAGUS: 1 pound = 3 cups chopped

BEANS (STRING): 1 pound = 4 cups chopped

BEETS: 1 pound (5 medium) = 2½ cups chopped

BROCCOLI: 1 pound = 6 cups chopped

CABBAGE: 1 pound = 4½ cups shredded

CARROTS: 1 pound = 3½ cups sliced or grated

CELERY: 1 pound = 4 cups chopped

CUCUMBERS: 1 pound (2 medium) = 4 cups sliced

EGGPLANT: 1 pound = 4 cups chopped = 2 cups cooked

GARLIC: 1 clove = 1 teaspoon chopped

LEEKS: 1 pound = 4 cups chopped = 2 cups cooked

MUSHROOMS: 1 pound = 5 to 6 cups sliced = 2 cups cooked

ONIONS: 1 pound = 4 cups sliced = 2 cups cooked

PARSNIPS: 1 pound = 1½ cups cooked, puréed

PEAS: 1 pound whole = 1 to 1½ cups shelled

POTATOES: 1 pound (3 medium) sliced = 2 cups mashed

PUMPKIN: 1 pound = 4 cups chopped = 2 cups cooked and drained

SPINACH: 1 pound = ¾ to 1 cup cooked

SQUASHES (SUMMER): 1 pound = 4 cups grated = 2 cups sliced and cooked

SQUASHES (WINTER): 2 pounds = 2½ cups cooked, puréed

SWEET POTATOES: 1 pound = 4 cups grated = 1 cup cooked, puréed

SWISS CHARD: 1 pound = 5 to 6 cups packed leaves = 1 to 1½ cups cooked

TOMATOES: 1 pound (3 or 4 medium) = 1½ cups seeded pulp

TURNIPS: 1 pound = 4 cups chopped = 2 cups cooked, mashed

FRUIT

APPLES: 1 pound (3 or 4 medium) = 3 cups sliced

BANANAS: 1 pound (3 or 4 medium) = 1¾ cups mashed

BERRIES: 1 quart = 3½ cups

DATES: 1 pound = 2½ cups pitted

LEMON: 1 whole = 1 to 3 tablespoons juice; 1 to 1½ teaspoons grated rind

LIME: 1 whole = 1½ to 2 tablespoons juice

ORANGE: 1 medium = 6 to 8 tablespoons juice; 2 to 3 tablespoons grated rind

PEACHES: 1 pound (4 medium) = 3 cups sliced

PEARS: 1 pound (4 medium) = 2 cups sliced

RHUBARB: 1 pound = 2 cups cooked

SOWING VEGETABLE SEEDS

SOW OR PLANT IN COOL WEATHER	Beets, broccoli, brussels sprouts, cabbage, lettuce, onions, parsley, peas, radishes, spinach, Swiss chard, turnips
SOW OR PLANT IN WARM WEATHER	Beans, carrots, corn, cucumbers, eggplant, melons, okra, peppers, squashes, tomatoes
SOW OR PLANT FOR ONE CROP PER SEASON	Corn, eggplant, leeks, melons, peppers, potatoes, spinach (New Zealand), squashes, tomatoes
RESOW FOR ADDITIONAL CROPS	Beans, beets, cabbage, carrots, kohlrabi, lettuce, radishes, rutabagas, spinach, turnips

A Beginner's Vegetable Garden

The vegetables suggested below are common, easy-to-grow crops. Make 11 rows, 10 feet long, with at least 18 inches between them. Ideally, the rows should run north and south to take full advantage of the sun. This garden, planted as suggested, can feed a family of four for one summer, with a little extra for canning and freezing or giving away.

ROW	
1	Zucchini (4 plants)
2	Tomatoes (5 plants, staked)
3	Peppers (6 plants)
4	Cabbage

ROW	
5	Bush beans
6	Lettuce
7	Beets
8	Carrots
9	Swiss chard
10	Radishes
11	Marigolds (to discourage rabbits!)

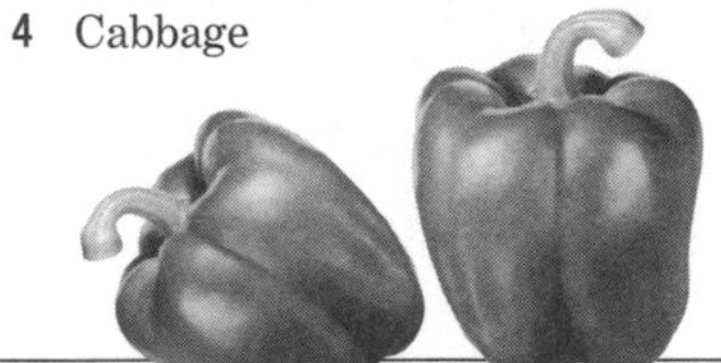

REFERENCE

TRADITIONAL PLANTING TIMES

- Plant **CORN** when elm leaves are the size of a squirrel's ear, when oak leaves are the size of a mouse's ear, when apple blossoms begin to fall, or when the dogwoods are in full bloom.
- Plant **LETTUCE, SPINACH, PEAS,** and other cool-weather vegetables when the lilacs show their first leaves or when daffodils begin to bloom.
- Plant **TOMATOES** and **PEPPERS** when dogwoods are in peak bloom or when daylilies start to bloom.
- Plant **CUCUMBERS** and **SQUASHES** when lilac flowers fade.
- Plant **PERENNIALS** when maple leaves begin to unfurl.
- Plant **MORNING GLORIES** when maple trees have full-size leaves.
- Plant **PANSIES, SNAPDRAGONS,** and other hardy annuals after the aspen and chokecherry trees leaf out.
- Plant **BEETS** and **CARROTS** when dandelions are blooming.

WHEN TO . . .

	. . . FERTILIZE	. . . WATER
BEANS	After heavy bloom and set of pods	Regularly, from start of pod to set
BEETS	At time of planting	Only during drought conditions
BROCCOLI	3 weeks after transplanting	Only during drought conditions
BRUSSELS SPROUTS	3 weeks after transplanting	At transplanting
CABBAGE	3 weeks after transplanting	2 to 3 weeks before harvest
CARROTS	In the fall for the following spring	Only during drought conditions
CAULIFLOWER	3 weeks after transplanting	Once, 3 weeks before harvest
CELERY	At time of transplanting	Once a week
CORN	When 8 to 10 inches tall, and when first silk appears	When tassels appear and cobs start to swell
CUCUMBERS	1 week after bloom, and 3 weeks later	Frequently, especially when fruits form
LETTUCE	2 to 3 weeks after transplanting	Once a week
MELONS	1 week after bloom, and again 3 weeks later	Once a week
ONION SETS	When bulbs begin to swell, and when plants are 1 foot tall	Only during drought conditions
PARSNIPS	1 year before planting	Only during drought conditions
PEAS	After heavy bloom and set of pods	Regularly, from start of pod to set
PEPPERS	After first fruit-set	Once a week
POTATO TUBERS	At bloom time or time of second hilling	Regularly, when tubers start to form
PUMPKINS	Just before vines start to run, when plants are about 1 foot tall	Only during drought conditions
RADISHES	Before spring planting	Once a week
SPINACH	When plants are one-third grown	Once a week
SQUASHES, SUMMER	Just before vines start to run, when plants are about 1 foot tall	Only during drought conditions
SQUASHES, WINTER	Just before vines start to run, when plants are about 1 foot tall	Only during drought conditions
TOMATOES	2 weeks before, and after first picking	Twice a week

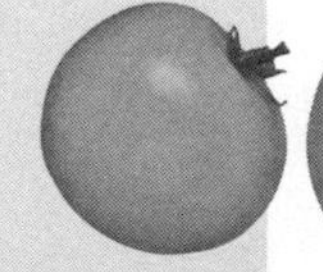

HOW TO GROW HERBS

HERB	START SEEDS INDOORS (WEEKS BEFORE LAST SPRING FROST)	START SEEDS OUTDOORS (WEEKS BEFORE/AFTER LAST SPRING FROST)	HEIGHT/ SPREAD (INCHES)	SOIL	LIGHT**
Basil*	6–8	Anytime after	12–24/12	Rich, moist	○
Borage*	Not recommended	Anytime after	12–36/12	Rich, well-drained, dry	○
Chervil	Not recommended	3–4 before	12–24/8	Rich, moist	◑
Chives	8–10	3–4 before	12–18/18	Rich, moist	○
Cilantro/ coriander	Not recommended	Anytime after	12–36/6	Light	○◑
Dill	Not recommended	4–5 before	36–48/12	Rich	○
Fennel	4–6	Anytime after	48–80/18	Rich	○
Lavender, English*	8–12	1–2 before	18–36/24	Moderately fertile, well-drained	○
Lavender, French	Not recommended	Not recommended	18–36/24	Moderately fertile, well-drained	○
Lemon balm*	6–10	2–3 before	12–24/18	Rich, well-drained	○◑
Lovage*	6–8	2–3 before	36–72/36	Fertile, sandy	○◑
Mint	Not recommended	Not recommended	12–24/18	Rich, moist	◑
Oregano*	6–10	Anytime after	12–24/18	Poor	○
Parsley*	10–12	3–4 before	18–24/6–8	Medium-rich	◑
Rosemary*	8–10	Anytime after	48–72/48	Not too acid	○
Sage	6–10	1–2 before	12–48/30	Well-drained	○
Sorrel	6–10	2–3 after	20–48/12–14	Rich, organic	○
Summer savory	4–6	Anytime after	4–15/6	Medium rich	○
Sweet cicely	6–8	2–3 after	36–72/36	Moderately fertile, well-drained	○◑
Tarragon, French	Not recommended	Not recommended	24–36/12	Well-drained	○◑
Thyme, common*	6–10	2–3 before	2–12/7–12	Fertile, well-drained	○◑

*Recommend minimum soil temperature of 70°F to germinate

** ○ FULL SUN ◑ PARTIAL SHADE

REFERENCE

GROWTH TYPE
Annual
Annual, biennial
Annual, biennial
Perennial
Annual
Annual
Annual
Perennial
Tender perennial
Perennial
Perennial
Perennial
Tender perennial
Biennial
Tender perennial
Perennial
Perennial
Annual
Perennial
Perennial
Perennial

DRYING HERBS

Before drying, remove any dead or diseased leaves or stems. Wash under cool water, shake off excess water, and put on a towel to dry completely. Air drying preserves an herb's essential oils; use for sturdy herbs. A microwave dries herbs more quickly, so mold is less likely to develop; use for moist, tender herbs.

HANGING METHOD: Gather four to six stems of fresh herbs in a bunch and tie with string, leaving a loop for hanging. Or, use a rubber band with a paper clip attached to it. Hang the herbs in a warm, well-ventilated area, out of direct sunlight, until dry. For herbs that have full seed heads, such as dill or coriander, use a paper bag. Punch holes in the bag for ventilation, label it, and put the herb bunch into the bag before you tie a string around the top of the bag. The average drying time is 1 to 3 weeks.

MICROWAVE METHOD: This is better for small quantities, such as a cup or two at a time. Arrange a single layer of herbs between two paper towels and put them in the microwave for 1 to 2 minutes on high power. Let the leaves cool. If they are not dry, reheat for 30 seconds and check again. Repeat as needed. Let cool. Do not overcook, or the herbs will lose their flavor.

STORING HERBS AND SPICES

FRESH HERBS: Dill and parsley will keep for about 2 weeks with stems immersed in a glass of water tented with a plastic bag. Most other fresh herbs (and greens) will keep for short periods unwashed and refrigerated in tightly sealed plastic bags with just enough moisture to prevent wilting. For longer storage, use moisture- and gas-permeable paper and cellophane. Plastic cuts off oxygen to the plants and promotes spoilage.

SPICES AND DRIED HERBS: Store in a cool, dry place.

COOKING WITH HERBS

BOUQUET GARNI is usually made with bay leaves, thyme, and parsley tied with string or wrapped in cheesecloth. Use to flavor casseroles and soups. Remove after cooking.

FINES HERBES use equal amounts of fresh parsley, tarragon, chives, and chervil chopped fine. Commonly used in French cooking, they make a fine omelet or add zest to soups and sauces. Add to salads and butter sauces, or sprinkle on noodles, soups, and stews.

HOW TO GROW BULBS

	COMMON NAME	LATIN NAME	HARDINESS ZONE	SOIL	LIGHT*	SPACING (INCHES)
SPRING-PLANTED BULBS	**Allium**	*Allium*	3–10	Well-drained/moist	○	12
	Begonia, tuberous	*Begonia*	10–11	Well-drained/moist	◑●	12–15
	Blazing star/ gayfeather	*Liatris*	7–10	Well-drained	○	6
	Caladium	*Caladium*	10–11	Well-drained/moist	◑●	8–12
	Calla lily	*Zantedeschia*	8–10	Well-drained/moist	○◑	8–24
	Canna	*Canna*	8–11	Well-drained/moist	○	12–24
	Cyclamen	*Cyclamen*	7–9	Well-drained/moist	◑	4
	Dahlia	*Dahlia*	9–11	Well-drained/fertile	○	12–36
	Daylily	*Hemerocallis*	3–10	Adaptable to most soils	○◑	12–24
	Freesia	*Freesia*	9–11	Well-drained/moist/sandy	○◑	2–4
	Garden gloxinia	*Incarvillea*	4–8	Well-drained/moist	○	12
	Gladiolus	*Gladiolus*	4–11	Well-drained/fertile	○◑	4–9
	Iris	*Iris*	3–10	Well-drained/sandy	○	3–6
	Lily, Asiatic/Oriental	*Lilium*	3–8	Well-drained	○◑	8–12
	Peacock flower	*Tigridia*	8–10	Well-drained	○	5–6
	Shamrock/sorrel	*Oxalis*	5–9	Well-drained	○◑	4–6
	Windflower	*Anemone*	3–9	Well-drained/moist	○◑	3–6
FALL-PLANTED BULBS	**Bluebell**	*Hyacinthoides*	4–9	Well-drained/fertile	○◑	4
	Christmas rose/ hellebore	*Helleborus*	4–8	Neutral–alkaline	○◑	18
	Crocus	*Crocus*	3–8	Well-drained/moist/fertile	○◑	4
	Daffodil	*Narcissus*	3–10	Well-drained/moist/fertile	○◑	6
	Fritillary	*Fritillaria*	3–9	Well-drained/sandy	○◑	3
	Glory of the snow	*Chionodoxa*	3–9	Well-drained/moist	○◑	3
	Grape hyacinth	*Muscari*	4–10	Well-drained/moist/fertile	○◑	3–4
	Iris, bearded	*Iris*	3–9	Well-drained	○◑	4
	Iris, Siberian	*Iris*	4–9	Well-drained	○◑	4
	Ornamental onion	*Allium*	3–10	Well-drained/moist/fertile	○	12
	Snowdrop	*Galanthus*	3–9	Well-drained/moist/fertile	○◑	3
	Snowflake	*Leucojum*	5–9	Well-drained/moist/sandy	○◑	4
	Spring starflower	*Ipheion uniflorum*	6–9	Well-drained loam	○◑	3–6
	Star of Bethlehem	*Ornithogalum*	5–10	Well-drained/moist	○◑	2–5
	Striped squill	*Puschkinia scilloides*	3–9	Well-drained	○◑	6
	Tulip	*Tulipa*	4–8	Well-drained/fertile	○◑	3–6
	Winter aconite	*Eranthis*	4–9	Well-drained/moist/fertile	○◑	3

* ○ full sun ◑ partial shade ● full shade

DEPTH (INCHES)	BLOOMING SEASON	HEIGHT (INCHES)	NOTES
3–4	Spring to summer	6–60	Usually pest-free; a great cut flower
1–2	Summer to fall	8–18	North of Zone 10, lift in fall
4	Summer to fall	8–20	An excellent flower for drying; north of Zone 7, plant in spring, lift in fall
2	Summer	8–24	North of Zone 10, plant in spring, lift in fall
1–4	Summer	24–36	Fragrant; north of Zone 8, plant in spring, lift in fall
Level	Summer	18–60	North of Zone 8, plant in spring, lift in fall
1–2	Spring to fall	3–12	Naturalizes well in warm areas; north of Zone 7, lift in fall
4–6	Late summer	12–60	North of Zone 9, lift in fall
2	Summer	12–36	Mulch in winter in Zones 3 to 6
2	Summer	12–24	Fragrant; can be grown outdoors in warm climates
3–4	Summer	6–20	Does well in woodland settings
3–6	Early summer to early fall	12–80	North of Zone 10, lift in fall
4	Spring to late summer	3–72	Divide and replant rhizomes every two to five years
4–6	Early summer	36	Fragrant; self-sows; requires excellent drainage
4	Summer	18–24	North of Zone 8, lift in fall
2	Summer	2–12	Plant in confined area to control
2	Early summer	3–18	North of Zone 6, lift in fall
3–4	Spring	8–20	Excellent for borders, rock gardens and naturalizing
1–2	Spring	12	Hardy, but requires shelter from strong, cold winds
3	Early spring	5	Naturalizes well in grass
6	Early spring	14–24	Plant under shrubs or in a border
3	Midspring	6–30	Different species can be planted in rock gardens, woodland gardens, or borders
3	Spring	4–10	Self-sows easily; plant in rock gardens, raised beds, or under shrubs
2–3	Late winter to spring	6–12	Use as a border plant or in wildflower and rock gardens; self-sows easily
4	Early spring to early summer	3–48	Naturalizes well; a good cut flower
4	Early spring to midsummer	18–48	An excellent cut flower
3–4	Late spring to early summer	6–60	Usually pest-free; a great cut flower
3	Spring	6–12	Best when clustered and planted in an area that will not dry out in summer
4	Spring	6–18	Naturalizes well
3	Spring	4–6	Fragrant; naturalizes easily
4	Spring to summer	6–24	North of Zone 5, plant in spring, lift in fall
3	Spring	4–6	Naturalizes easily; makes an attractive edging
4–6	Early to late spring	8–30	Excellent for borders, rock gardens, and naturalizing
2–3	Late winter to spring	2–4	Self-sows and naturalizes easily

SUBSTITUTIONS FOR COMMON INGREDIENTS

ITEM	QUANTITY	SUBSTITUTION
Baking powder	1 teaspoon	¼ teaspoon baking soda plus ¼ teaspoon cornstarch plus ½ teaspoon cream of tartar
Buttermilk	1 cup	1 tablespoon lemon juice or vinegar plus milk to equal 1 cup; or 1 cup plain yogurt
Chocolate, unsweetened	1 ounce	3 tablespoons cocoa plus 1 tablespoon unsalted butter, shortening, or vegetable oil
Cracker crumbs	¾ cup	1 cup dry bread crumbs; or 1 tablespoon quick-cooking oats (for thickening)
Cream, heavy	1 cup	¾ cup milk plus ⅓ cup melted unsalted butter (this will not whip)
Cream, light	1 cup	⅞ cup milk plus 3 tablespoons melted, unsalted butter
Cream, sour	1 cup	⅞ cup buttermilk or plain yogurt plus 3 tablespoons melted, unsalted butter
Cream, whipping	1 cup	⅔ cup well-chilled evaporated milk, whipped; or 1 cup nonfat dry milk powder whipped with 1 cup ice water
Egg	1 whole	2 yolks plus 1 tablespoon cold water; or 3 tablespoons vegetable oil plus 1 tablespoon water (for baking); or 2 to 3 tablespoons mayonnaise (for cakes)
Egg white	1 white	2 teaspoons meringue powder plus 3 tablespoons water, combined
Flour, all-purpose	1 cup	1 cup plus 3 tablespoons cake flour (not advised for cookies or quick breads); or 1 cup self-rising flour (omit baking powder and salt from recipe)
Flour, cake	1 cup	1 cup minus 3 tablespoons sifted all-purpose flour plus 3 tablespoons cornstarch
Flour, self-rising	1 cup	1 cup all-purpose flour plus 1½ teaspoons baking powder plus ¼ teaspoon salt
Herbs, dried	1 teaspoon	1 tablespoon fresh, minced and packed
Honey	1 cup	1¼ cups sugar plus ½ cup liquid called for in recipe (such as water or oil)
Ketchup	1 cup	1 cup tomato sauce plus ¼ cup sugar plus 3 tablespoons apple-cider vinegar plus ½ teaspoon salt plus pinch of ground cloves combined; or 1 cup chili sauce
Lemon juice	1 teaspoon	½ teaspoon vinegar
Mayonnaise	1 cup	1 cup sour cream or plain yogurt; or 1 cup cottage cheese (puréed)
Milk, skim	1 cup	⅓ cup instant nonfat dry milk plus ¾ cup water

ITEM	QUANTITY	SUBSTITUTION
Milk, to sour	1 cup	1 tablespoon vinegar or lemon juice plus milk to equal 1 cup. Stir and let stand 5 minutes.
Milk, whole	1 cup	½ cup evaporated whole milk plus ½ cup water; or ¾ cup 2 percent milk plus ¼ cup half-and-half
Molasses	1 cup	1 cup honey or dark corn syrup
Mustard, dry	1 teaspoon	1 tablespoon prepared mustard less 1 teaspoon liquid from recipe
Oat bran	1 cup	1 cup wheat bran or rice bran or wheat germ
Oats, old-fashioned	1 cup	1 cup steel-cut Irish or Scotch oats
Quinoa	1 cup	1 cup millet or couscous (whole wheat cooks faster) or bulgur
Sugar, dark-brown	1 cup	1 cup light-brown sugar, packed; or 1 cup granulated sugar plus 2 to 3 tablespoons molasses
Sugar, granulated	1 cup	1 cup firmly packed brown sugar; or 1¾ cups confectioners' sugar (makes baked goods less crisp); or 1 cup superfine sugar
Sugar, light-brown	1 cup	1 cup granulated sugar plus 1 to 2 tablespoons molasses; or ½ cup dark-brown sugar plus ½ cup granulated sugar
Sweetened condensed milk	1 can (14 oz.)	1 cup evaporated milk plus 1¼ cups granulated sugar. Combine and heat until sugar dissolves.
Vanilla bean	1-inch bean	1 teaspoon vanilla extract
Vinegar, apple-cider	—	malt, white-wine, or rice vinegar
Vinegar, balsamic	1 tablespoon	1 tablespoon red- or white-wine vinegar plus ½ teaspoon sugar
Vinegar, red-wine	—	white-wine, sherry, champagne, or balsamic vinegar
Vinegar, rice	—	apple-cider, champagne, or white-wine vinegar
Vinegar, white-wine	—	apple-cider, champagne, fruit (raspberry), rice, or red-wine vinegar
Yeast	1 cake (⅗ oz.)	1 package (¼ ounce) or 1 scant tablespoon active dried yeast
Yogurt, plain	1 cup	1 cup sour cream (thicker; less tart) or buttermilk (thinner; use in baking, dressings, sauces)

TYPES OF FAT

One way to minimize your total blood cholesterol is to manage the amount and types of fat in your diet. Aim for monounsaturated and polyunsaturated fats; avoid saturated and trans fats.

MONOUNSATURATED FAT lowers LDL (bad cholesterol) and may raise HDL (good cholesterol) or leave it unchanged; found in almonds, avocados, canola oil, cashews, olive oil, peanut oil, and peanuts.

POLYUNSATURATED FAT lowers LDL and may lower HDL; includes omega-3 and omega-6 fatty acids; found in corn oil, cottonseed oil, fish such as salmon and tuna, safflower oil, sesame seeds, soybeans, and sunflower oil.

SATURATED FAT raises both LDL and HDL; found in chocolate, cocoa butter, coconut oil, dairy products (milk, butter, cheese, ice cream), egg yolks, palm oil, and red meat.

TRANS FAT raises LDL and lowers HDL; a type of fat common in many processed foods, such as most margarines (especially stick), vegetable shortening, partially hydrogenated vegetable oil, many commercial fried foods (doughnuts, french fries), and commercial baked goods (cookies, crackers, cakes).

Calorie-Burning Comparisons

If you hustle through your chores to get to the fitness center, relax. You're getting a great workout already. The left-hand column lists "chore" exercises, the middle column shows the number of calories burned per minute per pound of body weight, and the right-hand column lists comparable "recreational" exercises. For example, a 150-pound person forking straw bales burns 9.45 calories per minute, the same workout he or she would get playing basketball.

Chore	Calories/min/lb	Recreational
Chopping with an ax, fast	**0.135**	Skiing, cross country, uphill
Climbing hills, with 44-pound load	**0.066**	Swimming, crawl, fast
Digging trenches	**0.065**	Skiing, cross country, steady walk
Forking straw bales	**0.063**	Basketball
Chopping down trees	**0.060**	Football
Climbing hills, with 9-pound load	**0.058**	Swimming, crawl, slow
Sawing by hand	**0.055**	Skiing, cross country, moderate
Mowing lawns	**0.051**	Horseback riding, trotting
Scrubbing floors	**0.049**	Tennis
Shoveling coal	**0.049**	Aerobic dance, medium
Hoeing	**0.041**	Weight training, circuit training
Stacking firewood	**0.040**	Weight lifting, free weights
Shoveling grain	**0.038**	Golf
Painting houses	**0.035**	Walking, normal pace, asphalt road
Weeding	**0.033**	Table tennis
Shopping for food	**0.028**	Cycling, 5.5 mph
Mopping floors	**0.028**	Fishing
Washing windows	**0.026**	Croquet
Raking	**0.025**	Dancing, ballroom
Driving a tractor	**0.016**	Drawing, standing position

FREEZER STORAGE TIME

(freezer temperature 0°F or colder)

PRODUCT	MONTHS IN FREEZER
FRESH MEAT	
Beef	6 to 12
Lamb	6 to 9
Veal	6 to 9
Pork	4 to 6
Ground beef, veal, lamb, pork	3 to 4
Frankfurters	1 to 2
Sausage, fresh pork	1 to 2
Ready-to-serve luncheon meats	Not recommended
FRESH POULTRY	
Chicken, turkey (whole)	12
Chicken, turkey (pieces)	6 to 9
Cornish game hen, game birds	6 to 9
Giblets	3 to 4
COOKED POULTRY	
Breaded, fried	4
Pieces, plain	4
Pieces covered with broth, gravy	6
FRESH FRUIT (PREPARED FOR FREEZING)	
All fruit except those listed below	10 to 12
Avocados, bananas, plantains	3
Lemons, limes, oranges	4 to 6
FRESH VEGETABLES (PREPARED FOR FREEZING)	
Beans, beets, bok choy, broccoli, brussels sprouts, cabbage, carrots, cauliflower, celery, corn, greens, kohlrabi, leeks, mushrooms, okra, onions, peas, peppers, soybeans, spinach, summer squashes	10 to 12
Asparagus, rutabagas, turnips	8 to 10
Artichokes, eggplant	6 to 8
Tomatoes (overripe or sliced)	2
Bamboo shoots, cucumbers, endive, lettuce, radishes, watercress	Not recommended
CHEESE (except those listed below)	6
Cottage cheese, cream cheese, feta, goat, fresh mozzarella, Neufchâtel, Parmesan, processed cheese (opened)	Not recommended

PRODUCT	MONTHS IN FREEZER
DAIRY PRODUCTS	
Margarine (not diet)	12
Butter	6 to 9
Cream, half-and-half	4
Milk	3
Ice cream	1 to 2

FREEZING HINTS

FOR MEALS, remember that a quart container holds four servings, and a pint container holds two servings.

TO PREVENT STICKING, spread the food to be frozen (berries, hamburgers, cookies, etc.) on a cookie sheet and freeze until solid. Then place in plastic bags and freeze.

LABEL FOODS for easy identification. Write the name of the food, number of servings, and date of freezing on containers or bags.

FREEZE FOODS as quickly as possible by placing them directly against the sides of the freezer.

ARRANGE FREEZER into sections for each food category.

IF POWER IS INTERRUPTED, or if the freezer is not operating normally, do not open the freezer door. Food in a loaded freezer will usually stay frozen for 2 days if the freezer door remains closed during that time period.

PLASTICS

In your quest to go green, use this guide to use and sort plastic. The number, usually found with a triangle symbol on a container, indicates the type of resin used to produce the plastic. Call **1-800-CLEANUP** for recycling information in your state.

PETE

NUMBER 1 • *PETE or PET (polyethylene terephthalate)*

IS USED IN . . . . microwavable food trays; salad dressing, soft drink, water, and juice bottles

STATUS . . . . hard to clean; absorbs bacteria and flavors; avoid reusing

IS RECYCLED TO MAKE . . . carpet, furniture, new containers, Polar fleece

HDPE

NUMBER 2 • *HDPE (high-density polyethylene)*

IS USED IN . . . . household cleaner and shampoo bottles, milk jugs, yogurt tubs

STATUS . . . . transmits no known chemicals into food

IS RECYCLED TO MAKE . . . detergent bottles, fencing, floor tiles, pens

V

NUMBER 3 • *V or PVC (vinyl)*

IS USED IN . . . . cooking oil bottles, clear food packaging, mouthwash bottles

STATUS . . . . is believed to contain phalates that interfere with hormonal development; avoid

IS RECYCLED TO MAKE . . . cables, mudflaps, paneling, roadway gutters

LDPE

NUMBER 4 • *LDPE (low-density polyethylene)*

IS USED IN . . . . bread and shopping bags, carpet, clothing, furniture

STATUS . . . . transmits no known chemicals into food

IS RECYCLED TO MAKE . . . envelopes, floor tiles, lumber, trash-can liners

PP

NUMBER 5 • *PP (polypropylene)*

IS USED IN . . . . ketchup bottles, medicine and syrup bottles, drinking straws

STATUS . . . . transmits no known chemicals into food

IS RECYCLED TO MAKE . . . battery cables, brooms, ice scrapers, rakes

PS

NUMBER 6 • *PS (polystyrene)*

IS USED IN . . . . disposable cups and plates, egg cartons, take-out containers

STATUS . . . . is believed to leach styrene, a possible human carcinogen, into food; avoid

IS RECYCLED TO MAKE . . . foam packaging, insulation, light switchplates, rulers

7

OTHER

NUMBER 7 • *Other (miscellaneous)*

IS USED IN . . . . 3- and 5-gallon water jugs, nylon, some food containers

STATUS . . . . contains bisphenol A, which has been linked to heart disease and obesity; avoid

IS RECYCLED TO MAKE . . . . custom-made products

HOW MUCH DO YOU NEED?

WALLPAPER

Before choosing your wallpaper, keep in mind that wallpaper with little or no pattern to match at the seams and the ceiling will be the easiest to apply, thus resulting in the least amount of wasted wallpaper. If you choose a patterned wallpaper, a small repeating pattern will result in less waste than a large repeating pattern. And a pattern that is aligned horizontally (matching on each column of paper) will waste less than one that drops or alternates its pattern (matching on every other column)

TO DETERMINE THE AMOUNT OF WALL SPACE YOU'RE COVERING:

- Measure the length of each wall, add these figures together, and multiply by the height of the walls to get the area (square footage) of the room's walls.
- Calculate the square footage of each door, window, and other opening in the room. Add these figures together and subtract the total from the area of the room's walls.
- Take that figure and multiply by 1.15, to account for a waste rate of about 15 percent in your wallpaper project. You'll end up with a target amount to purchase when you shop.
- Wallpaper is sold in single, double, and triple rolls. Coverage can vary, so be sure to refer to the roll's label for the proper square footage. (The average coverage for a double roll, for example, is 56 square feet.) After choosing a paper, divide the coverage figure (from the label) into the total square footage of the walls of the room you're papering. Round the answer up to the nearest whole number. This is the number of rolls you need to buy.
- Save leftover wallpaper rolls, carefully wrapped to keep clean.

INTERIOR PAINT

Estimate your room size and paint needs before you go to the store. Running out of a custom color halfway through the job could mean disaster. For the sake of the following exercise, assume that you have a 10x15-foot room with an 8-foot ceiling. The room has two doors and two windows.

FOR WALLS

Measure the total distance (perimeter) around the room:

(10 ft. + 15 ft.) x 2 = 50 ft.

Multiply the perimeter by the ceiling height to get the total wall area:

50 ft. x 8 ft. = 400 sq. ft.

Doors are usually 21 square feet (there are two in this exercise):

21 sq. ft. x 2 = 42 sq. ft.

Windows average 15 square feet (there are two in this exercise):

15 sq. ft. x 2 = 30 sq. ft.

Take the total wall area and subtract the area for the doors and windows to get the wall surface to be painted:

400 sq. ft. (wall area)
- 42 sq. ft. (doors)
- 30 sq. ft. (windows)
328 sq. ft.

As a rule of thumb, one gallon of quality paint will usually cover 400 square feet. One quart will cover 100 square feet. Because you need to cover 328 square feet in this example, one gallon will be adequate to give one coat of paint to the walls. (Coverage will be affected by the porosity and texture of the surface. In addition, bright colors may require a minimum of two coats.)

METRIC CONVERSION

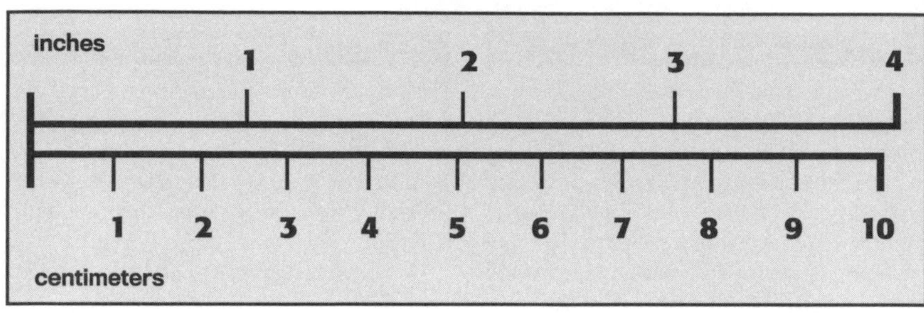

U.S. MEASURE	X THIS = NUMBER	METRIC EQUIVALENT	METRIC MEASURE X THIS = NUMBER	U.S. EQUIVALENT
inch	2.54	centimeter	0.39	inch
foot	30.48	centimeter	0.033	foot
yard	0.91	meter	1.09	yard
mile	1.61	kilometer	0.62	mile
square inch	6.45	square centimeter	0.15	square inch
square foot	0.09	square meter	10.76	square foot
square yard	0.8	square meter	1.2	square yard
square mile	2.59	square kilometer	0.39	square mile
acre	0.4	hectare	2.47	acre
ounce	28.0	gram	0.035	ounce
pound	0.45	kilogram	2.2	pound
short ton (2,000 pounds)	0.91	metric ton	1.10	short ton
ounce	30.0	milliliter	0.034	ounce
pint	0.47	liter	2.1	pint
quart	0.95	liter	1.06	quart
gallon	3.8	liter	0.26	gallon

If you know the U.S. measurement and want to convert it to metric, multiply it by the number in the left shaded column (example: 1 inch equals 2.54 centimeters). If you know the metric measurement, multiply it by the number in the right shaded column (example: 2 meters equals 2.18 yards).

Where Do You Fit in Your Family Tree?

Technically it's known as consanguinity; that is, the quality or state of being related by blood or descended from a common ancestor. These relationships are shown below for the genealogy of six generations of one family. *–family tree information courtesy of Frederick H. Rohles*

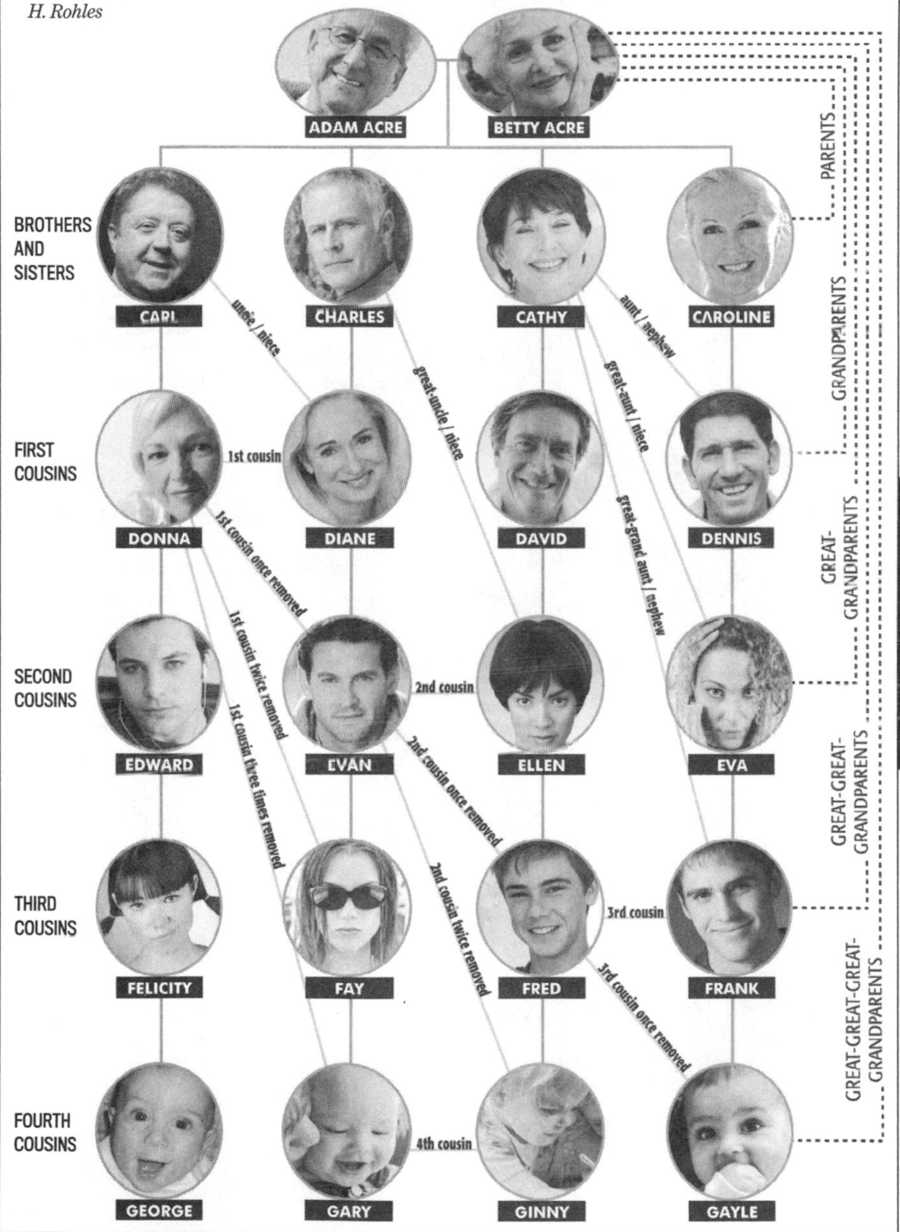

REFERENCE

The Golden Rule

(It's true in all faiths.)

Brahmanism:
This is the sum of duty: Do naught unto others which would cause you pain if done to you.
Mahabharata 5:1517

Buddhism:
Hurt not others in ways that you yourself would find hurtful.
Udana-Varga 5:18

Christianity:
All things whatsoever ye would that men should do to you, do ye even so to them; for this is the law and the prophets.
Matthew 7:12

Confucianism:
Surely it is the maxim of loving-kindness: Do not unto others what you would not have them do unto you.
Analects 15:23

Islam:
No one of you is a believer until he desires for his brother that which he desires for himself.
Sunnah

Judaism:
What is hateful to you, do not to your fellow man. That is the entire Law; all the rest is commentary.
Talmud, Shabbat 31a

Taoism:
Regard your neighbor's gain as your own gain and your neighbor's loss as your own loss.
T'ai Shang Kan Ying P'ien

Zoroastrianism:
That nature alone is good which refrains from doing unto another whatsoever is not good for itself.
Dadistan-i-dinik 94:5

–courtesy of Elizabeth Pool

REFERENCE

FAMOUS LAST WORDS

Waiting, are they? Waiting, are they? Well–let 'em wait.
(To an attending doctor who attempted to comfort him by saying, "General, I fear the angels are waiting for you.")
–Ethan Allen, American Revolutionary general, d. February 12, 1789

A dying man can do nothing easy.
–Benjamin Franklin, American statesman, d. April 17, 1790

Now I shall go to sleep. Good night.
–Lord George Byron, English writer, d. April 19, 1824

Is it the Fourth?
–Thomas Jefferson, 3rd U.S. president, d. July 4, 1826

Thomas Jefferson–still survives . . .
(Actually, Jefferson had died earlier that same day.)
–John Adams, 2nd U.S. president, d. July 4, 1826

Friends, applaud. The comedy is finished.
–Ludwig van Beethoven, German-Austrian composer, d. March 26, 1827

Moose . . . Indian . . .
–Henry David Thoreau, American writer, d. May 6, 1862

Go on, get out–last words are for fools who haven't said enough.
(To his housekeeper, who urged him to tell her his last words so she could write them down for posterity.)
–Karl Marx, German political philosopher, d. March 14, 1883

Is it not meningitis?
–Louisa M. Alcott, American writer, d. March 6, 1888

How were the receipts today at Madison Square Garden?
–P. T. Barnum, American entrepreneur, d. April 7, 1891

Turn up the lights, I don't want to go home in the dark.
–O. Henry (William Sidney Porter), American writer, d. June 4, 1910

Get my swan costume ready.
–Anna Pavlova, Russian ballerina, d. January 23, 1931

Is everybody happy? I want everybody to be happy. I know I'm happy.
–Ethel Barrymore, American actress, d. June 18, 1959

I'm bored with it all.
(Before slipping into a coma. He died 9 days later.)
–Winston Churchill, English statesman, d. January 24, 1965

You be good. You'll be in tomorrow. I love you.
–Alex, highly intelligent African Gray parrot, d. September 6, 2007